IN DEFENSE OF KANT'S *RELIGION*

Indiana Series in the Philosophy of Religion
Merold Westphal, editor

In Defense of Kant's *Religion*

Chris L. Firestone and Nathan Jacobs

FOREWORD BY NICHOLAS WOLTERSTORFF

INDIANA UNIVERSITY PRESS
Bloomington & Indianapolis

This book is a publication of

Indiana University Press
601 North Morton Street
Bloomington, IN 47404-3797 USA

http://iupress.indiana.edu

Telephone orders   800-842-6796
Fax orders   812-855-7931
Orders by e-mail   iuporder@indiana.edu

The paper used in this publication meets the minimum
requirements of American National Standard for Information
Sciences—Permanence of Paper for Printed Library Materials,
ANSI Z39.48-1984.

Manufactured in the United States of America

Library of Congress Cataloging-in-Publication Data
Firestone, Chris L., date
In defense of Kant's religion / Chris L. Firestone and Nathan
Jacobs ; foreword by Nicholas Wolterstorff.
p. cm. — (Indiana series in the philosophy of religion)
ISBN 978-0-253-35217-0 (cloth : alk. paper)
ISBN 978-0-253-22014-1 (pbk. : alk. paper)
1. Kant, Immanuel, 1724–1804. Religion innerhalb der
Grenzen der blossen Vernunft. 2. Philosophy and religion.
I. Jacobs, Nathan. II. Title.
B2792.F57 2008
210.92—dc22
2008005973

1 2 3 4 5   13 12 11 10 09 08

To Elizabeth and Heather

[The First Command of all duties to oneself] is "know (scrutinize, fathom) yourself," . . . in terms of your moral perfection in relation to your duty. That is, know your heart—whether it is good or evil, whether the source of your actions is pure or impure, and what can be imputed to you as belonging originally to the substance *of a human being or as derived (acquired or developed) and belonging to your moral* condition.

Moral cognition of oneself, which seeks to penetrate into the depths (the abyss) of one's heart which are quite difficult to fathom, is the beginning of all human wisdom. For in the case of a human being, the ultimate wisdom, which consists in the harmony of a human being's will with its final end, requires him first to remove the obstacle within (an evil will actually present in him) and then to develop the original predisposition to a good will within him, which can never be lost. (Only the descent into the hell of self-cognition can pave the way to godliness.)

Immanuel Kant, *The Metaphysics of Morals* (6:441)

Contents

Contents

Foreword

In Defense of Kant's Religion, by Chris L. Firestone and Nathan Jacobs, joins the rather long list of commentaries on Immanuel Kant's late text, *Religion within the Boundaries of Mere Reason,* as among the most challenging and illuminating, perhaps as *the* most challenging and illuminating.

Kant's *Religion* has the deserved reputation of being one of the most profound and suggestive, yet also problematic, texts in the entire Kantian corpus. It is profound in its analysis of our human moral condition. Our condition is not merely that we all do things we ought not to do, so that we are guilty of having done this wrong thing and of having done that wrong thing. Our condition is that there is something evil about ourselves; there is in us a propensity or disposition to act against the moral law. We are not committed to the moral law as our supreme incentive. We are committed to obeying the moral law only as long as doing so does not seriously interfere with what we judge to be to our personal advantage. Radical moral evil has somehow become attached to our species—by a free choice, otherwise it would not be *moral* evil.

The fundamental question that Kant's analysis raises for him is whether, in spite of our deplorable moral condition, there is ground for moral hope. A good many commentators, myself included, have thought we spied conundrums of various sorts in the details of Kant's answer to that question. Others have emphasized these conundrums less than the various points at which Kant's answer appears to be out of accord with his critical philosophy as a whole.

In part 1 of their discussion, Firestone and Jacobs provide a masterful review of the secondary literature on Kant's *Religion;* the review is masterful both in its coverage and in its analysis of the various positions that have been staked out pro and con the coherence of Kant's *Religion* internally and with the rest of his philosophy. The question that emerges forcefully is whether it is possible to interpret the text in such a way as to save it from the barrage of charges that have been fired against it. Is Kant's *Religion* a coherent text of critical philosophy?

With these charges in mind, in part 2 of their discussion Firestone and Jacobs engage in a close and deep reading of Kant's text, informed by a knowledge of the relevant parts of the philosophical climate of the day. What emerges is a Kant very different from the one we thought we knew, more metaphysical, more willing to engage in speculative theology, less dismissive of actual religion. A good many of the conundrums that commentators have thought they spied are dissolved; whether all of them are is not yet clear to me. But the position that emerges is also strange, so strange that many of us will wonder whether this could really be what Kant had in mind. The great merit of Firestone and Jacobs's discussion is that they rub our skeptical noses in the text; over and over they point to what Kant actually said.

A central feature of their interpretation is that they interpret literally what most, if not all, of us have taken to be metaphorical. I have in mind especially, though not only, their interpretation of what Kant says about humanity's *prototype*. Most commentators, again I include myself, have taken Kant to be speaking metaphorically here; he did not believe that there actually is a prototype. But the authors provide what is, to my mind, conclusive evidence that Kant was not speaking metaphorically; it was his view that there really is an eternal prototype of humanity. The existence of that prototype is an essential component within his explanation of how it can be that we, who harbor radical evil, yet have ground for moral hope.

Kant studies have experienced a number of jolts in recent years, stimulated by close and deep reading of all of Kant's major texts and by knowledge of the philosophical and intellectual climate within which Kant worked. My own guess is that Firestone and Jacobs will prove to have delivered as big a jolt as anyone. After one has worked through their interpretation, it is no longer possible to read the text of Kant's *Religion* in the way one did before. We won't all immediately jump onto the bandwagon; the Kant that emerges is too strange. We will wonder whether there's not some other way of reading the text, not yet thought up, that preserves the profundity and dissolves the conundrums while making Kant less strange. Until that other way emerges—I am not at all confident that it ever will—this interpretation has the merit not only of dissolving most if not all the conundrums but of offering us the best close, deep, and intellectually imaginative reading of the text that we have.

Nicholas Wolterstorff
Noah Porter Professor Emeritus of Philosophical Theology, Yale University
Senior Fellow, Institute for Advanced Studies in Culture, University of Virginia

Acknowledgments

From its inception seven years ago, this project has received help from a variety of laypeople, scholars, and universities. The order of acknowledgement here is more chronological than hierarchical, but all contributed significantly to the successful completion of this project. We are deeply indebted to everyone mentioned and want to convey our sincere appreciation.

In 2001, Peter Byrne challenged us to give a careful reading of Immanuel Kant's *Religion within the Boundaries of Mere Reason* and to come to grips with the manifold criticisms leveled against it. Although we do not understand the text as he does, this project would never have begun without his insistent skepticism and demand for top scholarship. Jeanette Hsieh, David Fergusson, Michael Partridge, and John McDowell served as a counterbalance to Byrne's skepticism in these early stages of research. Their persistent confidence in the end result of our efforts ensured that Byrne's skepticism did not yield despair.

We are thankful to those who offered insightful comments at a special meeting of the Eastern Division of the Society of Christian Philosophers in 2006, including John Hare and David Sussman. We were also helped immensely by the editors and anonymous reviewers at the University of Chicago's *Journal of Religion*, who were a great encouragement, but whose comments made clear to us that the defense of *Religion* we intended would require a book. In addition, we would like to thank Nicholas Adams, John Cooper, Scott Erdenberg, Richard Muller, Dylan Pahman, Stephen Palmquist, Philip Rossi, James Smith, and Kevin Vanhoozer, whose help at various points in the process spurred on and enhanced our efforts.

From an institutional vantage point, we want to thank Trinity College (Deerfield, Ill.) and Calvin College (Grand Rapids, Mich.). Trinity College supported this project with a sabbatical leave, modest grant, and course reduction. During that sabbatical leave we discovered the governing metaphor of the book and were able to produce our proposal for Indiana University Press. Calvin College was equally valuable throughout. We think particularly of the *Communitas Summer Research Program*. For two amazing summers, the *Communitas* hospitality team took great care to see that we had the best possible research environment for this work. Their assistance accelerated our progress and contributed greatly to the end result.

Acknowledgments

Lee Hardy, Merold Westphal, and Nicholas Wolterstorff gave this project its much-needed push to the finish. Hardy and Westphal reviewed the manuscript with expert eyes, providing invaluable insights and encouragement. Wolterstorff served as our skeptical and yet charitable interlocutor over the last two years of writing and revising. We felt the volume would not be ready for press until it received his seal of approval, and we are delighted that, after much work, we were able to win his support.

Finally, we thank our families, especially Elizabeth and Heather. Your patience over many days of long research hours, with impromptu research trips across states, and with continual writing and rewriting, has, in the truest sense, made this project possible. Without your loving support and encouragement, we would never have completed this book.

Note on Text Quotations

Throughout this volume, we have made every effort to adopt the new Cambridge University Press (CUP) translation of Kant's works. In the rare case that an alternative translation is utilized, the full publishing information is cited in endnotes. Adjustments to the Cambridge translations or alternative renderings by the authors are based on *Kants gesammelte Schriften*, edited by the Royal Prussian/German Academy of Sciences. For the sake of consistency and ease of reference, we have standardized all citations, so that they refer to the German *Akademie* (Ak) pagination, which can be found in the margins of *The Cambridge Edition of the Works of Immanuel Kant*. These citations are embedded within the body of the text throughout. A selected bibliography can be found at the close of this volume.

The Cambridge Edition of the Works of Immanuel Kant
Paul Guyer and Allen W. Wood, General Editors

Correspondence. Ed. and trans. Arnulf Zweig (Cambridge: Cambridge University Press, 1999).

Critique of the Power of Judgment. Ed. Paul Guyer, and trans. Paul Guyer and Eric Matthews (Cambridge: Cambridge University Press, 2000). (Cited as "third *Critique*.")

Critique of Pure Reason. Ed. and trans. Paul Guyer and Allen W. Wood (Cambridge: Cambridge University Press, 1997). (Cited as "first *Critique*.")

Lectures on Metaphysics. Ed. and trans. Karl Ameriks and Steve Naragon (Cambridge: Cambridge University Press, 1997).

Opus Postumum. Ed. Eckart Förster, and trans. Eckart Förster and Michael Rosen (Cambridge: Cambridge University Press, 1993).

Practical Philosophy. Ed. and trans. Mary J. Gregor (Cambridge: Cambridge University Press, 1996). This text includes, among other works, *Groundwork of The Metaphysics of Morals* (cited as *Groundwork*), *Critique of Practical Reason* (cited as "second *Critique*"), and *The Metaphysics of Morals*.

Religion and Rational Theology. Ed. and trans. Allen W. Wood and George di Giovanni (Cambridge: Cambridge University Press, 1996). This text includes, among other works, *Religion within the Boundaries of Mere Reason* (cited as *Religion*), *The Conflict of the Faculties* (cited as *Conflict*), and "Lectures on the Philosophical Doctrine of Religion" (cited as "Lectures on Religion").

Theoretical Philosophy, 1755–1770. Ed. and trans. David Walford (Cambridge: Cambridge University Press, 1992). This text includes, among other works, "Dreams of a Spirit-Seer Elucidated by Dreams of Metaphysics" (cited as "Dreams").

People vs. *Religion*

After more than two hundred years of deliberation, the jury is still out on how to best understand Immanuel Kant's major text on religion, *Religion within the Boundaries of Mere Reason*.[1] Some interpreters are resolute in downplaying the significance of *Religion* to Kant's philosophical portfolio. By focusing on various aspects of his sociopolitical context and early anti-metaphysical tone, they dismiss the text by appealing to Kant's hidden motivations: he was simply writing either to placate the Prussian censors so that his views on religion could be published or to appease the religious sensitivities of his manservant, Lampe, who had been severely shaken by the conclusions of the *Critique of Pure Reason*. Other interpreters, however, warmly accept *Religion* into the fold of Kant's critical philosophy. They focus, in a more positive sense, on Kant's Pietistic Lutheran upbringing, arguing that his chief intent was either to move certain Christian essentials into the safe confines of reason alone or to establish the contours of a rational religious faith in accord with both his religious convictions and mature critical philosophy. Whatever we make of these disparate arguments, the jury of contemporary Kant interpreters remains deadlocked over how best to understand Kant's *Religion*.

In *Kant and the New Philosophy of Religion*, the case is made that there are essentially two interpretive trends regarding Kant's philosophy of religion in the field of Kant-studies—one is principally negative toward religion and theology, while the other affirms religion and theology.[2] For ease of reference, the editors called these two trends "traditional" interpretations and "affirmative" interpretations. Interpretations designated "traditional" are primarily negative in

1

their assessment of the prospects of grounding religion and theology in the Kantian paradigm. Traditional interpreters have a wide range of positions on the place of God in Kant's philosophy: some, such as Allen Wood and Denis Savage, argue that Kant's philosophy is basically deistic;[3] others, including Keith Ward and Don Cupitt, think Kant's philosophy is most amenable to theological non-realism;[4] and still others, such as Matthew Alun Ray and Yirmiahu Yovel, argue that Kant's philosophy supports either atheism or agnosticism but nothing more.[5] Despite their differences on the exact nuances, all these interpreters agree that Kant's philosophy works decidedly against those who would seek to gain a foothold for religion and theology in reason; and, at the end of the day, they find that Kant's philosophy of religion offers no real help in overcoming this basically negative thrust.

Contrary to their negative counterparts, theologically affirmative interpretations of Kant typically hold that Kant's philosophy provides a rationale for God-talk and religious faith. But the case cannot be made without looking beyond the first *Critique,* and sometimes to Kant's writings both before and after 1781. These affirmative readers usually make a point of capturing a sense of the whole of Kant's philosophical enterprise—something that is lost when too strong an emphasis is placed on the first *Critique.* The arguments articulated and defended among these theologically affirmative interpretations vary greatly, but all within this camp agree that this diversified theological affirmation is the real legacy of Kant. Ronald Green, Ann Loades, Stephen Palmquist, Adina Davidovich, John Hare, Elizabeth Galbraith, and others have therefore argued that traditional interpretive approaches to Kant on religion and theology are wholly inadequate.[6] If the affirmative camp is right, traditional interpretations are either shortsighted or negligent. They either miss the plethora of positive resources for grounding religion and theology in Kant's philosophical paradigm or plainly bungle opportunities for understanding Kant's more metaphysically robust insights as genuine contributions to the critical philosophy.

The editors' conclusions in *Kant and the New Philosophy of Religion* regarding these interpretive trends were fourfold: (1) based on a select assortment of first *Critique* principles, those espousing some form of traditional interpretation unanimously deny the possibility of grounding religion and theology in Kant's philosophy; (2) these traditional renderings of Kant comprise the "largest unified minority report" on how to interpret his philosophy of religion, but, when all relevant data are considered, they represent neither the majority in the field of Kant-studies nor the most accurate interpretation of Kant on religion and theology; (3) cogent arguments exist for thinking Kant's critical writings, taken as a whole, provide the grounds needed for positive incorporation of religion and theology into Kant's philosophical program; and (4) the hermeneutic superstructure of the traditional interpretation is in need of renovation, if not outright demolition, and the basis for an affirmative grounding of religion and theology in Kant's philosophy needs to be more adequately articulated.

Our purpose here is to make a significant advance on points three and four by providing a comprehensive interpretation of Kant's *Religion* that defends it against recently mounting charges of incoherence. Our interpretation and defense is set in the context of a civil trial that considers arguments from both the traditional and the affirmative camps. We will call forward witnesses from each side in order to draw out the best evidence for and against *Religion*. While we believe this classic text to be innocent of the charge of incoherence, clearly the quantity of negative research on *Religion* casts a dark shadow over its inner workings. Thus, in dialogue with this expert testimony, we will develop an interpretation that, we believe, sheds new light on the text and exonerates it from the charges of its critics. Our goal is to demonstrate in a comprehensive manner that, when all relevant resources are brought to bear, a full acquittal of Kant's *Religion* is the only reasonable verdict.

While it is true that the jury is still out on Kant's philosophy of religion as a whole, a strong team of interpreters has, in recent years, assembled for the prosecution of Kant's *Religion*. Smattered throughout the literature are essays and books, which argue that the key "insights" of *Religion* are fundamentally flawed. Philip Quinn writes of Kant's "remarkable antinomy" in *Religion*, and Nicholas Wolterstorff finds Kant's rational religion so stocked full of "conundrums" that the coherence of his arguments is under threat at nearly every turn.[7] Such critics highlight the way Kant's reasoning often appears conflicted, if not outright contradictory: Kant suggests we have a predisposition to good as well as a natural propensity to evil; he suggests we have an evil disposition that is innate yet freely chosen; he thinks we are in need of divine grace, but we must in effect earn this grace.

Many see this dissonant talk as the inevitable result of synthesizing an Enlightenment, moralist system that is concerned with rights and obligations and assumes *ought* implies *can* with a biblical worldview that presumes human depravity and humanity's need for divine grace.[8] As a result, traditional interpreters find serious problems in attributing much importance to *Religion* for Kant's philosophical paradigm, and thus move for a guilty verdict: not only does Kant's *Religion* appear incoherent at key junctures, but even its fundamental aspirations seem at cross purposes. Therefore, *Religion* should be separated from the critical philosophy proper and relegated to the gallows along with Kant's less significant work.

Gordon Michalson's publications are perhaps the best example of this traditional push. Michalson presents some of the most thoroughgoing analyses of the challenges facing Kant's philosophy of religion. In the light of his findings, Michalson submits, "Kant's position is a nest of tangles," "riddled with inconsistencies," and "sufficiently problematic" so as to lead to an "entire set of wobbles."[9] While a number of witnesses for the prosecution will be called throughout our survey of current scholarship, Michalson's work will provide us with the main arguments for the incoherence of *Religion*. As star witness in the case against *Religion*, Michalson will serve as chief interlocutor for our defense.

We should note that not all negative witnesses will be welcome at this hearing. Some negative witnesses are hostile to the idea that Kant has anything positive or constructive to say about historical faith, and thus presume at the outset that *Religion* is necessarily a rehashing of Kant's established moral philosophy, which is taken to be incompatible with revealed religion. Yirmiahu Yovel examples this interpretive strategy in *Kant and the Philosophy of History*. According to Yovel, "Almost every positive idea that Kant has to express under the title of rational religion has already been expressed in his ethics, while what is new in the *Religion within the Limits of Reason Alone* (1793) is mainly an uncompromising attack upon existing religions and an attempt to eliminate them from the historical scene."[10] To the extent that *Religion* adheres to Kant's critical philosophy, traditionally understood, Yovel thinks it must be read exclusively through the lens of the moral philosophy, and this means *Religion* is essentially "destructive" to revealed religion. To accept such an overtly pessimistic view of Kant's philosophy of religion, however, one must simultaneously take an artificially low view of Kant's religious sincerity—something Kant took to be an important part of his personal integrity.[11] Such hostile witnesses, who would so clearly testify against the grain of Kant's religious convictions, will not be admitted into the courtroom of deliberation. In building our defense, we will instead examine only those interpretations of Kant that take his philosophy of religion seriously, but still dispute its nature and coherence.

Any defense of Kant's *Religion* must come to grips with one of the central and immediate difficulties inherent in the task. This difficulty concerns what Philip Rossi calls the "theological spectacles" of the interpreter.[12] Given the complexity and diversity of *Religion* and the inevitable subjectivity of the interpretive process, interpreters tend to see in Kant what is amenable to their own theological stance. This is true not only for persons of religious conviction and theists generally, but also for atheists, agnostics, and non-realists. To be sure, interpreters exist in the field of Kant-studies who wear what might be called a-theological spectacles, which have just as much potential for skewing the meaning of the text as affirmative theological spectacles—Yovel would be one obvious example. No one is immune to this sort of criticism. How, then, do we overcome the potential for a deadlock based on hermeneutic subjectivity? We submit that if the interpretive task is to remain fair and to have hope of succeeding, interpreters must revisit the text in a context of open rational discourse and careful textual analysis. The evidence we offer in defense of *Religion* therefore consists first and foremost of careful textual analysis in dialogue with some of the very best interpretations of the last century.

This being said, anyone who has given close consideration to the details of *Religion* will be aware that theological spectacles are not the only hindrance to a unified reading of the text. It cannot be denied that Kant's writings are partially to blame for the fragmented interpretive landscape of Kant-studies. Those who would see a moral reinterpretation of Christianity, where the central tenets of the faith are reduced to picturesque portrayals of moral struggle, can find scattered support in Books One and Two of *Religion*. Those wishing to see *Religion* as an effort to reduce religion to morality, which results in either the abolition of religion or an emergent religious pluralism, can find choice passages in Book Three. Anyone wanting to emphasize Kant's political vision, which strips the state of its ties to ecclesiastical faith and presses toward the League of Nations, can find useful passages in both the latter portions of Book Three and parts of Book Four. None of this is to say that these disparate themes represent an accurate rendering of *Religion*. Rather, they speak more of Kant's tortured vocabulary, complex German, philosophical subtleties, and diverse corpus, all of which, when taken together, allow for understandings of *Religion* that, when pressed by the exegetical specifics, make Kant's writing seem excessively convoluted. Portions of *Religion* seem contradictory and can give the impression that the text is a Gordian knot—presenting a never-ending set of difficulties that, rather than being untangled, must be cut. The text, to many, seems not only unintelligible, but also theologically negative and metaphysically destructive. However, Kant's arguments are far more positive and constructive than these isolated passages would indicate; and they are certainly more subtle and complex than a "face-value" reading admits. Therefore, acknowledging the inevitable hermeneutic complexities of the interpretive task, we seek to offer a reading of *Religion* that is firmly based on the internal textual specifics—rather than some prior understanding of Kant's critical goals—and resolutely aimed at yielding a coherent whole. Our only self-aware hermeneutic rudder is the rule of charity, which presumes that the best reading of the textual specifics is the one that makes Kant's claims most cogent.

Before outlining the basic structure of this work, important to note at the outset is that, in our defense of *Religion*, the content of Kant's arguments begins to look remarkably Christian. Despite this result, we will not present *Religion* as an apologetic for the Christian faith. Such a characterization, we believe, would be wrongheaded. In our understanding of *Religion*, Christianity comes out in a better position than other historical faiths, and we believe Kant, in this sense, offers "rational assistance" to Christianity. However, Kant's tone throughout *Religion* is clearly not defensive of any historical faith; instead, Kant's tone suggests an uncompromising, and, in many ways, offensive assessment of historical religion. The relationship between Kant's *Religion* and Christianity is, from a Christian perspective, a mixed bag. In the positive sense, Kant's project bears a striking similarity to the Christian gospel; and Kant ultimately affirms Christianity (at least as taught by Jesus himself) as a rational religion, seeing the relationship between "New Testament" Christianity and "Old Testament" Judaism (as Kant understands it) as the sort that ought to exist between rational religion and historical faith. On the negative side, Kant's project, in exalting the dictates of reason over historical faith, undercuts the historical element of Christianity, nullifying (or at least suspending purely rational assent to) a great many things that Christians have understood to be essential to their faith. Defending the internal coherence of *Religion* from an expository vantage point and commending its desirability for Christianity are two entirely different matters, and we will, in this volume, focus exclusively on the former.[13]

The outline of this work is as follows. Chapters 1, 2, and 3 make up part 1, "Perspectives on Kant's *Religion*." In chapters 1 and 2, we will consider the testimony of key Kant interpreters as important background information for understanding the indictment against *Religion*. These witnesses will testify regarding two questions, the answers to which are crucial for making an informed decision about the nature and purpose of the text. The first question, taken up in chapter 1, regards the metaphysical motives behind *Religion*. As a critical philosopher (as opposed to a pre-critical philosopher or dogmatic metaphysician), was Kant primarily positive or negative about the prospects for metaphysics? To answer this question, we will call Vincent McCarthy, Stephen Palmquist, Keith Ward, and Allen Wood to the stand. The second question concerns the philosophical character of *Religion*. Are there ample resources for grounding *Religion* in the critical corpus, and if so, are these resources sufficient to show the text to be a genuine contribution to Kant's philosophical program? To answer this question, we will call, in chapter 2, Philip Quinn, Nicholas Wolterstorff, Ronald Green, Adina Davidovich, John Hare, and Bernard Reardon to the stand. Part 1 culminates in chapter 3 with the testimony of star witness for the prosecution, Gordon Michalson. While Green, Davidovich, Hare, and Reardon offer renditions of *Religion* that help give some sense of direction and stability to Kant's arguments, despite the negative evidence presented by Quinn, Wolterstorff, and others, Michalson's testimony casts a shadow of suspicion over the argumentative specifics. Michalson's summary of the indictment lays out a comprehensive and yet-unanswered set of difficulties that any interpretation must overcome if Kant's *Religion* is to be judged coherent and of lasting significance to the field of philosophy of religion.

While part 1 examines two key dimensions of the case as understood by Kant interpreters and provides the final indictment of *Religion*, part 2 provides a thorough defense of this classic text. Chapter 4 begins this defense by focusing on key resources in the critical philosophy and in *Religion* itself that are important preliminary considerations for understanding the shape of *Religion* and its theological talk. They are Kant's notions of pure cognition, the two experiments identified in the Second Preface of *Religion*, and the moral disposition, which is a point of concern throughout *Religion*. We make the case that these features of Kant's argument are present at the earliest stages of *Religion* and are crucial to keep in mind throughout in order to understand the text as a coherent work of philosophy of religion, and one consonant with Kant's critical philosophy. Chapter 4 will thus serve as our opening statement in defense of *Religion*. Following this opening statement, chapters 5, 6, 7, and 8 present the four exhibits central to our defense. Each of these chapters is dedicated to our interpretation of one of the four books of *Religion* —chapter 5 sets forth our interpretation of Book One, chapter 6 sets forth our interpretation of Book Two, and so on. Collectively, they address the specific issues in the indictment and make the case that a coherent understanding of *Religion* is possible.[14]

Employing the rule that Kant's arguments are "innocent until proven guilty," we contend in our closing statement that the reading provided in the previous chapters casts reasonable doubt on the charges of incoherence brought against *Religion* and, in this light, move for an acquittal. Our interpretation and defense shows that, although Kant may be charged at points with constructing a somewhat unclear or even convoluted text, his argument is essentially consistent. That said, we will not be suggesting that *Religion* is without blemish. Difficulties remain. However, what becomes clear from our analysis is that the difficulties with *Religion* are more like the age-old problems germane to Greek philosophy and Christian thought than they are contradictions of the kind suggested by readers like Michalson. Even though Kant's *Religion* is not a perfect text, we will show it to be innocent of the charges brought against it, and, on this basis, rest our case in defense of Kant's *Religion*.

PART 1.
PERSPECTIVES ON KANT'S *RELIGION*

1

The Metaphysical Motives
behind *Religion*

Our purpose in part 1 is to examine recent scholarship on Immanuel Kant with a view to understanding the basic issues at stake when interpreting *Religion* and to present the major components of the case against its coherence. In pursuit of these objectives, we will cross-examine a number of the main Kant experts of the last forty years, asking of their work some basic questions concerning the content and context of Kant's philosophy of religion: What, if any, metaphysical motives lay behind the exposition of Kant's philosophy? Does *Religion* emerge out of a philosophical program that is fundamentally for or against the rational incorporation of religious faith? What characteristics of Kant's critical philosophy support the specific arguments of *Religion,* and which ones militate against them? And how does Kant's critical philosophy both enhance and limit the way *Religion* can be interpreted? The answers to these questions are leading indicators for determining how *Religion* should be interpreted, and thus for discerning the consistency or inconsistency of its arguments. They constitute what we call the *metaphysical motives* behind and *philosophical character* of the text. They also provide the conceptual backdrop for *the indictment* of *Religion* on the charges of patent and pervasive incoherence. These three aspects of the case (the metaphysical motives, the philosophical character, and the indictment) make up the three major divisions of part 1.

By covering this preliminary ground in some detail, we provide a backdrop, not only for the case against *Religion,* but also for its defense, which we take up in earnest in part 2. If the testimony of part 1 indicates that the metaphysical motivations behind *Religion* are incompatible with or contradictory to the critical philosophy, such evidence will support the charge that the text is fundamentally flawed. If, on the other hand, the testimony regarding the philosophical character of Kant's work provides resources for an interpretation of *Religion* that shows it to advance positively on the critical philosophy, we will have good reason to think the arguments of *Religion* are coherent. The indictment against *Religion* thus rests on showing that when its metaphysical motives and philosophical character are properly understood, the text becomes unstable and falls under the weight of internal and irreconcilable conundrums, while an adequate defense of *Religion* depends on showing that Kant's metaphysical motivations and the philosophical character of *Religion* support an interpretation of the text that overcomes the so-called conundrums.

We begin in this chapter by cross-examining two opposing positions on the historical situation and psychological state of Kant and the impact these considerations have on his philosophy of religion. Vincent McCarthy is decidedly pessimistic in his evaluation of the metaphysical motives behind *Religion*. He understands *Religion* to be a text in tension, conceptually trapped between Lutheran Pietism and Enlightenment rationalism. In trying to graft what is essential to the former onto the latter, Kant inevitably creates irresolvable difficulties for his philosophy as a whole and his philosophy of religion in particular. Stephen Palmquist's position on *Religion* directly opposes McCarthy's testimony. Palmquist understands the text to be consistent with Kant's intention of developing a critically viable form of religion in the midst of a revolutionary new way of understanding philosophy. Palmquist traces this "critical religion" from Kant's pre-critical essay "Dreams of a Spirit-Seer Elucidated by Dreams of Metaphysics" to the *Opus Postumum*, describing this development in Kant's thinking as "Critical Mysticism." For Palmquist, *Religion* is best thought of as a transcendental analysis of hope that is consonant with the Copernican nature of Kant's critical philosophy and caps off Kant's critical study on the possibility of religious experience.

With these two interpretations providing a backdrop for understanding the metaphysical motives behind *Religion*, Keith Ward and Allen Wood are called to the stand to provide mediating positions. Ward finds something true in both sides of this debate. With Palmquist, Ward argues that Kant wants to arrive at some critically viable form of rational religious faith. However, with McCarthy, Ward thinks that Kant's theoretical strictures put Kant into a conceptual straitjacket without a critically satisfying means of escape. Despite Kant's desire to make room for faith and the existence of certain existential tendencies in Kant's thinking on religion and theology, Ward does not see how Kant can get beyond moral formalism and theological non-realism when viewing religion from the point of view of the theoretical and practical philosophy. Kant's denial of theoretical knowledge of God and later practical postulation of

God set up, for Ward, a Copernican version of "Hume's fork." One can either rely on empirical judgments for the establishment of rational foundations for theology or look to the postulation of God for purely moral purposes. In the end, however, neither choice is satisfying as a *rational* foundation for religion and theology.

Allen Wood's testimony is very different from Ward's. Wood avers that sufficient critical warrant exists in the *Critique of Pure Reason* for thinking that Kant intends to develop rational religious faith in a way that moves beyond theological non-realism. God, for Kant, cannot be known like objects of experience. Nevertheless, Wood shows that Kant's conception of God in the first *Critique* contains the notion of the *"ens realissimum"* and argues that this basic conception of God "comes about in the course of our attempt to conceive the conditions for the 'thorough determination' of things."[1] Wood argues additionally that certain things, such as "knowledge, volition, and moral goodness," can be predicated of God.[2] This conception of God in the first *Critique* serves as the cornerstone for the development of rational religious faith as a morally grounded and existentially significant religious epistemology. Unlike Palmquist, however, Wood thinks that Kant's rationalistic faith in God cannot amount to mysticism. Instead, Wood's early work presents Kant as a theist, forwarding a substantial argument that traces Kant's reasoning from the first antinomy of the *Critique of Practical Reason* on through to *Religion*. It supports the view that Kant's philosophy grounds not an abstract and sterile theism but a moral faith in a benevolent, gracious, and "living God." Wood argues, in short, that Kant's understanding of *moral faith* develops according to a clear logic into *rational religious faith*.

Witness for the Prosecution: Vincent McCarthy

Vincent McCarthy's *Quest for a Philosophical Jesus* provides a good example of the traditional approach to interpreting Kant's *Religion*.[3] The way McCarthy approaches *Religion* is less expository and more analysis of Kant's upbringing, his intellectual influences, the evolution of *Religion* as a text, and the relationship between *Religion* and the critical philosophy proper. The picture McCarthy paints presents *Religion* as an attempt to create a synthesis between Kant's early Lutheran Pietism and Enlightenment rationalism.[4] This synthesis is not understood by McCarthy as an affirmative theological maneuver or a Christian apologetic, however. McCarthy understands Kant to have "the far more ambitious goal of scrutinizing all religion from the standpoint of moral reason and penetrating to its central and deepest truths."[5] Even so, McCarthy believes that, despite expressing an intent to evaluate critically all forms of religion, Kant was unable to break free of his Christian heritage and, with it, the European bias against other religions. What Kant therefore provides in the end is a rationalist version of a theology of symbol that unabashedly and uncritically promotes Christian concepts and imagery, despite its underlying intention to place all religion under the authority of reason.[6]

At bottom, McCarthy finds an irresolvable conflict in Kant's desired synthesis between rationalism and the anthropology of Pietism. The Enlightenment represented an almost naïve optimism regarding humanity's ability to attain moral ideals, while Pietism retained a sober (and almost somber) understanding of human depravity and the limits of human ability to affect moral renewal. As is well known, Kant sides conceptually with the latter in Book One of *Religion*, forwarding his now famous (or perhaps infamous) doctrine of "radical evil." Yet, McCarthy understands Kant, in embracing human depravity, to be inadvertently bringing tension into his relationship with both rationalism and Pietism: the theological doctrine of depravity was shunned by the rationalists, who recognized radical evil as a crippling blow to humanity's hope of moral progress, while at the same time, Kant's highly rational approach to themes such as radical evil roused suspicion in religious Pietists, who harbored mistrust in the "enlightened" faith of reason.[7] McCarthy's interpretation of *Religion* thus views the text as a bold attempt to bring diametrically opposed starting points together, the result of which is both a rationalistic antinomy regarding human moral progress and a radical reconstruction of the Christian religion along Copernican lines.

Undergirding McCarthy's interpretation is a supposition regarding Kant's "properly" critical writings: only those works bearing the word "Critique" constitute properly critical philosophy, according to McCarthy. McCarthy's position is that, in *Religion*, Kant moves beyond what is allowed under first and second *Critique* strictures, violating Kant's own limitations on God-talk without a sufficient critical rationale. For this reason, McCarthy is convinced that *Religion* occupies a position outside the confines of the critical philosophy. Since, for him, Kant's discussion of God, grace, revelation, and redemption is a plainly uncritical endeavor, driven by non-philosophical motivations, McCarthy finds no convincing grounds for theology in Kant's thinking. Instead, McCarthy views Kant's religious talk as just that—religious talk, which is empty speculation according to Kant's philosophical framework.[8] This ungrounded discourse is precisely what McCarthy thinks is so problematic about *Religion*.

Since the critical philosophy unravels all God-talk, *Religion* cannot be an application of the critical philosophy to religion. Kant's religious talk, argues McCarthy, is neither historical theology nor transcendental philosophy; it is, instead, the byproduct of a deeply religious man's desire to reunite the discipline of philosophy with the essential elements of a beleaguered Christianity. Kant's chosen means for achieving this reunification is the moral philosophy. McCarthy sees a gradual development in Kant's thinking on religion and theology, beginning with the postulation of God in the second *Critique*. God the postulate emerges because "reason cannot conceive the attainment of the highest good . . . unless there is a highest intelligence."[9] This postulate has nothing to do with religion or theology, however. McCarthy's position is that, for Kant, "a God-idea gives us only knowledge of our own mind . . . and no knowledge whatsoever of the reality of God."[10] The God concept as a formal moral postulate never escapes pure subjectivity. The actual existence of God is not necessary for Kant; all that matters is "what God is for us as moral beings."[11]

Despite the theological non-realism his reading entails, McCarthy recognizes that Kant's understanding of God develops beyond a mere postulate in the *Critique of the Power of Judgment*, becoming a transcendental necessity for moral purposiveness.[12] McCarthy points to Kant's May 4, 1793, letter to Stäudlin, in which Kant indicates that *Religion* addresses the question, What may I hope? This question is the third of the four questions that Kant's philosophical program intended to answer. According to McCarthy, hope enters Kant's philosophical purview in force, not in the third *Critique*, where nature and freedom are considered simultaneously, but in *Religion*, where radical evil makes its appearance. In showing us incapable of fulfilling our moral duty, *Religion* finds the highest expression of hope in the possibility that God would choose to overcome evil: "One must hope and indeed one can hope, and such hope is practical. For it honeys the rim of the cup of duty and cuts short the danger of despairing of ever being well-pleasing to God, precisely the despair that could result from the consciousness of radical evil."[13]

Despite Kant's apparent logic in moving from radical evil to the question of hope, the doctrine of radical evil seems, to McCarthy, unabashedly and unjustifiably borrowed from historical Christianity. McCarthy writes, "[T]here is an unexpressed unity [in *Religion*] constituted by the one subject matter that is constantly referred to but never systematically addressed: the Christian religion. Christianity stands in the background of the entire work, frequently enters the discussion indirectly and occasionally more directly. But in neither fashion is its entry adequately accounted for."[14] Even though radical evil may serve as the catalyst for Kant's introduction of religion into the realm of hope, McCarthy points out that this way of addressing the third question—What may I hope?— radically revamps Kant's earlier answer to the second question, What ought I to do? If humans are incapable of doing what they ought to do, Kant's *ought-implies-can* principle no longer stands. Insofar as *Religion*, in this way, cripples Kant's moral philosophy and does so via a starting point that cannot be critically deduced, McCarthy sees *Religion* as decidedly uncritical and far removed from the fourth *Critique* many expected.[15] Kant's *Religion* seeks to carve out room for religion in general and Christianity in specific, but this project is hardly an account of religion within the boundaries of mere reason. If Kant ever gave such an account, McCarthy thinks it the second *Critique*.

From the foregoing we can identify the four main claims that frame

McCarthy's interpretation: (1) the critical philosophy does not allow room for the kind of God-talk or theology we see in *Religion*; (2) given the decidedly uncritical nature of the text, *Religion* is not a fourth *Critique*; (3) the starting point of *Religion* (viz., radical evil) is in no way deducible from the critical philosophy, and must therefore be a theological import from Kant's early Pietism; and (4) the importation of the Christian doctrine of original sin undoes the *ought*-implies-*can* principle and requires a shift in focus from the individual autonomy of the critical philosophy to a new foundation for moral hope.[16]

With these guiding principles in hand, the specifics of McCarthy's interpretation of *Religion* unfold. Book One begins with radical evil, which McCarthy views as a philosophical restatement of the Christian doctrine of original sin.[17] McCarthy understands Kant as making a straightforward attempt to parallel the story of Adam in Genesis with a rational account of human depravity. Human beings begin in a natural state of goodness (or *pre*-disposition) and this natural state is the one to which human beings are destined to return. Evil, however, has entered all of humanity. McCarthy sees this entrance as different from the Christian notion of inherited sin and equally distinct from the "social fall" of Rousseau. Kant instead holds that every individual is responsible for his or her own moral fall. Radical evil is universal only because every individual tends to fall freely into evil: "Kant's notion of radical evil is everyman's original sin, the product of his own misused freedom that has placed self-love above the moral law."[18] Thus, McCarthy's Kant accepts the "truths" of original sin (humanity begins good, falls into evil, and this fall is universal), but rejects the doctrine's historical content and hereditary character—while humanity universally falls into evil, this is not due to the transgression of a single ancestor but due to each individual's free willing of evil.

To be sure, radical evil is not meant to explain *why* humans universally choose evil—the choice itself is inscrutable. The doctrine, from what McCarthy can tell, is merely an empirical observation: we see evil in human history and our daily lives. But by introducing the problem of radical evil, Kant makes room for a divine solution. The introduction of God becomes necessary in the face of humanity's moral impairment, for if humans are incapable of becoming morally upright on their own, outside intervention is needed. "Many can grasp the moral law without God or religion," suggests McCarthy, "but [Kant] cannot realistically conceive of man's overcoming radical human weakness without God."[19] The difficulty, of course, is that McCarthy sees no justification for the introduction of radical evil, and even finds significant reasons to avoid the doctrine: (1) radical evil is entirely contrary to Kant's a priori principles, "good . . . is the natural state [of man] and . . . is known a priori,"[20] and (2) radical evil constitutes the biggest disruption to Kant's critical philosophy since it "disturbs the otherwise clear and rounded Kantian system and alters the understanding of religion that would otherwise issue."[21] In the end, however, McCarthy thinks such inadequacies are immaterial to Kant, in that Kant's goal is not the rational engagement of evil, but the introduction of a hope friendly to Lutheran Pietism.

The introduction of hope comes in Book Two, where the notion of grace first appears. According to McCarthy, grace is as inevitable in Kant's Christian-ized conception of religion as evil. This is not to say, of course, that grace is a critically derived, a priori concept. Rather, grace is a doctrine that asserts itself as necessary in the face of evil. The difficulty, however, is that certain concepts of grace are unwelcome in Kant's program, specifically those that threaten moral responsibility—the cornerstone of practical reason. As a result, McCar-thy understands Kant's philosophy of religion to entail a semi-Pelagian con-cept of grace—God offers grace, but this offer is extended only to those who do all in their power to earn it.[22] In the eyes of God, this earned grace is extended to moral converts at conversion. Our turn to the good, evidenced in our subsequent moral progress, gives us reason to hope that, despite our inevitable periodic failings, we will be judged well-pleasing to God. In other words, Kantian hope is hope that God will choose to count our turn to the good and our subsequent struggles sufficiently well-pleasing in themselves. Such grace is distinct from supernatural assistance to fulfill the law, for grace comes in response to the moral agent's turn to the good in the form of an affirmative judgment, not prior to the moral agent's turn to the good as assistance to initiate this turn.

In addition to the basic concepts of grace, McCarthy tries to account for two other significant themes that we find in Book Two: (1) Kant's renewed interest in the human disposition and (2) Kant's extensive use of Christic images. Regarding the former, McCarthy is dismissive. He acknowledges Kant's frequent references to the disposition and the apparent link between the disposition and grace, but for McCarthy, "Such language does not clarify Kant's philosophical teaching at all; it rather confuses it."[23] As for Kant's appar-ent Christology, McCarthy relies on symbolic theology for his explanation. He thinks that in Book Two what Kant intends to offer is a philosophical rein-terpretation of the Gospel of John in keeping with the reinterpretation of original sin in Book One of *Religion*. Book Two opens with talk of the Word, which is the Son of God, and moves on to describe a Christic figure Kant calls "the prototype of perfect humanity." Jesus Christ is presented in this symbolic theology as the first to withstand evil.[24] The Christic narrative is a metaphor, offering moral agents a picture of perfect humanity; it offers a "stimulus to action" for moral converts, and in this way provides grace for moral improve-ment. To be sure, this stimulus is not efficacious because of some redemptive action in history. Kant's emphasis, according to McCarthy, is always and only on our duty to conform to this symbol, a conformity which itself constitutes the suffering that atones for radical evil in the eyes of God. Redemption is not brought about by a historical Christ-figure; redemption is self-redemption worked out in our mirroring of the symbol that is Christ.[25]

Despite the emphasis McCarthy places on individual duty in *Religion*, he recognizes the communal thrust of Book Three. Kant suggests that humans must band together in effort to form an ethical commonwealth. In McCarthy's assessment, this emphasis on community is an offshoot of the universal nature of the moral law. The need for a universal moral community arises from the convergence of the universal moral law and the universal epidemic of radical evil. The reality of evil, for Kant, does not change what we ought to do, but it certainly changes our ability to do it, and therefore a communal effort is necessary for hope of ever overcoming radical evil.[26] This communal emphasis provides a way for Kant to justify the existence of both the church and sacred Scripture in expressly Christian terms. The church is a necessary vehicle for transporting individuals with moral faith to an ethical commonwealth; it promises to transform Kant's collection of redeemed moral individuals into a people of God.

In McCarthy's assessment, this linking of Enlightenment philosophy with Christian ecclesiology does not provide a critical rationale for historical religion. Ultimately, Kant wants philosophy to be the final authority for church doctrine and biblical interpretation.[27] With interpreters such as Yirmiahu Yovel, McCarthy understands Kant's goal to be the eventual disposal of the church since it is merely a vehicle for the instantiation of pure religion. A church can be a true church only if "it recognizes itself as transitional and as the imperfect vehicle of pure religion."[28] Kant thus advocates the rational purification of ecclesiastical bodies as they assume their vehicular role for moral religion. His vision, on McCarthy's reading, is one in which Christianity is purged of miracles and mysteries, as well as matters of atonement, grace, and sacramental ritual. This purging is not the outright removal of such doctrines from the faith but the symbolic reinterpretation of them set in motion in Books One and Two of *Religion*.[29]

McCarthy sees Kant moving in Book Four from a purely symbolic theology to a more historical discussion of Jesus. While Kant understands the historicity of Jesus to be significant, in Book Four it becomes clear that this significance is not the kind most Christians affirm. Jesus is hailed only as the first teacher of true religion. Kant engages various sayings of Jesus with a view to showing Christianity (as originally expounded) to be in keeping with rational religion. Whether this crediting of Christianity is justified is doubtful to McCarthy, for Christian doctrine was smuggled in at the beginning of *Religion*; thus Kant's affirmation of Christianity at the end of *Religion* is dubious in its circularity. McCarthy sees the analysis of Christianity in Book Four as merely one of many echoes of Kant's Pietistic roots:

> Kant's repeated singling out of Christianity and Christ (even when he does not refer to them by name) are, in fact, unjustified by his method of inquiry. A philosophical consideration of religion may, of course, look at historical religion and, indeed, should do so. But Kant looks all too instinctively at

Christianity, so much so that one finally recognizes that his interest in Christianity underlies his philosophical inquiry into religion. Were he evenhanded, he would have to investigate at least parallel material from other historical religions. His standpoint is clear, however, even if unsupported: he regards Christianity as the only truly moral religion. Thus his continued interest in highlighting its moral content and in transforming or eliminating less praiseworthy elements is evident throughout.[30]

Kant's Pietistic roots, in McCarthy's view, do not allow for an evenhanded assessment of religion. Instead, these roots drive Kant toward a favorable assessment of Christianity from the outset.[31]

In the end, McCarthy thinks virtually all the religious innovations in *Religion* betray Kant's desire, stemming from childhood, to carve out room for Christian faith despite its incongruence with the critical philosophy. As McCarthy summarizes, "Kant's treatment of Christ comes in the aftermath of the publication of the epoch-making Reimarus *Fragments*, edited by Lessing, in which Jesus and his disciples were depicted as schemers and deceivers. Thus, as Despland notes, 'Kant was at the beginning of a series of thinkers for whom it became clear that Jesus must either be reinterpreted or lost.' In part, Kant tried to save Jesus from the *Aufklärer*."[32] In *Religion*, the entire endeavor of rescuing the Christian faith from the *Aufklärer* progresses, in McCarthy's view, under tension at each stage—the tension between the autonomous will and radical evil, the tension between the individualism of the second *Critique* and the ethical community of *Religion*, and the tension between the need for the church and the need to disband dogma and religious practice. McCarthy sees these tensions throughout as reflective of the greatest tension in *Religion*, namely, Kant's desire to merge his Pietistic roots with his critical philosophy. The implication is that only moral reason and God as postulate constitute legitimate developments in Kant's philosophy. The rest of Kant's rational religion must be interpreted either as adhering closely to moral reason and theological non-realism or as positing something novel and fundamentally out of step with the critical philosophy. Kant's philosophy of religion is thus either reductive toward historical religion or productive in an anti-critical way. But in either case, it remains in fundamental opposition to both religious experience and historical religion, despite Kant's metaphysical motivations.

Witness for the Defense: Stephen R. Palmquist

What makes Stephen Palmquist's testimony significant is that, rather than approaching the text with the skeptical lenses afforded by McCarthy, Palmquist argues that Kant genuinely intends to establish a rational basis for religious experience and practice, and this intent is present from the earliest manifestations of his critical philosophy. In other words, *Religion* is not an afterthought for Kant; it is the natural outcome of his philosophical quest, tempered by years of critical reflection and religious conviction. Contrary to McCarthy, Palmquist does not see a sharp break between Kant's Pietistic upbringing and Enlightenment culture. Instead, Palmquist argues for a smooth transition. The gulf between Kant's pre-critical, rationalist metaphysics and Kant's groundbreaking transcendental philosophy is not nearly as great as some would suggest. Palmquist argues for a close connection between Kant's pre-critical interest in mysticism and the later development of his transcendental philosophy and theology.

Key to this interpretation is Palmquist's recasting of one of the most contentious essays Kant ever wrote, "Dreams" (1766). Kant wrote the essay in response to an encounter with the writings of Swedish mystic Emanuel Swedenborg. Swedenborg is famous for his contributions to numerous fields of inquiry, from science and politics to philosophy and religion. However, Swedenborg's more fantastic claims seemed to intrigue Kant most. Kant waited anxiously for, and then reportedly bought, Swedenborg's *Arcana Coelesti*, an expensive multi-volume treatise documenting Swedenborg's extraordinary mystical experiences and inspired interpretations of these experiences. Although Kant read *Arcana Coelesti* with great interest, unclear is what influence the specifics of the book had on Kant. Kant was apparently less than impressed on the whole, and—perhaps feeling a bit swindled—wrote "Dreams" in order to lambaste Swedenborg's writings, averring that they "contain not a single drop of reason" (2:360).

The traditional way of handling Kant's understanding of Swedenborg is to take the language and tone of "Dreams" at face value. Such an approach indicates that Kant (under the influence of the newly encountered writings of David Hume) disavowed his earlier intrigue with the Swede's mystical musings and clairvoyant experiences. "Dreams," on this reading, is prima facie evidence that Kant held at best an ambivalent view of Swedenborg's corpus and publicly expounded visions, and at worst a resolutely antithetical view toward the enthusiasm (*Schwärmerei*) that Swedenborg examples. What is often pointed out is that Kant's criticism of Swedenborg's "mystical" accounts focuses on their lack of philosophical rigor. Kant's language is at times harsh and his tone often sarcastic, and this too is marshaled as clear support for the traditional understanding of Kant's position. Often interpreters take this firm rejection of Swedenborg's writings to mean that Kant was against the very possibility of any kind of mysticism whatsoever.[33] Credibility is added to such an interpretation when one realizes that Kant later did not include "Dreams" in a book of his collected writings—presumably because he was somewhat embarrassed by the essay.

Palmquist begins his interpretation of "Dreams" by acknowledging that Kant rejects most of Swedenborg's claims as critically untenable. Palmquist suggests, however, that the reason for Kant's uncharacteristically harsh treatment of Swedenborg's work is not clear. Limiting ourselves to what Kant actually writes, we discover that Kant is clearly against mysticism of a certain kind, namely, fanatical forms of mysticism that attempt to usurp reason's authority and superstitious kinds of mysticism that attribute special powers to worldly things without good reason (see 2:360). But Palmquist points out that although Kant condemns Swedenborg's writings as an ad hoc mixture of both of these bad forms of mysticism, he does not disavow all forms of mysticism. The "tone" of "Dreams" is often over-interpreted and made to say as much. But Palmquist contends that the lack of a blanket rejection of mysticism in "Dream," when coupled with a careful look at the more positive material that runs parallel to this work in the critical philosophy, gives reason to think Kant may have developed a positive position on mysticism in his subsequent writings.

Palmquist believes that a positive case for the initial stages of "Kant's critical mysticism" can be made by comparing "Dreams" with the first *Critique*. In describing the content of "Dreams" as it relates to Swedenborg's writings, Palmquist insists, "Many of the important doctrines of his Critical philosophy are foreshadowed in this book (*and*, using rather different language, in Swedenborg's own books)."[34] For instance, in one passage in "Dreams" Kant outlines two advantages to maintaining a critical approach to metaphysics, both of which sound very much like his emphasis on critical inquiry and rational limitations in the first *Critique*. The first advantage is the neutralization of mystics such as Swedenborg, who enlist reason to support theories about hidden properties of things without reasonable cause (see 2:367). The second advantage, according to Kant, "consists both in knowing whether the task has been determined by reference to what one can know, and in knowing what relation the question has to the empirical concepts, upon which all our judgements must at all times be based. To that extent metaphysics is always a science of the *limits of human reason*" (2:367–68).

Other passages in "Dreams," Palmquist points out, foreshadow the central themes of the second *Critique* (see, e.g., 2:369–73). For example, in a series of rhetorical questions, Kant asks, "What, is it only good to be virtuous because there is another world? Or is it rather the case that actions will one day be rewarded because they are good and virtuous in themselves? Does not the heart of man contain within itself immediate moral prescriptions?" (2:372). Material links like these provide support for Palmquist's contention that Kant's encounter with the writings of Swedenborg is more constructive than typically thought.[35] Rather than understanding "Dreams" as a work of either "pre-critical" or "critical" philosophy, Palmquist sees it as a transitional writing. It exhibits the kind of critical balance and resourcefulness important to Kant's early writings and anticipates features integral to his later transcendental or "Copernican" writings.

Palmquist argues that the main difficulty in finding something positive in Kant's critical engagement with mysticism is that interpreters often read

"Dreams" and the first *Critique* as compatible "Copernican" rejections of mysticism. Yet, for Palmquist, "Dreams" represents a pre-Copernican mixture of perspectives in which Kant vents his critical frustration with his inability to cope satisfactorily with Swedenborg's claims. The question of knowledge commanding Kant's attention in the first *Critique* led to the formulation of a theoretical account of reason in which mysticism finds no secure foothold. Palmquist writes, "The fact that 'glimpses [of "the infinity in the finite and the universality in the individual"] are distrusted' by Kant is taken by most interpreters as a distrust of immediate [religious] experience, when in fact Kant's expression of distrust in such 'glimpses' always relates to their inadequacy when viewed from reason's theoretical standpoint, the standpoint that aims at and depends on empirical knowledge."[36] This does not mean that, as the critical philosophy developed, Kant remained unable to find a suitable place for religious experience and practice, however. On the contrary, Palmquist sees this concern to place religious experience and practice as present throughout the Kantian corpus and finally brought to critical completion and fruition in Kant's writings on religion and posthumous writings.

The posthumous writings, or *Opus Postumum*, are important for Palmquist's interpretation of Kant because these papers demonstrate, more clearly than any other writings, Kant's intention to complete his philosophy as a systematic whole, including God, man, and world within its architectonic parameters. The third *Critique* and *Religion* constitute the third part of Kant's plan, and, as we will see, this placement is integral to Palmquist's interpretation of *Religion*. However, the question of man—including man's place in the world and relationship to God—is never fully addressed as a final synthesis within the critical architectonic. The *Opus Postumum*, while incomplete and tentative at best, show that Kant was indeed interested in providing a complete and critical account of reason that incorporates God, man, and world into one system. When this fact is coupled with a careful analysis of Kant's metaphysical transition from the pre-critical writings to the critical philosophy, it appears that Kant sought from beginning to end to include a critical account of religious experience at the transcendental boundaries of reason.

Palmquist's technical name for this final movement in Kant's thought is the "Transcendental Perspective."[37] Palmquist contends that this is the one overarching perspective that is important for understanding the nature and extent of Kant's philosophy and its overall relationship to the philosophy of religion. The Transcendental Perspective does not have a special relationship to any single *Critique*, but is the perspective governing all of them. Palmquist puts it thus: "There is no 'transcendental standpoint'—i.e. no separate *Critique* corresponding to the transcendental perspective—because this perspective forms the Transcendental Perspective which governs *all* the [perspectives] on the very highest level on which the principle of perspective operates in Kant's System."[38] The Transcendental Perspective critically "unpacked" consists of an empirical standpoint in the first *Critique*, a moral standpoint in the second *Critique*, and a combined aesthetic/teleological standpoint in the third *Critique*. As Palmquist writes, "This over-arching 'Transcendental (or "Copernican") Perspective', which is based on the assumption that the subject imposes certain a priori conditions on the object, defines the systematic context into which all three Critical systems fit."[39] The Transcendental Perspective proceeds on the assumption that religious experience is experience of a special kind: according to Palmquist, Kant's God is assumed to be the ground of being, and as such funds experience in each of its forms. Religious experience, therefore, is fundamentally distinct from all other forms of experience—scientific, moral, and aesthetic. In a word, it is *mystical* and bound up with the transcendental nature of bare reason as a whole.

For our purposes here, we need not go into the details of Palmquist's interpretation of the critical philosophy.[40] Neither Palmquist's case for Kant's "critical mysticism" nor the significance of the *Opus Postumum* to the critical philosophy is at issue here. What Palmquist's interpretation adds by way of testimony that McCarthy overlooks is the positive utility of the many religiously and theologically affirmative resources in Kant's work. So far, we have focused on Palmquist's case for positive metaphysical motives behind the construction of the critical philosophy. Palmquist's case for the positive incorporation of *Religion* into the critical philosophy depends less on these holistic considerations and more on the role of the third *Critique*. According to Palmquist, the third *Critique* in particular is what allows Kant to transform mere moral faith into a critically robust form of rational religious faith.

Palmquist presents the third *Critique* as "the crowning phase of [Kant's] entire System."[41] According to Palmquist, "in the *Critique of Judgment* Kant argues that the opposite standpoints of nature (our causally-determined, theoretical knowledge) and freedom (our self-determined, practical action) are *synthesized* by various forms of existential judgment."[42] Palmquist points to a lengthy appendix in the third *Critique*, where Kant explains how this synthesis provides a foundation for "moral theology," where God can be seen as more than a "deistic watchmaker." He instead becomes a *"living God*, who can be encountered—albeit, symbolically—in just such forms of human experience as are examined earlier in the book."[43] The judicial, or third, standpoint of transcendental reason, brings critical culmination and existential import to the architectonic substructure of Kant's entire philosophical system and, as such, is crucial for determining the meaning of *Religion*.

The problem of unity is highlighted in the third *Critique* (see 5:176) and manifests itself in a distinctly religious form in Book One of *Religion*. Without aesthetic and teleological judgment, nature would appear blind to human moral striving, and human moral striving would appear queer to nature. Unless reason has within its faculties a source of hope, it becomes unstable. The third *Critique* brings harmony to reason through the experience of beauty and sublimity, and these experiences provide us with a sense of purposiveness that compels human judgment to contemplate the meaning of the highest good. This is, of course, not new to Kant's way of thinking. He had already highlighted the significance of the highest good in the first antinomy of practical reason in the second *Critique*. In the third *Critique*, however, the issue of the highest good comes to the fore and eventually leads Kant to consider religion. In this way, the third *Critique* becomes the crowning phase in Kant's critical trilogy, setting the stage for a transcendental building process, meant to stabilize the fact-value divide and initiate a critical approach to philosophy of religion.

Palmquist is sensitive to the shortcomings of interpretations that understand *Religion* to somehow reduce religion to morality in an eliminative way. (Eliminative reduction occurs when "one special way of explaining something is not only necessary, but *self-sufficient*, so that it can actually replace, or *explain* away all other explanations.")[44] However, Palmquist suggests that understanding *Religion* in such a decisively moral way makes Kant's arguments appear radically inconsistent. And it would be better, in the light of the perspectival nature of Kant's philosophical program leading up to *Religion*, to see *Religion* as an answer to the question, What may I hope? and as requiring third *Critique* resources for its interpretation. According to Palmquist, "[*Religion*] ought to be viewed as itself a transcendental *Critique of Religion*—i.e., as an attempt to delineate the *boundary* between true religion and false religion by setting forth the *necessary conditions for the possibility of religious experience.*"[45] In this way, *Religion* presents a prolegomena to "Critical Mysticism."

These considerations surrounding the critical philosophy and its relationship to Kant's metaphysical motivations set the stage for Palmquist's interpretation of *Religion*. According to Palmquist, there exists a plethora of "perspectival" considerations in *Religion* that Kant imports from the critical philosophy. Put simply, Palmquist suggests that each of the four books of *Religion* is best understood as a manifestation of one of four different perspectives emanating from the critical philosophy—the transcendental, logical, empirical, and hypothetical perspectives, respectively. Each of these four perspectives branches out into three distinct moments in Kant's argument. Thus, *Religion*, for Palmquist, has a kind of architectonic structure (not unlike Kant's Critiques) that, when properly understood, reveals the essence of bare reason as it applies to religious experience. A summary of this twelve-fold structure is displayed in "Figure VII.8: Kant's Circle of Religion" of *Kant's Critical Religion*. To unpack all the idiosyncrasies of Palmquist's approach to *Religion* would take us well beyond the confines of the required testimony. Instead, we will here take only a brief look at the contours of each book in *Religion*, according to Palmquist's reading, and home in on Kant's arguments regarding the moral disposition found therein.

Palmquist takes the central question of Book One of *Religion* to be, Is human nature originally good or evil? Kant's answer to this question, argues

Palmquist, is two-sided. On the one side, when we refer to the "potential that resides in every human being . . . we must regard human nature as originally good."[46] This is how Palmquist understands Kant's talk of "the predisposition." On the other side, if "the question refers to the *actual* state of every human person in their first (and subsequent) moral act(s), then we cannot avoid the conclusion that an original ('radical') evil exists in every human nature."[47] Humans in this sense are "evil by nature." Palmquist summarizes, "Kant never explains the origin of 'radical evil' . . . , but merely sets it up as a sign of the inscrutability of evil's true origin."[48]

Book Two, by contrast, asks, How can an *evil* person *become* good? Kant's answer again, says Palmquist, involves two parts. First, "no matter how good we are, we cannot be good enough to please God."[49] God is holy and perfect; we are unholy and flawed. The gulf is too big to be traversed by mere human effort. Second, "by acting morally we render ourselves *susceptible* of 'higher and, for us [i.e., for bare reason] inscrutable assistance.' "[50] Kant, thinks Palmquist, holds that we can hope to become pleasing to God by acting morally, and in doing so we make ourselves susceptible to divine assistance in our moral deficiencies. Book Two, according to Palmquist, is essentially an argument for the claim, "*grace is a necessary condition of becoming good.*"[51] We must believe in grace because the integrity of our moral dispositions depends on it. "The solution to the problem of personal evil," argues Palmquist, "rests on an inscrutable element in the system: the notion that there is a higher moral Being who will assist us in our moral weakness, thus making practical faith . . . effective."[52] The practical personification of God's gracious provision is "the 'ideal of moral perfection' that exists in every human person as an 'archetype' and 'can give us power.' "[53] That is, Palmquist assumes that all humans have within them an idea of a morally perfect person, and this idea can help spur on moral converts in their moral striving. According to Palmquist, there is no rational explanation for the existence of this concept of a morally perfect person within us, "other than to assume it is an inscrutable gift from some higher moral power."[54]

Whereas Books One and Two consider the rational dimension of religion by way of the existence of inscrutable evil in human nature and faith in divine (and equally inscrutable) moral assistance, Book Three displays Kant's "concern for establishing the context for the expression of the good heart in the real world of *experience* . . . [by] adopting . . . an *empirical* religious perspective."[55] Palmquist understands the empirical perspective to be demonstrated explicitly in Kant's turn to social or communal considerations, or what Kant calls "the ethical commonwealth." Kant likens the ethical commonwealth to a church with both invisible and visible dimensions. It is the duty of human beings with good hearts to band together and form their kindred, invisible unity into a visible kingdom of God on earth. According to Palmquist, "The empirical perspective . . . concludes . . . by making 'empirical faith,' also known as 'historical ecclesiastical faith,' a necessary element of genuine religion."[56] The rest of Book Three shows how the empirical insights of reason "are to be *applied* in a real, historical religion."[57] For Palmquist, "like radical evil and the assistance-giving archetype in the first two stages, the details of the divine organization of the church must be 'filled in' by some historical tradition."[58] Christianity is Kant's religion of choice in this regard.

Palmquist places Book Four of *Religion* under the rubric of the hypothetical perspective of reason insofar as it "establishes the conditions under which the church, as given in [Book Three], can serve God, despite the limitations of earthly existence."[59] True service to God constitutes the direct activity of bare reason or natural religion, while indirect service to God is a product of revealed religion. Indirect service, as a sort of non-moral "add-on," has its place in any thoroughgoing analysis of religion as the clothing of pure religious faith. However, when it is understood to be somehow self-sufficient or detached from natural religion, it shades off into pseudo-service to God and religious delusion. Natural religion alone is necessary to please God; revealed religion, on the other hand, is made up of an admixture of both moral action and morally indifferent action. Morally indifferent action, according to Palmquist, plays a "supporting role" in the quest for true religion by providing a dispositional context that promotes moral action.[60] Yet, Kant's main concern in Book Four is to properly prioritize natural and revealed religion, and point out where religion goes wrong when it misprioritizes these features.

Looking deeper into this basic structure to Palmquist's reading of *Religion*, we find first Palmquist's understanding of the disposition. Palmquist defines the generic human disposition as "the timeless ground of a person's maxims at any given point in time."[61] Precisely what this means for Palmquist is difficult to determine. Although he seems initially satisfied with maintaining this somewhat paradoxical definition, he takes Kant's aims in *Religion* to require an explication of the human disposition in order to get at the transcendental conditions of religious experience and the contours of critical religious belief. As Palmquist draws out Kant's understanding of the disposition, he contrasts the human disposition with the original predisposition. The predisposition, says Palmquist, is "the timeless ground of a person's maxims at the very *outset* of life, before any moral actions have been performed,"[62] while the human disposition is essentially a combination of the "predisposition" and what we might call the "disposition proper." When, however, the disposition is considered in its original state of goodness, it is thought of as an indeterminate predisposition to good. When the disposition is considered subsequent to its employment in nature it is thought of as the disposition proper, which has been determined by human freedom. This second way of considering the disposition is what Palmquist thinks Kant has in mind when he says humans are "evil by nature." When the human disposition, which is originally good, is employed in nature, it naturally inverts the moral order of incentives and displays an evil character. And this inversion is what makes way for the indwelling of radical evil.

Palmquist thus understands the logic of Kant's argument to endorse a kind of double-aspect understanding of the human disposition: the disposition is viewed in either its original state of innocence or its existential state of evil. Hovering between these two aspects, we find what Kant calls "the propensity to evil." The propensity to evil, like the disposition, has two dimensions—a noumenal and a phenomenal dimension. The former is the sense in which radical evil is innate, "indwelling" us, as Palmquist puts it, while the latter is the phenomenal exercise of the will, where we have "actively *chosen* [evil] even though we are essentially passive recipients of the 'indwelling' of radical evil."[63] While what it means to display a phenomenal propensity to evil may be clear enough, the noumenal act that gives rise to this propensity is less clear. Palmquist recognizes that Kant takes the propensity to evil to be rooted in a subjective ground for the exercise of freedom that is chosen prior to any exercise of freedom in time, and this is the "noumenal act" that gives rise to the phenomenal propensity to evil.[64] As Palmquist points out, a noumenal act, by definition, is inscrutable; thus we have no explanation of why each individual chooses evil. We can only affirm, says Palmquist, the paradoxical reality that this noumenal act is contingent and yet universal—every human contingently chooses evil.[65] Radical evil is thus "a mystery not unlike the mysteries of pure intuition and freedom, both of which Kant regards as basic facts of human nature that must simply be acknowledged, and cannot be proved or explained by reason."[66] For this reason, radical evil is the noumenal complement to the phenomenal propensity to evil, affecting the turn from the predisposition to the disposition proper and creating a situation in which each human disposition must be converted to the good.[67]

Conversion, on Palmquist's reading, is not a mere intellectual acknowledgement of radical evil and of the need to change our ways. Rather, conversion is a "radical *conversion* of one's disposition," a conversion equally radical as the movement away from the predisposition to good.[68] As for the possibility of such conversion, we must hold it possible, Palmquist submits, because duty demands it. This said, conversion is not to be naively thought of as a re-turn back to the original state of human disposition. To the contrary, it is a turning toward the good in full realization of the inevitable pitfalls and failings associated with even the most radical moral striving.

Palmquist admits the presence of profound paradoxes in *Religion*. In fact, the thrust of Palmquist's argument seems to be that Kant's intent in Book One is to show that we necessarily meet with certain paradoxes from the perspective of reason alone. On the one hand, Kant believes that it must be within our power to obey the moral law and, by extension, convert our disposition back to the good. On the other hand, Kant asserts that, despite a lingering "seed of goodness," evil is "*not to be extirpated* by human forces" (6:37). This paradoxical account of the human condition requires that we believe in divine aid as the only reasonable way forward. How God could provide the kind of assistance that preserves human autonomy and moral self-determination is a mystery, but mystery is part and parcel of the mysticism Palmquist sees in Kant.

Resting a philosophy of religion on mystical foundations may appear folly according to the analytic logic of Kant's detractors, but this makes perfect sense according to the synthetic logic of Kant's critical mysticism. When nature and freedom are considered simultaneously, we are driven to reflection on the question of hope in the context of felt harmony. Palmquist sees the third *Critique* as providing an insufficient account of this harmony and the religious feeling that is often associated with it. *Religion,* as a transcendental critique of the possibility of religious experience, therefore offers a way forward. Once we recognize that the human predicament is fundamentally paradoxical, a *Religion*-styled narrative of evil and redemption, based on moral fortitude and divine grace, becomes a rational answer to the question of hope. According to Palmquist's interpretation of *Religion,* both grace and moral striving are required for the hope of salvation. Grace is the theoretical means and moral striving is the practical means. They can never be thought of at the same time, however, for to do so would yield a contradiction. From the point of view of judicial reasoning, the nature of the relationship between grace and moral striving is inscrutable.[69] Mystery and inscrutability are, therefore, the hallmarks of Palmquist's interpretation of Kant's philosophy of religion. He understands them to have intellectual credibility because, for Kant, religion is rooted in the paradoxical and ineffable phenomenon of religious experience at the outer bounds of reason transcendentally considered.

Witness for the Prosecution: Keith Ward

Palmquist's strategy for interpreting *Religion* emerges out of his interpretation of Kant's critical philosophy as a whole. It relies on showing a relationship between the beginning and end of Kant's career as a professional philosopher and, in this context, showing how *Religion* fits into the critical philosophy as an extension of the arguments in the second and third *Critique.* Keith Ward accepts many of the main features of this type of interpretation. His key interpretative text, entitled *The Development of Kant's View of Ethics,* moves from the pre-critical writings to the *Opus Postumum* in a way very similar to Palmquist's work. Nevertheless, Ward arrives at diametrically different conclusions than Palmquist. Ward's rendition of Kant's journey casts suspicion on the overt optimism reflected in Palmquist's testimony. Ward argues that Kant was never able to get beyond a purely formal expansion of his ethical theory and that a continuous thread of theological agnosticism, not mysticism, permeates Kant's critical writings from beginning to end. Like Palmquist, Ward grants that some optimism exists in the first *Critique* regarding the status of transcendental idealism and the eventual development of a critical approach to religion and theology. "[Kant] holds open," avers Ward, "the future possibility of a final synthesis of human knowledge under necessary principles,"[70] and Ward grants that Kant's motives behind completing the system are never far removed from his religious convictions. Unlike Palmquist, however, Ward does not think that Kant provides a feasible architectonic capable of grounding critical religious theory. Kant's ethics and philosophy of religion are built on the shifting sands of rational and religious concepts, and from the point of view of the critical philosophy proper, no way exists to make coherent sense of Kant's writings on religion.

In a moment, we will examine how Ward tracks the evolution of Kant's position on ethics from "Dreams" (1766) to *Religion* (1793). An important preliminary note, however, is that this analysis is set in the context of a careful assessment of the biographical and historical origins of Kant's thought. Ward, like McCarthy, thinks these details dramatically color Kant's ethical theory and place it in a conceptual quagmire from which Kant was never able to escape. In the opening pages of his treatment, Ward zeros in on the tension between Kant's Pietistic Lutheran upbringing and the philosophical rationalism of his university education. According to Ward, "A vital key to the understanding of Kant's views is the fact that his parents were both devout members of the Pietist Church."[71] Kant's parents had "set before him, from his earliest years, an example of simple piety at its best; and his deepest religious convictions never moved far from this idea of the religious life."[72] But, as Ward points out, Kant also experienced a darker side of Pietism at Protestant school. At school, Kant learned that outward piety was to be valued more than inner sincerity, that emotional intensity was more significant than moral worth, and that his sins should be his constant focus.[73] This experience eventually loosened the grip of religion on Kant's intellectual life.

As Kant's schooling continued, philosophical rationalism became another important influence on his ethical and religious thought. Kant was introduced to this intellectual pathway when he enrolled at the University of Königsberg, and it became an enticing alternative to Pietism. Christian Wolff and Martin Knutzen were important catalysts in this regard. Wolff systematized and elaborated on the work of Leibniz, and he provided the standard texts in the areas of logic and metaphysics during Kant's formative years. Knutzen was Kant's esteemed teacher at university. He utilized Wolff's texts and teachings, and was influential in guiding Kant toward rationalism in his philosophical inquiries. "Knutzen himself," Ward writes, "managed to combine Pietism and rationalism; and the combination of simple faith and rigorous intellect is very characteristic of his greatest pupil."[74] Ward takes the mix of Pietism and rationalism to be the driving influence behind the development of Kant's ethics, and the chief reason why Kant eventually runs into trouble in *Religion*. According to Ward, "It is plain that the combination of these two schools of thought is not easily achievable. There is the difference of an era between the man of faith, who lives by Divine revelation and self-abnegation; and the man of the Enlightenment, for whom reason is the final judge in all matters, even those of religion."[75]

Like Palmquist, Ward begins his analysis of Kant's metaphysical motivations for writing *Religion* with "Dreams." Unlike Palmquist, however, Ward argues that the tone and force of the language in this essay combine to launch a frontal attack on metaphysics as represented in the work of Emanuel Swedenborg, and Ward understands this attack to spill over into Kant's account of metaphysics generally considered. "Dreams" marks a time in Kant's life, argues Ward, when encounters with the metaphysical pretensions of the day came to a head, bringing into collision Pietism and rationalism in the work of Swedenborg. In the end, metaphysical speculation became the very epitome of all that is wrong with religion from the point of view of reason, and, as a result, Kant came to the conclusion that the pursuit of moral perfection was the only meaningful aim in human life. Accordingly, "One might see the main argument of the *Dreams* . . . as being to establish the independence and logical priority of morality over theoretical speculation."[76]

Ward contends that "*Dreams* marks the nadir of Kant's metaphysical interests" and the true source of Kant's turn toward morality in his later writings.[77] Metaphysics does not emerge again in the degree present in Kant's pre-critical writings until the moral theology of the second *Critique*, and there it takes a very different form. This new form erases virtually all of the robust realism of Kant's earlier and more conventional work in theology in favor of a kind of moral formalism, conducive to the transcendental nature of reason. Ward notes that the task of establishing an a priori universal science, though begun in the first *Critique*, does not receive Kant's full attention until *Groundwork of the Metaphysics of Morals* and the second *Critique*. In the meantime, Kant's theoretical philosophy puts his thought at some remove from the rational religious realism of his pre-critical work. According to Ward, the critical Kant became more of an agnostic in his religious and theological convictions, looking to formulate the rational essence of religion rather than ground the empirical dimension of religion.

All this is not to say that Ward is insensitive to the many aspects of Kant's philosophy that carry positive implications for faith. Citing Kant's *Lectures on Ethics*, for example, Ward points to how Kant explicitly affirms, "though ethics cannot depend upon metaphysical or theological belief, it necessarily gives rise to theological belief and cannot exist without it."[78] Yet, in Ward's estimation, while clearly positive in theological intent, little of Kant's pre-critical metaphysics actually survives the Copernican revolution. In the development of Kant's ethics, Ward understands Kant to start from a position of theoretical agnosticism and gravitate gradually toward moral non-realism. Kant's rational foundations for theology correspond directly to the support they receive from his moral theory and the lack of support (and outright antagonism) they receive from his theoretical philosophy. For this reason, they remain merely a formal aspect of his moral development.

Ward's emphasis on the formal in morality and his conclusion that Kant's thinking on theology lacks any real metaphysical content has clear implications for the way in which Ward interprets *Religion*. Ward cannot hold that *Religion* develops Kant's moral thought in ways that excavate the rational grounds for religious faith; the development of Kant's ethics, thinks Ward, always ends up with the postulation of God as a merely formal component of morality. As Ward puts it, "The imagined supposition of a supreme moral intelligence thus helps to regulate our attitudes in specific ways, as dictated by morality itself."[79] The rest of Kant's philosophy of religion only supports these postulates, adding nothing to them that they do not already possess on their own. Moreover, there is no possible correlation between the concept of God (and immortality) and reality; the concept of God and any further dissemination of its meaning is a mere figment or fiction. Ward summarizes this way: "not only is talk of God 'empty' or purely formal—being not founded on sense perceptions—it is necessarily inapplicable to the object it attempts to conceive. So there is no question that a noumenal object might *correspond* to these ideas of reason."[80]

In line with this assessment, Ward argues that *Religion* is meant simply to expound on and, in a sense, vindicate the formal nature of the moral theory. When the reality and profundity of our moral failure threatens to destabilize practical reason, religious reasoning of the kind we find in *Religion* provides us with helpful and novel moral resources. According to Ward, "the only important thing in religion is that which is common to all religions, obedience to the moral law and hope of grace to remedy man's seemingly inevitable moral deficiencies. Beyond this a man may believe what he pleases, as long as he does not regard the specific observances of his own religion as in themselves an especially pleasing service to God, or as any more than 'a means of awakening within us a godly disposition.'"[81] In Ward's interpretation of Kant, moral character and obedience are at some remove from religious belief and practice. The latter serve as only a help-maid to the former. As long as religion promotes human moral striving (or at least does not lead to moral deficiency), the content of and rituals behind belief are not significant.[82]

In this light, it is not hard to see how Ward's contextualized reading of *Religion* parallels the work of McCarthy, while yielding a blanket dismissal of interpretations such as Palmquist's. Ward's interpretation of *Religion* presents a highly critical account of Kant's position, where *Religion* is understood as a book written by a man seeking to come to terms with two opposing positions on religion and theology.[83] For Ward, "there remains in Kant to the end that tension of freedom and rational intelligibility, Wolffian rationalism and individualistic Pietism, from which he started."[84] Kant's chief concern in *Religion*, under this reading, is to stabilize the moral quest by translating Christian concepts into ones that are useful for moral purposes. In Book One of *Religion*, Kant begins with the philosophical translation of the Christian doctrine of original sin:

> Kant here seems to commit himself fully to the Christian doctrine of original sin; and his version of the theory retains all the paradoxes of the orthodox account. Evil is innate; but man is responsible for it. It is ineradicable, but every particular action is original and totally free; so each new evil act is an original fall from innocence. He accepts the biblical story of the Fall, treating it as a temporal allegory depicting a non-temporal, intelligible reality.[85]

Kant gives the title *radical evil* to his moral translation, identifying original sin as every individual's decision to invert the moral order of incentives and subordinate the moral law to other considerations. On Ward's account, radical evil is "the existential genesis of the Fall in every man; Adam is a symbol to explain our innate evil propensity."[86] The symbol of the Fall communicates that "man was seduced and is not fundamentally corrupt."[87] This picture of a fall from a higher state assures us that, while we, as humans, bear a corrupt heart, there also lingers remnants of "a good will; and so hope remains of a return to the good."[88] The symbol of the Fall becomes, for Ward, both the sober assessment of humanity's tendency to diverge from the moral law and a glimmer of hope that a return to the good may be possible. Radical evil is thus the aperture through which the rest of Kant's translation takes place.

The tension between human corruption and moral redemption requires divine grace. Grace comes through both a fresh conversion to the good and the individual's determination to band together with others committed to being good so that moral progress can proceed. As such, grace must be thought of as something that comes only as a result of a continual, phenomenal demonstration of an inner conversion to the good; that is, grace "must be won through one's own efforts."[89] In short, one "wins" grace through conversion.

Conversion, on Ward's reading, is a continual putting off of the old self for the sake of the new; its realization is never certain, for it can only be inferred from "one's actual moral improvement in life."[90] Given this uncertainty, grace, like the Fall, becomes an important symbol for Kant's moral economy. The grace symbol assures us that the imperfect life is judged not on the basis of its inherent perfection, or even its approximation of perfection; rather, the grace symbol assures the moral convert that our moral life is judged on the basis of its overall character. Insofar as this character testifies to an inherently good disposition made to appear imperfect by ongoing phenomenal deficiencies, we can hope to find mercy. As Ward puts it, "An ever-defective but endless advance may be judged by an intellectual intuition to be perfect as a whole, because of its underlying disposition. . . . As phenomenon, man is permanently deficient;

yet, as noumenon, he is essentially holy, through a change of heart."[91] Grace is not a foreign divine influence, on Ward's reading, but a symbol, encouraging radical and continual rededication of the will to the moral law as supreme incentive. Grace thus constitutes a formal addition to reason, occupying the same intellectual space as the other religious postulates of moral reason.

To Ward's mind, Kant's entire argument centers on Christian symbols and their usefulness in developing the anatomy of moral postulates. These symbols should be read not as Kant's commendation of wishful thinking, but as necessary features of the moral philosophy. "Religious doctrines are implied in morality," Ward contends, "in so far as they symbolize this struggle [i.e., a warfare of good and evil], its origin and its outcome, in the individual's life."[92] Without employing religious symbols, the moral philosophy would be nothing more than abstract formalism. Religious symbols and aesthetic ideas, thinks Ward, share an important characteristic: "they express what is indefinable in a particular mental state in such a way that it can be communicated to others."[93] When the moral law is confronted by competing sensual incentives, religious symbols are able to counteract their potentially corruptive influence. They put flesh on the internal, dispositional struggle of every man—the human will is conflicted, and symbols help to bring this struggle and the possibility of its solution into sharp relief.

To be sure, Ward's interpretation of Kant understands symbol to depend only accidentally on history. Reason does not require empirical argumentation for the justification of symbols or necessitate that symbols be taken from a specific historical faith (e.g., Christianity). As far as our moral improvement is concerned, there is no point to considering whether Jesus ever existed, for example. The symbol of the prototype works just as well with or without the historical personage. Jesus may well be "the 'archetype of the pure moral disposition,' which all men must imitate in themselves";[94] and it may be true that, in the act of conversion, the new man undergoes suffering brought on him by the sins of the old man, a suffering "the Christian story of Jesus on the Cross symbolizes."[95] But the story (or symbol) itself does not provide anything of substance to the process; and presumably, Kant could draw religious symbols from any historical faith—even though his "European biases" likely made other religious images a non-option for him.

With this picture of *Religion* before us, we come to Ward's testimony regarding the success of Kant's project. The fact that the symbol of divine assistance is required for moral striving should not be taken to mean that Ward finds Kant's understanding of grace to be coherent relative to the critical philosophy as a whole. To the contrary, Kant's use of the grace symbol is precisely where Ward thinks Kant's account begins to run aground. Divine assistance is "incomprehensible" from both the theoretical and practical vantage points. We could never know that God gave us assistance, and the moral philosophy itself cannot coherently be conceived to rest on such assistance since we cannot construct maxims around what God might do. Nevertheless, on Kant's view, we need "a complete reversal of the ordering of incentives we have intelligibly chosen, a conversion of the intelligible act, so that the moral law can be re-established as sole adequate incentive of all our maxims."[96] This sets up grace as a "mystery" in *Religion*: "The basic mystery, in this sense, is that regarding what God may do to supplement our moral inabilities, to bring about the *summum bonum*."[97] For Ward, much of what we find in *Religion* is the symbolic rendering of this mystery. So, for example, "the Devil symbolises the power of one's own evil choice; Heaven and Hell symbolise the radical gulf between the pure and impure will; the Holy Spirit becomes our confidence in our own moral disposition; and Christ symbolises that moral perfection which is the final end of creation."[98] One of the rather dubious outcomes of this symbolism, however, is that the mystery of grace makes conversion unattractive. Essentially, Ward argues that the symbols of grace are so extreme they are more likely to prompt despair than to stir moral striving, and, in the end, our epistemic limitations prevent all assurance that an actual change in disposition has taken place anyway.[99]

Other more serious and fundamental irregularities, specifically regarding conversion, linger just below the surface of *Religion*. Ward highlights these difficulties in a series of questions:

> Suppose that at one time, T1, a man has happiness as his determining incentive; at T2 he takes the moral law as incentive; and at T3 he returns to happiness. Has he had a change of heart and back again? For Kant, man must be totally good or bad; so how does one determine the ultimate maxim—by counting empirical acts and balancing them up? And how can there be a change of heart in a timeless, unchanging intelligible world? Or how can infinite progress really be equivalent to actual perfection? Can we be sure that all men are regenerate? That the process is one-way and will be completed? If the punishment is infinite, must the new man sacrifice for eternity? And how can one man intelligibly decide both ways at once?[100]

Such tensions create a severe instability in *Religion* and cast suspicion on the success of Kant's efforts to merge moral formalism and religious doctrine. Ward sees these tensions as having their roots in Kant's Pelagianism, which, in *Religion*, comes to rely on an inscrutable and insistent belief in God's grace and forgiveness.[101] This uneasy juxtaposition drives the forensic analysis of atonement in Kant's philosophy of religion, where humans are charged with doing as much good as possible and hoping that God will make up the difference. In the end, however, Ward thinks one of the few intelligible things about Kant's account of grace is that it ends in contradiction—what Ward calls "the contradiction of grace and spontaneity."[102] The introduction of depravity and grace into Kant's account of the human will produces "an antinomy . . . between the necessity for atonement before the evil disposition can be overcome, and the necessity that good works should proceed from faith, if one is to hope for atonement."[103]

In addition to these internal difficulties, Ward finds a fundamental tension between Kant's moral formalism and religious realism.[104] Realism in Kant's religious convictions runs headlong into Kant's philosophical strictures on knowledge of God and the fact that God and immortality are mere ethical postulations.[105] In the development of Kant's ethics, tensions and contradictions like these rule the day. On Ward's interpretation, "Kant's view of ethics ends, in the *Religion* and the *Opus Postumum*, in a tangle of contradictions and antinomies, in which Kant is constantly saying what is on his own terms unsayable, and saying it in contradictory ways."[106] When Kant tries to express a deeply religious ethics in radically humanistic terms, the whole project must finally end in conundrums and contradictions. Ward sums up his critique as follows:

> Perhaps the main factor which does render the *Religion* in the end an unsatisfactory work is not Kant's introduction of religious concepts into morality, but his humanistic faith in the unbounded power of pure reason, both to disclose the truth about man's moral situation, and to overcome innate evil in its own power. It is clearer to those who stand in a different culture and age from Kant how much his basic view of ethics derives, not from a supposed eternal reason, but from a rather over-zealous Pietistic, and certainly Christian, background.[107]

Ward finds Kant's project in *Religion* to fail, both in its tendency to violate Kant's own rational principles and in its internal quagmires. Ward thus testifies that the entire dilemma stems from Kant's metaphysical and religious motives, which were never completely purified from the Pietistic religious tendencies of his youth, and only create tension with Kant's more sober rationalist predilections.

What Ward's testimony shows is that Kant wants to ground religion, even the Christian religion, within the confines of the critical philosophy and that Kant has a certain amount of critical resources for doing so. In this sense, Ward agrees with Palmquist. However, Kant runs into the insurmountable problem of precisely how to ground religion in reason, given the sharp and very decisive divide between phenomena and noumena in his transcendental philosophy. By Ward's lights, Kant's rationalistic ethics are what came to matter most to Kant's religious worldview, and these ethics capture much, if not all, of the essence of Kant's religious motivations. When schematized, however, this essence becomes purely formal moral postulation. Ward cannot understand Kant as a critical mystic in the same way Palmquist does because Kant is clearly a transcendental rationalist with an expressed aversion to mystical enthusiasm. Like Palmquist, Ward senses Kant's continuing optimism throughout the first *Critique* and right through to *Religion*, but this optimism in no way alleviates the tension between rationalism and religion that characterizes Kant's work.

Any linguistic similarities between Swedenborg's writings, the first *Critique*, and the unfinished notes on Kant's desk, simply do not tip the scales toward mysticism. Ward thus sides with McCarthy. *Religion* is an expression of the conflict between Kant's positive metaphysical motivations and his negative rationalistic predilections, and is riddled with conundrums because of it.

With this telling assessment of Kant's metaphysical motives and their consequences for the philosophy of religion before us, we turn now to consider one final testimony concerning the metaphysical motives behind *Religion*. This testimony comes on behalf of the defense and is that of the early Allen Wood, who promotes a more optimistic view of these matters. But, as we will see, Wood approaches the topics of Kant's metaphysical motivations from a vantage point quite distinct from the foregoing testimonies.

Witness for the Defense: Allen W. Wood

As an interpreter of Kant's philosophy of religion, Allen Wood has two distinct phases to his career. In his early work, which includes his highly influential books *Kant's Moral Religion* (1970) and *Kant's Rational Theology* (1977), Wood understands Kant's philosophical system as religiously and theologically affirmative in a strong sense.[108] Wood's general thesis is this: "Kant's argument for the rational inevitability of the idea of an *ens realissimum* is an original and well thought out one, making use of concepts that belong to the metaphysical tradition."[109] Wood interprets Kant as a theological realist and advocate of rational religious faith in a "living God," contending, "it would be a great mistake to see in the God of Kant's moral faith no more than an abstract, metaphysical idea. For Kant, moral faith in God is . . . the moral man's *trust in God*."[110] For the early Wood, there is no doubt that "Kant's position is not to be described as 'deistic.'"[111] Instead, Wood describes Kant's position as "moral theism." More recently, Wood has defended a less affirmative portrait of Kant. Wood's essays "Kant's Deism" and "Rational Theology, Moral Faith, and Religion" argue that Kant's philosophy of religion and rational theology shade off into deism, and eventually yield a straightforward program "to abolish the church's hierarchical constitution."[112] Wood defines a deist as "a believer in a natural religion founded on unaided reason, but not in a revealed religion, a religion founded on a supernatural revelation through scripture," and then sets out to show how Kant's philosophy of religion resonates with this kind of deism on a variety of fronts.[113] Considering Wood as a witness for the defense of Kant's *Religion*, we focus primarily on the early Wood.[114] Here we find Wood's most substantial treatment of *Religion* and a consistent set of arguments that effectively counter the pessimistic, non-realist interpretation of Keith Ward. In part 2, we will return to Wood's later work in the context of developing our own interpretation (which is more in line with the early Wood) and defending it from traditional challenges.

Despite marked differences in how their interpretations unfold, Ward and Wood begin with somewhat similar insights on the nature of God in the first *Critique*. Wood agrees with Ward that "[t]he term *idea* is borrowed by Kant quite consciously from Plato . . . [and] refers to any of several concepts formed a priori by our rational faculty, to which no possible experience can correspond."[115] Wood also agrees that, "since our concept of God is an idea of reason, no sensible content corresponding to it can ever be given. This concept is thus an 'empty' or 'problematic' one, a concept incapable of serving as a vehicle of (empirical) knowledge."[116] Kant's epistemology, on the face of it, would thus appear to entitle us to say very little about God. Nevertheless, Wood's understanding of Kant's conception of God finds its own moorings in a fairly traditional and rationalistic conception of God.[117] According to Wood, "the most proper idea of God . . . [is] as a supremely perfect being or *ens realissimum* . . . [which] comes about in the course of our attempt to conceive the conditions for the 'thorough determination' of things, that is, the unconditionally complete knowledge of them, or the thoroughgoing specification of the properties belonging to them."[118] Wood thus grants that the idea of God is a problematic one, but not an impossible one or mere figment. Even though reason presents the idea of God empty of direct sensory determination, the idea provides the principal transcendental resource for the thoroughgoing determination of things in the world and a chief resource for understanding human beings as purposeful participants in the world.

Referring to difficult principles surrounding knowledge of God in Kant's theoretical philosophy, Wood writes:

> These strictures, however, do not really apply to some predicates, such as those based on the categories, or on the "pure derivative concepts," such as duration and change. For although such concepts are "empty" ones in their application to noumena, they are nevertheless available to us a priori as formal elements of our concept of a thing or object in general. Kant gives the name "ontological predicates" to these "a priori realities" which belong to God in virtue of the fact that they "refer to the universal attributes of a thing in general."[119]

Wood's point is that, even though Kant's denial of theoretical knowledge makes literal language about God problematic from the empirical point of view, it does not mean that we are cut off from such language about God, all things considered. Belief in the existence of God, which first emerges as a problematic in the theoretical philosophy, finds rational warrant as the critical philosophy advances into its practical and judicial phases. We can get God in mind, thinks Wood, and utilize the concept as a necessary condition for a thoroughgoing transcendental determination of reason in its various employments. Practical reason and, later, judicial reason allow for the establishment of rational faith on transcendental grounds by raising the questions of the necessary conditions for the possibility of right action and moral hope. In other words, Wood contends that the formal elements of Kant's rational subjectivity enable a transition from the empirical to the moral without relegating moral theology to the realm of theological non-realism. Theoretical reason presents the idea of God as one necessarily inherent in reason, and "Kant has only respect for our natural interest in the content of this idea and our theoretical curiosity about the existence or nonexistence of an object corresponding to it."[120]

The argument for moving from theoretical to practical reason to establish belief in God (rather than the factual existence of God) is closely tied to Kant's irrefragable belief in humanity's moral disposition and the meaningfulness of the world. Wood writes, "According to Kant, we believe in God because this belief harmonizes with, and is rationally required by, our moral disposition to pursue the highest good."[121] Inasmuch as human identity is wrapped up in an a priori commitment to belief in the reality of a moral disposition and commitment to living as though the world has moral order, Kant is likewise committed to a robust faith in God. As Wood puts it, "Kant was convinced that an upright moral disposition rationally required belief in a moral world, purposively ordered by a supremely wise and morally perfect being, very much along the lines of traditional theistic religions."[122] Practical reason thus tips the scales, which were at first perfectly balanced by the theoretical philosophy, toward belief in God and makes it possible for a critical extension of transcendental theology. According to Wood, "Moral faith, in Kant's view, requires 'theism,' the belief in a 'living God,' a being endowed with knowledge and free volition, who governs the world wisely according to moral laws. . . . Transcendental theology, says Kant, is an indispensable 'propaedeutic' to a fuller theology, but remains 'idle and useless' from a moral-religious point of view unless supplemented by it."[123]

Like Ward, Wood recognizes that there is a strong sense of theological subjectivity in Kant and that the question of the existence or nonexistence of God is an open-ended one on the basis of the first *Critique* alone. Yet, Wood submits that this appearance of agnosticism is offset by the moral argument for God's existence, which aims not at knowledge but at faith. Wood is careful to show that belief in God is rooted in transcendental recesses of the theoretical philosophy as much as it is in purely moral considerations, but moral considerations are pivotal to understanding Kant's theism as an advance beyond both non-realism and deism. Wood sums up his point this way: "Kant's justification of theism must be sought not only in the moral and existential considerations leading to practical faith, but also in the theoretical dialectic which is supposed to furnish this faith with a clear and compelling conception of its natural object."[124]

Chief among these moral considerations is the connection Wood sees between moral actions and beliefs about God and immortality. Wood notes that "according to Kant, when a person announces his intentions to pursue a certain end, and undertakes a certain kind of action in pursuit of that end, he *presupposes, implies* or *commits himself* to the belief that the end in question is at least *possible* of attainment through the action he is taking toward it."[125] Wood uses several examples to demonstrate that there is a close connection between what one believes and one's chosen course of action—a physician, for example, treats a patient with a view to the real possibility of alleviating pain or curing an ailment, and without an implicit belief in the possibility of a success- ful treatment, the physician is not really acting as a physician. Likewise, when- ever we act, we presuppose a rule or maxim that aims at some achievable and final state of affairs, and, "according to Kant, there is one end, called the 'highest good,' which is 'an a priori necessary object of our will and is insepara- bly related to the moral law.' We cannot abandon the pursuit of this end without ceasing to obey the moral law altogether, and this end is therefore *morally* 'necessary.'"[126] Kant's moral argument for belief in God thus depends on the viability of human moral striving and its being closely tied to the attainability of the highest good.

Kant's movement from purely moral considerations to a hybrid view of moral and religious considerations as the ground of rational faith hinges on the conception of the highest good. In the "Antinomy of Practical Reason," Kant contends that "if the highest good is not possible of attainment . . . 'then the moral law which commands that it be furthered must be fantastic, directed to empty imaginary ends, and consequently inherently false.'"[127] The highest good is the end of moral action and belief, and its possibility provides the linchpin of Wood's understanding of the link between morality and religion. Kant's logic here utilizes a *reductio ad absurdum practicum* argument (which Wood terms the *absurdum practicum* argument for short). The argument is based on the possibility and attainability of the highest good. Wood explains: "Suppose I deny either the existence of God or of a future life. Now if I deny either of these, I cannot conceive of the highest good as possible of attainment. But if I am to obey the moral law, then I must pursue the highest good. Thus the moral law requires me to pursue an end which I cannot conceive possible of attainment. Therefore the moral law is 'false' and I am under no obligation to obey it."[128] Since the moral law is the condition for obligation and is uncon- ditionally binding, the *absurdum practicum* argument must lead to an antin- omy. Wood points out that the *reductio ad absurdum* strategy is not a logical one or one that leads to inconsistent judgments, but is practical. This kind of logic is more "personal" than logical; the main issue relates to our moral nature. For Wood, "The moral arguments . . . justify a 'subjective' faith, in that they are founded not on objective proof or evidence but on a personal, but rationally commanded, decision to adopt a morally upright course of life."[129] To deny the existence of either God or immortality is to make oneself a *Bösewicht* (a scoundrel). Moral faith is thus primarily personal and subjective, rather than impersonal and objective.

Because Wood finds that God and immortality must be postulated if we are to escape an *absurdum practicum*,[130] moral faith, on Wood's reading, is at once theoretical and practical:

> [I]t is *theoretical* reason which assumes the existence of a God and a future life. But for the practical postulates to function as theoretical explanations of the possibility of the highest good, we would require more knowledge of these objects than can be given in mere transcendental concepts of them, which is all theoretical reason can give us. The postulates of God and immortality, then, must allow us to "conceive" the possibility of the highest good in some distinctly practical way, which does not involve us in theoretical claims which we would have to justify by appealing to something beyond transcendental ideas as they are given to us.[131]

This conceiving of the possibility of the highest good is tantamount to a theoretical commitment based on moral considerations, for as Wood points out, "in postulating the existence of a God and a future life, we make a theoretical commitment, a belief in the reality of *some* supersensible existence adequate to the possibility of the highest good, which takes a definite form only by means of the transcendental ideas of God and immortality."[132] The idea of God, on Wood's interpretation of Kant, thus has a "practical function" as a postulate, which raises it from mere theoretical possibility to the status of the proper object of moral faith. Moral faith, however, is not merely formal faith; it involves convictions of the will with theoretical ramifications.[133]

The role of immortality in this scheme is that moral reason needs the postulate of immortality in order to hope for a steady progression toward goodness. From a practical point of view, good actions can be intentionally pursued only under such a belief. Yet, Wood contends that a careful analysis of the first antinomy of practical reason reveals the insufficiency of the postulate of immortality in one important sense: it facilitates a pursuit of the moral life or the performance of good acts, but it does not account for the nature of our moral dispositions. In other words, the postulate of immortality solves only part of the problem, namely, the part that allows moral reason, considered on its own, to move forward unhindered. It leaves unanswered "how this endless progress (or the disposition corresponding to it) fulfills the supreme condition of the highest good. Until we know this," Wood continues, "the first antinomy of practical reason cannot be regarded as fully resolved. And because Kant does not treat this matter in the second critique, his discussion of the first antinomy at this point must be regarded as incomplete."[134] The resolution of the antinomy, on Wood's account, must wait for Kant's critical analysis of humanity's moral disposition in *Religion*.

Wood understands *Religion* to be the natural byproduct of the practical need to unpack the nature of the moral disposition and its relationship to the ideas of God and immortality as transcendental objects. Because of Kant's *absurdum practicum* argument, God and immortality are to be thought of as "immanent" in moral volition. This "way of thinking" is crucial for understanding the substructure of rational religious faith. Wood calls this way of thinking a "moral outlook" that practical reason commends regarding the transcendental ideas of God and immortality. Since these objects are intimately tied to moral volition and are subjectively necessary, Wood suggests that we must look to the nature of the moral agent in order to provide a robust accounting of moral faith: "If we are to discover Kant's true conceptions of God and immortality as objects of moral faith, then, we must go beyond the transcendental ideas of God and immortality, and beyond the *absurdum practicum* argument itself, to a consideration of the function that moral belief, moral faith, fulfills immanently in the frame of mind of the moral agent."[135] Transcendentally speaking, we are warranted in believing that God exists and that, in addition to the ontological predicate *ens realissimum*, certain things can be said of God, even if they cannot be known as objects of theoretical cognition. This realization allows Kant to move with confidence into matters of religion in pursuit of an answer to the question of how the human disposition actually fulfills the supreme condition of the highest good. Kant, in *Religion*, seeks to demonstrate "the practical possibility of the final end of morality."[136] Without such a demonstration and belief, Wood concludes, "I would have to deny my own real nature and its eternal moral principles, I would have to cease being a rational human being."[137]

While Wood focuses much of his interpretation of *Religion* on Books One and Two, he begins by addressing Book Three. Understanding rational religious faith under the rubric of moral theism the way Wood does might tempt one to think that Book Three is the real focal point of Kant's argument. For example, Kant could be understood as advocating in Book Three a new form of religion (viz., rational religion) meant to replace all forms of empirical religion. Wood argues, however, that "Kant is not recommending, as Auguste Comte was later to do, that men should found a *new* religion, with no other basis than an abstract philosophical one. To attempt such a thing would not only be quixotic, but would ignore the fact that men already have, albeit in an imperfect way, attempted to form moral communities of this kind."[138] The image Kant uses is not horizontal or lateral, but one involving the motif of essence. On Wood's assessment, "Pure religious faith is . . . not the *alternative*, the 'opposite' of ecclesiastical faith. Rather, it is the true and rational *essence* of ecclesiastical faith. Ecclesiastical faith is the 'vehicle,' the 'conducting substance,' of pure rational faith; it is the 'shell' (*Hülle*) which contains the rational kernel of pure religious faith."[139] In Book Three, true religion has *both* pure and empirical parts. Empirical religion bases itself on some purported divine revelation, but it also contains principles that are independent of historical tradition or sacred literature. These principles "recommend themselves to men universally, and base their claim solely on moral reason."[140] A central aim of *Religion*, then, is to show that "Men must 'set free' pure religious faith from its 'shell'" and explicate how this can be done.[141]

Although Wood begins with Book Three, his point is not to highlight its centrality but merely to place its arguments relative to Kant's more decisive work on the human moral disposition in Books One and Two. Before moving directly into Wood's interpretation of Books One and Two, worth noting is that Wood recognizes and resists the tendency of many of Kant's interpreters to see Kant's pure religious faith as a "compromise" between Christianity and faith rooted in moral reason. Contrary to interpreters such as McCarthy and Ward, Wood suggests that "Kant makes claims of this sort because, in his view, Christianity is 'represented as coming *from the mouth of its first Teacher* not as a statutory but as a moral religion.'"[142] *Religion*, on Wood's interpretation, cannot be properly understood merely as a philosophical adaptation of Christian symbols "unless we dismiss all attempts at 'rationality' as mere 'rationalizations' or claim that history itself is a product of metaphysical 'reason.'"[143] For this reason, the young Wood is emphatic, "we cannot assume that Kant's pure religious faith is *based* on the historical tradition from which his conception is drawn."[144] Rather, we must assume that Kant's rational religion is based on Kant's rational arguments unless we are persuaded by the evidence to conclude otherwise.

Turning to Wood's interpretation of Books One and Two, we find that his analysis of Kant on human depravity and moral redemption is logically driven by the problems and resources already presented in the practical philosophy. Following this practical trajectory, Kant set out on the critical quest to understand the nature of the human disposition and its rational relationship to God and immortality. If humanity's moral disposition is to be found good, it must have a way of meeting its objective in the highest good. Kant's critical access to the issue centers around the concept of moral perfectibility: "In the *Religion*, Kant reopens the whole question of man's moral perfectibility, and attempts to give a more complete answer to this question than he did in any of his earlier works."[145] The concept of man's moral perfection in the context of God, freedom, and immortality is a propaedeutic to any reasonable conception of the highest good, and it can be brought into sharp relief only on the backdrop of Kant's doctrine of radical evil. The doctrine of radical evil is not the result of some scheme to address religious topics while pacifying the religious censors, nor is it an emergent property subconsciously rooted in Kant's Pietistic religious upbringing; the doctrine of radical evil, according to Wood, is rooted in a very real problem in Kant's critical philosophy: How do I hope in the highest good when the objective end of morality is fundamentally threatened by a rebellious will?

In Book One, Kant sets out to understand the nature of the moral disposition. His conclusion is that human beings are evil by nature, but not by necessity. Key to understanding this distinction is the further distinction Kant makes between predispositions and propensities. The predispositions, on Wood's reading, comprise the heading under which human incentives for moral action fall.

The goodness or evil of some chosen maxim "consists in its 'form,' in the 'order' or 'subordination'; of the incentives it contains."[146] Wood is clear that "if a man is to be said to be 'by nature' good or evil, this goodness or evil cannot consist in the predispositions bound up with the *possibility* of human nature." The predispositions do not themselves determine the nature of the disposition—that is, whether it is good or evil. Everything hinges, for Wood, on "the actual use man makes of his capacities."[147] In other words, a person's predispositions, even the predisposition to personality (which makes one "susceptible" to the moral law as supreme incentive) are only "a condition for the possibility of being good or evil, and his possession of it cannot render him actually good or evil."[148] We must make a decision with regard to the order of incentives and the supremacy of the moral law. Radical evil is "found in man's use of his capacities through his power of free choice, his *Willkür.*"[149]

One of the main issues of concern in Book One surrounds the nature and location of the subjective ground for the power of choice (*Willkür*). Wood recognizes the importance of Kant's critical examination of human nature in this regard: "Kant, along with Hume, sees that moral accountability of man depends on his possession of a fixed character or disposition."[150] To explain this fixed character, Wood turns toward a broad empirical analysis of maxim-making by individuals, noting that "The subjective ground or highest maxim is also 'ultimate' for Kant in the sense that every man can be said to have it; it can be 'predicated of man as a species' (though not derived from the concept of man as a species)."[151] Kant's aim in analyzing humanity's moral disposition is to stake a decisive claim, rather than a vague generality about the human race. What Kant wants is a universally valid conclusion—something that is true and applicable to the human race generally. Wood makes the point this way: "When Kant says that man is evil 'by nature,' he does not mean to *explain* evil, but only to point out the *universality* of evil in man."[152]

At this crucial juncture in the argument, Wood's reading of *Religion* understands Kant to be reasoning from principally empirical rather than rational considerations. On Wood's assessment, "Kant thus looks for evidence supporting the claim that all men, without exception, exhibit a propensity to evil; and he finds such evidence in 'the multitude of crying examples which experience of the actions of men puts before our eyes.'"[153] This issue will become a significant point of contention as we move into the indictment and defense of Kant's *Religion*, but suffice it to say for now, Wood takes Kant's argument for the universality of evil to be an inductive effort "to show the *universality* of evil, to show that all men, despite the many differences between them, exhibit a radical propensity to do evil."[154] Whether or not this way of arguing justifies Kant's conclusion is not clear and does not seem to be an issue of concern for Wood. He takes Kant's unflinching acceptance of the argument as proof enough of Kant's belief in its cogency.

Being satisfied with his conclusion that human beings are evil by nature,

Kant considers the "subjective conditions for the possibility of the development of moral good in man."[155] According to Wood, a consistent interplay exists in Kant's account between the subjective conditions that define the human being and the empirical character of the human being. Our empirical character pursues the good by way of "gradual reform, a slow progress from bad to better. But goodness of will as it must be found in man's highest maxim, his supersensible moral character."[156] Yet, Wood argues that this inner reform cannot be understood as a gradual reform, for the human disposition is singular and definite. As Wood puts it, "the goodness of will . . . requires not a 'change of practices (*Sitten*),' but rather a 'change of heart' establishing a *good disposition* (*Gesinnung*) as the supreme ground of our maxims."[157] The human agent must undergo a revolution in disposition, which again establishes the moral law as its supreme incentive.

A key point in Wood's reading of Book Two is that, while Kant's plethora of language regarding a "conversion," "revolution," "change of heart," or "transformation of one's cast of mind" carries with it the notion of temporal change, the change of heart (conversion) is in fact not temporal. Rather, such talk, by Wood's lights, refers to an inference one can make about an individual's atemporal character, involving the decision to "*break* with the evil he observes in himself by an 'incessant counteraction' against the evil propensity in his nature."[158] The "change of heart" itself, however, is not temporal. The good disposition has an unchangeableness about it that contrasts with the empirical character, and the only assurance we have that such a break has taken place is the observance of a "gradual temporal reform."

With Wood's account of conversion before us, we reach Kant's introduction of the concept of divine grace. Here, Wood highlights John Silber's problem with Kant's appeal to grace and atonement, to wit, that grace and atonement violate the moral law. Wood's stance on this issue is clear: "Silber says that 'Kant could see clearly the incompatibility of forgiveness' with his moral philosophy. But this is precisely what Kant did not 'see.' "[159] Wood suggests that forgiveness ("a forgiving disposition") is "a morally good quality in man's nature" and "that a 'conciliatory spirit' (*Versöhnlichkeit*) is a duty of virtue for all men."[160] According to Wood, "we recognize that it is altogether *right* and *good* that men should be forgiven, that forgiveness accords with true morality, and that reason itself is on the side of mercy rather than of 'abstract moral rectitude.' "[161] Given that reason approves of forgiveness as good, Wood thinks we can readily attribute this same type of goodness to God—especially in the context of moral conversion. We humans may, therefore, have no "legal claim" to forgiveness, but divine forgiveness, nonetheless, is "a moral and a just verdict," for it is a verdict based on something real and genuinely pleasing to God, namely, the good disposition.

Toward the end of Wood's interpretation of *Religion*, we find a cooperative vision of moral renewal: "Man justifies *himself* insofar as he does everything in his power to become good; but God, for the sake of man's disposition to holiness, forgives him the evil which is not in his power to undo, and by this justifying verdict renders the disposition equivalent to that of moral perfection which is the unconditioned component of the highest good."[162] Wood moves quickly through Kant's account of atonement and analysis of punishment and justification, striking for what he calls "the postulate of divine grace." Wood states, "God's grace must be presupposed if an *absurdum practicum* is to be avoided as regards the unconditioned component of the highest good."[163] For Wood, trust in divine forgiveness is a central aspect of Kant's understanding of moral faith. Such faith is justified in *Religion* by an extension of the *absurdum practicum* argument. Divine grace is needed to resolve the first antinomy of practical reason, and therefore, it must be granted the status of a postulate of practical reason. "In faith," Wood concludes, "the moral agent places his rational trust not only in God's beneficence as world-creator and wise providence as world-ruler, but also in God's just forgiveness as the moral judge and the loving and merciful Father of mankind."[164] Such is the outcome of Kant's philosophical employment of practical reason, according to the early Wood, and the basis for Kant's moral theism. In light of Wood's testimony, we have reason to take pause and consider the very real possibility that Kant's metaphysical motivations may in fact be philosophically pure and conducive to a rationally responsible philosophy of religion.

2

The Philosophical Character of *Religion*

The expert testimony surrounding the metaphysical motives behind Immanuel Kant's *Religion* leaves us at something of an impasse between Kant's desire
to ground religion in the rational resources of the critical philosophy and the
philosophical strictures that militate against it. The first *Critique* shows signs
that Kant's philosophy promotes both a chastening of traditional theological
endeavors and a fashioning of a new transcendental approach in their place.
The chastening can be easily understood as part of Kant's denial of proof for
(and against) the existence of God in the first *Critique*, but the fashioning of
Kant's new transcendental theology is harder to articulate and requires an
examination of his writings before and after the first *Critique*, coupled with the
kind of comprehensive and innovative interpretation we find in Wood's early
work. Certainly, one cannot make sense of Kant's turn to religion and theology
on the grounds of the first *Critique* alone. The brilliance of Wood's interpretation is that it employs resources from Kant's moral and religious writings to
articulate a forceful argument for the essential coherence of Kant's vision in
the face of charges of ethical formalism and fundamental incoherence. The
careful reader will notice, however, that in order to see the way forward toward
coherence in the sense of Wood, we have had to move some distance away
from a consideration of Kant's motivations for writing *Religion* and square into
the details surrounding the philosophical character of *Religion*. In this chapter, we turn directly to the question of whether Kant has sufficient philosophical resources to ground religious faith in reason.

Philip Quinn and Nicholas Wolterstorff are the first two experts called to the stand. They will serve as witnesses for the prosecution concerning the philosophical character of *Religion*. Each will testify to significant problems that remain in the text, even on the most charitable interpretations. Rather than attacking Kant's *Religion* on motivational grounds, Quinn and Wolterstorff move into the textual specifics, probing the viability of Kant's arguments from both philosophical and theological angles. They present a series of debilitating conundrums in Kant's *Religion* that emerge as a result of the conflict between the tenets of Kant's practical philosophy (e.g., the *ought*-implies-*can* principle and God as the "great Paymaster"[1]) and the tenets of Kant's philosophy of religion in *Religion* (e.g., radical evil and divine grace). The dual testimony of Quinn and Wolterstorff casts suspicion on the content of Kant's arguments in *Religion* by drawing out inconsistencies internal to the text and between the text and Kant's other writings. The conclusion of this testimony is that Kant's philosophy of religion, under the resources so far developed and employed, simply does not work.

To the extent that the testimony of Quinn and Wolterstorff proves convincing, those seeking to defend *Religion* will have to provide new resources and interpretive lenses for reading *Religion*. On behalf of the defense, we then call Ronald Green and Adina Davidovich to the stand. In viewing *Religion* through distinct critical lenses, these two Kant experts offer alternative ways of unpacking Kant's resources for rational religious faith.[2] Unlike McCarthy and Palmquist, Green and Davidovich make less of the psychological and contextual circumstances in which Kant wrote *Religion*, and more of the critical writings themselves. Green emphasizes new resources for understanding Kant's turn to rational religious faith in what he refers to as the "relentless logic" of Kant's moral philosophy. This carries over into how Green understands *Religion*. Green sees the text as a logical extension of Kant's practical philosophy. Where the practical philosophy, when actually employed, presents us with a moral and prudential dispute over right conduct, the logic behind Kant's critical method turns to rational religious faith in order to adjudicate the dispute. Reason is thus logically driven to religious faith, on Green's account, when practical reason and human inclinations meet the empirical realities of human experience.

Davidovich, on the other hand, turns to the "creative logic" of Kant's aesthetic and teleological philosophy. By drawing on the third *Critique* and the teleological portion of Kant's critical philosophy, Davidovich argues that rational religious faith is part of a broader contemplative process meant to bridge the gap between nature and freedom. *Religion* should thus be interpreted as Kant's contemplative presentation of religion as a realm of meaning—a cognitive extension of Kant's theoretical and ethical philosophy that unifies them with purpose. Green and Davidovich thus supply new interpretive lenses by which to understand *Religion* and offer interesting ways forward. However, in the end, we will argue that the testimony of both Green and Davidovich, though innovative and insightful, does not decisively counteract the very specific objections leveled by Quinn and Wolterstorff. If Kant's *Religion* is to be acquitted of some of the most damaging charges against it, the defense must present additional evidence that more precisely determines, and thereby vindicates, the argumentative character of *Religion*.

To fill this gap in the defense, we will consider testimony regarding an interpretative thesis that has recently been gaining momentum in the field of Kant-studies, namely, what we will call the *"Religion*-as-Translation" thesis. *Religion*-as-Translation presents the text not as an extension of Kant's arguments in the critical philosophy, but as a translation of the Christian faith. While we have seen, in the previous chapter, interpreters draw on Kant's Lutheran upbringing as an explanatory hypothesis for why Kant wrote *Religion*, Bernard Reardon and John Hare have taken considerable strides toward constructing a more precise account of Kant's methodological engagement with Christianity under the *Religion*-as-Translation thesis. By drawing on Kant's talk of two experiments in the Second Preface of *Religion* as well as Kant's talk of the pure rationalist in Book Four of *Religion*, Reardon and Hare offer a picture of the text that, while distinct from Kant's purely critical philosophy, does not violate the critical philosophy. Rather, *Religion* becomes a treatise covering the type of interplay between theology and philosophy Kant thinks necessary for those who would remain loyal to a purported revelation. But, as we will show, this interpretative strategy, while offering a means for explaining Kant's often paradoxical and seemingly novel arguments in *Religion*, runs into serious difficulties surrounding both the significance (or relevance) of *Religion* and the success of Kant's experimentation in *Religion*.

In short, while we find in these philosophical character witnesses advances in our understanding of the critical resources for deciphering *Religion*, problems surface when these interpretations are compared with the exegetical specifics of Kant's writings and when closely scrutinized for internal consistency. Although enlightening in the way they open up possibilities for understanding certain aspects of *Religion*, none of these interpretations provide the kind of treatment of *Religion* necessary to face the multi-faceted objections and internal inconsistencies pointed out by critics like Wolterstorff and Quinn. In the next chapter, Gordon Michalson will further expand and clarify these objections and inconsistencies, putting them in the form of an indictment of Kant's *Religion*.

Witnesses for the Prosecution:
Philip Quinn and Nicholas Wolterstorff

In his essays "Conundrums in Kant's Rational Religion" and "Is It Possible and Desirable for Theologians To Recover from Kant?," Nicholas Wolterstorff brings to the fore a series of difficulties with Kant's philosophy of religion in general and its appearance in *Religion* in specific.³ In the latter essay, Wolterstorff draws out a central difficulty for any effort to construct a Kantian theology, namely, the strictures on God-talk and God-thought set forth in Kant's critical philosophy. The former essay compliments this God-talk concern by bringing into sharp relief those problems internal to Kant's philosophy of religion as developed in *Religion*. Philip Quinn's work resonates with Wolterstorff's pessimistic assessment of the philosophical character of *Religion*, even though Quinn is somewhat positive regarding Kant's overall contribution to the realm of philosophy of religion.⁴ Quinn's criticisms of *Religion* center principally on Kant's introduction of grace and Kant's concepts of moral conversion and moral hope in Book Two of *Religion*. Such criticisms can be found in Quinn's triad of essays "Original Sin, Radical Evil and Moral Identity," "Christian Atonement and Kantian Justification," and "Saving Faith from Kant's Remarkable Antinomy."⁵ Throughout this section, we will consider the overlapping testimonies of Wolterstorff and Quinn.

In approaching *Religion*, Wolterstorff presumes an intended continuity with Kant's critical work. Wolterstorff thus sees Kant's project as necessarily centering on "rights and obligations" and the preservation of the *ought*-implies-*can* principle of the moral philosophy. Kant's inquiries into religious and theological matters in *Religion* must, therefore, (1) uphold what Wolterstorff calls "the Stoic maxim"—*man must make himself whatever he is to become morally*—and (2) develop within the limits of what practical reason tells us about God (viz., God is our moral judge and supremely concerned with rights and obligations).⁶ When we approach *Religion* with these lenses, a number of fundamental problems emerge, most of which surround Kant's use of grace in Book Two.

Highlighting Kant's emphasis on human responsibility, Wolterstorff notes, "[in *Religion*] Kant repeatedly affirms the Stoic maxim that a person's moral worth is determined entirely by that person himself. 'Man himself,' he says, 'must make or have made himself into whatever, in a moral sense, whether good or evil, he is or is not to become.'"⁷ The Stoic maxim reiterates what the *ought*-implies-*can* principle tells us, namely, that humanity is both responsible for and capable of fulfilling its moral obligations. The introduction of radical evil, thinks Wolterstorff, violates the basic assumptions underlying the Stoic maxim and the *ought*-implies-*can* principle. Kant's practical philosophy bears an implicit Pelagianism, which, on the face of it, is incompatible with the type of moral corruption espoused in the doctrine of radical evil. Rather than abandoning the practical philosophy, however, Kant attempts to take the bit in his mouth by introducing divine assistance amid the insights of practical reason.

Despite Kant's best efforts to retain both the Stoic maxim and divine grace, Wolterstorff sees a lingering difficulty in this tension. In conceding the need for divine assistance and forgiveness in the face of our inevitable failings, Kant implicitly concedes that the *ought*-implies-*can* principle is misguided. If it is the case that our nature is corrupt and God must "alter our moral status for the better," and if it is also the case that we need forgiveness for *inevitable* moral failings, then it follows that without God's assistance we are incapable of fulfilling the *oughts* commended by practical reason.[8] *Ought* apparently does not imply *can*. In order for *Religion* to be taken seriously, therefore, Wolterstorff suggests that Kant must answer the rather troubling question, how can we alone be the source of our moral worth and simultaneously require divine assistance and forgiveness to generate such worth? As Wolterstorff points out, "To affirm the Stoic principle is to affirm something which contradicts the claim that God wipes out guilt."[9] In the end, Kant's turn to divine grace appears incompatible with his practical philosophy, and Kant must choose between the two: either the former is overly optimistic and misguided, or the latter is wrongheaded, but the two cannot be held in tandem. This unsavory dichotomy casts suspicion on Kant for ever beginning a project like *Religion* without acknowledging an explicit break with his critical work.

Quinn raises a similar criticism in his essay "Saving Faith from Kant's Remarkable Antinomy." Pointing to the Stoic maxim, Quinn suggests that Kant's use of divine grace counters the idea that an individual creates his or her moral worth. For Kant, moral worth must emerge from the individual and be the product of her spontaneous use of freedom. Hence, Quinn contends, "grave difficulties stand in the way of assuming that human efforts to become worthy of membership in the kingdom are susceptible of such supplementation, for the assumption appears to contradict Kant's view that moral worth derives entirely from the kind of free action that is in no way influenced by external determinants."[10] Aside from grace moving contrary to the *ought-implies-can* principle generally, the introduction of divine assistance strips any resulting moral progress of the value it would yield. The convert does not and cannot gain new moral worth from her moral progress, for the resulting good is not the product of her own freedom but the product of another aiding agent.

Kant's claim that we must earn (or make ourselves worthy of) divine grace, according to Quinn, only compounds this difficulty. Quinn recognizes that Kant's introduction of divine assistance carries an implicit admission that we cannot, on our own, become truly good (as Wolterstorff's objection above points out); thus, we must exert ourselves morally in order to prompt a dispositional revolution in ourselves, thereby making ourselves worthy of divine assistance. Yet, Quinn wonders how the initiation of a dispositional revolution is any less difficult than becoming a better person. If the prompting of this revolution is no less difficult, then it would seem that to initiate the radical change of our moral demeanor, we also need God's aid. But, as Quinn points out,

> [a] regress appears to be in the offing. It would seem that bringing about such a revolution is no easier than becoming a better person if one has brought upon oneself an evil propensity that corrupts the very ground of one's maxims, and so the former task would seem to require divine assistance if the latter does. But then, on Kantian assumptions, it appears that

divine aid with carrying out a revolution in disposition will be forthcoming only if one first does something else on one's own to make oneself worthy of receiving such aid. No matter how this other deed that must be done is specified, the question of how it is possible for an agent in whom the ground of maxims is corrupt to perform it will arise. If this deed in turn is only possible for such an agent with divine assistance, then yet another deed must first be performed to render the agent worthy of that assistance.[11]

Essentially Quinn has difficulty seeing how a radical change or revolution, such as is required to make us worthy of divine grace, can be any less difficult than the path we must tread after this revolution, and thus it seems the need for divine initiative cannot be avoided. God must be first mover in both moral conversion and the life lived according to this conversion.

Recognizing Kant's practical resources, Quinn suggests that Kant can offer the response (per the *ought*-implies-*can* principle) that there must be something in our power to begin the process, for the process itself is required of us—that is, "Duty requires this of us, Kant supposes, and duty demands nothing of us that we cannot do."[12] Such a response helps soften this particular conundrum, but it still begs the question: What is the difference between the initial goodness we must conjure to make ourselves worthy of grace and the goodness that follows after grace has come? If the initiation of goodness is within our power, it seems peculiar to suggest that the goodness to follow is not. The former, if as radical as Kant suggests, would seem to require grace for its occurrence just as much as the latter. But if grace is not required for this radical moral shift, why is grace needed at all?

Wolterstorff too notes a difficulty surrounding Kant's notion of "earned grace." The difficulty Wolterstorff highlights regards the conflict between the concept of *grace*, as typically utilized in theological circles, and its application in *Religion*. In Christian theology, grace is most often linked with the sovereignty of God. God renders grace, by definition, without obligation; he retains complete freedom over whether to offer grace or whether to withhold it. As the apostle Peter points out, "God did not spare angels when they sinned, but sent them to hell, putting them in chains of darkness to be held for judgment" (2 Pt 2:4). God was under no obligation, it is traditionally held, to treat humanity differently. None can expect or demand grace; God offers it freely as a gift or not at all. "Earned grace" is simply oxymoronic in any form, for "required grace" (if "required" means *required of the grace-giver*) is a contradiction in terms.

In *Religion*, however, Kant introduces grace as if it were a necessary postulate of practical reason. As Wood argues, "The doctrine of divine grace is necessary . . . and it must therefore be accorded, along with freedom, immortality, and God's moral governance of the world, the status of a postulate of practical reason."[13] For Kant, grace is not freely offered by God and revealed as an a posteriori fact of history; instead, grace is a necessary facet of the order of rights and obligations that is revealed to reason a priori. But to make grace a priori, Wolterstorff submits, is to make grace something other than grace. Kant's God does not choose to forgive; Kant's God is required (for whatever reason) to forgive those who fail morally but offer a good effort nonetheless. Although Wood is prepared to accept this position on God's nature, arguing that "God, for the sake of man's disposition to holiness, forgives him the evil which is not in his power to undo,"[14] Wolterstorff submits that such a picture of grace violates what is most essential to the theological conception of grace, namely, the divine freedom that grants it. In the end, "Kant cannot have it both ways: he cannot hold that we can expect God's forgiveness, since God's failure to forgive would violate the moral order of rights and obligations, and also hold that God's granting of forgiveness is an act of grace on God's part."[15]

The merger of grace and practical reason is not the only problematic conjunction in Kant's account of moral hope in *Religion*. In "Original Sin, Radical Evil and Moral Identity," Quinn highlights what he thinks is an inconsistent triad in Books One and Two of *Religion*:

(1) The evil of the supreme maxim is freely chosen, independent of all temporal conditions, and is inextricable by human force.
(2) A moral agent can have only one supreme maxim, which is either good or evil; the maxim cannot be morally neutral or morally bifurcated—a position Kant calls "moral rigorism."
(3) Moral conversion is a revolution in disposition, where the evil supreme maxim is replaced with a good supreme maxim.

Quinn draws out the inconsistency of the triad by bidding his readers to think of an individual who has undergone a revolution of disposition—the type of revolution Kant says is possible and necessary for moral hope. In such an individual, Quinn points out,

> [e]ither a morally good supreme maxim coexists . . . with a morally evil supreme maxim, or it does not. If it does, then that human has two supreme maxims, one good and the other evil, and his or her moral character is a mixture of good and evil, which contradicts the thesis of rigorism. If it does not, then either that human has not adopted a morally evil supreme maxim or that human had at one time adopted a morally evil supreme maxim and at some later time given it up and replaced it with a morally good supreme maxim. But the assumption that that human has not adopted a morally evil supreme maxim contradicts the part of the thesis of radical evil which asserts that every human has adopted a morally evil supreme maxim. And the supposition that that human had at one time adopted a morally evil supreme maxim and at some later time given it up contradicts the part of the thesis of radical evil which asserts that a morally evil supreme maxim, because it is the product of an act independent of all temporal conditions, is inextricable once adopted.[16]

In short, Quinn finds that by conjoining radical evil, moral rigorism, and moral conversion, Kant lands himself in an overt contradiction when affirming the possibility of moral renewal.

By showing the inconsistency of this triad, Quinn does not merely want to demonstrate that Kant is trapped in a paradox or minor inconsistency. Rather, Quinn intends to show that Kant's efforts to outline a viable account of moral conversion fail outright. As Quinn puts it, "What the argument does show is that there is no possible world in which (i) the thesis of rigorism is true, (ii) every human adopts a morally evil supreme maxim, and (iii) some human adopts a morally good supreme maxim."[17] Quinn recognizes Kant's attempt at a practical defense of moral hope—*It may seem that moral conversion is impossible if we begin from evil, but if we ought to, then we can*—but insofar as the triad can be shown to run into blatant contradiction, Kant's practical arguments are necessarily false. Kant cannot allow practical reason to appeal to the *ought*-implies-*can* principle, since, as Quinn's triad shows, to affirm moral conversion is to affirm a logical impossibility. If the *ought*-implies-*can* principle is applied to the topic of conversion, it should, according to Quinn's argument, be used only to show we ought not to affect a change in our moral disposition because we cannot. For this reason, Quinn concludes, "Kant's attempt to rationalize the Christian doctrine of original sin must be judged a failure because his theory of radical evil is inconsistent with the conjunction of two other claims equally central to his mature practical philosophy, the thesis of rigorism and the thesis of moral revolution."[18]

Surrounding Kant's account of the process of moral renewal, Quinn finds a further difficulty. Quinn recognizes that when discussing how a moral convert can be justified (in the theological sense) before God, Kant emphasizes dispositional revolution as the source of this possibility. "But," as Quinn reads Kant, "a switch of supreme maxims from evil to good is bound to leave a gap between noumenal disposition and phenomenal deeds."[19] That is, the revolution of disposition will not yield ideal conduct, but manifests itself in time "as unending progress from bad to better."[20] In admitting the progressive nature of moral renewal, Kant admits an inevitable gap between the moral ideal demanded by the moral law and the moral convert who adopts a good disposition. Quinn recognizes, however, that Kant's view of moral goodness is indicative of unbending commitment to the moral law in all circumstances—duty must *always* take precedence. Therefore, as Quinn points out elsewhere, "we must, if we wish to attribute to Kant a consistent view, understand reversals of the moral order of the incentives broadly as *any* failure to preserve the proper subordination of the incentives of inclination to the moral incentive."[21] True moral goodness, then, is identical with moral perfection in Kant's world. And in this light, even if Kant admits that one can lay hold of a new disposition, "it looks as if the ideal of complete moral perfection remains elusive for such a person, since such a person will not lead a life completely and faultlessly in harmony with the good disposition he or she has acquired."[22]

Clear enough is Kant's admission that a person continues to lack moral perfection after conversion, but this concession raises a question for Quinn: "How . . . are we to be morally justified in the eyes of God?"[23] Quinn summarizes Kant's answer in a way typical of the traditional understanding of *Religion*.[24] In Quinn's view, Kant essentially appeals to divine omniscience. God sees the heart and perceives the goodness of the disposition directly as an atemporal whole, as opposed to a temporal upward movement. Moreover, the moral convert, in undergoing a dispositional revolution, changes moral identity; he is morally a "new man." This moral revolution itself serves as a type of atonement, as the new man enters on a path of suffering that accompanies the pursuit of the good. Such suffering serves as a type of atonement for the moral debts of the "old man" and procures for the new man a surplus of righteousness.[25] The difficulty Quinn sees with such a solution, however, is that Kant presents moral conversion as humanity's universal moral obligation—such a response to radical evil is what we ought to do. Yet, if the process of moral conversion is really a moral obligation, how can it yield a surplus of righteousness? Even if successful, the moral convert has only done what every human ought to do—and (per the previous difficulty) does not even do this as well as one should. Quinn thus submits: "[I]t would seem that acquisition of a good disposition could not produce a surplus of good over and above what is morally obligatory sufficient to pay the debt of sin. How is it possible for the good disposition to make satisfaction for sin if in acquiring it one is doing no more than the moral law demands?"[26]

For such reasons, Quinn concludes that Kant's account of moral conversion cannot provide a sound basis for either moral atonement or any so-called surplus of righteousness. Moral conversion is merely a moral obligation, which is imperfectly embodied by even the best of moral converts. Moreover, Quinn goes to great lengths to show that Kant, in rejecting the transfer of moral merits (positive or negative), cuts his philosophy off from all other forms of atonement.[27] Therefore, in the end, it seems moral faith can do nothing other than appeal to blind forgiveness in the sense of Wood's interpretation: God simply wipes out the debt of sin. Yet, both Wolterstorff and Quinn find it problematic for Kant to introduce such a bald concept of forgiveness into his rational understanding of God. Assuming Kant is justified in following practical reason to key insights about God, we have the difficulty that nowhere prior to *Religion* does practical reason commend the predicate *forgiving* of the deity. As Wolterstorff notes regarding Kant's pre-*Religion* theology, "all we know of God is that God honors and ensures the requirements of morality—i.e., of rights and obligations."[28] In light of this rather limited store of practical insights into the divine nature, Wolterstorff thinks we must wonder "why, in Kant's scheme, God would ever do such a thing as forgive."[29] If practical reason tells us that we ought to fulfill the dictates of the moral order, and experience tells us that we fail to do so (even if some slowly improve in their efforts over time), why should we expect to ever find mercy?

Examining such a question under the guide of Kant's critical work, we should expect only judgment and condemnation from God: We are obligated to fulfill the moral law; we are capable of fulfilling the moral law; but we do not fulfill the moral law. To suggest that God, who is supremely concerned with upholding the moral order, would offer some judicial fudging in our favor simply because our efforts to do good improve slightly with time seems an odd concession in the Kantian scheme. Were Kant able to appeal to inherited sin, he may have some grounds for inferring divine mercy—there is a sense in which our failings are necessary—but given Kant's unwavering Pelagian assumptions, our failings can be attributed to nothing other than our own free choice. If, then, God forgives, he merely shows himself to be unjust: he simply chooses not to punish the morally corrupt. As Quinn points out, "The moral law demands that each of us acquire such a perfect righteousness of our own, and so everyone of us is able to acquire such righteousness. Hence, anyone who does not acquire such perfect righteousness but instead disobeys the moral law becomes a sinner by free choice. But a sinner by free choice stands condemned in the sight of God and has earned a divine decree of condemnation."[30]

Christian theology has affirmed historically that God must, for the sake of his own justice, not simply forgive, but atone—that is, he must pay off the debt of sin and impute to the convert a foreign righteousness, namely, the righteousness of Jesus Christ. But if Quinn is right in his claim that Kant's model of self-atonement fails, then God's acquittal of a guilty individual would constitute judicial corruption. "Such laxness," Quinn points out, "would be a moral outrage; a righteous judge would never behave in this indulgent fashion."[31] John Silber punctuates this very point when he writes, "[I]f the individual has done all he can, he does not need grace. And if he has not, even Kant agrees he should not get it."[32] Essentially, Quinn (with Silber) sees Kant caught in a devastating dichotomy: either Kant must concede that the *ought*-implies-*can* principle is misguided, so that when one has done all one can morally he or she still is in need of forgiveness, or the one who falls short of the moral ideal and is in need of grace has fallen short by her free choosing and in no way deserves grace. Kant's practical philosophy points toward the latter, making grace capricious and unjust, while the former makes Kant's introduction of grace an implicit concession that his practical philosophy is wrongheaded.[33]

Behind many of the problems identified in *Religion* thus far lies a common denominator, which Wolterstorff identifies in "Is It Possible and Desirable for Theologians to Recover from Kant?" namely, the nature of the transcendental philosophy itself. Without the possibility of knowledge of God and God's actions in history, Kant's discourse about God's gracious acts toward humans seems almost beside the point. According to Wolterstorff, the Kantian strictures on human knowledge and experience set forth in the first *Critique* appear to make theological discourse that is actually about God impossible.[34] Wolterstorff's pessimism is rooted in the problems the traditional interpretation creates for meaningful God-talk. Wolterstorff explains the traditional view of the Kantian strictures on knowledge by employing "the metaphor of a boundary."

Since, as Wolterstorff puts it, "knowledge of objects is limited to what we could in principle experience," we cannot have knowledge of what we cannot experience.[35] The metaphor of a boundary identifies the boundary line between what we can know and what is beyond our ability to know. This sets up a bifurcated worldview made up of *things as they appear* and *things as they are in themselves.* The forms of intuition (viz., space and time) and the forms of conception (viz., the twelve categories) are the structural features that constitute knowable objects and separate the knowable from the unknowable. God, freedom, immortality, the soul, and the *Ding an sich* are beyond our ability to know in any meaningful way. Therefore, while Kant may have "[denied] knowledge in order to make room for faith" (Bxxx), Wolterstorff submits that the only examples of faith that seem to fit Kant's philosophical paradigm are those that shade off into agnosticism, non-realism, or perhaps radical fideism.

Wolterstorff thinks the God-talk problem points not to a serious difficulty for theology but to a serious inadequacy in Kant's philosophical system. Kant clearly wants to say things about God in his writings on religion—a point that is evident in Kant's talk of divine grace. Yet, speaking of Kant's critical writings and their reception, Wolterstorff notes:

> There are many options to explore for the interpretation of God-thought and God-talk. Many options have in fact been explored, Kant himself being the first of such explorers. From Kant's late book, *Religion within the Bounds of Reason Alone,* and from his unpublished Lectures on Philosophical Theology, it becomes clear that Kant not only thought that we could get God in mind, but that we were entitled to predicate a good many things of God. Thus Kant's own option turns out to be relatively non-skeptical. On this occasion I do not propose describing it. It is complex, at many points hazy, and has proved not at all compelling, even for Kantians— which of course explains why so many other options have been explored. Though many theologians and philosophers have found Kant's problem, along with the philosophical framework generating that problem, compelling, few have found his solution compelling.[36]

Wolterstorff thus divulges his own inclination, which is to simply dispose of the Kantian paradigm. Wolterstorff's comments at the close of the essay are telling:

> At the end of our books about God, those of us who are not Kantians will discuss how it is that we human beings can think and speak about God. That for us is an important matter of intellectual curiosity. But not a matter of agony. We empathize with those who experience the Kantian agony, but we do not share it. If one believes that one's car is in good running order, one does not spend the whole day tinkering under the hood to determine whether it could possibly be in good running order, and if so, how. One gets in and drives off. Along the way one might discuss with one's passengers how it is that this old car runs—especially if *they* thought it wouldn't![37]

In short, Wolterstorff thinks it self-evident that we can speak about God and engage in meaningful theological discourse—such is common sense—and if the consequence of Kant's philosophy is an insatiable anxiety over how theological talk is possible, this represents a strike against the Kantian paradigm, not theology. Kant may find that humans are in need of divine assistance, but, given Kant's philosophical strictures, such an assertion about God's activities is simply impossible.

In the end, the testimony of Wolterstorff and Quinn suggests that even if we grant the legitimacy of Kant's introduction of radical evil in Book One of *Religion* (which is itself a difficult concession), this shift in the Kantian framework serves the single purpose of offering a catalyst for Kant's appeal to divine grace. Yet, because practical reason commends only a form of Pelagianism that stands opposed to grace, the introduction of grace forces Kant into a debilitating dichotomy: either what practical reason tells us about humanity's moral capacities is misguided, or the apparent human tendency to diverge from the moral law indicates that none can expect to be found pleasing to God—or perhaps that we are not obligated to follow the moral law perfectly. Grace, in the Kantian scheme, radically disrupts what the *ought*-implies-*can* principle tells us about human freedom, while also moving contrary to the limited store of theological insights about God supplied by practical reason. To suggest that God would somehow offer grace is an anomaly in Kant's world that lacks justification (presuming the practical philosophy is upheld), and the form it takes, given Kant's effort to hold fast to the Stoic maxim, also ends up violating the very concept of grace, traditionally understood—what we need, but can neither presume upon nor create for ourselves, is earned by our own striving and comes to us necessarily. In the end, such conflicted results prove detrimental to the whole of *Religion*, for the introduction of grace stands as the centerpiece of the entire work.

Witness for the Defense: Ronald M. Green

In the light of Quinn's and Wolterstorff's testimony, we find that, when we read *Religion* as an addendum to Kant's critical philosophy, its philosophical character cannot stand up to close scrutiny. Although Wood provides helpful arguments for the text's incorporation into the critical philosophy, Quinn and Wolterstorff demonstrate that the structure of Kant's argumentation in *Religion* is flawed. If no counter evidence is forthcoming, Kant's philosophy of religion will be found guilty as charged. We must, therefore, consider whether there is an alternative way of harmonizing *Religion* with the critical philosophy. In the remainder of this chapter, we will consider three alternative ways of incorporating *Religion* into the Kantian paradigm to see if the philosophical character of *Religion* can rebut the testimony of Quinn and Wolterstorff and vindicate the text of the charge of incoherence.

In contrast to the interpretations so far addressed, Ronald Green's understanding of Kant's philosophy of religion depends on the transcendental logic of Kant's critical philosophy. In particular, Green focuses his attention on the inner workings of practical reason. Although Kant's critical writings emphasize what Green calls practical reason's moral viewpoint, practical reason is necessarily composed of three interrelated "points of view"—the moral, the prudential, and the religious. Green believes that each point of view is important for Kant's system, though the latter two (i.e., the prudential and religious) are only implicit in it. The implicit nature of these two viewpoints should not, however, lead the interpreter to think that they are somehow less important to Kant's thought. According to Green, the internal logic of Kant's thinking depends on rightly understanding these points of view, and by understanding their implications for Kant's critical philosophy, we can understand the internal consistency of both the critical philosophy and Kant's philosophy of religion.

Green contends that the logic of transcendental philosophy suggests that the three practical points of view, taken together, bridge the gap between freedom and nature. This bridge of the fact-value divide establishes the location of the philosophical basis for religion and theology. The first point of view, which provides the surface structure of practical reason, is moral reasoning. In answering the question, What ought I to do? reason is naturally led to seek the ideal answer from a point of view that suppresses or even ignores our own "special needs and desires." This viewpoint of practical reason is what Green calls "a direct expression of reason."[38] Moral reasoning orients us to knowledge of the ideal action in any situation (subject, of course, to the limits of one's knowledge of the facts). An ideal action is a selfless act of doing on behalf of others, not in the sense of completely ignoring the self, but in viewing oneself as just one amongst others affected by the decision; "It asks us to choose as though we might be any of the people affected by our conduct."[39] Green believes that the impartial/moral point of view is the only viewpoint of practical reason that legitimates the categorical imperative as a constitutive principle of practical reason.[40]

Despite the crucial role that the categorical imperative plays in Kant's moral philosophy, it was not the only principle that Kant thought necessary for practical reason to know what to do in a given situation. Green believes the second half of the second *Critique* shows that happiness is related to practical reason in a way that transforms its inner workings into a new point of view.

> Now we learn that happiness plays an important, indeed indispensable, role in moral reasoning. In addition to the categorical imperative, Kant tells us, practical reason has as its presupposition and requires belief in the attainability of the "Highest Good," understood as the proportionate and exceptionless union of virtue and happiness. Without a constitutive role for the Highest Good, [Kant] says, morality would lack a complete object and moral striving itself would become empty and vain.[41]

Green contends that Kant's discussion of happiness and the highest good at this crucial juncture implies that practical reason has, or at least should have, deeper structural levels than the moral point of view alone (which he believes is constituted without reference to happiness and the highest good). In the second stage of practical reason, prudential reasoning urges us, given the reality of our individual situations in the actual world, to choose according to our "personal concerns," just as impartial reasoning compels us to do what we ought to do. This self-centered employment of reason is what Kant would later develop into his theory of radical evil.

Below the surface of moral deliberation, personal happiness ineluctably transforms the inner workings of practical reason and constitutes a completely different and competing point of view. When personal happiness is seriously considered in moral deliberation, moral reasoning becomes prudential reasoning. One might say that in the same way that moral reasoning answers the question of duty by emphasizing duty to others, prudential reasoning answers the question of conduct by emphasizing the duty that we have to ourselves. When reasoning prudentially, we are compelled to act according to our own special needs and desires because "impartiality before the social array of desires can cause all or most of my desires—and the most important among them—to be suppressed."[42] Prudential reasoning condones selfishness when selfishness is necessary to maintain our personal interests in the real world.

Admitting happiness into moral deliberation does not, according to Green, degrade virtue; it merely makes practical reason honest. When theoretical reason encounters the world, we learn that we not only have knowledge of things as they appear but also have desires in relation to those things. Theoretical reason in a sense transforms moral reasoning—which prior to this transformation might have been called the "pure" practical reason of virtue—into prudential reasoning, or a more genuine form of practical reason based on personal happiness. And this complete transformation sets up a conflict in practical reason. In difficult situations, impartial and prudential reasoning compel us to choose diametrically opposed courses of action. If these two employments of practical reason were our only recourse, we would find ourselves in constant turmoil. Difficult moral decisions would provide so much internal tension that reason's only "reasonable" way forward would be to seek an even deeper level of practical deliberation. Here, the concept of the highest good becomes vitally important.

Employing what Kant designates an "object" of practical reason in the second *Critique* (see 5:4 and 115), Green suggests that the idea of the highest good can have a constitutive role in practical reason. All that is necessary, in Green's opinion, to secure such a role for the highest good are the postulates God and immortality, fully clothed in culturally contingent religious beliefs and practices. They allow us to act on behalf of the highest good, knowing perfectly well that it may not be achievable in this life: "There is, in fact, no third use of reason that can adjudicate the conflict between morality and prudence. But it may be that there is another way of handling the dispute between reason's two employments, *one that involves showing that no dispute really exists.*"[43] Religious reason, constituted by the highest good and supported by religious adherence, does not adjudicate the conflict; it simply views the situation in a whole new way. This new way is rooted in the religious beliefs and practices emerging out of the cultural/linguistic context of history. We can believe in the reality of our central religious doctrines because reason demands these beliefs as a stabilizing bridge between theory and practice, prudence and impartiality.

Reason employed religiously insists that the discrepancy between morality and prudence is "only apparent, not ultimate." Religious reason teaches us that the only rational way forward in decisions that affect our special needs and desires is to believe that moral retribution and rewards are certain. "Just as a belief in retribution eases the apparently insuperable opposition between prudence and morality," notes Green, "so religious beliefs can make it rational to renew our dedication to moral effort even as we realize the difficulty of this task and the failures that loom before us."[44] Because reason necessarily finds itself in conflict between the action of virtue and the action of happiness, only the postulation of a moral will greater than our own and faith in this postulate can guarantee that virtue and happiness will ultimately be brought together in their proper proportion. "Kant's total argument," Green contends, "drive[s] us to the realization that his own transcendent resolution, as offensive as it may be, is the one to which reason is ineluctably driven."[45] Religious reason, in short, allows us to embrace the internal strife caused by practical reason's other two employments by urging us to act morally and by promising to justify our actions through faith in postulated religious beliefs. Green therefore sees transcendental belief as grounded in the relationship between the practical conflicts of reason and the theological beliefs of actual religious traditions.

Green's approach to Kant's philosophy of religion offers an intriguing way of viewing Kantian religion as the inevitable trajectory of the logic of the second *Critique*. The difficulty we face, however, is that Green's approach offers few argumentative specifics from *Religion*. In order to determine whether Green's second *Critique* window is really capable of handling the more detailed objections leveled by Quinn and Wolterstorff, we would need to follow the second *Critique* trajectory, along with Green's rough outline of Kantian religion, into the argumentative details of *Religion*. Green, however, does not provide a detailed accounting of *Religion*. Therefore, as it stands, he can only offer an alternative starting point for reading *Religion*; his testimony cannot, in itself, rebut the testimony offered by Kant's critics. To the extent that the greatest difficulties facing the text heretofore are internal to Kant's arguments, this lacuna in Green's approach seems a serious limitation for its serving to vindicate *Religion* of the charges of incoherence.

Glaringly absent from Green's understanding of Kantian religion, for example, is a detailed explanation of the doctrine of corruption. For Green, Kant's notion of corruption is best understood as a break in the logical precision of reason and the will to act on such a break.[46] For Kant, however, human depravity presents itself as more than a mere break in the precision of reason; it is a volitional act whereby humans will an inversion of the moral order of incentives. Such evil is *radical*, according to Kant, and threatens the possibility of realizing a good disposition, the achievement of the highest good, and the stability of moral reason in general. Hence, the introduction of and the solution to radical evil form the primary focus of *Religion*. Green's interpretation is strong on its critical justification for the rational necessity of religious belief, but is weak on understanding the specific content of Kant's rational religious faith surrounding the notion of human depravity. Green only offers a way of critically placing the logical possibility of an evil volition, while leaving unclear how we are to understand so radical a view of human depravity as found in *Religion*.

One way of applying Green's approach to *Religion* would be to interpret the incentives outside of the moral law, which Kant discusses in *Religion*, as matters of prudential concern. Radical evil would, then, be a rubric under which the supremacy of prudential reasoning falls: practical reason considers the moral law as sole and supreme incentive, thereby constituting a good disposition, while prudential reasoning subordinates the moral law to personal happiness and other considerations, thereby giving rise to a corrupt disposition. The difficulty with such an approach, however, is twofold. First, it is not clear that the incentives talked about in *Religion* are merely matters of consideration for Kant. Rather, as Wood points out, the incentives are linked with the predispositions, which represent basic human inclinations—animality, for example, funds the inclination to self-preservation and hence procreation. Such inclinations are not linked with personal happiness, but are more closely associated with humanity's basic biological makeup. To therefore equate the incentives with prudential reasoning would be misdirected.

Second, Green seems to think that prudential reasoning takes dominance in human reasoning merely by virtue of the human being placed in nature. Practical reason *transforms* into prudential reason by virtue of theoretical reason's recognition of personal desires regarding empirical things. A transformation of the sort Green describes presents itself as inevitable, given the meeting of the human person and his or her context. Yet, such a transformation is far removed from Kant's talk of radical evil as a freely chosen maxim for the exercise of freedom in general. Radical evil would be necessary on this rendering, but Kant is explicit in rejecting it.

This is not to mention Green's lack of assistance in placing (and defending) Kant's introduction of divine grace, which gives rise to the majority of the conundrums numerated above. Therefore, if the above formulations are, in fact, what Green's approach offers when applied to the specifics of *Religion*, then it seems we are no better able to handle the conundrums of Quinn and Wolterstorff with Green's assistance—and we may only find ourselves facing fresh difficulties in this approach.

Witness for the Defense: Adina Davidovich

Where Ronald Green finds the ground of religion and theology in reason's practical employment, Adina Davidovich finds an alternative ground in reason's faculty of judgment. Davidovich offers an interpretation of Kant's philosophy of religion that draws attention to the fact that, in the context of the first and second *Critique*, the faculty of judgment has no constitutive function; yet, in the third *Critique*, aesthetic and teleological judgment work together to form a kind of judicial reasoning. According to Davidovich, the faculty of judgment is the supreme faculty of reason, and judicial reasoning is the supreme employment of reason. They generate the human capacity to contemplate or reflect by poetically fusing feelings and concepts, thereby harmonizing nature and freedom. "Kant is led to a position that we can only characterize as the *supremacy of contemplation* over both practical and scientific concerns," Davidovich explains.[47] She draws a close connection between the work of judicial contemplation and the writing of *Religion*. Contemplation as such is the constituent feature of religion as a realm of meaning, the chief means by which Kant's philosophy of religion develops, and the bridge built between theory and practice.[48]

The significance of Kant's third *Critique* for Davidovich comes to the fore early in her book *Religion as a Province of Meaning: The Kantian Foundations of Modern Theology*. In the chapter entitled "The Conflict between the Interests of Reason," she argues that even though Kant held at one point to the primacy of practical reason, the third *Critique* reveals this was not his final position. As Kant's philosophical program developed, the transcendental method of reason (which first modeled transition in Kant's move to the second *Critique*) demanded a third *Critique*. The basis for this demand can easily be seen if we think of Kant's philosophy in a bifurcated form, where Kant's Copernican revolution, as an answer to Hume's dilemma of causality, becomes as much a problem for philosophy as it is a solution. In Hume, the connection between repeatable observations and scientific knowledge rests on the mere feeling that there exists a necessary connection between the two, but for Kant, causality and freedom constitute different realms of human experience. When considered simultaneously they become overtly conflicted a priori constituents. Hume's philosophy leaves an inductive gap, while Kant's philosophy, considered as a whole, appears to be on the verge of transcendental contradiction. According to Davidovich, this edging toward contradiction gives sufficient cause to expect from the third *Critique* a means of unifying the whole transcendental system of philosophy.

As with Hume, Kant turns, in the third *Critique*, to *feeling* to resolve the problem of a gap. Feeling, for Kant, is not limited to the empirical context, but refers more fully to an experience of beauty and the sublime in the context of hope and the highest good. His expressed intention is to find the a priori constituents for the faculty of judgment:

> Now whether the **power of judgment,** which in the order of our faculties of cognition constitutes an intermediary between understanding and reason, also has *a priori* principles for itself; whether these are constitutive or merely regulative (and thus do not prove the power of judgment to have its own domain), and whether the feeling of pleasure and displeasure, as the intermediary between the faculty of cognition and the faculty of desire, gives the rule *a priori* (just as the understanding prescribes *a priori* laws to the former, but reason to the latter): it is this with which the present critique of the power of judgment is concerned. (5:168)

Of course, the relative success of Kant's third *Critique* is a long-standing debate in the field of Kant-studies. Realizing this fact, Davidovich begins her interpretation with a frontal assault on the common assumption that the primacy of practical reason is a cornerstone of Kant's philosophy. According to Davidovich, Kant asserts the primacy of practical reason only over theoretical reason, and he asserts this primacy only because of the stifling effects of the conflict between our inclinations (theory) and the moral law (practice).[49] Davidovich does not see in Kant the kind of resources Green finds; and since Kant explicitly addresses the gap between nature and freedom only in the third *Critique*, it is there, argues Davidovich, that we should expect Kant's unification of nature and freedom.

Kant appears to confirm this line of reasoning in 5:175–76: "Now although there is an incalculable gulf fixed between the domain of the concept of nature, as the sensible, and the domain of the concept of freedom, as the supersensible . . . there must still be a ground of **unity** of the supersensible that grounds nature with that which the concept of freedom contains practically." In reference to this hypothetical ground of unity in the Introduction of the third *Critique*, Davidovich points to a later passage where the faculty of judgment, in its aesthetic sense,

> sees itself, both on account of this inner possibility in the subject as well as on account of the outer possibility of a nature that corresponds to it, as related to something in the subject itself and outside of it, which is neither nature nor freedom, but which is connected with the ground of the latter, namely the supersensible, in which the theoretical faculty is combined with the practical, in a mutual and unknown way, to form a unity. (5:353)

Davidovich identifies the "something" in this passage as the notion of a "supersensible substrate" by which "Kant accounts for the universal validity of the judgments of taste."[50] She goes on to suggest, "The analysis of taste thus becomes a decisive stage in the restoration of unity to our cognitive powers."[51] This designation of taste as decisive can be misleading if taken literally in the context of Davidovich's overall interpretation and thus needs clarification.

In Davidovich's way of interpreting Kant, aesthetic judgment is "decisive" only in the sense that it paves the way for an even more decisive role of teleological reflection. She supports this interpretive strategy by comparing the layout of the third *Critique* to that of the first *Critique*. "According to my interpretation of the first part of the *Third Critique*," Davidovich writes, "the task of the analysis of judgments of taste is analogous to the aesthetic of the *First Critique*. Like the discussion of space and time, the analysis of the judgments of taste is a propaedeutic. It paves the way for the study of teleological judgments."[52] The purpose of this first-*Critique*/third-*Critique* comparison is to argue that the role of aesthetics in Kant's philosophical economy is subordinate to that of teleology.

Davidovich applies this vision of Kant's philosophical program to *Religion* in her essay "How to Read *Religion within the Limits of Reason Alone*." There, Davidovich posits "that *Religion* is, in essence, a concrete elaboration of Kant's more abstract discussion of the reflective thought (contemplation) about God, an idea which is the main focus of his third *Critique*."[53] Utilizing third *Critique* resources, she supports her thesis by arguing that reason has three powers, as opposed to the conventional two—the power of reflection along with the powers of understanding and the moral will. The power of reflection bridges the gap between theory and practice by providing a necessary link between these two domains. She recognizes that the common approach to *Religion* is to understand it as correlative to Kant's moral philosophy, but this approach is precisely what she believes leads to problems of coherence. Her emphasis on the third *Critique* promises to provide new resources for smoothing over many of these difficulties. As she puts it, "Many themes in Kant's discussion of religion, especially his notion of grace, which have taxed the exegetical ingenuity of his interpreters, emerge as elliptical allusions to doctrines he developed in third *Critique*."[54]

Under Davidovich's reading of *Religion*, the central theme of the text is the problem of humanity's need for a change of heart, so that we may act on our duty in a world full of competing prudential concerns. Given the phenomenon of sin and our duty to aspire to a moral commonwealth, Kant is faced with a series of questions that reason must answer: "Can we reform our hearts to moral perfection? Can we ever regard ourselves as worthy members of the kingdom of morals even though we have all sinned? What punishment do we deserve for our past sins and how can we atone for them?"[55] Answers to such questions are beyond the reach of reason in its theoretical or practical employment; nevertheless reason must both ask and answer them. Thus, Kant's philosophy is driven toward answering questions usually reserved for theology, and "[t]his," according to Davidovich, "is the task of religious reflection."[56] Such reflection is ultimately what gives rise to Kant's much-maligned appeal to divine grace. Although Davidovich admits that the introduction of grace signals new frontiers for Kant, she suggests that Kant has at least two good reasons for moving in this direction: (1) Kant "brings to the fore the realization that in order to overcome evil and sin, we must undergo a total change of heart," which seems beyond mere human effort; and (2) "Kant's speculative question reflects the fact that humans cannot avoid asking themselves what they may hope for in life."[57]

Davidovich's movement to religious reflection highlights her belief in the threefold structure of Kant's philosophical program. Her strategy for supporting this turn to reflection is based on Kant's insistence that there are certain questions that reason must address lest it be shown impotent in dealing with life's most pressing concerns. Dealing with these questions leads us to reflect on possible solutions, and, while the point of this reflection is not to determine answers with anything like certainty, the idea is to bridge the gap between nature and freedom with reflections on (or visions of) hope. This, in Davidovich's estimation, is what *Religion* is all about. Thus, Kant is not appending new elements to his moral theory or flirting with empirical theology. On the contrary, Kant is reflecting religiously on possible solutions to the problem of sin and the question of hope.

If *Religion* is taken as religious reflection, Davidovich thinks Kant is justified in appealing to divine aid. Davidovich submits that "it is only in light of his discussion of the reflective recognition of the transcendental unity of Nature and Freedom (in the third *Critique*) that Kant can appeal (in *Religion*) to divine assistance in the perfection of the human heart."[58] Reflection is the key to understanding the coherence of Kant's appeal to divine aid in spite of his insistence on moral (and even regenerative) autonomy. "Reason can adopt the idea of the supernatural complement to moral insufficiency, neither in maxims of thought nor in maxims of action," admits Davidovich; yet, "Kant maintains that it may be available to the good will" and "this belief of Reason, this faith, is *reflective*."[59] In other words, whatever Kant means when he talks about divine aid being available to the good will (and Davidovich takes Kant to be enigmatic on this point), reflective faith should be understood as a non-dogmatic complement to reason in its quest for moral hope. Reflective faith, unlike reason's other faculties, offers its insights in order to "strengthen the will (*Willkür*) to execute the moral decree by providing for it a concrete vision of the final moral end."[60] Wood makes a similar point regarding Kant's understanding of the highest good: "there is one end, called the 'highest good,' which is 'an a priori necessary object of our will and is inseparably related to the moral law.'"[61] The difference between them is simply that, for Davidovich, reflective images of grace should not be subjected to dogmatic scrutiny, where, for Wood, the highest good must be more exactly determined if it is to function as the final end of moral action.

The results of this insight are important insofar as they provide a significant rejoinder to traditional claims that Kant's account of grace is inconsistent. Davidovich argues, "[I]f we read Kant's discussion of grace (defined as reflective faith) against the background of the third *Critique*, we shall realize that reflective faith in grace is a trust that, ultimately, nature is contrived to make possible the only object which is an end in itself: i.e., a moral being."[62] When we look at the beginning of Book Two of *Religion*, what we need to understand, according to Davidovich, is that Kant is situating his solution to human failure not only in the moral resources and benefits of the good will (whatever they may be) but also in reflection on religion as a province of meaning unto itself. As Davidovich remarks, "All that reflective faith allows us is to believe that our nature makes our rebirth possible. Kant calls it 'grace' because this reflection depends on thinking of God as the moral designer of the universe."[63] Since the third *Critique* identifies thought of a moral governor of the universe as the supreme principle of reflective judgment and reason determines that rebirth is possible, Kant has all the cognitive ballast necessary to support his appeal to divine aid.

In this sense, Davidovich's way of reading *Religion* as a continuation of the third *Critique*'s efforts to bring unity to reason provides an overview for understanding Kant in a more coherent fashion. Human beings need to believe in divine aid in order to overcome paralyzing doubts about the possibility of moral rebirth and betterment, and reflective faith allows us to picture the world as a place in which divine aid can occur: "Kant's project in [both *Religion* and the third *Critique*] is to show that a *good will* is possible, not that moral *action* is possible."[64] However, reflective faith "cannot be adopted in maxims of action, it does not determine the will and does not infringe on its autonomy."[65] Reflective faith merely allows us to believe that the will, which at some point has chosen evil, can become good again. And this belief provides a clearer understanding of the place of forgiveness. As Davidovich points out, "Forgiveness is no longer an arbitrary indulgence, but an acknowledgement that moral reform leads to a better life and the realization of the kingdom."[66] Such beliefs are a large step toward answering the question that pulses through the heart of Kant's philosophy of religion: What may I hope?

In addition to grace being understood in a less objectionable fashion on Davidovich's interpretation, we can better see why Kant employs positive language toward historical (or empirical) religion. Historical religion has a pedagogical purpose for the moral life. Davidovich sees historical religion as "a nexus of dogma and ritual that provides the required expedients."[67] It offers "an eschatological picture of world history" in the form of a "concrete image," and "depict[s] a world in which divine providence promises the final realization of moral ends, the ideas of Reason acquire concretization in the agent's mind and are no longer marginalized as mere idealizations that have little to do with real life."[68] Similarly, Kant's use of Christic imagery serves to concretize the moral ideal in human form. "Using the power of reflection," Davidovich writes, "we can perceive the events of Jesus' life as an exemplification of the moral life, and this perception provides us with an impetus to strive and follow Jesus' example."[69]

Religion, by Davidovich's lights, is Kant's best effort to reflect on the purposiveness felt in the aesthetic dimension of human experience and to articulate (or make concrete) the religious implications of this purposiveness. Problems with inconsistency are genuine problems for Kant, but they are not problems that necessarily emerge from the critical philosophy. They emerge only from time and experience, and in the particular reflections of the human imagination. They are therefore germane to the discursive intellect of humans concerned with the question of hope. It really does not matter on Davidovich's interpretation whether or not Kant's particular claims in *Religion* actually cohere with one another; it only matters that we believe they *could* cohere in some form. Of course, this removes the arduous task of showing *Religion* to be coherent. Coherence, according to Davidovich, is an important consideration in Kant's thinking, but it is not the most important. Foremost for Kant in the writing of *Religion* is the process of stabilizing reason by discerning the meaning of the highest good.

Although her arguments on a number of points are weighty, Davidovich's proposed replacement of Kant's primacy-of-practical-reason doctrine is not without its problems. If contemplative reason did actually become primary for Kant in the years after writing the second *Critique*, why did he neither recant the original doctrine nor defend the supposedly new doctrine? And why are his later writings on religion at least as prone to a moral interpretation as they are to a poetic interpretation? Davidovich's arguments are most convincing in establishing the necessity in Kant's mind for a unifying perspective of reason, but they are less than convincing in demonstrating that this new third perspective either could or should become primary in Kant's sense of the word.

In addition, while it is true that the second half of the third *Critique*, like the first half, has both analytic and dialectic chapters—thus signaling a significant critical function—it is not true (or at least not self-evident) that the "Critique of Aesthetic Judgment" is a propaedeutic to the "Critique of Teleological Judgment." If anything, the details of their functions in the third *Critique* suggest quite the opposite. Aesthetic judgments serve to unite freedom and nature through feeling (see 5:178), and the role of teleological judgments is to lead us to understand such feelings as being full of purpose; they "affect" metaphysics from a philosophical point of view by treating science and morality as a "propaedeutic" to theology (see 5:417). Davidovich oftentimes seems to confuse this relationship and in so doing limits the theological perspective to the point of view of poetic philosophy.

Paul Guyer, in *Kant and the Claims of Taste*, offers a clear account of the relationship between aesthetic and reflective judgments in Kant's judicial philosophy. He writes, "We may use the theory of reflective judgment to interpret Kant's model of aesthetic response, but not to identify the *a priori* principle of aesthetic judgment."[70] To identify the a priori principle of aesthetic judgment via reflective judgment is to unravel (i.e., to make objective) that which by its very nature is enigmatic (i.e., subjective or inter-subjective).[71] If Davidovich chooses to appeal to aesthetic judgment as that instance in which reflective unity is experienced, then taste, and not contemplation, must be the essence of Kant's judicial solution to the problem of unity.[72] The aesthetic experience of the subject is what, according to Kant, occasions a smooth transition from theory to practice, not the meaningfulness attributed to that response by reflective judgment. Reflective judgment helps us understand how it is humanly possible to conceive of a unity between the theoretical and practical perspectives of reason; aesthetic judgment provides the unity that we actually experience. Through the feeling of harmony (*purposiveness*), which is totally mysterious (*without a purpose*), we experience certain things as "beautiful."

All this is not to say that reflective judgment is superfluous or nugatory. Davidovich understands that "[t]o be able to recognize spatio-temporal events as moral acts, we need to be able to contemplate nature in terms of final causes."[73] The main feature of reflective judgment is not to constitute or actualize aesthetic judgment, but to demonstrate that it is *possible* to ascribe purposiveness to those ineffable feelings of harmony that are so real to those who experience them. It fills in the teleological blind spot of judicial reason with a creatively constructed, humanly oriented *possibility*. Davidovich's doctrine of contemplation, however, replaces Kant's emphasis on aesthetic judgment over teleological judgment with a synthesis of reflection and feeling in which the former gains constitutive priority over the latter. For Davidovich, contemplation becomes the highest faculty of reason in Kant's philosophy, and this conflation confuses speculative poetry with critical philosophy, thereby exceeding the critical bounds of Kant's transcendental philosophy.

Davidovich's approach to *Religion*, though a resourceful alternative to merely moral interpretations, is hardly satisfactory in either its understanding of the third *Critique* or its handling (or lack thereof) of the textual details of *Religion*. Some of Kant's critics may admit that Davidovich's emphasis on the third *Critique* is potentially helpful for understanding Books Three and Four of *Religion*—particularly the divisions entitled "Philosophical representation of the victory of the good principle in founding the Kingdom of God on earth" and "Historical representation of the gradual establishment of the dominion of the good principle on earth." However, interpreters such as Quinn and Wolterstorff (and most certainly Michalson, whom we will look at in the next chapter) are likely to find Davidovich's interpretation much less persuasive in accounting for Books One and Two, given (1) how susceptible these portions of *Religion* are to moral interpretations and (2) how conflicted these Books appear to be, both internally and relative to the insights of practical reason. When stretched to interpret the whole of *Religion*, reflective faith, as construed by Davidovich, appears to come into conflict with *moral* faith, and offers in return only an enigmatic vision of hope lacking in coherent content. At best, applying Davidovich's interpretation uniformly and comprehensively to the text can give us only a way of glossing over and ignoring the problems of coherence in *Religion*, not a way of solving such problems.

Witnesses for the Defense:
Bernard M. G. Reardon and John E. Hare

A third testimony rounding out the defense of the philosophical character of *Religion* presents the text as a moral translation of the Christian religion. While McCarthy and Ward have already touched on this approach, the interpretive strategy we will consider here should not be confused with the ones they adopt. McCarthy views *Religion* as an awkward mingling of Christianity and moralism, while Ward views *Religion* as a moral and purely conceptual use of Christian symbols. The interpretation examined in this section sees a far more precise and cogent methodology at work in Kant's engagement of Christian theology and, as a result, finds a good deal of coherence in Kant's conclusions. As mentioned in the opening of this chapter, we call the thesis that lies behind this approach the "*Religion*-as-Translation thesis" (or "*Religion*-as-Translation," for short). *Religion*-as-Translation was first taken up in earnest by Bernard Reardon in his 1988 book *Kant as Philosophical Theologian*.[74] John Hare has, more recently, adopted this thesis in *The Moral Gap: Kantian Ethics, Human Limits, and God's Assistance* and subsequent writings.[75] As we will see, *Religion*-as-Translation offers some assistance in explaining the various anomalies in *Religion*. At the end of the day, however, the approach is fraught with its own set of difficulties—which we will show at the close of this section.

Reardon's treatment of *Religion* in *Kant as Philosophical Theologian* constitutes the second half of a two-part treatment of Kant's philosophy of religion. The first part, "The True Basis of Theism," offers Reardon's understanding of the practical philosophy as the rational grounds of Kant's philosophy of religion. The second part he calls "Interpreting Christianity," which refers to the edifice Kant builds on these grounds in *Religion*. Although Reardon's treatment of *Religion* does not display the pessimism of Kant's detractors, Reardon's placement of *Religion* remains, by and large, traditional. Reardon recognizes that Kant, per his May 4, 1793, letter to Stäudlin, intends *Religion* to answer the third part of Kant's threefold inquiry, What can I know? What ought I to do? and What may I hope? (see A804–805/B832–833), but Reardon takes it as evident that *Religion* was not part of Kant's original intent. Reardon thinks it clear that the first *Critique* was itself written with a view to answering all three questions, since "[a]t the outset [Kant] conceived no clear distinction between the practical reason and the theoretical, but only between a practical and a theoretical *use* of the pure reason."[76] With Kant's realization of the problems implicit in so simplistic a conception, however, the second *Critique* needed to be produced. As for the third *Critique*, Reardon sees it as "little else than an extended appendix to its two predecessors and is only so called because of its author's love of system and symmetry."[77] *Religion*, like *The Metaphysics of Morals* and "The Metaphysical First Principles of Science," is, in Reardon's view, an "application of the critical principles to a particular sphere of thought."[78] In playing this role,

Religion is meant to unite historical religion with "the most pure practical reason."

Important to note is that Reardon distinguishes between the sphere of philosophy and the sphere of revealed religion. Reardon sees the former as dealt with in the critical philosophy, while the latter is a new sphere to which the critical philosophy is applied in *Religion*.[79] This new sphere is what introduces both the anomaly of radical evil and its solution, since, in Reardon's estimate, reason offers no a priori assistance regarding human depravity. The difficulty, of course, is that Kant is aware that he cannot simply turn to revealed religion as a sphere of knowledge. Therefore, *Religion*, as Reardon sees it, embodies Kant's attempt at a middle ground between a priori principles and revealed religion. What is this middle ground? Reardon offers the following synopsis:

> Kant's purpose . . . is . . . to show that the Christian religion, in its historic lineaments, is conformable with what he calls "moral theology," resting on a new metaphysics of the practical reason. What *Religion within the Limits of Reason Alone* offers us is, accordingly, a reinterpretation of Christianity solely in terms of moral values. "Revealed" religion may thus be seen to embody truths which dogmatic metaphysics is unable to convey on its own account. . . . [The critical philosophy] presents criteria by which the traditional content of Christianity is itself to be judged. For what is contrary to reason is to be rejected . . . ; although it should also be recognized that reason may yet sanction certain beliefs which it cannot expressly justify.[80]

Essentially, Reardon sees Kant attempting to reinterpret Christianity in a way fitting to the tenets of the first and second *Critique*. In the process, Kant concedes certain imported doctrines that, while not defensible by critical means, may not be offensive to the moral sphere and may even be of positive utility to its aspirations.

In defense of this understanding of *Religion*, Reardon points to 6:12 of the Second Preface, where Kant speaks of two experiments. The first experiment centers on the explication of a pure religion of reason, while the second looks at a specific example of revealed religion and tests it to see how well it conforms to the religion of reason. Although Reardon does not go into great detail regarding these two experiments, he seems to understand the first experiment as something Kant has already carried out in the critical philosophy and the second experiment as a reference to *Religion* as a whole. What this means is that, from the outset, Kant is reinterpreting Christianity along purely moral lines—radical evil is a translation of original sin, the prototype of perfect humanity is a translation of Christ, and so on.[81] On this score, *Religion*-as-Translation, in the sense of Reardon, has much in common with the interpretation of Ward.

Hare adopts this same reading of the Second Preface of *Religion*, stating it explicitly in a number of places. One concise statement of this reading and its implications can be found in his 1999 essay, "Augustine, Kant, and the Moral Gap." There Hare writes:

> In the preface to the second edition of *Religion within the Limits of Reason Alone* Kant suggests that we try the experiment of thinking of revelation as like two concentric circles. In the inner circle is the religion revealed to pure reason and in the outer circle (the region of the larger circle not covered by the smaller) the revelation to historical faith. The experiment will be successful if we can show that the contents of the two areas are not only consistent with each other but have the sort of unity that means that a person who follows the prescriptions of the one will also be following those of the other. To demonstrate this kind of consistency and unity, he proposes to translate the central items of the historical faith into language available to the philosopher in the inner circle. This translation will use the moral concepts, which operate (as reason always does) without the use of singular terms.[82]

Hare emphasizes Kant's discussion of historical faiths as a vehicle for rational religion (or the pure religion of reason) in Book Three, pointing out, "This latter [i.e., the pure religion of reason] is all that is necessary for saving faith; but there may be many people (including Kant himself) who have been introduced to this pure rational religion by the Bible."[83] The idea behind this approach to *Religion* is that Kant felt a certain level of continuity exists between aspects of Christian theology (as he knew it) and his own moral philosophy; and thus, the experiment of *Religion* presumes that, while the content of the pure religion of reason may be more concise and limited in scope than the doctrines of a historical faith, what the religion of reason entails can be found within historical Christianity. Hare calls the second experiment (i.e., *Religion*) "a kind of raiding party; leaving the inner circle, we investigate the outer circle to see if we can bring back any doctrines found there into the domain of pure reason by translating them under appropriate constraints."[84] Hence, the imagery of concentric circles is meant to make plain Kant's grounding presupposition that the tenets of his moral philosophy represents a sphere of moral insight that is contained within the larger sphere of Christian doctrine.

In keeping with this construal of the Second Preface in particular and *Religion* in general, Reardon argues that Kant's title, *Religion within the Boundaries of Mere Reason*, is an indicator of Kant's intent not to form a rational religion within the limits of reason, but to examine a particular historical religion (viz., Christianity) from within his own philosophical sphere— that is, from within the boundaries of reason alone: "What [Kant] has in view is Christianity as he knew it. . . . But this means that his approach to Christianity is not primarily theological; his interest is, rather, in the church as an institution and in the religious beliefs commonly held and taught. Indeed Kant makes little or no attempt to adopt the standpoint of the academic theologian."[85] Hare also affirms Kant's intent to avoid playing the role of "academic theologian," suggesting instead that what Kant's experiment in *Religion* exemplifies is the stance of the "pure rationalist"—a form of rationalism Kant discusses in the opening of Book Four of *Religion*. As Hare puts it, "there is in fact a perfectly good interpretation of [Kant] that uses a label he himself invented, namely 'pure rationalist.' To be a pure rationalist in his sense is to accept special revelation but not to regard this acceptance as necessary for every rational agent."[86] *Religion*, therefore, is fueled by Kant's Lutheran upbringing, as many of Kant's critics have argued, but, according to Hare, Kant does not intend the illegitimate importing of Christian doctrines into his moral philosophy. Rather, Kant intends to translate the core Christian doctrines into terms that are acceptable to the moral philosopher, and he attempts this translation in order to show the presence of rational religion within the broader sphere of Christian theology.

The translation is applied to the central doctrines of Christianity: creation, fall, redemption, ecclesiology, and eschatology. Kant's second experiment is thus to abstract from these doctrines whatever essential, rational truths they may contain. Hare relates the way this experiment unfolds to the categorical imperative. He emphasizes the way the categorical imperative abstracts from experience. It considers the specific act in question and abstracts the act into a universal moral law that offers a moral precept without reference to any specific historical situation or individual. In like manner, Hare sees Kant's notion of translation moving forward: "Suppose that we now try to understand the central doctrines of the historical faith, namely creation, fall, redemption, and second coming, 'in the light of the moral concepts.' This would mean that they have to be understood without reference to the Garden of Eden or Sinai or Calvary."[87] This method of translation thus makes plain why Kant's religious talk in *Religion* seems strikingly Christian, but utilizes terms that are Kant's own (e.g., *radical evil, the prototype, the ethical commonwealth*, etc.).

Even with the guide of translation, Reardon admits, "The contents of *Religion within the Limits of Reason Alone* are set out according to what appears to be a rigorously consistent scheme, but the exposition of it in detail is not always so clear and well-arranged; sometimes the procedure is confusing, while certain important topics that one would have expected to form an essential part of the text itself are simply relegated to lengthy notes."[88] Having said this, both Reardon and Hare attempt to make plain the specifics of the text in a way that captures Kant's "rigorously consistent scheme." Hare, in particular, attempts to utilize the distinct spheres of revealed religion and practical reason as a way of mediating some of the well-known difficulties that emerge in *Religion*. On Hare's reading, it is perfectly normal that Kant sounds Pelagian at one moment because he is speaking from the inner circle of practical reason, and Augustinian at another moment because of the way he uses the outer sphere of revealed religion. This is not an analytic contradiction but a linguistic quagmire created as Kant moves between spheres in his first, second, and sometimes even "third" experiments.[89]

Under the *Religion*-as-Translation thesis of Reardon and Hare, *Religion* becomes a philosophical account of "the struggle between good and evil in human nature."[90] Kant's explication of this struggle begins with the doctrine of evil. Contrary to the "prevailing optimism of the Age of Reason," Kant, in his translation endeavor, endorses "the complaint as old as history" that the world lies in evil.[91] The doctrine of radical evil, Reardon notes, contrasts starkly with the attitude of Kant's time: "the Christian doctrine of original sin was usually dismissed by the men of the Enlightenment as a noxious superstition and a device of priestcraft."[92] Given Kant's Enlightenment heritage, his introduction of an innate tendency toward evil in human nature is "challenging to the verge of paradox."[93] The translation motif helps explain *why* Kant introduces radical evil (per his translation of original sin), but beyond this, Reardon can only bid his readers to rethink whether "[radical evil] is really such an alien intrusion," given that Kant uses this doctrine as the basis for "a rigorously moralistic interpretation of religion."[94]

Hare offers some additional assistance in explaining Kant's starting point of radical evil. He notes Kant's recognition of "Spener's problem." As Hare summarizes it, Philipp Jakob Spener raised the problem of "how can we become *other* men and not merely better men."[95] Spener essentially asks whether true moral transformation is possible, given that we, as humans, begin with an apparent inclination to diverge from the moral law. And this question, in turn, points to a (practically) unsettling conclusion: "If the morally good life is one that we cannot live, because of the corruption of our initial dispositions, then it seems it is not a life that we ought to live."[96] One way of avoiding this dilemma is to deny the corrupt disposition, but, as Hare points out, "Kant is not willing to do this."[97] Hare does not make explicit why Kant is not willing to go this route (nor does Reardon offer much in this regard).[98] But presumably, radical evil emerges as an assumption resulting from Kant's translation of the Christian doctrine of original sin. This dilemma, Hare suggests, explains why Kant paints humanity as beginning with a corrupt disposition and yet possessing a seed of goodness that can be developed and nurtured into goodness. The starting point of *Religion* is, therefore, a conflict "between the good maxim, which subordinates the inclinations to duty, and the evil maxim, which reverses this order of incentives."[99] The anthropology that emerges is a kind of Manicheism of maxims.

Both Hare and Reardon distinguish between the disposition and the competing maxims. The disposition is the inclination toward one of two maxims— the good maxim or the evil maxim. "*Both* of these maxims reside in the will," Hare argues, "and a fundamental choice has to be made between them."[100] Our choice in this regard is what determines the moral character of our disposition, and, in this sense, whatever our moral nature, we are culpable: "The choice for the evil maxim is a choice of our wills and is thus imputable to us."[101] Yet, because Kant is unwilling to embrace a type of Pelagianism in which humans are born morally neutral, he asserts that the choosing of the corrupt disposition is a choice of the will that precedes all exercise of freedom in time. As a result, the corruption of radical evil, while freely chosen, is an innate corruption: "We are *born* with the propensity to evil."[102] In these two tenets (innateness and freedom), we find the inscrutability of free will. As Reardon points out, because the disposition is rooted in freedom (despite its innateness), radical evil cannot be explained in terms of a cause; it merely presents itself as a universal human tendency: "one is unable, so to speak, to go behind a free act in order to explain it; which is why one cannot rightly talk of it as *caused*."[103]

Having affirmed humanity's universal depravity, Kant is not satisfied to leave humans with merely an innate disposition to evil. Instead, as Reardon puts it, "What Kant himself proposes . . . is a *tertium quid*, a mediating doctrine avoiding either of the two extreme positions [i.e., humans are *wholly* good or *wholly* evil] by arguing that man is by nature *part* good *part* bad."[104] What Reardon has in mind here is Kant's notion of the predispositions to the good, which constitute the seed of goodness in human nature that lies alongside the evil disposition. Hare takes this same approach, suggesting that, while we are born with the propensity to evil, "it is also true [for Kant] that we are born with the predisposition to the good (what Luther calls 'the seed of uprightness')."[105] Moral hope, under such a reading, depends on the sprouting of this seed of goodness into a good disposition.

Because of this conception of human nature and moral renewal, both Reardon and Hare suggest that we must reconsider how we understand Kant's affirmation of rigorism—*humanity must be either good or evil; it cannot be both or neither* (see 6:22–24). As Reardon sees it, Kant's affirmation of rigorism is not meant to be descriptive of the state of human nature (i.e., we are either wholly good or wholly evil), but of the type of disposition one must display if moral renewal is possible: "You cannot . . . fulfill the moral law by adopting both good maxims and bad simultaneously."[106] If we are to be remade morally, Reardon argues, we must press ahead in an effort to display a disposition that is devoted solely to good maxims in all respects; and our display of this new disposition must not be accidental, but the result of a decisive deed of freedom. Reardon writes, "For were man totally evil the moral imperative would have no meaning for him, whereas he in fact does recognize the command of duty even in his corrupted state. The moral law still faces him, and he understands, at least basically, what its demands are. This implies that his original disposition for good is ineradicable, and on the strength of it he has it in him to change his evil condition to one of good."[107] The good predispositions, then, provide for both Reardon's and Hare's interpretations the means for preventing radical evil from obliterating the moral order.

This emphasis on a decisive turning from evil brings us to the topic of moral conversion. Moral conversion cannot be a gradual one, representing a subtle transition from good to evil over the course of time. As Reardon's understanding of rigorism has already suggested, conversion must be "as radical . . . as the original act of sin."[108] It must manifest a new moral resolve, an inward moral change, which represents "a fundamental reorientation of the individual's life."[109] Here, Reardon and Hare see Kant finding a specific use for the incarnation. According to Reardon, the idea of incarnation provides a unique resource for presenting to the human mind "the humanly realized moral ideal in all its perfectness."[110] And therefore, on Reardon's reading, "[Kant] insists that the only way for man to please God and gain salvation is through a practical faith in the incarnate Son of God; a faith, that is, whereby he makes his own the disposition of which the incarnate is the ideal exemplar."[111] Conversion itself embodies a death to sin, where the moral convert exerts all his or her moral resources to manifest this Christic ideal and parts ways with the corrupt disposition. As also Hare affirms,

> There is, Kant points out, considerable sacrifice involved in this revolution. There is the pain of discipline, the remorse, and the reparation. The new man, we can say, takes these sacrifices vicariously as a punishment on behalf of the old man, who properly deserves them. As in the traditional Christian account it is the innocent who suffers on behalf of the guilty.[112]

Assuming the break is successful, the moral convert has become a "new man," distinct from the "old man" under sin, and the process of renewal itself serves as a type of personal atoning for past sins.

Justification, under the translation reading, becomes rooted in divine omniscience, which beholds the whole of this atoning process—the convert's future progress and the true nature of the convert's heart.[113] Hare and Reardon each emphasize slightly different nuances in Kant's translation of justification, but these nuances are not incompatible. Hare emphasizes God's ability to look on the heart of the moral convert and behold the new disposition: "The heart, as it is seen by God after justification, is 'essentially well-pleasing to him,' even though all we experience in our lives is a gradual process of reformation or improvement, not a revolution of the will."[114] Reardon, on the other hand, points to God's ability to behold the whole life span of the moral convert, and thus, impute righteousness to the convert that is not yet manifest, namely, the convert's future righteousness in the life to come:

> [F]or Kant the "non-temporal" adoption of an altogether new maxim has to be succeeded by a course of conduct, indefinitely prolonged, that will result in an actual state of moral goodness. . . . In the sight of God, who "penetrates the intelligible ground of the heart"; and who comprehends the unending process of ethical amelioration as a unity, it is equivalent to being actually good, or as a theologian would put it, to be *accounted* righteous before God.[115]

Despite the difference in emphasis between Hare and Reardon on this point, clear enough in both schemes is that justification, when translated, is not the imputation of the foreign righteousness of Christ but God's decision to count the moral convert righteous based on the inward disposition (per Hare) and upward moral progress (per Reardon), despite her inevitable failings throughout the moral process.

A word should be said here regarding divine grace. To this point, it may seem that Reardon's and Hare's respective accounts of the Kantian translation of Christianity lacks all reference to divine assistance. But this would be a misreading. Reardon certainly affirms that Kantian conversion "is a purely moral one, depending entirely, it would seem, on the individual's own resolution and firmness of will."[116] Yet, both Hare and Reardon recognize (and attempt to draw out) Kant's emphasis on divine assistance in the process of moral renewal. Reardon puts it this way: "Some supernatural aid, [Kant] grants, may be necessary for a man's becoming good, or at least better, but whether this co-operation consists merely in the abatement of hindrances or affords positive assistance, Kant by no means qualifies the principle that 'a man must first make himself worthy to receive it,' and must lay hold of this aid."[117] On Reardon's account, Kant recognizes the need for grace, but neither rejects the Stoic maxim—*a man ought to make himself into whatever he is to become morally*—nor speculates as to how exactly this assistance is rendered.

Hare, likewise, attempts to construe the Kantian introduction of grace in a way that does not violate the Stoic maxim. Key to Hare's approach is the distinction between the practical and religious spheres identified in the Second Preface. Hare suggests, "It is the translation process that accounts for Kant sounding both Augustinian, when he is talking about the outer circle, and hyper-Pelagian, when he is talking within the inner circle, the religion of pure reason."[118] From the outer circle, Hare tells us, Kant recognizes the need for divine grace, given the corruption of human nature. God must assist us if we are to become good—"the need for supernatural cooperation is granted here in response to Spener's problem."[119] Yet, the inner circle represents the dictates of practical reason. From a practical perspective, we cannot construct maxims based on divine grace, for maxims concern what we will do, not what other agents (e.g., God) might do on our behalf. Hence, Hare points out that in the Stoic maxim, "Kant . . . is not saying that we ought not to believe in works of divine grace. On the contrary his view is that we are required to believe in them. What he says is that reason cannot adopt divine grace into its maxims."[120] Reardon recognizes this same nuance when he writes,

> Taken in its usual theological meaning of a supernatural power operating on a man's will, grace is a concept that cannot itself be brought within the limits of reason. . . . Nor is it possible even to accord the idea a *practical* application, since such a use of it would presuppose a positive effort for good *on our part*; whereas merely to wait upon the operation of grace implies exactly the opposite, because then the accomplishments of good would be not our own act but that of another. . . . Therefore, although we

are not in a position to deny that works of grace do occur, they must remain incomprehensible to us, and so can have no place in a religion circumscribed by reason.[121]

In short, the translation project affords Kant the opportunity to appeal to divine grace, per the doctrines of the Christian faith and the condition that demands it (viz., radical evil). But in the end, practical reason cannot offer any prescription for the application of divine grace; it can at best acknowledge only its possibility and bid moral agents to make themselves worthy of this grace through moral striving.

The translation model clearly helps in alleviating some of the difficulties implicit within *Religion*. If Kant is, in fact, engaging Christian doctrine and translating it into moral language, the introduction of radical evil and the peculiar form it takes (e.g., evil is innate but freely chosen) begin to have some level of explanation—Kant is attempting to merge the premises of Christianity (e.g., humanity is innately corrupt) with the transcendental insights of practical reason (e.g., a moral predicate, such as *evil*, presumes freedom). Moreover, the anomalies of Kant's introduction of divine grace and his appeal to what appears to be a veiled (or a not so veiled) Christology are readily explained. We may even acknowledge Hare's insight that Kant's language seems conflicted at times because he oscillates between two distinct spheres—the practical sphere and the sphere of revealed religion. Despite these aids, the translation reading of *Religion* is not without its own set of serious difficulties.

The first problem that emerges for the *Religion*-as-Translation thesis surrounds the question of relevance. The later Allen Wood is helpful in fleshing out this specific difficulty. In his essay "Kant's Deism," Wood, like Hare, emphasizes the vehicular role of historical faith for Kant: "The historical function of ecclesiastical faith is to serve as the *vehicle* for pure rational religion. But it is also the *shell* in which rational religion is encased and from which it is humanity's historical task to free the religion of reason."[122] The latter point is what Wood has in mind when he calls Kant a deist. Wood does not mean that Kant fully embraces all that is traditionally identified with deism. Rather, "Kant's deism" refers to the basic Kantian assumption that natural religion is possible apart from supernatural revelation. Wood summarizes, "Essential to any deism is the view that there is such a thing as rational or natural religion, religion based on natural reason and not on supernatural revelation. Kant clearly holds that there is rational religion in this sense."[123] Not only is rational religion possible in Kant's world, but it is (practically) sufficient. There is no *need* for supernatural insight into our duties toward God; practical reason tells us what God demands. "Kant is emphatic," Wood tells us, "that there need not be any special duties to God in order for there to be religion. . . . What does seem requisite to religion is that (1) we have duties, (2) we have a concept of God, and (3) we are capable of regarding our duties as something God wills us to do."[124] As Wood sees it, Kant holds that all three requirements for religion are sufficiently supplied by reason. All rational beings who "use their reason honestly" can do the will of God and please him merely by adhering to the moral law.[125]

Wood's point is important when one recognizes that, according to Hare, the *Religion*-as-Translation thesis shows Kant to be a "pure rationalist." Given Kant's deism, however, Wood finds Kant's introduction of pure rationalism suspect. As is well known, in Book Four of *Religion* Kant distinguishes between naturalism, supernaturalism, rationalism, and pure rationalism. As with most Kant interpreters, Wood thinks Kant's rejection of both naturalism and supernaturalism is clear enough. But Wood thinks Kant's distinction between the rationalist and the pure rationalist is a bit hazy. Since Kant thinks that reason sufficiently reveals the will of God, the pure rationalist must maintain, argues Wood, "that God has given us certain commands supernaturally while denying that we are morally bound to carry them out."[126] Such a position seems superfluous to Wood, and thus he concludes that Kant's inclusion of pure rationalism was merely a way of rhetorically "cushioning [Kant's] evident denial of pure supernaturalism."[127]

Hare, of course, denies Wood's claim that pure rationalism is a position inserted merely to cushion Kant's denial of supernaturalism.[128] The pure rationalist, in Hare's assessment, represents a legitimate position that reflects Kant's own embrace of Christian revelation, via translation, in *Religion*.[129] Hare forwards three levels of evidence to support the pure rationalist reading of Kant, which we will return to in our treatment of Book Four. But regardless of whether Hare's defense of pure rationalism is convincing, Wood's point should not be missed. Even if Kant's motives are not as disingenuous as Wood's assessment of the pure rationalist would indicate, Wood highlights a serious question of relevance for *Religion*, if it is, in fact, what Reardon and Hare take it to be. Hare concedes Wood's basic premise that, for Kant, the pure religion of reason is all that is required for saving faith.[130] Hare also admits that, even if Kant is justified in carrying out a project of translation per the pure-rationalist rubric, we should not see "acceptance [of Kant's translation] as necessary for every rational agent."[131] In this light, we may wonder what, if anything, *Religion* adds to Kant's corpus. This is the question of relevance on which Wood harps. Translating Christianity is not required by Kant's system—unless, of course, one is inclined to embrace the Christian religion along with Kant's philosophy—nor is any of the content of the translation required for "saving faith." *Religion*, on this reading, offers only Kantian permission to hold to a certain form of Christianity (viz., morally translated Christianity) in the wake of the critical philosophy. The implication of such concessions is that one may take or leave *Religion*; it adds nothing of consequence to the pure religion of reason. Even if Hare is right in attributing the title *pure rationalism* to Kant's project and applying this rendering of pure rationalism to *Religion*, Wood's assessment of pure rationalism (viz., as a position that draws from revealed religion tenets to which no one is obligated to adhere) still stands; the pure religion of reason gains nothing from translating Christianity, and the results are binding on no rational agent. Perhaps the only benefit to seeing *Religion* as translation, then, is that it enables the clean dismissal of a text that traditional readers have sought to dismiss on other grounds.

In addition to the question *Religion*-as-Translation raises over the value of Kant's project, the results themselves cast suspicion on the success of Kant's experiment. As Hare points out, "The experiment will be successful if we can show that the contents of the two areas are not only consistent with each other but have the sort of unity that means that a person who follows the prescriptions of the one will also be following those of the other."[132] If such is the criterion for success, it seems evident that Kant's project fails. On the point of consistency, we have, at the outset, the introduction of radical evil, a doctrine that was recognized at its conception to be radically alien to Kant's critical philosophy. As Goethe complained to Herder in his June 7, 1793, letter, after Kant had gone to such great lengths to remove all prejudices from his philosopher's cloak, he "slobbered on it with the blot of radical evil so that even Christians would be enticed to kiss its hem."[133] The *Religion*-as-Translation thesis offers no explanation of why radical evil is introduced, except that innate corruption is a presupposition of Christianity. Yet, given that such innate corruption is starkly at odds with the *ought*-implies-*can* principle of practical reason, it seems the experiment is doomed to failure before it ever begins—the two spheres are at odds on their very first premise.

Reardon expresses one way of responding to this concern, namely, by appealing to the results of Kant's experiments as evidence that radical evil is not so alien to Kant's system. In other words, if radical evil gives way to a robust moral religion, is it really at odds with the practical philosophy? One cannot deny, however, that key to assessing the results of Kant's second experiment is coming to terms with the introduction of evil and grace within Kant's existing philosophical framework. While the distinct-spheres motif may be helpful in explaining why Kant oscillates between his practical Pelagianism and themes of depravity and grace, what is not clear is how Kant's distinct spheres serve to justify the introduction of radical evil and grace, all things considered. Yes, Christianity is a major world religion and likely the only one Kant was familiar enough with to utilize in such an experimental fashion, but surely other religions (perhaps even Judaism) would fare better. The distinct spheres simply do not address Quinn's and Wolterstorff's conundrums surrounding the entrance of radical evil and the subsequent introduction of divine forgiveness and assistance into the Kantian scheme: (1) if grace is needed, then *ought* does not imply *can*; (2) under the guide of practical reason, we have no reason to think God would show grace; and (3) Kant's presentation of grace moves contrary to the very definition of grace.

Regarding the first conundrum, the conflict between the theological notion of grace and the practical assumption that *ought* implies *can* may be explicable under the distinct spheres, but it does not thereby become reconcilable. The distinction of spheres only draws out the stark difference (and perhaps outright incompatibility) between Kant's critical philosophy and the theology he attempts to "translate." And this difference raises the same question sparked by the doctrine of radical evil: can Kant's translation be successful if the basic assumptions between the distinct spheres he puts in dialogue are fundamentally at odds with one another? The second conundrum also finds no justification under the translation reading of *Religion*. Grace is introduced because of Kant moving *outside* the sphere of practical reason—that is, because Kant introduces radical evil. From within the practical sphere, Kant has no reason for introducing divine grace. Regarding the third conundrum, while the distinct spheres may make grace historical (rather than a priori), Kant's doctrine of grace is still contrary to theological understandings of grace under the *Religion*-as-Translation thesis. Under Kant's translation, the only thing practical reason can say about grace is that we must make ourselves worthy of it; that is, moral converts must *earn* grace. Even if the translation avoids forcing the hand of God, it nevertheless distorts grace in the inner sphere, making it something to be laid hold of (or earned) by human effort—a concept contrary to the notion of a free gift that comes despite what we deserve.

These difficulties with Kant's use of grace bring us to one of Hare's own grievances about *Religion*. By Hare's own admission, "Kant's actual translation *fails* . . . [insofar as] . . . the pure religion of reason fails to do the work he needs it to do in answer to Spener's problem."[134] Hare makes plain that he, like many critics, thinks Kant does not have critical resources for introducing grace. Hare's comments on this point are worth quoting at length:

> Kant's translation failed to do the work he needed it to do in answer to Spener's problem. He is faced with a dilemma. Either he is going to allow himself within the pure religion of reason to make use of the appeal to extrahuman assistance, or he is not. If he does not, and this is the first horn of the dilemma, he is left with Spener's problem and the antinomy of practical reason. . . . The problem is that he has to show us *that* he can appeal to extrahuman assistance. If he cannot show us this, we will be left inside the inner circle with the violation of the principle that "ought implies can," since the overcoming of our adherence to the evil maxim, which reverses the proper order of incentives, "could occur only through good maxims, and cannot take place when the ultimate subjective ground of all maxims is postulated as corrupt."[135]

Kant, in short, may admit grace is necessary, but he has no critical resources by which he can appeal to extra-human assistance. Hare thus echoes Wolterstorff's concern that grace is an illegitimate resource for the practical philosophy—If we alone can make ourselves what we are morally, how does God assist us? Like Palmquist, Hare makes an appeal to inscrutability, suggesting that

"Kant can legitimately say that speculation about this matter is out of bounds to human reason, going beyond the limits of human understanding."[136] The bigger difficulty for Kant, in this light, is the Stoic maxim. Hare attempts to avoid this difficulty by saying that Kant does not deny grace; he simply denies that we can adopt it into our maxim.[137] Yet, Quinn points out that, for Kant, the Stoic maxim is not merely perspectival, but constitutive of the nature of moral goodness itself. If we are to be morally good, we alone must be the source of that goodness. The predicate *moral* requires that the individual's goodness be generated by a deed of that individual's own freedom.

Perhaps Kant could adopt a notion of freedom similar to what we find in Augustinian theology—God renews, changes, or heals the will, so that it may choose the good.[138] Such a conception of grace and the will would enable Kant to attribute the good will to God and yet retain the predicate *moral*; yet, as Hare goes on to point out, unless grace comes via some prior merit, the divine decision to assist becomes arbitrary, and the relationship between grace and works is not a moral relationship.[139] The notion of earned grace once again raises both Wolterstorff's concern that Kant's use of the concept violates the very definition of grace (i.e., *grace, by definition, is not earned or given by obligation*) as well as Quinn's criticism that if we are incapable of doing the good required of us and thus need grace, the initial earning of grace must also come by grace; thus, the relationship between God's giving of grace and our earning grace runs the risk of falling into an infinite regress.

The *Religion*-as-Translation reading offered by both Reardon and Hare helps make sense of the text and place it within the Kantian corpus, and the *Religion*-as-Translation thesis even offers some assistance with regard to Kant's sometimes conflicted vocabulary. But this reading in no way alleviates the conundrums; it only serves to explain why they emerge. In the end, Kant's project still fails. Moreover, the nature of the project, given Kant's surrounding philosophical assumptions regarding the sufficiency of rational religion, raises serious questions over whether Kant's project in *Religion* offers any real contribution to the Kantian paradigm. It seems the only benefit of this type of translation approach is that it helps place *Religion* within the Kantian corpus, casting light on the conundrums in a way that avoids making Kant appear philosophically sloppy, while also showing how Kant's philosophy applies directly to the prevailing religion of the time. But such results do not lead to the acquittal of *Religion*. The text, on this reading, has in no way come to be a genuine contribution to Kant's thought, for one may take or leave Kant's experiment (and given lingering conundrums, it may best be left). We therefore remain at some remove from ranking *Religion*, as the early Wood does, "as one of the great achievements of the human intellect," even with the *Religion*-as-Translation approach.[140] *Religion* is merely a failed and awkward experiment Kant once attempted due to his lingering religious loyalties. Even if a better translation defense were possible (and we are not sure it is), it would still marginalize *Religion*, in terms of both value and contribution. Thus, even with *Religion*-as-Translation, we fail to achieve the type of vindication of *Religion* promised in our introduction, namely, a defense that solves the conundrums and yields a reading that shows the text to have a contributing status in Kant's philosophy. In our next chapter, we turn to Gordon Michalson, who, as star witness for the prosecution, presents a comprehensive overview of the charges against *Religion*, charges a defense such as ours must answer.

3

The Indictment of *Religion*

Having cross-examined expert witnesses on the metaphysical motives behind and the philosophical character of *Religion*, we turn now to a final testimony on the part of the prosecution. Gordon Michalson's work on Immanuel Kant provides something of a watershed for current research in this regard, and therefore, Michalson may rightly be identified as the prosecution's star witness. His testimony will outline the indictment of the text. Two main works compose the heart of Michalson's interpretation of *Religion* and offer a detailed synopsis of some of the major objections to its coherence. They are *The Historical Dimensions of a Rational Faith* (1979) and *Fallen Freedom: Kant on Human Autonomy and Moral Regeneration* (1990).[1]

Two years prior to the publication of *The Historical Dimensions of a Rational Faith*, Michalson penned "The Role of History in Kant's Religious Thought."[2] In that essay, Michalson focuses specifically on Book Three of *Religion*, where Kant commends the coming together of moral converts in an effort to form an ethical commonwealth and discusses the usefulness of revealed religion for propagating moral truth. Adopting an interpretive strategy akin to *Religion*-as-Translation in the sense of Reardon and Hare (but in a markedly more pessimistic form), Michalson presumes that all of Kant's theological talk beyond what is found in the moral philosophy amounts to imagery borrowed from some historical faith, which has been schematized by moral reason. Historical faith is meant to serve a vehicular or "mediating role" in disseminating the moral philosophy, not an essential role in the development of Kant's thought. According to Michalson, after having "demolished the pretensions of a metaphysically-based natural theology" in the first *Critique* and translated "religious concepts from metaphysical categories to ethical terms" in the second *Critique*, Kant's main objective in *Religion* is to establish this vehicular role for historical faiths in the propagation of rational religion.[3]

This essay set the tone for Michalson's later work on *Religion*. Since Michalson understands Kant's arguments in *Religion* to represent a moral reinterpretation of a historical faith, meant to disseminate the philosophy of the second *Critique*, the later Michalson sees little room for genuine philosophical development in *Religion*. Like Hare and Reardon, Michalson sees Kant's apparent use of Christian theology as arising simply because Kant was raised in a predominantly Christian context and, as a result, chose Christianity as the historical faith for his religious experiment and the further development of his philosophy of religion. As we saw in chapter 2, Hare and Reardon find that Christianity provides at least some positive resources for Kant's understanding of moral faith, despite a lack of persuasive critical reasoning. Michalson, however, does not allow for such optimism. He identifies deep and debilitating problems that emerge the moment Kant's philosophy of religion moves into matters of depravity, redemption, and grace, and these problems snowball into a mountain of conundrums that Kant's philosophy proves insufficient to scale.

In *The Historical Dimensions of a Rational Faith*, Michalson develops his earlier essay-length analysis of Book Three of *Religion* into a complete interpretation and critique. Michalson's overall position is somewhat neutral toward the significance of Kant's philosophy of religion for the critical philosophy proper. On the one hand, he makes the case that *Religion* is best understood as a complete text and an important contribution to Kant's philosophy; on the other hand, he argues that Book Three presents tensions that threaten to undermine the integrity of Kant's philosophy of religion. Later, in *Fallen Freedom*, Michalson tackles Books One and Two and develops his interpretation and critique of *Religion* into a full-blown assault on its coherence. In the process, Michalson displays a noticeably more pessimistic tone regarding the coherence of Kant's arguments in *Religion* than he did in his earliest work. In "The Role of History in Kant's Religious Thought," the early Michalson sought to undo the common misunderstanding that Kant's philosophy of religion is purely reductive toward historical faiths. But with the development of *The Historical Dimension of a Rational Faith* and *Fallen Freedom* (and more recently, *Kant and the Problem of God*), Michalson's reading of Kant and Kant's impact on theology progressively degenerates into unabashed pessimism.

In what follows, we lay out Michalson's testimony regarding *Religion* in the form of seven core objections to its coherence. We call them "The Predisposition-Propensity Conflict," "The Innate-but-Freely-Chosen Predicament," "The Universal-Contingent Puzzle," "The Stoic-Saint Dilemma," "The Before-and-After Problem," "The Hermeneutic Circularity Crisis," and "The

Unnecessary Necessity Paradox." These seven objections (along with the subsidiary objections noted in the earlier testimony of Quinn and Wolterstorff) constitute the overall indictment of Kant's *Religion*. Any interpretation of *Religion* that pronounces Kant's arguments coherent and compatible with the critical philosophy must overcome these objections. In part 2 of this work, we will present our defense of *Religion* on the backdrop of these objections.

The Predisposition-Propensity Conflict

The first conundrum or "wobble" Michalson notes stems from Kant's "troublesome terms 'predisposition' (*Anlage*) and 'propensity' (*Hang*)."[4] As Michalson sees it, "The burden of the first two Books of the *Religion* is to examine these fundamental features of human nature and their relationship to one another."[5] Yet, in examining the relationship between humanity's natural predispositions and propensity to evil, Michalson finds serious ambiguities that cast suspicion on Kant's vision of our moral nature, and these difficulties, Michalson thinks, are constitutive of many of the inconsistencies in *Religion*.

Michalson understands human predispositions as inclinations that belong to the very concept of human nature. The predispositions represent basic human "potentialities." These predispositional potentialities are three in number: animality, humanity, and personality. Each has a close connection with humanity's natural inclinations, which range from our predisposition to procreate (stemming from the predisposition to animality) to our predisposition to have respect for the moral law as supreme incentive (stemming from the predisposition to personality). Within these predispositions, there are gradations; some predispositions require a significant level of intellect and are uniquely human, while others require less intellect and may be shared in common with other sentient creatures. Michalson suggests that in pointing out this gradation in our inclinations and potentialities, "Kant is evidently trying to devise a kind of calculus of sensuousness here."[6] Michalson sees Kant's catalogue of predispositions as identifying the hierarchy and relationship between the lower potentialities and the highest of all potentialities, namely, the potential to treat the moral law as supreme incentive.

The goal of Kant's "calculus of sensuousness," according to Michalson, is to vindicate the lower order of human nature from moral guilt—all our predispositions are good in themselves. At the same time, however, Michalson notes that Kant's discussion of lower inclinations and potentialities is clearly intended to have some explanatory role in Kant's treatment of radical evil. These lower inclinations still have a hand, as it were, in humanity's movement away from the moral law as supreme incentive. Michalson writes, "what I think we are seeing—although admittedly not very clearly—is Kant trying to theorize a bridge between our sensuous nature and moral culpability, a bridge that leaves sensuousness blameless, when taken by itself, while still managing to refer to it in the account of moral evil."[7]

On Michalson's reading, Kant's goal is unquestionably to root moral evil in freedom, not in some purely biological or physiological pull. The predispositions constitute certain potentialities in humanity, and there can be no doubt that, while these potentialities "are fixed," what we do with our predispositions is "not fixed."[8] Thus, for Kant, the human individual's exercise of freedom must be responsible for evil. Be this as it may, Michalson's instincts are that, despite this concerted effort to vindicate the predispositions from moral blame, Kant intends humanity's natural predispositions to have a significant explanatory role in his account of radical evil. Kant is attempting to schematize the human person so as to allow for an explanation of radical evil via our natural inclinations. In the process, however, "Kant must walk a fine line between attributing moral evil to something naturally given in human nature and attributing it to some force or capacity utterly irrelevant to basic human nature."[9]

Kant, as Michalson envisions him, is caught between his tendency to make the sensuous aspects of human nature a feature of radical evil and his desire to exempt from blame humanity's sensual inclinations. For Kant's project to work, our individual exercise of freedom must be the culprit behind radical evil, otherwise evil would be a necessary component of human nature. Conversely, unless Kant makes use of the sensual nature as a device for explaining evil, he can give no account of the origin of evil. As Michalson points out, lower incentives, which are tied up with our lower inclinations, are what draw us away from the moral law as supreme incentive. Freedom may choose evil of its own accord, but without sensuality, the moral law would always win out as supreme incentive, given the working assumptions carried over from Kant's practical philosophy. Kant is thus forced to link freedom implicitly with sensuality as a cause of sorts, while simultaneously maintaining enough distance between sensuality and freedom to avoid making the choosing of evil a matter of raw necessity.

In the end, Michalson thinks Kant's "calculus of sensuality" simply does not add up. While Kant may be justified in emphasizing freedom in order to avoid making evil necessary, the problem Michalson sees is that this gap makes Kant's notion of a *propensity* to evil resulting from the inverted order of incentives unintelligible. Michalson writes:

> We now learn that the idea of a propensity suggests the way in which sensuous inclinations get the upper hand, so to speak, in the formation of maxims. To be sure, the propensity to evil does not explain how or why the subordination of the moral to the sensuous occurs. . . . Yet the propensity to evil does explain the sheer potentiality that is required for there ever to be moral evil in the world. This is significant, since Kant's theorizing about our original predispositions leaves a gap in respect of just this potentiality, in

light of his insistence that all of our predispositions are good in themselves. That is to say: Kant's theory of the predispositions accounts for all of our potential in life, *except* for our potential to become morally evil.[10]

Put in a slightly different way, if Kant insists on an infinite gap between freedom's choosing of evil and the sensual nature, so that freedom alone is to blame for evil, Michalson does not see how a free, spontaneous act can produce a general propensity in subsequent spontaneous acts. Freedom must have a partner in crime in this respect (viz., the sensuous nature) that limits freedom's spontaneity and draws it into evil as a course of habit. Only in this way would Kant be warranted in arguing for a general propensity in human nature. Without such a sister concept, freedom is always spontaneous and immune from propensities of any sort. To speak of freedom as if it could take on a propensity of any kind is problematic. Unless something outside of freedom binds the will, a propensity to evil must always refer to a continual spontaneous willing of evil, despite the ability of freedom to choose otherwise. The human propensity to evil is therefore a concept Michalson thinks in dire need of clarification and explanation, but Kant simply offers no clear explanation that Michalson can see in this regard.

In considering possible solutions, Michalson suggests that Kant could appeal analogically to something like addiction. Kant, when speaking about inclinations, refers at one point to savages having a tendency toward intoxication. Homing in on this example, Michalson suggests that perhaps Kant could construe the propensity to evil in a way similar to a propensity to drink: once alcohol has been tasted (an act presumably done without compulsion), a propensity toward intoxication can sometimes emerge. But Michalson finds even this type of explanation to be unhelpful: "[T]he analogy would then be an extremely selective one, since it is not offset by another analogy depicting a propensity for good. There is thus some confusion—or what one commentator has aptly called a 'lack of symmetry'—in Kant's account of moral motivation as it crystallizes in his theory of the propensities. There is no intrinsic reason why the notion of a propensity should have only a negative or evil connotation."[11] If moral decisions have compulsory properties and, for this reason, the tasting of evil creates a propensity toward like-acts, then Michalson wonders why Kant would not find that the tasting of goodness creates a similar compulsion in the opposite direction. Moreover, the idea that Kant intends the propensity to be compulsory seems to be in conflict with his notion that the propensity is the result of the ever-spontaneous exercise of freedom. Insofar as Kant insists on locating evil in the spontaneous will of humanity and vindicating the sensual nature of responsibility, "it is not clear," submits Michalson, "that we are any closer to grasping why Kant should be proposing that there is something natural and inevitable about the propensity to evil."[12]

Michalson sees a very similar conflict between freedom and the sensual nature in Kant's discussion of the varying gradations of evil. Kant lists three such gradations (viz., frailty, impurity, and wickedness). According to Kant, only wickedness is an overt decision to invert the moral order of incentives; both frailty and impurity constitute only inadequacies or weaknesses in the person's moral resources. Michalson is not sure how Kant can affirm the reality of frailty or impurity, however, since Kant identifies our propensity to evil with a willful inversion of the moral order of incentives that is causally disconnected from our lower inclinations. Since Kant remains steadfast in his declaration that freedom is responsible for humanity's moral failings, in what sense can Kant speak of humanity's moral resources proving inadequate due to frailty or impurity? As Michalson puts it, "We might say that, insofar as Kant's account of radical evil appears only to involve what he is here calling 'wickedness' (*Bösartigkeit*), it is not at all clear what the point of the other two degrees of evil is, or whether they are in fact examples of 'moral' evil."[13]

In sum, Kant's simultaneous use of good predispositions and a natural propensity to evil to describe humanity's corrupt state drives Kant's argument in *Religion* to a fork in the road. On one side, Kant must use his calculus of sensuousness as an explanatory device for introducing radical evil, while on the other side, Kant wants to retain the pure spontaneity of freedom as the sole source of our moral failings. If Kant needs the sensuous to account for the origin of evil, radical evil is divorced from freedom and becomes a non-moral necessity. But if Kant identifies the spontaneous exercise of freedom as the final cause of radical evil, he has no way of explaining evil as a propensity in human nature. The latter point is perhaps most significant. A propensity to evil must be nothing more than a human's willful and perpetual pursuit of evil, but Kant clearly does not want to define it in such terms. So long as Kant defends the fecundity of humanity's moral resources and finds the roots of evil in freedom alone, he can offer no explanation for our evil propensity, and "the absence of genuine argumentation for this crucial point," Michalson finds, "is one of the most outstanding features of the entire *Religion*."[14]

The Innate-but-Freely-Chosen Predicament

Michalson's second wobble concerns Kant's declaration that evil is both innate and freely chosen. The tension is captured in 6:38: "This *innate* guilt . . . is so called because it is detectable as early as the first manifestation of the exercise of freedom in the human being, but . . . must nonetheless have originated from freedom." According to Michalson, Kant has some explaining to do. On the one hand, Kant assumes evil to be present in human nature prior to any exercise of the will in time; on the other hand, he holds that humans are responsible for radical evil because we bring it upon ourselves through the exercise of freedom. Kant recognizes the tension, but, according to Michalson, seems satisfied to give no explanation whatsoever: "We shall say, therefore, . . .

that [radical evil] is *innate* in him; and yet we shall always be satisfied that nature is not to blame for it . . . but that the human being is alone its author" (6:21–22). Michalson thinks it is incumbent upon Kant to explain "the exact relationship between the free act by which the moral agent chooses his or her disposition, and the free acts arising out of the disposition in individual acts of maxim-making."[15]

It should be said that Kant's critics are not unified over whether this tension in Kant's account of radical evil is problematic. Wood endorses Kant's position, remarking, "I think we cannot help realizing that Kant's discussion of radical evil and grace ranks as one of the great achievements of the human intellect in attempting to give a rational account of the reconciliation of man to God";[16] and Quinn gives this lofty appraisal:

> I know of no rational reconstruction of the doctrine of original sin that preserves more of these [moral] intuitions than Kant's theory of radical evil does. Moreover, as far as I can tell, the theory is internally consistent or, more cautiously, is logically possible if it is logically possible for there to be human acts of will which are both absolutely spontaneous and independent of all temporal conditions.[17]

Other Kant interpreters, however, are dissatisfied with the tensions found in Kant's assessment of human nature. Ward, for instance, finds the only consistent feature of Kant's doctrine of radical evil to be that it "retains all the paradoxes of the orthodox [Christian] account [of original sin]."[18] And McCarthy likewise thinks that radical evil disturbs Kant's otherwise balanced moral outlook.

Michalson spells out two specific difficulties for Kant's innate-but-freely-chosen understanding of evil that are worth examining more closely. Firstly, Michalson, like Ward, thinks such a claim is viciously paradoxical. Kant's doctrine of the innate-but-freely-chosen disposition "would appear," argues Michalson, "to rob either 'freedom' or 'innateness' of its point."[19] Freedom carries a character of spontaneity and the possibility of choosing alternative courses of action, while innateness carries connotations of inevitability. Far from affirming our moral sensibilities, the combination of innateness and freedom creates a predicament that seems to shade off into contradiction.

Secondly, Michalson thinks Kant owes the reader an explanation of the relationship between the "single, timeless disposition that constitutes the definitive feature of one's moral condition" and "the worldly manifestation of the disposition in countless acts of maxim-making."[20] As Michalson sees it, Kant's philosophy prior to *Religion* presents a radically free (morally speaking) view of humanity, where Kant seems bent, at every turn, on defending the sufficiency of our moral resources—our freedom is always spontaneous, and since we *ought* to do good, we *can* do good. Kant's turn to the innate disposition, however, moves contrary to such a trend. Michalson writes:

> It is one thing to speak of moral evil as the potential product of an act of maxim-making. Indeed, one could even say that Kant is simply deducing moral evil transcendentally, since his theory of freedom clearly serves as the necessary condition of its possibility. . . . But it is quite another thing to claim that this immoral exercise of freedom points to something innate. A transcendental argument concerning the possibility of moral evil could well be a natural elaboration of Kant's theory of freedom. By contrast, the suggestion of the innateness of an underlying radical evil appears to shift us away from inquiry into freedom's possibilities to the idea of a limitation on freedom.[21]

Michalson finds the turn to the innate disposition to be contrary to Kant's prior views on freedom. Kant's transcendental theory of freedom allows for the kind of moral spontaneity that makes room for evil decision-making and even evil maxim-making. Yet, Kant's emphasis on innateness in *Religion* creates a division between individual acts of freedom in maxim-making (which had previously been Kant's focus) and the completely unique act of maxim-making that limits all subsequent uses of freedom. "If this distinction cannot be sustained," Michalson argues, "it is not clear how Kant can deduce the very notion of the disposition as something distinct from lower-order maxims."[22] In this light, Michalson concludes, "Kant's argumentative trouble stems mainly from his wanting to say that radical evil is both freely elected and 'innate.' "[23]

The Universal-Contingent Puzzle

Kant's emphasis on the spontaneous exercise of freedom raises one of the most troubling conundrums in *Religion*, to wit, "the puzzling question of why Kant should end up claiming that freedom will be *universally* exercised in this way."[24] As discussed earlier in the treatment of the predisposition-propensity conflict, Kant attempts to vindicate the predispositions from moral blame—our sensual nature, those inclinations that are natural to us as humans, cannot be the *cause* of evil; evil emerges solely from a spontaneous or, as Michalson says, "discrete" deed of freedom. Kant's commitment to the spontaneity of freedom makes Kant's subsequent claim that radical evil is universal puzzling, for "discrete acts of human freedom undertaken by countless multitudes of moral agents provide no connecting thread that would account for this universality."[25] Since, as Michalson puts it, "Kant's moral universe is a scene of innumerable idiosyncrasies," how can Kant make a claim regarding universality?[26] A common choosing of evil, it would seem, must be sheer coincidence; the choices of the will can be neither explained in terms of why the will has chosen as it has chosen nor systematized in anticipation of what it will choose.

Philip Quinn points out a virtually identical difficulty with the universality of radical evil in his essay "Original Sin, Radical Evil and Moral Identity." Quinn, like Michalson, recognizes that, since "the propensity to moral evil is a product of freedom, it cannot be an essential element in human nature as is the predisposition to good. If moral evil is to be attributed to mankind as a species, it must be a contingent and accidental attribute of each member of the species."[27] In other words, Kant's universal conclusion cannot be "justified by philosophical analysis of human nature."[28] Instead, Kant's arguments, Quinn points out, must be inductive in the sense of being rooted in an observation of humans generally. But such induction hardly secures Kant's conclusion that evil is universal. Quinn's comments on this puzzle are noteworthy:

> But it seems very improbable that a propensity to moral evil should be both a product of freedom and universal among mankind. Because the adoption of an evil supreme maxim is an absolutely spontaneous exercise of the will, it is antecedently likely that some people would have freely adopted a morally good supreme maxim while others adopted a morally evil supreme maxim. Even if it is impossible to assign numerical values to the prior probabilities of the various alternatives, it seems clear enough that the prior probability of all humans choosing freely a morally evil supreme maxim must be quite low.[29]

Quinn's use of probability language is helpful. Kant may be able to claim that it is *likely*, given our experiences in the world, that all humans have chosen evil. Kant can even assert that humanity's universal choosing of evil is mathematically possible, even if unlikely—there is at least one possible world in which all humans spontaneously choose evil without exception. But insofar as Kant's reasons for declaring the universality of this choice are inductive, the conclusion cannot be assured. Kant wants to assert with confidence that all who have ever lived have made this choice. Without some type of predetermined cause for this choice, however, Kant cannot declare its universality with any kind of certainty. This logical gap is true of the past, but is especially true of the future. Spontaneous and continuous acts of goodness will always be a possibility for free human beings, unless Kant can offer some cause or condition that makes the universal choosing of evil necessary. But this is precisely what Kant refuses to do. So long as the choosing of radical evil is a free, spontaneous choice, no claim of universality can be made.

Quinn attempts to offer a way of delivering Kant from this puzzle. Quinn's approach emphasizes Kant's use of the "rigorist criteria"—a disposition must be either good or evil; it cannot be morally neutral or morally bifurcated. Given this stark view of moral goodness, Quinn argues,

> it is made possible by the inevitable presence in humans of incentives of two kinds which can, and often do, come into conflict, and also a product of freedom, in that it consists of a free choice of a supreme maxim which does not always give obedience to the moral law pride of place over pursuit of the satisfaction of sensuous inclinations. And it seems reasonable enough to suppose that such a policy is, implicitly at least, universal among mankind.[30]

The exact nature of Quinn's argument is somewhat unclear. Either Quinn is attempting to say that the move to evil is necessary, given the makeup of mankind as a creature with competing incentives, or he is attempting to say that, because of the various incentives present in human experience, evil is *likely* universal. In the case of the former, however, evil is no longer moral, for it does not emerge freely; yet, in the case of the latter, we are still left without a clear universal conclusion—some may have chosen, or may still choose, the good over evil, even if the good is so difficult it likely has never been chosen. Thus, even in Quinn's supposed "way out," Kant is bound to deny either freedom in the origin of radical evil or the universality of evil.

Michalson recognizes this dichotomy and suggests that Kant's arguments are ineluctably driven to conclude that evil is necessary due to the influence of our lower inclinations. Kant attempts to avoid this conclusion by continually pointing to freedom as the cause of evil and by identifying humanity's pre-dispositions as good. Nevertheless, the calculus of sensuality Kant develops, Michalson believes, inevitably entails that evil is necessary. Michalson avers, "The question of why Kant claims that radical evil is universal must finally have at least part of its answer in Kant's deep suspicion of our bodies. For although he is careful not to blame moral evil on the sheer competition for control of character between sensuous and rational incentives: rationality would have no competition if it were not embodied."[31] And again:

> Radical evil can thus be viewed as the final result of Kant's latent resentment against the body, his philosophical chagrin that pure reason must cohabit with sensuousness. There is, after all, a profound connection between transcendental method and the "disembodied" standpoint—as though we "get it right," philosophically, only to the extent that we bracket (if not escape altogether) the conditions of our embodiment, as well as the effects of history.[32]

Michalson sees the body as the only "connecting thread" among moral agents who lapse into evil. "What is more," Michalson argues, "the definitive feature of a moral agent is the struggle to subordinate the incentives that emerge *because* we are embodied to the incentive arising out of reason."[33] Michalson recognizes Kant's efforts to strike a balance between using humanity's sensuality to explain evil and not blaming our sensuality for evil, but, in the end, Michalson finds the whole discussion misaligned. Kant's final conclusion—evil is universal—and his confidence in reason's endorsement of morality points to humanity's physicality as the only basis for Kant's conclusions: "We might say that the body provides freedom with its opportunity to go wrong."[34]

Here again, we see Kant at a fork in the road. He must choose between identifying the sensual nature of humanity (i.e., our natural predispositions and the incentives that bombard us as creatures of flesh) as causally responsible for radical evil and holding fast to the spontaneity of freedom. But, as already pointed out, in the former option, evil becomes necessary and is no longer *moral*, for it does not emerge from freedom. We can neither be held accountable for radical evil nor consider the predispositions naturally good. Such consequences are quite similar to those enumerated in our critique of Green in the previous chapter, and move so contrary to Kant's explicit assertions in *Religion* that few are willing to consider this option a legitimate interpretation of *Religion*. Even Michalson, who places Kant on this road for consistency's sake, does not think the results provide a balanced and cogent philosophy of religion. The second way open to Kant is no less problematic, however. If Kant's argument treats evil as the product of a spontaneous act of the will, which can find no causal basis outside the will itself, then Kant cannot defend the universality of radical evil. From a purely inductive standpoint, Kant can, at most, identify evil as a popular option for the majority of people; he can even admit to the possibility of its universality; but he cannot conclude that all who have lived (or will live) have chosen (or will choose) evil.

In robbing Kant of the universality of evil, this option also robs Kant of any postulate of divine grace—such as what we find in Wood's reading, for example. For Kant, postulates are not optional extras; they emerge in the face of insurmountable challenges to theoretical reason and teleological concerns. If radical evil is not universal and has no cause (it arises freely and could have been rejected), then there is no insurmountable challenge in the face of evil. The dominance of evil indicates only that a great many humans are ambivalent to the moral law but are (and were) capable of treating the moral law as supreme incentive. Said otherwise, those who are susceptible to radical evil merely show their freely chosen disregard for the moral law; they are not bound to evil, for they could have been good had they willed it. If such is the state of affairs for humanity, there exists no universal or insurmountable plight that bids a postulate of divine grace. To suggest that a postulate of grace presents itself on behalf of those who are morally ambivalent is questionable from a moral perspective and is certainly not the basis for a critical philosophy of religion.

In the end, if Kant were to reject the necessity of radical evil and part ways with its universality, the only practical resource he would have for assessing humanity's moral nature is the *ought*-implies-*can* principle. But this principle, which is the cornerstone for Kant's entire moral philosophy, tells us that humans are fully capable of developing without falling into radical evil. In such an assessment of human nature, grace, from a practical perspective, becomes an impossibility. Thus, if Kant were to set his foot to the road where evil is universal but freely chosen by each individual's spontaneous will, any argument that hinges on the introduction of the postulate of divine grace is bound to fail. But the only alternative is to accept the necessity of evil, which undercuts its moral status along with the basic principles of the moral philosophy. Such is the unsavory dichotomy of this puzzle.

The Stoic–Saint Dilemma

In the first section of the previous chapter, we discussed, from a variety of angles, the difficulties surrounding Kant's coupling of what Wolterstorff calls "the Stoic Maxim" and divine grace—a coupling that seems to either admit the falsehood of the *ought-*implies-*can* principle or make divine grace into a case of judicial fudging. To avoid belaboring the point, we will not reiterate the various difficulties that emerge from this aspect of *Religion*, except to say that Michalson is cognizant of many of the (roughly eight) difficulties noted by Wolterstorff and Quinn.[35] Michalson writes, "[T]he theory of radical evil appears to force him in an Augustinian direction, while his conception of grace or divine aid reintroduces an obviously Pelagian element based on human effort and merit."[36] Michalson agrees with Quinn and Wolterstorff that this awkward mixing of Augustinianism and Pelagianism calls into question Kant's assumptions regarding human autonomy. Michalson writes:

> Kant is delicately walking a fine line between autonomy and grace, free will and providence, appealing to the human dimension so as to have the result be a truly *moral* regeneration, while referring in vague but substantive ways to divine action so as to underwrite the possibility of what radical evil seems to make impossible. As I have been indicating all along, this is where Kant's position will wobble most severely, signaling his awkward posture between a modern commitment to autonomy and a received tradition framed in terms of biblical imagery.[37]

Michalson readily acknowledges that Kant's introduction of radical evil requires an appeal to grace. However, Kant's emphasis on maxim-making, practical reason, and human autonomy prevents this very appeal: "Kant more or less 'backs into' discussions of seemingly forbidden or philosophically irrelevant topics, and then, once there, he devises solutions to difficulties produced on the purely philosophical level. The key move, obviously, is the move that gets him on the initially forbidden ground."[38] Theologians inevitably need to discuss justification in the face of radical evil—the connection is a natural theological one—but Michalson questions whether this connection is at all Kantian. In the end, "it is not at all clear," says Michalson, "that Kant abides by his own strictures as he goes on to make use of the notion of divine aid in his account of moral conversion."[39]

In addition, Michalson, with Quinn, recognizes the difficulty of presuming, as Kant does, the possibility of moral conversion after having claimed that the disposition cannot be changed from evil to good by human effort. If the subjective ground for the exercise of freedom is presumed to be corrupt, and human effort cannot undo this corruption, how can Kant be justified in presuming that humans can exert themselves and produce a re-reversal of the moral order of incentives? Michalson summarizes the problem thusly:

> Notice to begin with how Kant begs his own question (concerning how someone with a corrupt disposition can become good again) by simply assuming at the outset of his answer that this transformation has already occurred. Just *how* someone "reverses, by a single unchangeable decision, that highest ground" of one's maxims (i.e., the disposition), is exactly what we want to understand, rather than what we can assume as a premise for discussing something else. Presumably, Kant cannot really answer this question without setting a free act of *Willkür* into an explanatory framework— but he is the one who has fashioned the question as though he is going to tell us.[40]

As Quinn points out, Kant presumes the possibility of moral conversion on practical grounds, but offers no explanation of the moral conversion itself—its possibility and prospects. While practical insight may be a legitimate Kantian tool in the face of epistemological limitations, what Kant has given us in his treatment of the doctrine of radical evil leaves us with no reason to believe that the disposition can be altered by human force. Kant appears to have run out of philosophical resources at this crucial juncture, and all he can do, thinks Michalson, is appeal to biblical language as a non-critical supplement to his philosophy of religion.

These and other difficulties drawn out by Quinn and Wolterstorff above highlight the problems that emerge under Kant's use of divine grace. Kant's introduction of radical evil and his concession that grace is needed for moral renewal shake his bedrock moral assumption that *ought* implies *can*. The awkward tension created in the effort to retain human autonomy amid the concession of moral depravity and our need for grace not only creates an instability in Kant's practical philosophy generally, it also casts a shadow of suspicion on Kant's introduction of the concept of grace. Within this shadow, quandaries over the role and nature of grace, as well as the justice of God in the application of grace, thrive. Quinn, Wolterstorff, and Michalson each aptly draw out such problems, and this complex host of issues together compose the Stoic-Saint Dilemma.

The Before-and-After Problem

The second major problem Michalson sees in Book Two is what appears to be a convoluted account of moral regeneration. In particular, Michalson's concern is that Kant's notion of moral conversion fragments human identity. It will be remembered that Ward presented this problem rhetorically:

> Suppose that at one time, T1, a man has happiness as his determining incentive; at T2 he takes the moral law as incentive; and at T3 he returns to happiness. Has he had a change of heart and back again? For Kant, man must be totally good or bad; so how does one determine the ultimate maxim—by counting empirical acts and balancing them up?[41]

Key to the Before-and-After Problem is the issue of timing: how can God be just to a person, who, over the spectrum of time, represents two morally distinct people? According to Michalson, Kant's account of regeneration combines divine justice and human identity over the course of moral transformation in a way that fragments the human person. Moral hope, for Kant, "culminates in the paradox that an act having no relation to time produces a moral agent who is materially different 'after' the act from 'before.' "[42] Kant, thinks Michalson, awkwardly mixes timelessness and time in *Religion:* the evil disposition is chosen through a decision not in time, while the moral agent converts to good *after* such a decision, indicating temporal succession in the disposition, and since Michalson understands Kant to provide no metaphysical connection between moral conversion and temporal succession, Michalson argues that the inevitable consequence of Kant's vision is that "every free act is for Kant a 'conversion.' "[43] That is, the temporal turn to the good, if constitutive of a change in disposition, is on par with equally temporal re-turns to evil, which must, then, also constitute a change in disposition.

Bernard Reardon draws out this same difficulty, though from a slightly different angle, when he writes:

> Yet how, if the individual's choice of new and good maxims is sincere, can he really—if infrequently—defy the moral law? Kant certainly would not have argued that conversion results in immediate virtue, in clearly recognizable 'newness of life'; he is only too well aware that the reform process is gradual; and he also concedes that a man can never be wholly sure of the genuineness or the durability of his change of heart. Thus there is bound to be moral failure, despite the recovered will to good. All the same, do not bad actions, on Kant's reckoning, proceed from the *radical* evil in human nature, so that the heart is not after all regenerate? . . . The theological doctrine [*coram Deo*] is not inconsistent with attributing conversion to the grace of God, and sin to the corrupted will of man. But Kant's effort to attribute both the good and the evil to one and the same human volition, which yet must adopt the maxim *either* of duty *or* of self-love, surely indicates a discrepancy in Kant's reasoning that does not admit of easy resolution.[44]

Concisely put, Reardon senses a difficulty in Kant's account of the moral life. Given his assumptions, how could Kant ever infer the presence of a good disposition in us? Kant's rigorist view of morality seems to make *any* act of evil evidence of a corrupt maxim—a point also noted by Quinn.[45] When this inference is coupled with the fact that Kant thinks moral failings are inevitable in "moral converts," one must conclude that moral conversion is impossible. The only other option is to go with Michalson and construe each free, moral decision as a change in disposition. As Michalson points out, however, conversion in this latter sense is not a moment where the individual definitively and finally changes, but is any and every change of heart where the good is chosen over evil; and each failing becomes a type of de-conversion.

Michalson argues that this multifaceted understanding of conversion causes Kant's account to fall into a crisis of human identity. Considered over time, the person who made the first moral choice to adopt an evil disposition is "numerically" different than the person who made the later choice to become good. Even if we can grant that Kant is able to account for the difference between the original human being who is not evil by nature and the same human who, by his free choice, becomes evil by nature, we still cannot account for the same human being who later embraces the good again. The individual becomes more than merely an old and new man, divided by a definitive decision in time; the individual ends up consisting of a series of moral individuals—the original, uncorrupted man, the corrupt man who is evil by nature, the moral agent who converts to the good, and the man who lapses again into evil. As Michalson states:

> On the one hand, the very idea of regeneration or conversion . . . suggests two distinct moral agents, a fallen and a redeemed one; while, on the other hand, morality's noumenal insulation from the effects of time suggests just one moral agent, due to Kant's inability to discriminate between "before and after" when he considers the agent as an intelligible . . . being. In the first instance, the resulting conceptual problem concerns the integration of the two different selves under a theory of personal identity that allows us to say that the regenerated agent really is the "same" person . . . as the guilty one. For if we cannot do this—if . . . we end up with two metaphysically distinct agents—it ultimately becomes unclear how we are intelligibly to relate the issues of fall and regeneration. . . . And in the second instance, the problem concerns showing that the agent was sufficiently different at one point (in time?) than at another for the very idea of moral conversion to have meaningful application.[46]

On Michalson's interpretation, each of these moral individuals serves a necessary role in Kant's account of moral redemption, but to hold all of them in tandem fragments the human person and makes Kant's account of fallenness and redemption unintelligible.

The Hermeneutic Circularity Crisis

The first conundrum Michalson points out with regard to Book Three surrounds the relationship between rational religion and historical religion. This relationship, he thinks, exposes an "unresolved tension" in Kant's thinking: "on the one hand, Kant's rationalistic predilections keep him from ever conceding that any particular historical aspect is soteriologically or pedagogically necessary for our religious life; but on the other hand, his principle of human limitations militates against the worldly satisfaction of those very same rationalistic predilections."[47] For Michalson, this tension between the rationalist's use of historical faith and rational religion itself resides most noticeably in

Kant's biblical hermeneutic. We find there a simultaneous appeal to the biblical narrative for support of Kant's moral philosophy and movement away from the biblical narrative when it imposes doctrines the critical philosophy is not prepared to accept. For Kant, the "moral" interpretation of the biblical text always takes precedence over whatever the biblical author might have intended. "Consequently," Michalson suggests, "any inquiry into Kant's rationale for deriving moral meaning from an historical text comes full-circle back to the problem of the imposition of potentially foreign meaning *on to* the text."[48] In other words, Kant wants biblical themes and ideas to inhabit his thought when philosophical concepts run out, or when these themes serve as a useful vehicle, but he also wants to interpret the Bible "morally" *as if* these moral ideas are present in the text, even when this most clearly is not the case.

Kant's engagement with the Bible thus sets up a vicious circularity that dictates the argumentation in *Religion.* Michalson summarizes this charge of circularity in a passage where he relates Kant's biblical hermeneutic to Kant's "experimental" inquiry into the merits of Christianity, mentioned in the Second Preface:

> The reason Kant's method of interpretation proves so unsatisfactory is that it betrays the circularity of his approach in *Religion.* . . . If Kant is committed to the presupposition that the rational elements . . . reside implicitly in any historical faith embraced by rational beings, then his experimental inquiry into revealed religion 'in light of moral concepts', with the aim of seeing whether this 'does not lead back to the . . . pure rational system of religion', loses its innocent and experimental character. The result of such an experiment is a foregone conclusion, given Kant's theory of practical reason. There is of course the possibility that certain particular historical faiths, like Christianity, may more completely approximate the religion of pure reason, but Kant seems committed to the claim that any historical faith whatever must contain at least a minimal aspect of rational religion.[49]

For Michalson, Kant's approach to historical faiths in general, and Kant's theory of biblical interpretation in particular, is illuminating only insofar as it reveals Kant's prior commitments that guide the entire procedure. "Every interpreter carries presuppositions," notes Michalson, "but in Kant's case, the presuppositions involved tend to predetermine not only the questions he asks the texts, but the answers he gets."[50] The only thing Kant can accomplish in his treatment of Christianity, therefore, is the reduction of biblio-historical Christianity to moral religion, for any affirmation of Christianity Kant offers is only an affirmation of a Christianity restructured to fit the Kantian moral framework.[51]

This crisis of hermeneutic circularity not only casts suspicion on Kant's project in *Religion,* it also creates significant difficulties for the *Religion*-as-Translation interpretation. If Kant's hermeneutic is such that it compels the reader to approach a religious text under the assumption that the text contains rational religion, while also allowing (and even obliging) the reader to manipulate and force the text to declare the truths of rational religion, even when such truths may not be present, then Kant's two experiments are not really experiments at all. They suggest, instead, a project bent on reducing the authorial intent of religious texts to some preestablished set of rational mandates. As we have already seen, Hare submits that Kant's position on the success of the experiments hinges on whether "we can show that the contents of the two areas [i.e., rational religion and historical religion] are not only consistent with each other but have the sort of unity that means that a person who follows the prescriptions of the one will also be following those of the other."[52] If, however, Kant is dedicated to finding rational religion (i.e., the inner sphere) in the sacred text of a "revealed" religion (i.e., the outer sphere), whether it is actually present or not, then any claim to a successful experiment is suspect. As Michalson suggests, Kant's approach presupposes the questions asked of the text as well as the answers to be given by the text. Given the circular nature of Kant's hermeneutic, Kant's experiment does not demonstrate the presence of rational religion in the given faith; it only shows the creative ability of human reason to find its desired meaning wherever it seeks it.

The Unnecessary Necessity Paradox

Michalson finds a second difficulty with Kant's arguments in Book Three, which is the last conundrum we will consider in this indictment. This final conundrum concerns the role Kant sees historical faiths playing in the progress of rational religion. Even if we grant that Kant can, in fact, relate historical faith and moral faith in the way that allows historical faith to be a vehicle for rational religion, according to Michalson, "The question which remains concerns the fate of this historical 'vehicle' once the moral element has been located and appreciated. It is here that we begin to touch upon the extremely crucial issue of whether or not an historical faith is somehow religiously necessary for Kant."[53] It appears there is a sense in which Kant takes historical faith to be necessary to humanity's moral and religious advancement, and yet Kant holds that historical faith is not necessary for rational religion. The difficulty, as Michalson sees it, is that "however strong a case one might make for the 'constructive' aspect of Kant's view of an historical faith, it can never warrant replacing the religion of the second *Critique* with a religion of revelation."[54] Clearly Kant holds that, like practical reason itself, rational religion is self-sufficient. But Michalson sees Kant's vision of transforming historical faiths into rational religions as edging toward the contention that humanity in some sense needs historical faiths. The irony, of course, is that Kant seems to advocate a time in the future where historical faith will no longer be needed. What precisely is Kant trying to accomplish by making historical faith a type of necessity, while at the same time holding firm to the conviction that only rational faith is soteriologically necessary for moral hope?

Michalson thinks there are two possible explanations of this need for historical faith in *Religion*. "On the one hand," Michalson suggests, "the necessity of an historical faith might be understood to mean the reliance of human salvation upon a particular historical event or series of events."[55] Such an understanding of *necessity* would indicate that Kant finds himself committed, for whatever reason, to the soteriological significance of a certain historical event (e.g., Christ's atoning work), which he holds outside the bounds of philosophical inquiry. Yet, as Michalson notes, "Kant is ultimately committed, not to the soteriological efficacy of anything contingent, but to the absolute reality and validity of something universal."[56]

The other possible meaning of necessity is more interesting to Michalson: "the necessity of an historical faith can be taken to mean the reliance of man upon revealed religion *up until* the time he is of sufficient intellectual maturity to appreciate a religion of pure reason."[57] On this interpretation, moral religion, or "the religion of the second *Critique*," is Kant's ultimate goal, and historical religion is necessary for its achievement. Any historical religion will do, so long as the goal of rational religion is kept at the fore. As Michalson summarizes, "The exact nature or content of these forms is immaterial; what is important is that we go through the stage represented by historical religion in order to reach the ultimate goal."[58] Kant's vision, under this interpretive option, is one of a purely moralistic society in which all formal or ecclesiastical religion is disbanded; however, Kant is sober enough to understand that a historical, intermediate period is inevitable. Michalson finds this understanding of necessity more plausible, but even here the problem of necessity remains. On Michalson's assessment, no clear explanation can be found in *Religion* of why such a historical-faith stage is required—and there is a significant difference between a stage's preceding rational religion and its being required for rational religion. Without an explanation of the necessity of this precursor, Michalson finds Kant's claim that rational religion is self-sufficient to be dubious.

Overall, Michalson's treatment of *Religion* sees Kant as fundamentally committed to human autonomy, stemming from a concern to defend the tenets of the theoretical and practical philosophy, while also importing new concepts to make it more amenable to religious and theological concerns. Yet, Kant's commitment to morality and human autonomy puts his philosophical program in a conceptual strongbox from which robust, meaningful theology cannot easily escape. Says Michalson: "[Kant] wants human autonomy to take over the role traditionally played by divine action in the creation of a good universe, with a corresponding displacement of the supernatural world by the noumenal realm where Kantian freedom enjoys its possibility."[59] This guiding presupposition fits well what Michalson finds throughout *Religion*, namely, a tension between moral responsibility and human depravity, human autonomy and divine assistance, the sufficiency of rational religion and the necessity of historical faith, all of which leads to numerous "wobbles" throughout the text and makes Kant's philosophy of religion both suspect and highly untenable.

PART 2.

THE DEFENSE OF KANT'S *RELIGION*

4

Kant's Philosophy of Religion Reconsidered—Again

In part 1, Perspectives on Kant's *Religion*, we surveyed six basic approaches to Kant's *Religion* in the literature, taking account of both the metaphysical motives behind *Religion* and the philosophical character of *Religion*. Regarding the motives behind *Religion*, Vincent McCarthy presented the text as caught in a tension between Enlightenment rationalism and Pietistic Christianity. He argued that Kant could not escape the web of conceptual conflict created when rational autonomy meets religious piety in Kant's philosophy of religion. Stephen Palmquist served as rebuttal witness. Palmquist testified that *Religion* has strong critical roots, which can be traced all the way back to the first *Critique*; and yet, it also has strong mystic roots. While these two sets of roots may seem to drink from different (and even opposing) streams, we must recognize, argued Palmquist, that Kant did not dismiss mysticism categorically, but only uncritical forms of mysticism. Keith Ward then testified in affirmation of much of what Palmquist utilized in defense of Kant; yet, Ward argued that Kant runs into the insurmountable problem of precisely how to ground religion in reason, given the sharp and very decisive divide between phenomena and noumena in the transcendental philosophy. In response to Ward, we heard the testimony of the early Allen Wood. Wood also testified to the critical foundation of *Religion*, but, unlike Palmquist, Wood found this ground in the necessary postulates of practical reason and the pursuit of the highest good. Wood testified that *Religion* offers a solution to Kant's *absurdum practicum* argument by introducing the notion of the moral disposition and the postulate of divine grace. When combined, these two developments in

Kant's thinking offer much-needed stability to Kant's philosophical paradigm. In the end, it seemed that, while Kant's motives in *Religion* certainly give reason to take pause and lead us to wonder what Kant's true intentions are, reasons exist for construing *Religion* as a possible (and very serious) candidate for inclusion in Kant's critical program. The testimony concerning Kant's motivations cleared the way for once again reconsidering Kant's philosophy of religion.

As far as the philosophical character of *Religion* is concerned, however, the case against *Religion* presented some significant obstacles. Philip Quinn and Nicolas Wolterstorff used Kant's phenomenal-noumenal divide and moral formalism to develop a full set of conundrums emerging out of the specific arguments in *Religion*. This dual testimony showed that the phenomenal-noumenal "boundary line" and the strict moral terrain of "rights and obligations" in Kant's philosophy make all talk of human depravity and divine assistance problematic from the outset. Ronald Green and Adina Davidovich each attempted to offer ways of overcoming these problems based on the second and third *Critique*, respectively. In the end, however, both witnesses underdetermined the specifics of the text and left us without a clear way of overcoming the accusations of Quinn and Wolterstorff. Bernard Reardon and John Hare offered a third way forward by employing the *Religion*-as-Translation thesis. Attempting to utilize Kant's Pietistic roots and apparent Christian imagery as a positive foundation for understanding Kant's project, Hare and Reardon characterized *Religion* as a philosophical experiment, where Kant examines a religious sphere from within the sphere of practical reason in order to see the degree to which the two spheres cohere. While the *Religion*-as-Translation thesis was helpful in explaining the conflicts that emerge in *Religion*, ultimately this testimony did less in the way of solving the texts' conundrums, and more in the way of seeing *Religion* as a failed experiment once attempted by Kant.

In the absence of clear rejoinders to the convicting testimony of Quinn and Wolterstorff, we found the philosophical character of *Religion* (that is, its argumentative details and their consonance with the critical philosophy) to be the most potent feature of the case against *Religion*. Having identified this philosophical character as the Achilles' heel of the aforementioned defenses, we heard from Gordon Michalson, the star witness for the prosecution. He presented the full indictment of the philosophical character of *Religion*. In addition to the difficulties identified by Quinn and Wolterstorff, Michalson drew out seven rather pointed conundrums in the argumentative specifics of *Religion*. These conundrums brought into sharp relief debilitating conflicts in Kant's notion of moral depravity, idea of the moral disposition, universal conclusion about human nature, view of human freedom, understanding of moral identity, biblical hermeneutic, and understanding of the relationship between religion and reason. Michalson's assessment of *Religion* established a myriad of charges that any effort to defend *Religion* with success must address. Only if this is done can *Religion* demonstrably be considered a work that carries on a consistent and coherent line of argumentation.

This bleak state of affairs serves as the backdrop for our defense of Kant's *Religion*, which we present here in part 2. In this chapter, we lay the foundation for our direct engagement with *Religion* in the chapters to follow, establishing the groundwork for how we approach the text. Chapters 5 through 8 will apply these insights directly to *Religion*, providing a careful treatment of Books One, Two, Three, and Four, respectively; and this defense of *Religion* will be shown throughout to counter effectively the catalogue of conundrums drawn out in part 1. The groundwork presented in this chapter has three points of focus: (1) cognition and rational faith, (2) Kant's two experiments, and (3) the moral disposition. By making plain our understanding of the relationship between these foci and Kant's philosophy of religion, we lay the foundation for how we understand the philosophical nature of Kant's arguments in *Religion*.

Pure Cognition and Rational Faith

In part 1, the God-talk problem was shown to lurk behind a number of the interpretations that understand Kant's philosophy of religion to be incoherent. For readers such as Ward and Wolterstorff, for instance, how Kant can talk about God in such an open and explicit way in *Religion* is enigmatic. Kant is either dribbling on his philosopher's cloak by importing doctrines from his Lutheran Catechism into his rationalist philosophy or illegitimately employing supposed truths from historical religion for the sake of reason alone. Either way, the results are curious and hardly satisfactory. The problem extends beyond merely the incoherence of *Religion*, however; it goes to the very heart of Kant's work on theology: how can we speak (or even think) of God in a way that actually refers to God? Neither Kant's ethics nor his philosophy of religion, suggest Kant's critics, provides stable grounds for such robust God-talk or God-thought.

Kant's philosophy, on Ward's reading, prohibits literal language about God, and relegates all such language to the formal confines of the moral philosophy. God and immortality are moral postulates with no actual (or even possible) connection with the world of immediate experience. How then can Kant begin speaking of God as though God exists when the fact of God's existence (or non-existence) cannot possibly be known? As we saw in chapter 2, Wolterstorff summarizes this problem with the metaphor of a boundary. This phenomenal-noumenal boundary line at the heart of Kant's epistemology means that God-talk can never be thought of as referring to God. If our language about God can never really be about God, then appeals to God's assistance and grace to remedy moral failings seem out of the question from the start, regardless of how problematic or non-problematic such appeals may be in their internal philosophical details.

One obvious response is that Kant has, from the first *Critique* onward, an a priori concept of God, namely, God as *ens realissimum*. As we saw in chapter 1, Wood, on the basis of this a priori concept, submits that Kant is able to transition cogently to practical reasons (rather than merely theoretical ones) for belief in order to develop a rational basis for faith. What interpreters of Kant's philosophy of religion need to show, however, is a rational way of linking Kant's conception of God in the first *Critique* with his method of argumentation and ever-expanding God-talk throughout *Religion*. Is there a common thread running throughout Kant's critical writings that leads from the first *Critique* to *Religion* and connects the various conceptions of God in Kant's philosophy with his philosophy of religion? If God-thought and God-talk have no definite connection with the theoretical philosophy, that is, no *linguistic* connection running throughout the critical corpus that grounds Kant's talk of God, then instability will likely be the hallmark of any and all interpretations of *Religion*.

A good way to approach this question of the critical linguistic foundation of *Religion* is to introduce it on the backdrop of a debate spawned by Peter Byrne's 1979 article, "Kant's Moral Proof of the Existence of God."[1] Byrne's article challenged the very possibility of a Kantian theology and spawned a dialogue instructive for our present purposes. This dialogue has value here because it clearly shows a lacuna in the way Kant's philosophy is commonly related to religious faith. In his article, Byrne makes the case for a fundamental flaw in the logic of Kant's movement from the "denial of knowledge" of God to some supposed "room for faith" in God. Byrne's central claim is that since, for Kant, "[k]nowledge that God exists is in principle impossible . . . it follows that we could never have any good reason for claiming to know that God exists";[2] and consequently, "[i]f one rules out knowledge of God as impossible in principle then one also rules out the possibility of faith, where this entails believing or thinking that God exists."[3] Byrne sees Kant's movement from knowledge to faith resulting in a formal contradiction:

1. If justifiable faith in God requiring the truth of "God exists" is possible, then the truth of "God exists" could in principle be established.
2. If the truth of "God exists" could in principle be established, then it is possible to have direct empirical evidence (i.e., knowledge) of God's existence;
3. Kant denies that it is possible to have direct empirical evidence (i.e., knowledge) of God's existence.
4. Therefore, Kant likewise denies that the truth of "God exists" could in principle be established (2–3).

5. Therefore, Kant denies that justifiable faith in God requiring the truth of "God exists" is possible (1 and 4).[4]

Byrne recognizes that Kant's attempt to circumvent this deduction focuses on practical reason. But, for Byrne, "practical considerations [that] fully justify his faith that God exists" are simply not possible.[5] Without some knowledge of God, faith in God is simply not rational.

In a response to Byrne's assessment, Don Wiebe argues that Kant's theology is rooted in "*cognitive* faith . . . [and] can quite legitimately, even if only in a weak sense, be referred to as religious knowledge."[6] Wiebe counters Byrne's concerns regarding the coherence of combining Kant's knowledge and faith doctrines with a novel attempt to unify the two. Wiebe's argument tries to put the two positions on the same cognitive plain. Wiebe calls practical reason "a practical function of the same reason [as theoretical reason]."[7] Kant's denial of knowledge in the first *Critique* creates a "cognitive vacuum" or "need" in reason, according to Wiebe, and practical reason is what fills in this vacuum or satisfies this need. Wiebe puts it thus: "Kant obstinately denies knowledge of the unconditioned. The cognitive vacuum at the apex of our system of knowledge must remain theoretically or speculatively empty; *but not thereupon completely cognitively empty.* If reason in its theoretical use cannot fill the vacuum, perhaps reason in its practical use can. The ideas of reason, that is, if not capable of theoretical justification may be capable of a practical justification."[8] The idea here is that the inherent logic of theoretical reason leaves an empty void in the area of knowledge, and this void has a discernable shape that the practical dimension of reason is able to fill. According to Wiebe:

> [I]f we are to avoid moral absurdity . . . this cognitive vacuum in our system of knowledge must be filled with something more than mere logical possibilities. Certain assumptions must be made, that is, if moral experience is not to be denied as illusory or the moral law invalid. Such assumptions or "postulates," as Kant designates them, can neither be affirmed nor denied but can be believed or disbelieved—they are "mere things of faith," objects for concepts whose objective reality cannot be proved.[9]

Wiebe's main point is that the "things of faith" are able to fill in the theoretical void in knowledge even though the "things of fact" cannot. Things of faith are "rational," argues Wiebe, but they do not constitute theoretical knowledge: "Acceptance of them is not justified on theoretical grounds but rather on practical grounds."[10]

In support of his thesis, Wiebe notes an interesting passage on faith from the third *Critique*:

> **Faith** . . . is reason's moral way of thinking in the affirmation of that which is inaccessible for theoretical cognition. It is thus the constant fundamental principle of the mind to assume as true that which it is necessary to presuppose as a condition for the possibility of the highest moral final end, on

account of the obligation to that, although we can have no insight into its possibility or into its impossibility. (5:471–72)

In highlighting the above passage, Wiebe draws our attention to the limits of theoretical reason and the resourcefulness of practical reason to fill out whatever knowledge is needed to complete reason's quest to understand. Wiebe's interpretation disassociates knowledge and faith according to the boundary between them and then argues that morality, when it fulfils its function, affords human beings a different kind of knowledge—a lesser knowledge called *practical* or *moral faith.*

The emphasis of Wiebe's account is thus on what moral faith can do for theoretical reason when the resources of theoretical reason have run out, but its desire to know remains. Moral faith can help us to make theoretical assumptions. What reason has, thinks Wiebe, is practical evidence for belief in God akin to theoretical evidence:

> [The] pronouncements [of practical reason] are not to be considered as the intuitive knowledge of theoretical reason, but rather as assumptions. However, when pure practical reason provides reality to these assumptions, transforming them into "postulates," some entry into the theoretical sphere is gained, but not such as to allow us to call postulates knowledge without some sort of qualification. Nevertheless, they are still more than mere assumptions.[11]

Wiebe argues that practical reason gains access to the theoretical sphere through the aperture supplied by the theoretical needs that, as Kant puts it, "reason admits it has." This aperture does not lead to theoretical reason proper, but to the wake left by the theoretical philosophy's "demolition" of the traditional proofs for God's existence. Kant's so-called demolition of these proofs creates room for practical reason to develop a notion of God that meets the needs of reason in a practical way. When we postulate God, we assume his existence for *moral* reasons. Although not theoretical knowledge, this postulation is, in Wiebe's account, a lesser form of knowledge based on moral considerations. It constitutes an assumption with a discernable theoretical shape and its own moral justification. Wiebe calls this lesser knowledge "moral faith."

The problem with Wiebe's thesis has to do with where it leads. Moral faith, by the light of Wiebe's argument, entails knowledge (or quasi-knowledge) of metaphysics: "a very important characterization of the nature of moral faith . . . [is] that through it we gain, in some small way, an *extension* of our theoretical knowledge."[12] In a response article, J. C. Luik directly contradicts Wiebe's central contention that faith involves an extension of human knowledge. He points out that the principal problem with Wiebe's interpretation is that in it, "the postulates are . . . not suppositions, subjective injunctions or maxims to act 'as-if' freedom, immortality and God were real, but rather, in effect, covert extensions of theoretical knowledge."[13] On Wiebe's interpretation, Kant's theoretical boundary line between phenomena and noumena is either not fixed or not impregnable, for the practical philosophy appears to be giving knowledge of things of which reason, in theory, can know nothing. Luik points to Kant's "What Is Orientation in Thinking?" to clarify matters: "Kant places the entire discussion of the 'concept of a First Being' within the context of a discussion of the 'need of reason . . . to presuppose and assume something which it may not pretend to know on objective grounds.' The 'need of reason,' Kant argues, provides us with nothing more than a 'subjective ground' for believing in the existence of God."[14] Luik also points out the way "Kant goes on to speak of rational belief in God's existence as 'a subjectively sufficient assent associated with the consciousness that it is an objectively insufficient assent; therefore it is *contrasted with knowledge*.'" This claim, Luik points out, contradicts Wiebe's main contention.[15] Luik's response to Wiebe ultimately leads to an affirmation of Byrne's assessment of Kantian moral faith: if Kant intended to arrive at belief in God, we must revise his well-known "denial of knowledge to make room for faith to denying *theoretical* knowledge to make room for practical knowledge."[16] Such a conclusion, however, cuts contrary to Kant's own epistemic strictures, and Luik thus concludes that there is in fact "quite literally no Kantian theology."[17]

Both Wiebe and Luik offer valid insights into Kant's transcendental theology, but there is an instructive and quite fundamental disconnect between their two positions that leads them to discuss at cross-purposes. This disconnect involves the identification of the words "knowledge" and "cognition." The root term for cognition, *erkennen*, may be (and usually is) translated "to come to know," or "to know." This use of *erkennen* was the most common use in the nineteenth and twentieth century and is the dominant understanding of the term in Kant-studies today. The common tendency when interpreting Kant is thus to assume that *Erkenntnis* is essentially a synonym for *Wissen* (knowledge), without any significant variance.[18] This use of *Erkenntnis*, or cognition, is certainly one present at the outset of Kant's critical period. According to the first *Critique*, all knowledge is traceable to the input of reason as it comes in contact with reality. Cognition provides reason with concepts and is the culmination of the synthetic processes that provide reason with knowledge. In this sense, the perception of empirical objects is dependent on human *cognition*. As Kant puts it, "the objects must conform to our cognition, which would agree better with the requested possibility of an *a priori* cognition of them, which is to establish something about objects before they are given to us" (Bxvi). In this conforming of objects to our cognition, knowledge of the world becomes possible. This aspect of Kant's transcendental philosophy is well established.

In recent years, however, a question has emerged over whether *Erkenntnis* is in all cases to be related to knowledge in the proper Kantian sense.[19] Rolf George, who has made significant contribution to this question, points out that

Johann Christoph Adelung's dictionary of 1793 (the same year as the publication of *Religion*) lists ten senses for the root *erkennen*.[20] George highlights two of these senses that should be of particular interest to the study of Kant. As already noted, *erkennen* may rightly be translated "to come to know," or "to know"; yet, another sense that George thinks significant "requires the direct object construction; in this sense the word means 'to represent it to ourselves clearly or obscurely, distinctly or indistinctly.' "[21] Unlike the way most today use *Erkenntnis* as "knowledge of empirical objects," George argues that "[t]o have *Erkenntnis* of a thing [in the time of Kant] was to have in one's mind a presentation, an idea, an image, a token referring to that thing."[22] In other words, cognition in its most basic sense simply means to be able to get something in mind. If an intuition is possible for a given cognition, then that cognition is appropriately categorized as a form of knowledge or possible object of experience—in the proper theoretical sense. But if no intuition is possible for a given cognition, then, for Kant, that cognition may be either an object of mere opinion (*Meinung*) or a possible object of belief (*Glaube*).

Kant unpacks the various distinctions between knowledge, opinion, and faith in the "Canon of Pure Reason" in the first *Critique* (A795–831/B823–59). The purpose of the "Canon" is to carve out space for what Kant means by *faith* in the face of both the strictures he has previously articulated regarding knowledge and those speculative positions that have only private validity and thus no rational foundation in the critical philosophy (what Kant calls "persuasion" [*Überredung*]). He defines knowledge, belief, and opinion as three forms of truth assertion. Opinions are the lowest-level form of truth assertion, since the one asserting some truth as an opinion is conscious of the assertion's objective and subjective insufficiency. Belief is somewhat like opinion in terms of its objective insufficiency, but it has a subjective sufficiency that opinion lacks. Belief is grounded in the transcendental nature of reason in its practical employment. This grounding is significant for Kant, not only because subjectivity is the foundation of all transcendental inquiry, but also because practical reason is primary for Kant and is the place where the rationality of religious faith must be established. Knowledge, of course, stands above belief, as it constitutes a truth assertion that is both objectively and subjectively sufficient, giving certainty. But this does not mean that truth assertions that are only subjectively sufficient (viz., belief) are examples of vacuous opinion. To the contrary, Kant maintains that such assertions yield legitimate "conviction" (*Überzeugung*). Kant thus lumps belief and knowledge together as properly rational enterprises emanating from "the two hemispheres of the *globus intellectualis*" while leaving opinion to the realm of idle speculation.[23]

In this light, we can see clearly why, according to Kant, "In judging from pure reason, **to have an opinion** is not allowed at all" (A822/B850), while having faith is a different story. Faith, for Kant, finds its rational grounds in morality and subsequent beliefs required for moral stability. With faith, it is absolutely necessary that something must happen, namely, that I fulfill the moral law at all points. The end here is inescapably fixed, and according to all my insight there is only a single condition under which this end is consistent with all the ends together and thereby has practical validity, namely, that there be a God and a future world. I also know with complete certainty that no one else knows of any other conditions that lead to this same unity of ends under the moral law. But since the moral precept is thus at the same time my maxim (as reason commands that it ought to be), I will inexorably believe in the existence of God and a future life, and I am sure that nothing can make these beliefs unstable, since my moral principles themselves, which I cannot renounce without becoming contemptible in my own eyes, would thereby be subverted. (A828/B856)

Kant makes clear in the "Canon" that rational faith in God and immortality is not just faith in possible objects or states of affairs but faith grounded on morally mandated principles of any critical understanding of reason. Such faith, Kant suggests, "is not *logical*, but *moral* certainty," which "rests on subjective grounds (of the moral sentiments)"; he asserts that it is "so interwoven with my moral nature, that I am under as little apprehension of having the former [i.e., belief in God and in another world] torn from me as of losing the latter [i.e., my moral nature]."[24] Precisely what constitutes the critical content of faith beyond these fundamental principles or beliefs is a matter that will require Kant to move beyond the first *Critique*. According to Kant, reason's quest to answer all of the relevant metaphysical questions systematically by a transcendental examination of pure reason is the driving force behind this process. What we know from the "Canon" are merely the bare moral grounds for faith (the moral law, God, and a future life), and only further critical inquiries into the faculties of reason can provide a thoroughgoing account of the rational superstructure of true religious faith.

Leslie Stevenson probes Kant's definition of faith in an essay entitled "Opinion, Belief or Faith, and Knowledge." Stevenson affirms the position that faith (*Glauben*) has a discernable place in Kant's philosophical economy, and is a plausible concept when understood in terms of the transcendental development of Kant's philosophical theology. Faith, Stevenson concludes, "is holding something to be true, and being practically but not theoretically justified in doing so."[25] The faith that Kant understands to be involved here is of a special kind, however: "The conviction is not *logical* but *moral* certainty, and, since it depends on subjective grounds (of moral disposition) I must not even say 'It *is* morally certain that there is a God', etc., but rather 'I *am* morally certain' etc." (A820/B857). Referring to this passage from the first *Critique*, Stevenson writes, "Here Kant strikes an existentialist note, giving us a sneak preview of his practical philosophy. It seems that the distinction between moral beliefs and theoretical beliefs about the supersensible is not between different propositions, but different styles of believing the same propositions: firmly believe in a moral way, unstably believe in the doctrinal way."[26]

For Kant, certain objects of cognition have no theoretical correspondence in experience, and thus no argument is objectively sufficient for belief in these objects. Yet, there are also objects of cognition that are possible objects of faith, and as such, these cognitions rise above the status of mere opinion: "I can think whatever I like, as long as I do not contradict myself but in order to ascribe objective validity to such a concept . . . something more is required" (Bxxvi). While certain non-empirical cognitions cannot have objective sufficiency, Kant does maintain that if reasons exist for deeming these cognitions subjectively sufficient, they can have objective validity. For Kant, we can think and talk about matters that have no direct empirical evidence (e.g., the nature of soul and the existence of God), and have many opinions about them; however, more is required to establish their subjective sufficiency as possible objects of rational conviction. This *more*, argues Kant, "need not be sought in the theoretical sources of cognition [although it can be so sought]; it may also lie in the practical ones" (Bxxvi). Throughout the first *Critique*, Kant's consistent concern is that we realize that what cannot be known in theory can, in principle, be cognized and become objects of conviction on other grounds. This convergence of cognition and conviction has as its source a form of reasoning that leads to faith, not knowledge, and Kant explicitly identifies the practical as its rational ground.

Kant's *Lectures on Metaphysics*, particularly "Metaphysik Mrongovius" (1782–83) and "Metaphysik Vigilantius" (1794–95), bring into sharp relief the direct practical connection between cognition and faith via two key distinctions. On the one hand, Kant makes clear the distinction between cognitions as objects of knowledge and all other forms of cognition; on the other hand, he distinguishes between cognitions as mere opinions and cognitions that are possible objects of faith. In "Metaphysik Mrongovius," for example, Kant makes the important distinction between pure cognition and empirical cognition: "This is quite useful in a science, to separate the cognition of reason from empirical cognition, in order to comprehend the errors all the more distinctly" (29:940). Empirical cognition indicates a process of judgment whereby intuitions and concepts are synthesized into knowledge. These cognitions are immediately convicting of the truth, and as such, should be distinguished so as not to lose sight of them in the process of rational deliberation on metaphysical matters. Pure cognition (or "the cognition of reason") involves the basic capacity of reason to get something in mind and the possible rootedness of these ideas in reason. Pure cognition can consist of idle speculations or mere opinions about virtually anything. But it can also, thinks Kant, refer to the proper objects of rational faith.

The anatomy of pure cognition and its relationship to faith is spelled out twelve years later in "Metaphysik Vigilantius" (written one year after the publication of *Religion*) and is worth quoting at length:

> Metaphysical cognitions must therefore be cognitions simply of reason, thus arise *a priori* through pure concepts of reason, i.e., the principles *principia* or grounds of cognition are so constituted that one connects the necessity of what one cognizes with the cognition itself, and the concepts are directed at objects that are not only cognized independently of all experience, but that also can never *possibly* become an object of experience. E.g., God, freedom, immortality. . . . [M]etaphysics thus has no *a posteriori* principles *principia*, but rather only *a priori*: they are given and are cognized through reason alone, but are not made (29:945).

Here, Kant makes plain not only that we can cognize God, freedom, and immortality, but also that such cognitions—if they are pure cognitions of reason—are not human creations or mere figments or opinions, but ideas that emerge in the natural course of reason's development at the outer bounds of human understanding. According to Kant, "Belief in God and another world is inextricably bound with the cognition of our duty, which reason prescribes, and the moral maxims for living according to it" (29:778); and again, "the existence of God and the hope of a future life can be cognized by any human being by common sense by considering nature and one's state. . . . But this is merely a practical faith" (29:938). Thus rational faith in God is not an arbitrary cognition or one necessarily relegated to mere opinion; rational faith is rooted both in the a priori cognition of God as *ens realissumum* and in freedom and the moral law as a priori constituents of practical reason.

In this link between cognition and faith, Kant juxtaposes his position with Plato's. According to Kant, "Plato assumed the innate ideas . . . [and] sensible representations, but he separated off as uncertain this source of cognition from the pure concepts of the understanding as the innate ideas *ideis connatis*, which he assumed as alone certain" (29:950). What Kant makes clear is that his criticism of Plato does not concern the innate ideas; rather, Kant's criticism is directed at the supposed epistemological status of these ideas. Says Kant: "The Principle of Plato, namely that by virtue of their previously possessed faculty of an intuitive understanding, human beings would still have the power to remember by their understanding back to previously held concepts, rests on a mistake . . . that he took pure *a priori* intuition *intuitus a priori puros* and *pure a priori* concepts *conceptus a priori puros* as the same" (29:954). What Kant thinks Plato should have realized is that, rather than taking the innate ideas as "certain" (i.e., as forms of knowledge), at best we only ever have critical access to pure cognitions as objects of rational belief.

Kant's understanding of the difference between cognized ideas and empirical knowledge thus distinguishes itself from Plato's by making only concepts that synthesize with intuitions objects of knowledge, while pure cognitions, even if a priori, must always remain outside the realm of *knowledge*. Reason's proper attitude toward pure cognitions is thereby two-pronged: they are either mere *opinions* (i.e., truth claims that have no objective or subjective support) or objects of *faith* (i.e., truth claims that have subjective support, and we must believe for rational/moral reasons but not empirical ones). In other words, Kant finds room for the critical incorporation of some cognized ideas in the transcendental recesses of reason as necessary conditions for the possibility of moral stability and moral hope. These ideas constitute the essential elements of rational religious faith. The philosopher can in this way, and only in this way, extend the application of reason beyond the realm of knowledge, and do so without becoming mired in mere opinion or metaphysical speculation. Sprinkled throughout *Religion* in Kant's talk of various practical ideas and concepts are indications that what Kant intends is a critical analysis of human cognition (*Erkenntnis*) as it pertains to religious belief and practice. Therefore, the above-outlined linking of cognition and faith, we maintain, is precisely the status of Kant's argumentation in *Religion*.

Kant's Two Experiments in *Religion*

In the Second Preface of *Religion*, Kant speaks of two "experiments" to be performed. The first experiment considers only what reason tells about the "pure religion of reason" (6:12)—that is, it considers only natural religion. The second experiment looks at a specific "alleged revelation" and compares its doctrines (*in abstracto*) to the doctrines of natural religion in order to "see whether it does not lead back to the same pure *rational system* of religion" (6:12). Because much hinges on the way these experiments are understood, the passage is worth quoting at length:

> Regarding the title of this work (since doubts have been expressed also regarding the intention hidden behind it) I note: Since, after all, *revelation* can at least comprise also the pure *religion of reason*, whereas, conversely the latter cannot do the same for what is historical in revelation, I shall be able to consider the first as a *wider* sphere of faith that includes the other, a *narrower* one, within itself (not as two circles external to one another but as concentric circles); the philosopher, as purely a teacher of reason (from mere principles *a priori*), must keep within the inner circle and, thereby, also abstract from all experience. From this standpoint I can also make this second experiment, namely, to start from some alleged revelation or other and, abstracting from the pure religion of reason (so far as it constitutes a system on its own), to hold fragments of this revelation, as a *historical system*, up to moral concepts, and see whether it does not lead back to the same pure *rational system* of religion. (6:12)

How we understand Kant's talk here—the nature of the experiments and the texts to which they refer—is of great importance to how we approach *Religion*.

As we saw in chapter 2, interpreters such as Reardon and Hare understand the first experiment, which explicates the pure religion of reason based on a priori principles, to refer to Kant's moral philosophy—principally *Groundwork* and the second *Critique*. The second experiment, which tests a purported revelation according to the sphere of reason to see whether it leads back to the same "pure *rational system* of religion," is an explanation, then, of what takes place within *Religion* as a whole.[27] What this means, as discussed above, is that, from the outset of *Religion*, Kant intends to translate the core Christian doctrines into terms that are acceptable to the moral philosopher, and he attempts this translation in order to show the presence of rational religion within the broader sphere of Christian doctrine. The translation is applied to the central doctrines of Christianity: creation, fall, redemption, ecclesiology, and eschatology. Just as the categorical imperative abstracts a moral precept from the particular moral situation in question, Hare and Reardon in like manner see Kant's notion of translation moving forward. Kant's religious utterances in *Religion* are philosophical abstractions of historical concepts whose content is being tested to find the degree to which they conform to the religion of reason. And, in the end, "The experiment will be successful if we can show that the contents of the two areas are not only consistent with each other but have the sort of unity that means that a person who follows the prescriptions of the one will also be following those of the other."[28]

By contrast to Hare and Reardon, we approach *Religion* under the assumption that both of Kant's experiments are present within *Religion*. Rather than presuming that Kant has articulated a complete system of rational religion in the *Groundwork* and second *Critique*, and thereby reading Kant's talk of depravity, redemption, ecclesiology, and eschatology as a moral translation of Christianity, we contend that Kant's arguments in Books One, Two, and Three of *Religion* are properly understood as an examination of the outer bounds of human cognition in an effort to address the question of hope under the guide of practical reason. If right, this indicates that the content of the first three books of *Religion* is not a series of addendums to Kant's critical philosophy or merely a permissible (though unnecessary) experiment performed on historical religion. Rather, Kant's examination of human nature, his doctrine of radical evil, his prototypical theology, and his vision of the ethical commonwealth are advances on his critical philosophy, without which it is incomplete. Such a perspective on Kant's insights in *Religion* aligns our interpretation more with the early Wood, who sees *Religion* as a necessary determination of the postulates of God and immortality emanating from Kant's moral philosophy, than with readers such as Hare or Reardon, who see *Religion* as independent of the moral philosophy. Regrettably, nothing in the Second Preface offers decisive indication of whether our understanding of the location of Kant's two experiments is more accurate than Hare's or Reardon's understanding.

Having said this, three noteworthy features of *Religion* point in favor of seeing Kant's experiments in the way we have presented them. The first indicator concerns what appears to be a pivot point in *Religion*, where Kant shifts the weight of his arguments away from the tenets of rational religious faith (or the first experiment) toward an examination of Christianity (or the second experiment). We find this transition in the introductory paragraphs of the First Part of Book Four. In 6:155, Kant argues that "a religion can be *natural*, yet also *revealed*, if it is so constituted that human beings *could and ought to have* arrived at it on their own through the mere use of their own reason"; then, in 6:156, Kant turns to "consider a revealed religion as yet *natural*, on the one hand, but on the other hand, a *learned* religion; . . . [and] test it and be able to sort out what, and how much, it is entitled to from the one source or the other." Following this *testing* language, Kant identifies New Testament Christianity as the "revealed" religion he will utilize in this test. Kant writes, "In our case this book can be the New Testament, as the source of the Christian doctrine of faith. In keeping with our intent, we now wish to expound the Christian religion in two sections—first, as natural religion, and then, second, as learned religion—with reference to its content and the principles found in it" (6:157).

Several things are noteworthy about this passage. First, Kant suggests that the expounding of the Christian religion is something he *now* wishes to engage, which indicates his consideration of Christian doctrine has heretofore not taken place. Second, Kant identifies the expounding of the Christian religion to take place in two parts, first as natural religion and second as learned religion; and these two divisions serve as the section headings of the divisions to follow, again indicating that the consideration of Christianity as natural religion has yet to occur in *Religion*. Third, the *intent* of Kant's examination of Christianity is identified in 6:156, where Kant speaks of testing a revealed religion to see how much of it falls to the side of natural religion and how much to learned religion. Kant's language of *testing* to sort out the extent to which the Christian religion can be viewed as containing the insights of natural religion fits well Kant's talk in the Second Preface regarding the second experiment and gives good reason to think that this point in Book Four marks *Religion*'s turning point to the second experiment.

A second reason to think both experiments are contained within *Religion* concerns Kant's Christic language. Kant's interpreters recognize that nowhere in *Religion* does Kant use the name "Jesus." Nevertheless, most Kant interpreters take as given that Kant is referring to Jesus of Nazareth, or at least drawing on the story of Jesus, when he speaks of the prototype of perfect humanity. Given his use of terms such as *the Son of God*, his reference to *the Word* (*the fiat!*), and his talk of the prototype as a divine being who condescends to humanity, thereby taking on humanity (see, e.g., 6:60), Kant's readers think it rather safe to conclude that Kant's *prototype* is Jesus of Nazareth. What is most interesting when considering the division of the two experiments we suggest, however, is that Kant's apparent reference to Jesus changes in Book Four. Following Kant's explicit turn to "New Testament Christianity," Kant refers to Jesus (the evident subject of Kant's exposition, given his quoting of Jesus from the synoptic gospels) as "the teacher of the Gospel" (see, e.g., 6:162). While this change in language may seem insignificant when *Religion* as a whole is presumed to be Kant's second experiment (e.g., Kant is merely changing terms for stylistic or thematic reasons), this change in a previously stable term (viz., *the prototype*) may be further indication that Kant makes a transition in Book Four from talk of a postulate of practical reason to talk of a specific historical figure.

Thirdly, in keeping with Kant's distinction between *the prototype* and *the teacher of the Gospel*, we may note that in 6:119, Kant distinguishes between "the appearance of the God-man," or "what in the God-man falls to the senses," and "the prototype lying in our reason." While we will not here discuss the details of this passage (our discussion of 6:119 appears in chapter 7), suffice it to say for now that Kant makes a clear distinction between faith in the prototype and faith in a purported appearance of the prototype: "The living faith in the prototype . . . refers . . . to a moral idea of reason. . . . By contrast, faith in this very same prototype *according to its appearance* . . . is not, as *empirical* . . . one and the same as the principle of the good life conduct (which must be totally rational)" (6:119). While Kant's focus here is on types of faith (rational versus historical or empirical), Kant does make plain that the prototype is "a moral idea of reason." This designation gives reason to think that the prototype is a postulate of practical reason, not merely a moral translation of a historical figure.

One potential hurdle to seeing the first three books of *Religion* as Kant's first experiment, however, is Kant's frequent use of Scripture throughout the early portions of the text. Three points should be kept in mind in this regard. First and foremost, Kant is explicit in the claim that the philosophical faculty is free to draw on any resources it likes, even the Bible, in its critical evaluation of reason, but such drawing does not mean that the use is dependent upon these resources. Kant writes:

> Among the sciences, however, there is, over against Biblical theology, a philosophical theology, which is an estate entrusted to another faculty. So long as this philosophical theology remains within the limits of reason alone, and for the confirmation and exposition of its propositions makes use of history, sayings, books of all peoples, even the Bible, but only for itself, without wishing to carry these propositions into Biblical theology or to change the latter's public doctrines—a privilege of the divines—it must have complete freedom to expand as far as its science reaches. (6:9)[29]

In this passage, we see Kant identifying the use of "history, sayings, books of all peoples, even the Bible," as legitimate resources for philosophical theology to draw upon, so long as in so doing, it remains within the limits of reason alone.

Wood concurs with this point, suggesting that there is no doubt Kant is drawing on the Christian tradition to expound his philosophy of religion: "But unless we dismiss all attempts at 'rationality' as mere 'rationalizations' or claim that all history itself is a product of metaphysical 'reason,' we cannot assume that Kant's pure religious faith is *based* on the historical tradition from which his conception is drawn. Whether this is so must depend on the strength of Kant's purportedly rational arguments, and not on the historical tradition in which his view stands."[30] Thus, while Kant may utilize biblical language and even quote Scripture, his arguments are not necessarily dependent upon such language and content or automatically outside the limits of reason alone. Kant reserves the right to philosophize by all available means and arrive at conclusions based on his seasoned transcendental methodology. This procedure is consonant with Kant's well-documented vocational objectives and is surely the appropriate direction for interpreters to head when trying to understand Kant's philosophy of religion.

Second, Kant also gives indication in the First Preface of *Religion* that he intends *Religion* to be (at least partly) in dialogue with theologians: "Now whether the theologian agrees with the philosopher or believes himself obliged to oppose him: let him just hear him out. For in this way alone can the theologian be forearmed against all the difficulties that the philosopher may cause him" (6:10). Given the theological interests of the audience, it would not be surprising to find Kant utilizing biblical language throughout the construction of rational insights, so as to pave the way for his later claim that Christianity stands up as rational when tested by the insights of reason—or, alternatively, his claim that Christians can adhere to rational religion while also adhering to the Christian faith. Kant's point is not to translate Christianity into morality, but, as a member of the philosophy faculty, to determine the nature and extent of rational religious faith by engaging the theology faculty in open rational discourse in pursuit of truth.

A third point to consider is that we find in Book Four of *Religion* Kant's affirmation of the claim that revelation, which cannot be viewed as impossible, could present itself as a catalyst for awakening truths already embedded in reason. Kant writes:

> Accordingly a religion can be *natural*, yet also *revealed*, if it is so constituted that human beings *could and ought to have* arrived at it on their own through the mere use of their own reason, even though they *would* not have come to it as early or as extensively as is required, hence a revelation of it at a given time and a given place might be wise and very advantageous to the human race, for then, once the thereby introduced religion is at hand and has been made publicly known, everyone can henceforth convince himself of its truth by himself and his own reason. (6:155)

Similarly, Kant indicates in *The Conflict of the Faculties*, "A philosophy faculty can . . . lay claim to any teaching, in order to test its truth" (7:28). Such statements indicate that Kant is not adverse to the idea that an insight (a rational insight) may be awoken by engagement with a purported revelation.

Therefore, while Kant presents the content of rational religion in the first three books of *Religion* as rationally grounded (these insights are based on the insights of practical reason), Kant may well have been awoken to these insights by his engagement with Christianity. If such is the case, it would be entirely appropriate for Kant to utilize Christian language when presenting the rational arguments for these insights.

In our treatment of *Religion*, therefore, we will engage Kant's arguments prior to 6:157 as rational arguments, rooted in practical reason and focused on the nature and *telos* of humanity's moral disposition. Our goal in engaging the first three books of *Religion* will therefore be to flesh out the exact nature of Kant's arguments in order to divulge the rationale underlying his conclusions. And, in our turn to Book Four of *Religion* (specifically, 6:157ff.), we will consider Kant's assessment of the Christian religion relative to the insights of the first experiment in Books One, Two, and Three.

The Moral Disposition and the Pursuit of Virtue

In this final section, we assess the centrality of the moral disposition to Kant's philosophy of religion and the link between humanity's moral disposition and the question of hope. Our aim in this assessment is to bring into sharp relief the philosophical lacuna we understand Kant to be filling with *Religion*. Our assessment of the philosophical significance of Kant's turn to the disposition offers the last preliminary consideration in our defense of *Religion*.

John Silber calls Kant's analysis of the moral disposition in *Religion* "the most important single contribution of the *Religion* to Kant's ethical theory, for by means of it he accounts for continuity and responsibility in the free exercise of *Willkür* and for the possibility of ambivalent volition, as well as the basis for its complex assessment."[31] While Silber is right to note the usefulness of Kant's turn to the disposition in addressing certain lingering quandaries in Kant's view of moral freedom, such as the prospects of "ambivalent volition," it is the emphasis on *continuity* in the exercise of *Willkür* that most interests us in this section. As Michalson points out, Kant distinguishes between the dispositional exercise of *Willkür* and particular acts that follow from it. Michalson raises two important questions in this regard: (1) Why does Kant distinguish between these two acts of *Willkür*? And, (2) given that the results seem to bind subsequent acts of moral decision-making, is Kant justified in making this distinction?

Silber's emphasis on *continuity* in moral decision-making, we believe, is pivotal to making sense of why Kant makes this distinction and ultimately of why Kant thinks the disposition is such a crucial assumption for practical reason. On this point of the dispositional continuity of our moral actions, Silber writes, "The dispositional act establishes the intelligible or noumenal character of the *Willkür*, whereas the specific acts establish its phenomenal character."[32] And again, "The dispositional act concerns the willing or the rejecting of the spirit of the moral law and establishes the *morality* of the acts of the *Willkür*, the underlying intentional ground of all its specific acts and therefore its character."[33] In this notion of underlying moral character, we begin to see why Kant understands the dispositional bent of an agent to be more fundamental to his or her moral standing than the character of the particular *deeds* they perform: Kant's dispositional philosophy in *Religion* offers a way of talking about an enduring moral character beneath specific moral acts, which prior to *Religion* seem to be without any necessary continuity in the Kantian framework.

The lack of continuity between moral acts becomes clear when considering Kant's comments on time in the "Lectures on the Philosophical Doctrine of Religion." There Kant lays out his view of time in contrast to God's eternity. Kant denies that God can exist within time, for God is "unalterable." As Kant continues, he juxtaposes the incompatibility of the divine existence and time with our creaturely temporality. In so doing, he makes plain that his view of time is one of successive duration, which gives to creaturely existence a mutative character. Kant writes, "For the existence of a thing in time is always a succession of parts in time, one after the other. Duration in time is, so to speak, a continuous disappearing and a continuous beginning. We can never live through a certain year without already having lived through a previous one" (28:1043–44). In other words, Kant's view of time enables the creature, as a being, to persist through the intervals of time, but there is no clear and concrete way of understanding how the moral conduct of an individual persists throughout time. At every moment the creature is changing. While a moral agent may perform evil at T2, have performed good at T1, and be in a position to choose between good and evil at T3, Kant seems to have no clear sense of how, without her having a moral nature, the character of her moral decisions endures or why past moral decisions should in any way factor into her later moral character. Moral character becomes merely an accidental property of each moment and is purely spontaneous, per the exercise of moral freedom.

The question we face, then, is what in Kant's philosophical worldview enables us to think of our series of moral acts as pressing toward a certain end? If each moral act is a very temporary part of an ever-changing series of successive moments, moral acts themselves have no enduring quality; only the moral agent in successive duration connects them. But without a moral nature within the agent, such acts are merely transient, accidental properties of the individual at each moment; the enduring agent has no enduring moral qualities. If no underlying moral nature exists, then the agent must be judged morally by a scale of cumulative good and evil—that is, the agent is good or evil based on what he or she happens to have chosen more often. To judge the agent good is merely to say that the spontaneity of the moral agent has fallen to the good more often than not. But this falling is ultimately an accidental property that says little or nothing about the agent as a moral *being*. Evil remains forever an equally real possibility. Yet, such a picture drives a rift between moral activity and the teleology of moral improvement (and ultimately perfection) Kant desires. The moral agent can in no way progress toward *being* good, if by this we mean the agent moves closer to having an enduring, subjective ground for the generation of maxims that is bent wholly toward the moral law. Kant must therefore develop a moral ontology. Without this development, at each instance forever on into the future, the moral agent's choosing remains purely spontaneous. The agent's collective decisions may slowly manifest a steady willing of the good (cumulatively speaking), but this does not alter the fact that the agent is always morally neutral (ontologically speaking) and as capable of declining into evil as ever before. Achieving moral perfection in such a scheme would be tantamount to persevering in an unbroken series of good choices, which is ultimately a moment-to-moment affair that is as achievable in this life as it is in the next, and is as fragile and perishable in the next life as it is in this life—any momentary choosing of evil breaks the chain of good choices. Kant's vision of moral teleology and perfection therefore requires Kant to develop a moral ontology, or philosophy of moral disposition, that provides enduring substance to our moral activity.

Silber recognizes the way a merely transient view of moral character endangers the notion of the highest good, which presumes a teleological direction to our moral actions. He writes:

> Continuity in disposition is essential to moral self-identity. Our moral self-consciousness would be fractured and dissipated into isolated intentions and actions if we did not relate them to one another by reference to their common ground of intention in disposition. Specific acts of *Willkür* have in themselves no direct inter-relation. . . . The establishment of a *moral* . . . relation between our actions depends upon viewing them as expressing, more or less accurately, the dispositional act of which we are not directly aware.[34]

Silber is quite right. The disposition provides a basis for uniting our moral activity and avoiding this disconnect between the moral agent, who persists through time, and her specific moral acts, which do not. Beneath our various spontaneous activities, there lies a moral posture or disposition that takes on a character indicative of our real moral bent. Our disposition is that *something* that underlies our particular moral acts; it enables us to think teleologically about our moral ends and assess in what sense we may morally improve. In other words, the disposition is something that we cognize as a way of understanding the continuity and integrity of our moral nature.

The early Wood also recognizes the link between moral perfection, the disposition, and teleology. Yet, in playing heavily on the notion of the highest good when drawing out the *absurdum practicum* argument, Wood fails to appreciate fully the significance of this link. His insights on these matters are, nevertheless, quite useful and worth examining. The connection between moral perfection and the disposition is brought out by the distinction Wood makes between particular acts (and even temporal moral character) and the type of moral *being* or *nature* that the disposition points toward. Wood writes, "[The moral man] must stake his hope on the permanence, the constancy, the absolute moral reality of this progress itself, since this alone—unlike his acts and his states of moral character in time—is capable of exhibiting some unqualified moral good."[35] This unqualified moral good points to the type of moral perfection Kant holds we must strive after and hope to achieve, for without the *possibility* of realizing this moral ideal, the highest good, with the ideals of the moral law, would drive us back toward the *absurdum practicum*.[36] According to Wood, "The moral man must hope, however, that somehow in this series [of moral acts] is manifested something more permanent, something which can stand as a moral reality and attest to an unqualified kind of moral perfection."[37] We must believe, thinks Kant, that we have a moral disposition and that this disposition can become good in some unqualified sense. Only in this way do we have a reasonable hope regarding the final aim of our moral striving.

Ultimately, Wood sees Kant's emphasis on the highest good requiring not merely belief in immortality but some aspect of the moral agent that persists throughout the series of moral actions and that provides the possibility of some concrete moral dimension to the human person that can be perfected. Wood recognizes that Kant's emphasis on something that endures in our moral character and underlies our various moral decisions is ultimately what paves the way for and is at the heart of Kant's notion of the disposition. Says Wood, "Something of our moral personality must persist beyond the particular acts and states of character manifested in the empirical world, if we are rationally to hold out any hope for the attainment of our moral final end as regards the goodness of our moral person. This permanent existence of our moral personality is described by Kant in his later writings as a man's supersensible 'disposition' (*Gesinnung*)."[38] In short, the highest good and moral progress suggests, not merely the belief that we can continue our pursuit of the moral ideal despite our lives being cut short before achieving this ideal, but also that there is something about us that persists throughout our moral striving that concretizes our moral efforts and can be perfected morally. This *something* is the disposition.

By offering a basis for moral continuity and a stable means for judging an agent's moral nature, Kant offers a clear way of thinking and speaking about the pursuit of moral perfection. The disposition is the enduring moral ontology of the human being that will be scrutinized by the divine judge and the place where moral perfection is made possible. In *The Metaphysics of Morals*, Kant identifies the purity of the moral disposition (i.e., one's devotion to the moral law as supreme incentive) and "fulfilling all one's entire moral end" as the very constituents of moral "perfection" (6:446). He sees this perfection as that which it is "a human being's duty to *strive* for" (6:446). But that a future life is required by this duty is all too apparent to Kant since, due to human frailty, this "*narrow* and perfect" duty is not to be reached *in this life* (6:446). Kant thus sees a very clear link between human perfection and our moral disposition, and quite plainly identifies this perfection as the teleological aim of our duty, which we may hope to achieve in a future life.

This understanding of the significance of the moral disposition begins to illuminate the way in which *Religion* addresses the question of hope. As is well known, Kant makes clear in his May 4, 1793, letter to Stäudlin that *Religion* is meant to address the question of hope—the third of his fourfold series of questions in the first *Critique*. The specific hope we understand Kant to have in mind here is the hope of attaining moral perfection, a good disposition, or complete virtue before a holy and just God. If this understanding is right, Kant's main concern in *Religion* is not to reconfigure the fundamental super-structure of the moral philosophy or to salvage the essentials of the Christian faith by some moral reinterpretation; rather, his main concern is to answer the question, How can I reasonably hope to become well-pleasing to God? This question takes Kant's transcendental philosophy beyond the practical question of merely *doing* good to the teleological question of what it would mean to *be* good.[39] The primary purpose of *Religion*, as we understand it, is to present Kant's dispositional philosophy. In short, what drives Kant's inquiries in *Religion* is a philosophical concern over whether or not we can hope that our moral striving will ever manifest a good disposition. Hence, from the outset, *Religion* focuses on how best to understand humanity's moral nature as it relates to the moral disposition. As we move into *Religion* in the following chapters, we will therefore approach the arguments of *Religion* as Kant's effort to conduct a practical assessment of humanity's moral nature (or disposition); and as this assessment begins to point in the direction of innate, universal corruption, we will see that this assessment requires Kant to address (under the guide of practical reason) the question of teleological hope for dispositional renewal.

Under this approach to *Religion*, Kant's argument in the first experiment takes on an hourglass shape. Books One, Two, and Three of *Religion* compose a problem-solution-vision components. In Book One, Kant begins his disposi-tional philosophy with a view to offering an assessment of how we must cog-nize our moral nature under the guide of practical reason. By utilizing tran-scendental insights surrounding the predicate *moral*, Kant is able to establish the parameters for how we must cognize humanity's moral disposition. From within these parameters, he contends that humanity universally possesses a corrupt disposition. Thus, while the disposition offers an enduring moral fea-ture to the human person, Kant's assessment is that this enduring feature points in the direction of radical evil. Practical reason therefore requires a basis for moral hope in the face of radical evil, and we find Kant supplying this ground in Book Two. There, we move into what we will call "Kant's prototypical theology," which offers a basis for moral renewal, progress, and even the possibility of perfection, despite radical evil.[40] The dispositional groundwork of Books One and Two paves the way for Kant's application of the dispositional philosophy in Book Three, where Kant develops the practical outworking of the dispositional philosophy in human community and in a world filled with historically grounded, empirical religions. Book Three rounds off Kant's sketch of the contours of rational religion, and enables him to move, in Book Four, to his assessment of the Christian religion (i.e., the second experiment) and his discussion of the ways in which historical faiths may best be purified and brought into conformity with rational religion. With this outline in hand, we turn in the following four chapters to our treatments of Books One, Two, Three, and Four of *Religion*.

5

Book One of *Religion*

With the parameters of interpretation of the previous chapter before us, we now move into Book One of *Religion*. We approach Book One under the presumption that Kant's arguments constitute not a translation of Christian concepts or imagery, or a merely symbolic or poetic theology, but the development of Kant's philosophical anthropology. Our goal in this chapter will be to understand Kant's arguments concerning radical evil from the perspective of practical reason. As discussed in the previous chapter, we will look at Kant's arguments as part of the first experiment, discussed in the Second Preface of *Religion*. Therefore, we read Kant's arguments as arguments with an underlying practical rationale. As Allen Wood puts it, "In the *Religion*, Kant reopens the whole question of man's moral perfectability, and attempts to give a more complete answer to this question than he did in any of his earlier works."[1] We will approach Kant's examination of human nature as linguistically and epistemologically representative of insights of pure cognition at the outer bounds of human understanding in answer to the question of hope.

In addition, we recognize Kant's focus on humanity's moral disposition (*Gesinnung*) in *Religion*, and, as discussed in the previous chapter, we see this focus as indicating a movement in Kant's thought away from the purely ethical question of what it would mean to *do* good, to the teleological question of what it would mean to *be* good. Because the disposition represents our "moral self-identity," to use Silber's phrase, and is that which establishes "a *moral* . . . relation between our actions," we see Kant's arguments, specifically in Book One, as addressing the question of our moral *nature* and its teleological perfectability.[2] That is, as Kant shifts focus toward the issue of moral ontology, he must examine what it means for a human to bear a moral nature that endures throughout time and can become truly good. In Book One of *Religion*, Kant offers an account of humanity's moral nature that seeks to remain true to both the concept of *nature* and the transcendental implications of the predicate *moral*. As we will see, this drives Kant to cognize the disposition as *innate* (per the concept of *nature*) and freely chosen (per the predicate *moral*). Moreover, insofar as the question of a *moral nature* concerns our overall posture toward the moral law, Kant is driven to cognize our moral nature as having a maxim or rule that establishes our posture toward the moral law as supreme incentive. Hence, the disposition must constitute *a deed of freedom that chooses a moral maxim, which serves as a rule for the entire exercise of freedom in time.* This supreme maxim constitutes our moral being, which Kant distinguishes from our particular moral acts in time.

In short, we take Book One to be principally an examination of humanity's moral nature meant to offer a philosophical anthropology of the human's moral makeup and to serve as groundwork for Kant's treatment in Book Two of the perfectability of this nature. We understand Kant's examination of our moral nature to consist chiefly of three parts: (1) the nature and commitments of the moral disposition, (2) the role and nature of humanity's natural predispositions, and (3) the cognizing of the moral disposition itself. Each of these features plays a role in developing Kant's philosophical anthropology and his well-known case for radical evil. Our treatment of Book One is divided into three sections, which correspond to these three main concerns. The first section regards Kant's case for moral rigorism, where moral reason ineluctably drives Kant to conclude that our moral nature must be either good or evil. This disjunctive makes way for Kant's analysis of the human species via "anthropological research" and his conclusion that we are evil by nature. We will focus on this aspect of Kant's argument in section two. Throughout both phases of his argument, Kant provides details regarding how we must cognize the disposition, details that make up the bulk of the anomalies in Book One (e.g., the innateness of the freely chosen disposition, its universality, and its distinctiveness from other maxims generated by *Willkür*). This material is brought together in the third and final section, where we provide a comprehensive account of how Kant thinks we must cognize humanity's corrupt disposition, given the course of his critical investigations in Book One.

Prior to moving into Kant's examination of our moral nature, a word should be said regarding the well-known *Wille-Willkür* distinction in Kant's work. Much has been made of this nuance in Kant, and, as a result, many translators have sought to make Kant's particular terminology evident to English readers (e.g., translating *Wille* as "will" and *Willkür* as "the power of choice"). In addition, many interpreters of *Religion* focus on the nuances between these words when attempting to navigate *Religion*. In his essay "The

Ethical Significance of Kant's *Religion*," Silber, for example, offers a (roughly) thirteen-page treatment of this nuance in Kant's thought.[3]

Throughout the examination to follow (and in subsequent chapters), we presume, more or less, the relationship between *Wille* and *Willkür* laid out by Henry E. Allison in *Kant's Theory of Freedom*.[4] Stated briefly, *Wille* can carry a general meaning and a particular meaning. In the general sense, *Wille* is a term for the will as a whole, *Wille* and *Willkür*. In the particular sense, *Wille* refers to the neither free nor unfree aspect of the will, which presents to the spontaneous aspect of the will the moral law as an incentive.[5] The center of spontaneity is what Kant calls *Willkür*, and is ultimately what generates maxims for the exercise of freedom.[6] As Allison summarizes, "Kant affirms unequivocally in the published text that only *Willkür* can be regarded as free and that *Wille*, which relates to nothing but the law (*der auf nichts anderes, als bloss auf Gesetz geht*), can be termed neither free nor unfree."[7] Our treatment of *Religion* will use *Willkür* interchangeably with "the power of choice," and *Wille* in only its specific sense, as a reference to the neither free nor unfree aspect of the will. Beyond these basic definitions, we will not focus on the nuances between *Wille* and *Willkür*. Suffice it to say that we do not find these nuances central to making sense of the difficulties in *Religion*, and the reasons for this will become clear as we move into our interpretation, particularly in section three of this chapter and beyond.

Kant's Case for Moral Rigorism

Book One of *Religion* opens with a contrast between what Kant takes to be two diametrically opposed worldviews—the predominant religious paradigm and the paradigm of the moralists. The former echoes the "complaint as old as history" that the world lies in evil (6:18). This ancient lament presumes something akin to the Christian narrative of the fall: humanity began in paradise and has since suffered a "decline into evil" (6:18). Such a perspective, Kant notes, contrasts starkly with the outlook of the moralists "from Seneca to Rousseau," who are of the "[m]ore recent . . . heroic opinion . . . that the world steadfastly . . . forges ahead in the very opposite direction, namely from bad to better" (6:18–20). The moralists' optimism, Kant admits, may be an accurate assessment of certain civil tendencies, but if the moralists intend to provide an accurate assessment of humanity's moral trajectory, Kant thinks it evident that they "have not drawn this view from experience" (6:20). To the contrary, "we may presume," Kant assures us, "that it is . . . just an optimistic presupposition" (6:20).

This juxtaposition of religious pessimism over human corruption and moralist optimism over the fecundity of our moral resources sets the stage for Kant's own examination of human nature in Book One. As indicated by Kant's reservations over the optimism of the moralists, Kant's concern in *Religion* is to offer a sober-minded assessment of the moral nature of humanity (as opposed to our socio-cultural abilities) that is practically grounded: does humanity (and the world) lie in evil, and, if so, do we possess the resources to press ahead from bad to better? Despite Kant's transparent skepticism over humanity's moral goodness, Kant does not immediately adopt the religious assumption that humanity is depraved. His goal is to move toward a more robust and rationally sound understanding of our moral nature. The pursuit of such an understanding is precisely what we find when Kant begins his examination of humanity's moral disposition in the opening pages of *Religion*.

As Kant considers the implications of humanity's having a moral disposition, it becomes clear that he intends to strike a balance between the idea of *nature*, as an innate governing principle, and the transcendental implications of the predicate *moral*, which points toward a freely chosen maxim. In seeking this balance, Kant cognizes the moral nature as a "subjective ground" for the exercise of freedom. This subjective ground, Kant submits, must itself be a *deed of freedom*, or, more precisely, the choosing of a moral maxim that serves as a rule for the entire exercise of freedom in time. This rule or maxim, as indicative of our moral nature, must likewise constitute an *innate* rule (per the concept of *nature*) that establishes our posture toward the moral law *in general*.

In *Religion* Kant defines moral *good* and moral *evil* by whether the moral law serves as supreme incentive in a given maxim. Therefore, the supreme maxim that establishes our moral nature must, Kant argues, concern whether our approach to maxim-making moves ahead with the moral law as supreme incentive or not. As Kant puts it:

> But lest anyone be immediately scandalized by the expression *nature*, which would stand in direct contradiction to the predicates *morally* good or *morally* evil if taken to mean (as it usually does) the opposite of the ground of actions [arising] from *freedom*, let it be noted that by "the nature of a human being" we only understand here the subjective ground—wherever it may lie—of the exercise of the human being's freedom in general (under objective moral laws) antecedent to every deed that falls within the scope of the senses. But this subjective ground must, in turn, itself always be a deed of freedom . . . Hence the ground of evil cannot lie in any object *determining* the power of choice through inclination, not in any natural impulses, but only in a rule that the power of choice itself produces for the exercise of its freedom, i.e., in a maxim. (6:20–21)

Under this guide, Kant explores several ways of construing this grounding maxim, and here we find his well-known discussion of moral rigorism.

In considering the nature of the supreme maxim, Kant begins by distinguishing the "moral rigorist" from the "latitudinarian." The former maintains a strict dichotomy with regard to humanity's moral nature— either humanity is good or humanity is evil; there can be no middle ground. The latter, by contrast, is a heading under which two "middle-ground" positions on our moral nature fall. The titles Kant uses for these middle-ground positions indicate that he has in mind the views of the latitudinarians of the seventeenth and eighteenth century, who, while holding fast to many doctrinal orthodoxies of the Christian faith, were suspected—whether legitimately or illegitimately—of semi-Pelagianism.[8] The first of these middle-ground positions Kant calls that of the "latitudinarian of neutrality," or the "*indifferentists*" (6:22). Indifferentism maintains that humanity's moral nature need not be good or evil, but can, in fact, be morally neutral—it is possible for the human to be neither good nor evil in her moral nature. The second middle-ground position is that of the "latitudinarian of coalition," or the "*syncretists*" (6:22). Syncretism represents a type of moral duality, where humanity is a hybrid—"partly good, partly evil" (6:20). These middle-ground positions are distinct from the disjunction that humanity must be either good or evil, which represents Kant's favored position, moral rigorism. Having said this, Kant's reasons for siding with rigorism are well argued and worthy of close examination. In order to grasp the nature of Kant's arguments, we must remember that Kant is exploring humanity's moral nature under the premise that *moral nature* is defined by a supreme maxim regarding the moral law in general. Thus, his investigation builds on the question of whether the notion of a morally neutral or bifurcated maxim is cogent.

Kant argues against indifferentism in two places. The first appears in a footnote in 6:23. There, Kant contends that there is no such thing as indifference to the moral law, for in attempting to define moral neutrality, or indifference, the definition inevitably proves identical with moral malevolence. Moral indifference, thinks Kant, would be possible only "if the moral law in us were not an incentive of the power of choice" (6:23). Foundational to Kant's philosophy, however, is the assumption that "the law is incentive" (see, e.g., 6:24 and 27). Said differently, Kant presumes that the moral law is continually presented by *Wille* to the power of choice (*Willkür*) as an incentive. The power of choice cannot, therefore, generate a maxim indifferent to the moral law. The only way for *Willkür* to produce a maxim indifferent to the moral law is by suppressing or rejecting *Wille's* presentation of the moral law as incentive. Thus, Kant concludes, "the lack of the agreement of the power of choice [*Willkür*] with [the moral law] . . . is possible only as a consequence of a real and opposite determination of the power of choice, i.e. of a *resistance* on its part" (6:23). Yet, resistance to the moral law signifies not neutrality but moral corruption. In short, Kant cannot conceive of a morally neutral maxim, for *Willkür* must, in its maxim-making, take a stance regarding the moral law as supreme incentive—either accepting this incentive as supreme or rejecting it. Kant thereby concludes that a morally neutral maxim (and thus a morally neutral disposition or supreme maxim) is simply impossible.

Kant's second argument against indifferentism, appearing in 6:24, also plays on the idea that the supreme maxim is a single rule regarding the moral law as supreme incentive. This second argument takes on a slightly different dynamic, however. The first argument is stated as a negative (neutrality is resistance to the moral law), whereas this latter argument is stated as a positive (neutrality is an elevation of competing incentives). Kant again begins with the assumption "the moral law is itself an incentive in the judgment of reason" (6:24). Using this premise, Kant suggests that a morally neutral supreme maxim cannot be coherently construed. If the moral law is not the sole determining ground of one's actions—that is, if the supreme maxim does not treat the moral law as supreme incentive—then, Kant submits, "an incentive opposed to [the moral law] must have influence on the power of choice of the human being in question" (6:24). Kant is clear that opposing incentives can have such influence only if one "incorporates the incentive (and consequently also the deviation from the moral law) into his maxim (in which case he is an evil human being)" (6:24). In other words, the moral law can find itself in competition with lower incentives only if the supreme maxim raises these lower incentives to a status equal to or higher than that of the moral law. Since one can misprioritize the order of incentives only by choosing to usurp the natural place of the moral law, "it follows," says Kant, "that [the deviant's] disposition as regards the moral law is never indifferent (never neither good nor bad)" (6:24).

One possible objection to Kant's distaste for indifferentism is that Kant confuses indifference, or even apathy, toward the moral law with moral neutrality. Kant is thus guilty of false identification by dubbing the "latitudinarian of *neutrality*" an "*indifferentist.*" Moral neutrality, one could argue, is better defined as the bald capacity for either good or evil; it does not point toward indifference.[9] Such an objection is useful in highlighting an important dimension of Kant's understanding of the moral nature. In committing himself to the idea of a moral nature and identifying the moral nature as constituted by a freely chosen supreme maxim, Kant is bound to think of the moral nature as more than mere capacity for good or evil. Kant must consider the moral possibilities for a maxim—in the case of indifferentism, can a maxim be morally neutral? If Kant rejects the idea of a supreme maxim and embraces instead moral neutrality in the sense of mere capacity, the result would be, not a morally neutral nature, but the absence of moral nature: no supreme maxim (and thus no enduring character) exists beneath our sorted moral acts. And this consequence would again result in a lack of unity to our moral activity. We would be left with only our diversity of spontaneous moral decisions and no enduring moral nature to unify them—which would bring us straight back to the difficulties mentioned in section three of the previous chapter. But once Kant embraces the practical and teleological need for an enduring moral nature, or disposition, and concludes that the predicate *moral* points in the direction of a freely generated maxim that underlies the exercise of freedom in time, Kant must consider the various ways this supreme maxim can be cognized. Kant's argument against indifferentism is not, then, an argument against raw moral capacity, but an argument that no maxim can be morally neutral.

Having eliminated the indifferentist position as a legitimate way of cognizing the supreme maxim, Kant moves on, in 6:24–25, to consider syncretism—humanity is partly good and partly evil. Kant thinks the notion of moral duality, like that of moral indifference, runs aground. His argument builds again on the singularity of the supreme maxim and the singularity of humanity's universal duty to incorporate the moral law as supreme incentive. As Kant points out, "the moral law of compliance with duty in general is a single one and universal" (6:25). Building on this premise, Kant does not see how the supreme maxim can simultaneously incorporate the moral law as supreme incentive, while also placing other incentives in competition with it. As Kant points out, if one "is good in one part, he has incorporated the moral law into his maxim"; yet, if such a one is simultaneously "evil in some other part," then it would follow that "the maxim relating to [the moral law in general] would be universal yet particular at the same time: which is contradictory" (6:24–25). In other words, the idea of a supreme maxim is the idea of a single maxim that underlies all moral decision-making and concerns the moral law as a whole. In order to selectively apply the moral law, one needs multiple particular maxims that concern the sorted applications of the moral law. While we certainly generate particular moral maxims, our situation-specific maxims are subsequent to and stand in contrast with the supreme maxim, for the *supreme* maxim concerns only one universal duty, namely, the duty to embrace the moral law generally as supreme incentive in all moral decision-making. This duty is either accepted or rejected. If the supreme maxim is a rule that allows for occasional deviation from the moral law, then this rule apparently does not incorporate the moral law as sole supreme incentive. And, by Kant's lights, such is the definition of moral evil, not moral bifurcation. Syncretism, like indifferentism, is therefore untenable, and Kant is left with moral rigorism—either the supreme maxim is good, or it is evil.

Taken in this way, Kant's argument for moral rigorism fits better the readings of interpreters such as Wood and Silber than it does with the reading of Hare and Reardon. For Hare and Reardon, Kant's argument for rigorism is meant to show that *particular* maxims are either good or evil; they cannot be morally neutral or morally mixed, and therefore, when engaging in our pursuit of moral renewal, we must seek to adopt only good maxims. As Reardon puts it, "You cannot . . . fulfill the moral law by adopting both good maxims and bad simultaneously."[10] Yet, insofar as we take Kant to be offering an account of our moral nature, which is constituted by a *supreme* moral maxim that underlies all particular maxim-making, we must side with Silber when he writes:

> On the level of mere observation, then, we judge the will on the basis of its specific actions, and we conclude that most if not all wills are both good and evil. Had we the omniscience of a divine judge, however, to observe the dispositional act, the basic intention which is the ultimate motive behind

all specific acts, this judgment would be supplemented. The disposition would be found to be either good or evil and its moral quality only more or less distorted by the specific acts which follow from it when the *Willkür* applies its dispositional intention to concrete moral situations.[11]

Kant's case for moral rigorism is therefore a case that maxims generally and the supreme maxim specifically cannot be morally neutral or morally bifurcated. As a single maxim regarding the moral law generally, either the supreme maxim must be good, or it must be evil; either the moral law is supreme incentive or it is not.

This "disjunctive proposition," as Kant calls it, clearly does not, in itself, constitute a complete conclusion. Despite Kant's indication at the opening of Book One that the presumption of human goodness is merely an optimistic presupposition, Kant is not satisfied to conclude just yet that humanity is evil by nature—even if this is the likely conclusion and one for which his philosophy of religion has become well-known. Kant's goal is to reach a more universal conclusion regarding the moral nature of humanity as a species or the human in his kind (*der Mensch in seiner Gattung*), which can be applied to every individual as innate. As Sharon Anderson-Gold puts it, "Kant explicitly maintains that the 'subject' of this discourse is not the 'particular individual' but the entire species."[12] For such a conclusion, Kant suggests that anthropological research (*anthropologischen Nachforschung*) is required. He writes:

> However, that by the "human being" of whom we say that he is good or evil by nature we are entitled to understand not individuals (for otherwise one human being could be assumed to be good, and another evil, by nature) but the whole species, this can only be demonstrated later on, if it transpires from anthropological research that the grounds that justify us in attributing one of these two characters to a human being as innate are of such a nature that there is no cause for exempting anyone from it, and that the character therefore applies to the species (6:25–26).

In what follows, Kant reaches such a conclusion about the species, and it therefore seems reasonable to presume that the developments following 6:26 constitutes the type of research Kant thinks necessary.

Having said this, we think it misguided to read Kant as merely looking out over human history in order to assess whether, all things considered, humanity generally tends more toward good or toward evil. Kant is not, in our assessment, placing human history on the scales of good and evil to see which is the more dominant tendency of our species. Yet, many of Kant's interpreters take his argument for radical evil to rest precisely on this sort of general observation. Michalson suggests the following about Kant's inference of radical evil:

> Quite simply, it is never clear why Kant thinks radical evil is universal, or the propensity to evil innate. At the point in the *Religion* where Kant makes these claims most explicit, he turns to empirical examples, as though offering a familiar "long melancholy litany of indictments against humanity"

will simply make manifest what we somehow intuitively know about the race. But of course there is utterly no way that Kant, above all, could legitimately generate a claim about intrinsic features of human nature from even the lengthiest list of empirical examples.[13]

Likewise, Quinn contends, "As Kant reads the historical evidence, it provides plenty of inductive support for such a presupposition [as radical evil]"; and again, "so Kant takes himself to have good inductive support for attributing a morally evil propensity . . . to mankind universally."[14]

We find it problematic to reduce Kant's argument for radical evil to a weighing of humanity's dominant moral tendency. Instead, we understand Kant to have a clear rationale supporting his assessment of our species' (universal) moral bent. Kant's turn to the concept of moral nature is the very thing that yields both the idea of a supreme maxim and Kant's subsequent conclusions in favor of moral rigorism, all of which lay the foundation for his assessment of humanity's moral bent. In other words, the supreme maxim and moral rigorism together comprise the transcendental parameters for assessing our moral nature, parameters that will lead Kant to his doctrine of radical evil. As for Kant's *anthropologischen Nachforschung* to follow, we take this to refer not to Kant's catalogue of humanity's historical ills in 6:33–34 but to Kant's examination of our natural predispositions, which must be accounted for when considering the nature of moral corruption from within Kant's transcendental parameters.

In this light, Kant's anthropological research is more of a philosophical anthropology that concerns itself with the role our natural predispositions play (or do not play) in moral corruption. As Gary Banham argues, "The question of the characterization of the human race is in fact not, despite appearances to the contrary, a mere pragmatic anthropology. . . . The subjective ground of the 'nature' of human beings is what Kant wishes to uncover. This entails that the type of enquiry that would need to be undertaken to discern the answer to this problem would have to be a *transcendental* philosophical anthropology."[15] In identifying Kant's anthropological research as philosophical anthropology, we are not, of course, suggesting that Kant's eventual conclusions regarding radical evil are detached from empirical observation. As we will see in the next section, Kant understands humanity's natural predispositions to be good, and a corrupt maxim cannot therefore be inferred from a purely philosophical anthropology. Empirical evidence that the moral order of incentives has been inverted is required. But Kant's empirical observation of our species must move ahead assuming a supreme maxim and moral rigorism, while also considering what our natural predispositions are and how evil is compatible with these predispositions. Only after Kant's examination of the supreme maxim, moral rigorism, and humanity's natural predispositions does Kant have the proper philosophical framework for assessing the moral character of our species. Therefore, with his understanding of the supreme maxim and his case for moral rigorism before us, we are now in a position to consider Kant's philosophical anthropology.

Kant's Anthropology and Humanity's Moral Bent

In 6:26, Kant presents the first tier of his anthropological research, which centers on what he calls humanity's "predispositions" (*Anlagen*). Predispositions are central to Kant's anthropology because they "belong to the possibility of human nature" (6:28). That is to say, the predispositions represent essential properties of the human person—the human rationally considered bears these natural inclinations. Here, Kant is clearly drawing on the biological connotations of the term *Anlage* during his time—hence his talk of the predispositions as *natural* (*Naturanlage*).[16] Kant defines the predispositions as "elements of the determination of the human being" (6:26). Put otherwise, predispositions represent natural inclinations, which make us susceptible to the draw of certain incentives. Yet, for Kant these natural inclinations do not, in themselves, determine the power of choice. As Michalson points out, "Goodness and evil are thus the result of what we do with these potentialities. Though the potentialities are fixed—in the sense that we cannot be held accountable for them—what we do with them is not fixed."[17] Michalson is quite right in identifying the predispositions as *potentialities*, for as Wood points out, "No man, says Kant, is *actually* good or evil on account of his possession of these predispositions. Hence, if a man is to be said to be 'by nature' good or evil, this goodness or evil cannot consist in the predispositions bound up with the *possibility* of human nature."[18] A predisposition, therefore, creates in humans only the natural *inclination* toward certain activity (e.g., procreation, the comparison of self with others, and susceptibility to the moral law as supreme incentive); and as part of the very concept of humanity, these natural inclinations cannot be "eradicated" (see 6:28).

Kant defines each of the predispositions relative to the level of cognitive aptitude they require. The predisposition to animality is a "merely *mechanical* self-love . . . for which reason is not required" (6:26). The predisposition to humanity is also a self-love, as a tendency to "judge oneself happy or unhappy" relative to others (6:27). But unlike animality, this predisposition requires a certain level of discursive reasoning since it *"involves comparison"* (6:27). The predisposition to personality stands out in contrast to both animality and humanity as "the susceptibility to [have] respect for the moral law *as of itself a sufficient incentive to the power of choice*" (6:27). This predisposition is unique because it exists for the sole purpose of provoking moral obedience. Here we find the hierarchy of predispositions that Michalson characterizes as Kant's "calculus of sensuousness."[19] Animality is clearly a lower inclination—evident from its title. It represents the baser inclinations of humanity to procreate. And the predisposition to humanity, while requiring a higher level of cognitive aptitude and standing above animality, does not rise to the dignity of the predisposition to personality, which gives humans the capacity to have respect for the moral law as supreme incentive.

Despite this hierarchy, Kant is emphatic that the predispositions cannot be credited for either moral goodness or moral evil. On the negative side, the predispositions are not to blame for moral corruption. Kant submits that the predispositions (and even the incentives to which they make us susceptible) are good in their original state; they stand in agreement with the moral law. By *agreement*, moreover, Kant does not mean that the predispositions simply avoid conflict with the moral law. Rather, he sees them (all of them) as invoking conformity to the moral law. "All these predispositions in the human being," Kant tells us, "are not only (negatively) *good* (they do not resist the moral law) but they are also predispositions *to the good* (they demand compliance with it)" (6:28). Contrary to Michalson's claim, the predisposition to animality, in itself, is not corrupting. There exist lawful and moral ways to act on this predisposition, and the same is true of the predisposition to humanity.

This said, Kant does not think the predispositions determine the will in the opposite direction either—that is, toward the good. Kant goes on to make plain that while the predispositions are essentially good, they can lead to corruption if misemployed. Since, as Michalson points out, what we do with our predispositions is not fixed, Kant admits that these natural inclinations can be (mis)used for immoral ends. For example, Kant suggests that the predisposition to animality, which promotes procreation, may give way to *"bestial vices of gluttony, lust and wild lawlessness"* (6:27); and, likewise, Kant suggests that the predisposition to humanity, which brings with it a tendency to compare oneself with others, may move from a search for "merely *equal worth* [with others]" to "an unjust desire to acquire superiority for oneself over others" (6:27). The predispositions, therefore, while essentially good, do not *necessitate* a virtuous employment.

The one exception to this rule is the predisposition to personality, which makes the human being susceptible to the moral law as supreme incentive. This predisposition serves only a moral purpose—namely, commending the moral law. Kant notes, "The human being can indeed use the first two [predispositions] inappropriately" (6:28), but the predisposition to personality is not susceptible to this type of misemployment. This is not to say that the predisposition to personality necessitates adherence to the moral law. Quite the contrary, the predispositions cannot be credited for either evil or goodness; thus, even the predisposition to personality must be grabbed hold of, otherwise its natural presence within humanity is of no value. As Wood notes, "Man's predispositions to personality, his moral accountability, is a condition for the possibility of being good or evil, and his possession of it cannot render him actually good or evil."[20]

One dimension of the foregoing that is not often drawn out in the literature is the connection between the predispositions and the incentives. By drawing a connection between the two—that is, by recognizing that our natural inclinations or predispositions are what make us susceptible to the draw of certain incentives—we are able to see the concern underlying Kant's movement from talk of the moral order of incentives to Kant's examination of humanity's essential inclinations. Kant's concern in vindicating the lower predispositions of guilt is to show that evil does not lie in our predispositions or even in the incentives that compete with the moral law for supremacy in the supreme maxim. All of humanity's essential inclinations, and even the incentives to which these inclinations make us susceptible, have an appropriate role to play in human experience. But because the order of incentives can be misaligned, these naturally good predispositions can be misemployed and yield vice.

The importance of this point is that Kant, in offering a "calculus of sensuousness," does not intend to *explain* radical evil, as Michalson suggests. Kant is quite clear that predispositions, as natural and essential (or even at times biological) features of the human person, are not inclinations we can be held accountable for having (see, e.g., 6:32). Rather, it seems, to our minds, that Kant's vindication of the predispositions is reflective of a type of Thomistic scheme. In his "Treatise on Law," Thomas submits that actions are always set in motion for the sake of obtaining some good, specifically related to felicity.[21] As Thomas notes, "Now the first principle in practical matters, which are the object of practical reason, is the last end: and the last end of human life is bliss or happiness."[22] Evil is done not for its own sake but out of a misguided pursuit of some good. Even self-destructive tendencies have good ends driving them, such as the end of suffering in the case of suicide, or a pleasure received from pain in masochism. The concern of the moral law, Thomas argues, is to guide humans to the good in an appropriate manner, fitting to human nature and our role in this world. In this scheme, evil is vacuous and almost parasitic, gaining its appeal only from an attachment to some genuine good, which has an otherwise appropriate (or lawful) application. Underlying this view is the Augustinian metaphysic, which defines evil as a privation of goodness (*privatio boni*).[23] Drawing on Plotinus, Augustine argues, "There is no such entity in nature as 'evil'; 'evil' is merely the name for the privation of good."[24] Thomas clearly adopts this metaphysic of good and evil, and in both Augustine and Thomas, the goal is to demonstrate that evil is not something positive.[25] To use Plotinus's phrasing, evil is "measurelessness as opposed to measure, of the unbounded against bound, the unshaped against the principle of shape, the ever-needy against the self-sufficing."[26]

Kant's account of our natural predispositions echoes this scheme. Our predispositions are good; they stand in conformity to the law and, when rightly employed, bid conformity to the moral law. Thus, just as Kant sees a natural link between happiness and moral uprightness—happiness is proportionate to virtue (see 5:110–11)—so there is a parallel between a proper employment of the predispositions and conformity to the moral law. The predispositions, when fulfilling their proper function, do not lead away from the moral law, but lead toward it. Humans can, nevertheless, seek the natural goods that our predispositions incline us toward through misguided, unlawful means. If this occurs, these otherwise good inclinations give rise to vice. Hence, animality, which creates a natural inclination for procreation, can become rampant licentiousness, but this is not the natural function of this predisposition; it is a perversion of a naturally good predisposition. In short, Kant's account of humanity's predispositions appears to be in one accord with the Augustinian/ Thomistic idea that evil is not done for evil's sake, but is a misguided quest for some genuine good. Or, as Kant himself puts it in 6:37, "The depravity of human nature is therefore not to be named *malice*, if we take this word in the strict sense, namely as a disposition . . . to incorporate evil *qua evil* for incentive into one's maxim (since this is *diabolical*), but should rather be named *perversity* of the heart, and this heart is then called *evil* because of what results" (see also 6:35).

When we look at Kant's talk of the predispositions from this vantage point, his intent is not, as Michalson suggests, to bring the predispositions to bear on the emergence of evil in an explanatory or causal fashion. Rather, Kant, like Thomas, examines the predispositions that make humans susceptible to (though not bound by) lower, non-moral incentives in order to show that *if* humanity's moral nature is corrupt, this corruption is not the result of *necessity*. Corruption is the result of a free and contingent decision to elevate lower incentives and thus invert the proper or moral order of incentives. Kant is well aware that if the statement *he is evil by nature* is derived "from the concept of the human being in general"—that is, from a predisposition that belongs to the very possibility of human nature—"then the quality [evil] would be necessary" (6:32). If Kant is to be open to the possibility that our moral nature is evil, his anthropology must first show that evil is "not a natural predisposition but something that a human being can be held accountable for" (6:32). Hence, Kant goes to great lengths to vindicate the predispositions and show that if humanity is corrupt, we are corrupt because our *Willkür* freely chose to subordinate the moral law to other incentives when generating our supreme maxim.[27] Kant's discussion of our natural predispositions serves as an anthropological safeguard against the *reality* of evil entailing the *necessity* of evil. Kant's point, in short, is that "[a]n evil heart can coexist with a will which in the abstract is good" (6:37).

The anthropological safeguard of humanity's good predispositions allows Kant to move into his discussion of moral corruption without the specter of necessity looming overhead. As has been said, Kant's basic definition of corruption is rooted in the order of incentives. As Wood puts it, "The goodness or evil of a maxim . . . consists in its 'form,' in the 'order' or 'subordination' of the incentives it contains."[28] Kant's point is that when one incorporates the moral law into a maxim alongside the "the law of self-love," one of these incentives must take priority. Or, put another way, one incentive "must be subordinated to the other as its supreme condition," for these incentives cannot "stand on an equal footing" (6:36). Since the moral law is rightly our supreme incentive, "this reversal of incentives . . . [is] contrary to the moral order" (6:36). This definition of corruption applies to all three "different grades" of corruption Kant names in 6:30 (viz., frailty, impurity, and depravity). When defining evil in these terms, Kant, like Augustine and Thomas, is able to define evil without making it a necessary feature of the human person and without making it a positive property. To use Kant's own words, the corrupt disposition "is therefore not . . . a disposition . . . to incorporate evil *qua evil* for incentive into one's maxim"; rather, it is a *"perversity* of the heart" (6:37). With this definition in hand, Kant is able to conclude that humanity's disposition is corrupt without robbing our moral nature of the predicate *moral* or robbing humanity of moral culpability. Thus, coming on the heels of his discussion of the predispositions, Kant offers his well-known and much maligned conclusion: "the propensity to evil is here established (as regards actions) in the human being, even the best" (6:30). Given the foregoing, this *propensity to evil* refers not to our natural predispositions, which are good, but to a tendency to give non-moral incentives a weight equal to or greater than the moral law. And this tendency results from a disposition (or supreme maxim regarding the moral law in general) that does not incorporate the moral law as supreme incentive.

As previously mentioned, many interpreters take Kant's conclusion that humanity is universally corrupt to be purely inductive. Kant, they suggest, merely considers the "multitude of woeful examples that experience of human *deeds* parades before us" (6:32–33). Certainly, there is an empirical dimension to Kant's conclusion. Kant certainly needs to look at humanity's behavior in order to assess whether humans operate as if under a rule that treats the moral law as sole supreme incentive or not. After all, if evil is not part of the very concept of humanity, how could Kant make a conclusion regarding human nature without observation? Or, to use Wood's words, "Kant has made it abundantly clear that we cannot hope to demonstrate by abstract reasoning that man is evil by nature; if we are able to predicate evil of the human species, or indeed of any particular person, we must somehow base this predication on what we can observe of the actions of men through experience."[29]

This being said, Kant's conclusion comes amid a series of transcendental insights regarding how to cognize humanity's moral nature. Kant examines human nature under the guide of the predicate *moral*. The question of a *moral* nature points Kant in the direction of a freely chosen supreme maxim for the entire exercise of freedom in time. This maxim, as we saw, concerns the single duty to regard the moral law as supreme incentive. Moreover, Kant's conclusions regarding moral rigorism require that the supreme maxim be either good or evil—either it incorporates the moral law as supreme incentive, or it does not. By the light of these parameters, Quinn is quite right when he states, "[W]e must, if we wish to attribute to Kant a consistent view, understand reversals of the moral order of incentives broadly as *any* failure to preserve the proper subordination of the incentives of inclination to the moral incentive and not narrowly as merely those failures which consist in subordinating the moral incentive to the incentives of inclination."[30] Kant therefore need not establish the radicality of evil in humanity by showing us to be grossly evil or by attempting to weigh the multiple examples of good and evil in the world on opposite sides of a moral scale. He need only consider the question of whether human behavior indicates that we operate (morally speaking) with the moral law as our supreme incentive or whether we occasionally consider other non-moral incentives in our moral decision-making.

Under such a strict definition of moral goodness, Kant's conclusion seems rather like common sense. Obvious enough is the fact that humans do not act according to the moral law as sole supreme incentive. Therefore, it is likewise obvious that under Kant's criterion humanity's disposition is evil. As Quinn rightly points out, Kant needs only a single instance of evil to justify this conclusion. It is not surprising, given Kant's parameters for defining moral corruption, that Kant would conclude, "the propensity to evil is here established (as regards actions) in the human being, even the best" (6:30). Even the most moral person fails at times to live up to the high standard of morality under Kant's strictures. Kant need not, therefore, go into "the formal proof that there must be such a corrupt propensity rooted in the human being, in view of the multitude of woeful examples that the experience of human *deeds* parades before us" (6:32–33). In 6:33–34, he nevertheless provides a sampling of some historical ills for any who may doubt such a conclusion. The conclusion that humanity's supreme maxim is corrupt serves as the climax of Kant's anthropological research and the heart of his well-known notion of radical evil: "This evil is *radical*, since it corrupts the ground of all maxims" (6:37).

Given this conclusion, we invariably run headlong into a series of major difficulties, previously mentioned in chapter 3. First, while it may seem obvious enough that humans, generally speaking, do not treat the moral law as supreme incentive, Kant cannot offer this conclusion with certainty if his conclusion is a purely inductive assessment of the moral nature human individuals spontaneously choose for themselves. Even if Kant's overtly rigid criterion for moral goodness makes it likely and even a matter of common sense that no human is good (*no one treats the moral law as sole supreme incentive*), Kant's vindication of humanity's predispositions and his unrelenting emphasis on the spontaneous exercise of freedom prevent this conclusion from being normative. As Michalson puts it, "Kant's moral universe is a scene of innumerable idiosyncrasies."[31] If the moral nature is an individual affair and the product of a spontaneous willing, the results cannot be schematized. Clearly Kant's argument, as Wood notes, is "designed to show the *universality* of evil, to show that all men, despite the many differences between them, exhibit a radical propensity to do evil."[32] But so long as radical evil is construed as a moral bent freely and contingently chosen by each individual and Kant insists that nothing requires the choosing of evil—it is spontaneously chosen—Kant cannot make a universal declaration regarding humanity's moral nature. Either Kant has set up a definition of goodness that makes a good disposition impossible (none are capable of being truly good and are *necessarily* evil), or a good disposition is possible, and it is therefore possible—and even likely—that some in the past (or the future) may have made (or will make) the moral law their supreme incentive. Kant clearly rejects the necessity of evil, so we are left with the latter, which stifles Kant's ultimate conclusion.

Second, we face Michalson's quandary concerning the *propensity* (*Hang*) to evil, which emerges alongside Kant's doctrine of radical evil. Kant clearly identifies the inversion of the moral order of incentives with humanity's propensity to evil: "if a propensity to this [reversal of incentives] does lie in human nature, then there is in the human being a natural propensity to evil" (6:37). Propensity, according to Kant, refers to an outworking of the supreme, enduring maxim in our particular maxim-making, and this outworking, says Kant, must be clearly "distinguished from a predisposition" (6:29). Unlike the predispositions, which are natural inclinations that the human cannot be held accountable for having and which (in the abstract) are good, the propensity to evil must be the resulting effect of an exercise of *Willkür* that subordinates the moral law to non-moral incentives. In this willful subordination, corruption emerges, as does the propensity to evil. But here we face another of Michalson's questions: If the inversion of the order of incentives is the result of a mere act of the will (it has no causal basis outside this, such as the predispositions, for example), what does it mean to speak of a propensity to evil? In other words, if nothing can compel the will to evil (evil emerges from unbound freedom), can a propensity be anything other than a repeated, spontaneous willing to subordinate the moral law to other incentives?

This question regarding Kant's notion of a propensity to evil also raises a third concern that Michalson notes regarding Kant's notion of gradations of corruption. As mentioned, Kant names three "different grades" of corruption (viz., frailty, impurity, and depravity). These forms of corruption range from weakness that sees the moral law as "subjectively" less potent than other incentives to a forthright tendency to "subordinate the incentives of the moral law to others (not moral ones)" (6:30). Yet, building on his criticism of propensity, Michalson wonders: If evil is ultimately chosen by the spontaneous exercise of *Willkür* and the natural predispositions (or sensual nature) of humanity are free from (causal) blame in the origin of evil, what sense does it make to speak of frailty and impurity? Such terms indicate failings as a result of weakness in what seems to be a type of overwhelming of the will. But such a notion of *overwhelming* is contrary to Kant's aforementioned assumption that freedom alone is to blame for evil. In order to address this triad of issues, we must transition into the details of how we understand a key movement in Kant's cognizing of the moral disposition, which helps overcome these difficulties.

Humanity's Moral Disposition

As we move into the final dimensions of Kant's understanding of the moral disposition, we have before us three major difficulties for Kant's argument:

1. How can Kant conclude that humanity is *universally* corrupt?
2. If evil has no causal basis outside a spontaneous exercise of freedom, what does it mean to say that we manifest a propensity to evil?
3. If evil has no foundation other than moment-to-moment spontaneity, how can Kant speak about frailty and impurity?

To answer these questions, we need the complete picture of Kant's vision of our moral nature, which heretofore has been treated only in part. It will be remembered that Kant's starting point is the supreme maxim. He first looks at the term *nature*, and argues that if our talk of a moral nature is indicative of a deterministic leaning, then *nature* is antithetical to *freedom* and "stand[s] in direct contradiction to the predicates *morally* good or *morally* evil" (6:21). Since, for Kant, morality and freedom imply each other, the *moral* disposition must be cognized as "a deed of freedom" (6:21); and this deed is the choosing of a maxim, or "a rule that the power of choice itself produces for the exercise of its freedom" (6:21). Moreover, this maxim, as *supreme*, is a single rule regarding the moral law generally, and ultimately defines our moral nature.

Moving deeper into Kant's understanding of our moral nature, we find Kant's talk of the "power of choice" (*Willkür*), which is the "formal ground of every deed" (6:31). *Willkür* is the spontaneous aspect of the will that generates maxims, and in the case of our moral nature, the supreme maxim. The exercise of *Willkür* is cognizable by reason alone, Kant tells us (see 6:31 and 39). He links this intelligible deed of *Willkür*, specifically as it relates to the disposition, with the "descent of an effect from its first cause" (6:39). He identifies this intelligible deed as the "*being*" of an act, which contrasts with its "*occurrence*" or "*cause in time*" (6:39). Kant does not spend much time explaining this language. Yet, very similar terminology can be found in the first *Critique*, specifically in "The Antinomy of Pure Reason."

While we will not here go into a detailed analysis of the "Antinomy," Kant's comments are instructive. Kant focuses on the distinction between that which is conditioned and that which is unconditioned. The phenomenal is always conditioned by space and time. Thus, if one were to seek something unconditioned, one would need to "look" outside of the phenomenal, as it were. When applying this distinction to the search for an unconditioned condition of a series of occurrences in time, the implication is that in order to trace an occurrence back to its condition, we must follow it back to an unconditioned condition. Such tracing, Kant submits, never allows for inference about the unconditioned condition as an *object*—as noumenal, we do not have such access to it. All we can infer, Kant tells us, is some grounding *rule* of which the unconditioned condition is constitutive, given what is phenomenally accessible.

What is intriguing about Kant's discussion is that he goes on to apply the search for unconditioned conditions to our use of freedom. As is well known, freedom is established on practical grounds according to its relationship to the moral law. And in the "Antinomy," Kant is clear as to why freedom cannot be empirically established: all choices, when assessed from an empirical vantage point, can be explained by prior causes and do not give reason to think of them as free (see A549–50/B577–78). Freedom, if real, must therefore be known transcendentally; and the power of choice (*Willkür*) is this transcendental side of freedom (see A548/B576). The power of choice constitutes the unconditioned condition of free acts (see A539/B568); and in keeping with Kant's earlier comments on unconditioned conditions, we may not know the power of choice as an object. *Willkür* is cognizable by reason alone, and what is cognized is only the rule of which it is constitutive. As the ground of our use of freedom, this rule must be a moral maxim (see A551/B579).

In the most basic sense, Kant offers a distinction between the use of freedom as it appears and freedom considered unconditionally. The former consists of "the **condition** of a successive series of occurrences" (A552/B580), and the latter refers to the power of choice, which is "**outside** the series of appearances" (A552/B580) and constitutes the free choosing of a maxim for the exercise of freedom in time. The picture is almost that of a moral cosmological argument. If we examine human actions empirically, we can simply trace them to a prior cause. Therefore, if we are to reach the unconditioned condition of this chain of acts, we must trace them back to a transcendental deed outside this series of occurrences. Freedom is thus known transcendentally, so that if we are to retain the idea of freedom, we must cognize a free, unconditioned ground for the use of freedom in time. And since we cannot know this ground as an object, we must examine the maxim of which it is constitutive. Thus, while Kant would not apply the phrase "prior to" to the power of choice, as this is a temporal term, the power of choice is the *beginning* of all uses of freedom in time (see A553–54/B581–82).

When we apply this understanding of the power of choice to Kant's talk of a supreme maxim in *Religion*, we notice a clear parallel. Kant's talk of a supreme maxim echoes the idea of tracing back all acts in time to the unconditioned condition of their occurrence; and this unconditioned condition serves as the "beginning" of this series of occurrences. Since the disposition cannot be known as an object, we must cognize the rule (or maxim) of which it is constitutive, given what follows in time. As Kant argues, "[E]ven though the existence of this propensity to evil in human nature can be established through experiential demonstrations . . . these demonstrations still do not teach us the real nature of that propensity" (6:35). We must look to the intelligible character or the being of the propensity. *Willkür*, as it relates to the supreme maxim, is the unconditioned condition that serves as a rule for the exercise of freedom in time. Since we see that the moral law is not our sole supreme incentive in time, we can infer that the rule, or supreme maxim, underlying these occurrences inverts the moral order of incentives. The disposition, or rule, to which we trace these occurrences is, then, "the ground antecedent to every use of freedom given in experience [and] . . . is . . . present in the human being at the moment of birth" (6:22). And again, "[I]f we wish to engage in an explanation of evil with respect to its *beginning in time*, we must trace the causes of every deliberate transgression in a previous time of our life, all the way back to the time when the use of reason had not yet developed, hence the source of evil back to a propensity (as natural foundation) to evil which is therefore called innate" (6:42–43). Present in this tracing back to the rule or moral disposition is Kant's tension between innateness and freedom.

Kant's assertion that the disposition must be rooted in a freely chosen maxim may seem to indicate that the dispositional bent of humanity is an individual affair—*we choose for ourselves our moral nature*. This is how Michalson, for example, takes it: "Kant will take us back no further than the foundational 'act' by which I choose my supreme maxim and freely establish the incentive structure influencing all my subsequent acts of maxim-making."[33] Since we tend to think of noumenon in the same way we think of phenomenon, the tendency is to think of the particular individual in question in the noumenal "realm" (whatever that may be). Noumenally, that individual possesses the power of choice, and what Kant must be espousing is a type of personal fall, where humans (noumenally considered) choose their disposition prior to any phenomenal exercise of freedom. Thus, when freedom is manifest in time, it reflects the noumenally chosen disposition that is empirically innate. Kant's notion of the disposition, in this light, parallels Gottfried Leibniz's idea that free decisions are the product of personal ontology or nature, and therefore the possibility of divine foreknowledge and preestablished harmony between free will and the causal nexus of our physical world is possible because free decisions are implicit in the pre-created souls of creatures.[34] The difference for Kant, however, is that since the disposition is the creature's *moral* nature, this pre-empirical nature must be freely chosen.

The difficulty with reading Kant's talk of the disposition as an individual affair, however, is not that it contradicts the tracing-back idea discussed above; the problem with this reading is twofold:

1. We find no explanation of how Kant expects to (and eventually does) arrive at a conclusion regarding humans universally.

    2. Such an individualistic examination of moral nature hardly
       amounts to an examination of the human *species.*

Both Quinn and Michalson, who each employ an individualistic reading of
Kant on the disposition, recognize that "[s]ince the propensity to moral evil is a
product of freedom, it cannot be an essential element in human nature as is
the predisposition to good. If moral evil is to be attributed to mankind as a
species, it must be a contingent and accidental attribute of each member of the
species."[35] Kant's arguments, as noted in chapter 3, must, on such a reading, be
rooted in an observation that humans more generally tend toward good or
toward evil. But such an observation hardly secures Kant's conclusion that evil
is universal. As Quinn aptly puts it:

> But it seems very improbable that a propensity to moral evil should be both
> a product of freedom and universal among mankind. Because the adoption
> of an evil supreme maxim is an absolutely spontaneous exercise of the will,
> it is antecedently likely that some people would have freely adopted a
> morally good supreme maxim while others adopted a morally evil supreme
> maxim. Even if it is impossible to assign numerical values to the prior
> probabilities of the various alternatives, it seems clear enough that the prior
> probability of all humans choosing freely a morally evil supreme maxim
> must be quite low.[36]

As already discussed, Kant can reasonably suggest that it *seems* most choose
evil; he can even say this *seems* to be the most common human choice; but
Kant cannot assert that radical evil is universal if his notion of the grounding
disposition is such that each individual chooses his or her own disposition and
his or her spontaneous exercise of freedom could have chosen the good. From
such a standpoint, no claim to the universality of evil can be made. If Kant
understands the disposition to be an individual affair, where each person noumenally chooses his or her own disposition prior to the exercise of freedom in
time, and this dispositional choice is made purely by unbound, spontaneous
freedom, Kant must allow for the possibility that some humans possess a good
disposition.

    F. W. J. Schelling understood this point quite clearly. In *Of Human
Freedom*, Schelling references Kant's notion of the moral disposition and affirms a reading of Kant that sees the disposition as a primordial, atemporal
determination of the will that is innate in human individuals in time. Schelling not only affirms this reading as an accurate rendering of Kant but adopts
this insight into his own system of objective idealism. Like Kant, Schelling
recognizes that freedom must be unconditioned by time; and thus, true moral
determination is transcendental.[37] Moreover, Schelling, with Kant (and
Hume before him),[38] sees the idea of a morally undetermined will to be
problematic, and thus recognizes the need for a prior moral determination
within acting agents. Schelling writes:

[T]here is no transition from the absolutely undetermined to the determined. . . . In order to be able to determine itself it would have to be already determined in itself; not indeed from the outside, since this would be in contradiction to its nature, nor from within by any merely accidental or empirical necessity. . . . But it would have to be determined by its own essence, that is by its own nature. This essence is no indefinite generality but definitely the intelligible essence of this specific human being.[39]

Schelling goes on to speak rather favorably about Kant's insight that the moral determination of creaturely nature must be a deed of freedom, outside of time and prior to all other deeds.[40] All of this makes way for Schelling's own peculiar rendition of the Christian doctrine of predestination. Schelling's version of the doctrine is very similar to the individualistic rendering of Kant's freely chosen disposition, where we each noumenally choose our personal moral nature; and this noumenally chosen moral nature becomes our innate moral destiny. Schelling, employing this reading of Kant, affirms the idea of a transcendentally self-determined will, or freely chosen disposition, which sets the tone for all subsequent moral activity in time. The freely chosen disposition is what Schelling calls the "free act which becomes necessity."[41]

Schelling argues, in keeping with the early tendencies of the post-Kantian German idealists, that the whole of creation is implicit in God's own being. Prior to creation, therefore, each individual was present in God, or the *Absolute*, and was able to determine his or her will, or moral nature, prior to being manifest in time. What one is in time is thus indicative of one's chosen moral, or dispositional, bent in eternity. "That Judas became a traitor to Christ," Schelling tells us, "neither he nor any creature could alter; nonetheless he betrayed Christ not under compulsion but willingly and with full freedom."[42] In short, Schelling follows Kant's notion of the need for a disposition (or determined will), and affirms that this determination must be a transcendental determination that is, in a sense, "prior to" our empirical exercise of freedom in time. But because Schelling presumes that each *individual* is present within the Absolute from eternity, there is no uniformity to the dispositions various individuals possess. Some bear a disposition of one kind; others bear a disposition of another kind.

Schelling's comments demonstrate sensitivity to the problem of offering a blanket conclusion about the human disposition when reading this decision as an individual affair. This sensitivity is well summed up in Schelling's quip at the opening of *Of Human Freedom:* "[A]ccording to an ancient but by no means forgotten tradition, the idea of freedom is said to be entirely consistent with the idea of system, and every philosophy which makes claim to unity and completeness is said to end in denying freedom."[43] Schelling recognizes that if the moral disposition is unique in each individual, then there can be no necessary uniformity to the human disposition—some may be good and some may be evil. If, therefore, the individualistic reading of the disposition is accurate, it seems Schelling is more consistent and sober-minded than Kant with regard to its nature; and ultimately, Kant's conclusions regarding the universality of radical evil and Kant's subsequent ideas that build on this universality must be rejected as wrongheaded. Even if all of recorded human history testifies to the dominance of evil, this does not remove the possibility that someone, somewhere, may have chosen a good disposition.

In this light, we think it necessary to consider a different option when reading Book One of *Religion*. Two ways forward present themselves. First, we may affirm with Michalson that, for the sake of consistency, Kant must blame the body for evil, thereby making radical evil necessary. This approach certainly offers uniformity to the human disposition and explains the universality of Kant's claim. However, as already mentioned, Kant is quite clear that the predispositions (whether lower or higher) are good and not the cause of evil. Our negative use of freedom is to blame. Moreover, Kant is clear that a predisposition is not something we can be held accountable for having; and thus, to blame the lower order of human nature for evil would be to move contrary to Kant's emphasis on freedom, his vindication of the predispositions, and his arguments against the necessity of evil. As Wood rightly points out, "Radical evil is not to be sought in man's predispositions, in the moral capacities of man as a finite rational being, but must, if it exists at all, be found in man's use of his capacities through the power of choice, his *Willkür*."[44]

The second way forward, which is the way we opt for, is to read Kant's assessment of our moral nature with an eye fixed on Kant's concern for the human species. Wood recognizes that Kant sounds, at key junctures, as if he is speaking in terms of an examination of the species as a whole: "Kant's language at this point might lead us to think that he is seeking some sort of explanation for the evil of the individual's will by tracing it to a 'propensity' characteristic of the species."[45] Wood goes on to reject this possibility, however, saying, "But this is definitely not the case."[46] Wood offers little elaboration as to why this is not a viable option;[47] and insofar as to reject this option is to leave us without an explanation of how Kant's conclusion regarding radical evil is legitimately universal—not to mention a whole host of other conundrums—we will utilize this avenue of interpretation in our defense of Kant's argument.

Though seemingly unorthodox to most readers, it may be that Kant's talk of species is not a nominalist notion of species, which constructs only artificial similarities between objects with no real substantial unity. It may instead be that Kant's talk of species has a realist, more Aristotelian character, that is, Kant's philosophical anthropology may in fact be an examination not of human individuals corporately considered but of the human species in a way akin to Aristotle's secondary substance. If this way of understanding Kant's position is right, the uniqueness of Kant emerges in that, by examining humanity as a species, he assigns to it a moral nature and thus, in keeping with the predicate *moral*, is bound to assign to our secondary substance the power of choice as well—at least with regard to the determination of our supreme maxim. Prior to the empirical activity of any primary substance (that is, any particular human), the secondary substance must generate a supreme maxim regarding the moral law in general, which is innate in all members of the species. If taken in this way, Kant's "moral cosmological argument," as we characterized it, is meant to trace all particular, empirical uses of human freedom to an unconditioned condition for the possibility of a moral nature of the human species; and it is the moral nature of the species that serves as the subjective ground for all particular uses of human freedom in time.

Prior to moving ahead with this interpretation, we should address one issue of cogency. One could argue that this solution is problematic insofar as it requires the secondary substance, *human,* to be a universal as well as an individual because the secondary substance is active. Two points should be noted in response to this potential concern. First, while we will not here go into a lengthy treatment of Aristotle on universals and individuals, suffice it to say that the relationship between universals and individuated form is a disputed one in Aristotle-studies. A strong history of interpretation exists that takes Aristotle to distinguish an individual (*tode ti*) from a particular (*kath' hekasta*). While a particular is non-repeatable and cannot be predicated of another object, a universal can be individual.[48] If individuation is understood in this way, it is possible to conceive of the secondary substance being individuated in the first particular human, actively determining the moral bent of the species prior to all particular exercises of freedom, and then being further individuated in the process of generation, bringing with it an innate disposition.

Second, Leroy E. Loemker has argued that the dominant concept of species in the early sixteenth century was Aristotelian in nature. Loemker points to Julius Caesar Scaliger as a prime example of the type of understanding dominant in the period: forms are immanent and individuated, being placed as "seeds" within matter, first *in potentia* and brought forth *in actu.* These "seeds" are then passed on and further individuated in the process of generation. Human concepts were therefore held to be signs of things known through contact with the individuated form.[49] Scaliger's not uncommon use of Aristotle thus "made Aristotle the founder of the preformation theory of generation."[50] Loemker notes that this Aristotelian understanding of species persisted into the seventeenth century (albeit with Platonic additions that we will return to in the next chapter), and he suggests that this understanding of species was dominant in figures such as Leibniz. Moreover, part of this realist view of species was the notion that "ideas are active or, as Leibniz put it, have an exigency to actualize themselves, and are therefore discoverable in things by scientific analysis."[51] In light of these historical trends preceding Kant, we should not think it strange to find Kant embracing a realist view of species, and understanding immanent form as active.

If Kant's argument is taken in the above way, then the exercise of *Willkür* in the context of the supreme maxim is very much like an Adamic Fall into sin. However, rather than the disposition being the product of one particular individual, such as Adam, the dispositional bent is chosen by the secondary substance, *human*, when first individuated and actualized in matter, prior to all particular exercises of freedom. Kant is, then, quite serious about his claim that our species is a moral species and thus has a moral nature; and he is equally serious in understanding the predicate *moral* to imply a freely chosen maxim, even if this means that the secondary substance, *human*, has a free choice to make, to wit, the choosing of our supreme maxim. The moral nature, or disposition, of the species is therefore innate in all empirical particulars because the secondary substance is universal in all particulars and further individuated in the process of generation (cf. 6:41–44). The free choice that determines the moral bent of humanity is, then, the free choice of the species, which inverts the moral order of incentives and, in so doing, generates a maxim that serves as the ground for all particular uses of freedom in time, which display an innate propensity to evil. As Kant states, "Whenever we therefore say, 'The human being is by nature good', or 'He is by nature evil', this only means that he holds within himself a first ground . . . for the adoption of good or evil . . . maxims, and that he holds this ground *qua* human, universally" (6:21).

The rationale behind this oddity is rooted in Kant's case for moral rigorism. Once the species is presumed to have a moral nature, and *moral nature* is cognized as a supreme maxim regarding the moral law in general, the species cannot be thought of as morally neutral, leaving the determination of the moral nature to various human particulars. Rather, once the species is said to have a supreme maxim, this maxim can be cognized only as good or evil; it is either for or against the moral law as supreme incentive; it cannot be morally neutral or morally bifurcated. That our species has a moral nature is therefore essential—moral neutrality is not a real possibility. Yet, the particular moral bent of the species is a matter of free determination. And thus, per the predicate *moral*, the species (in the secondary-substance sense), when first individuated, must determine its moral nature.

In this way, our culpability for the disposition resides in our participation or membership in the species. We cannot separate ourselves from our humanity; the properties of our species are *our* properties. This freely chosen disposition is thus part of the species in which we participate and is that which defines our common moral nature. The exact relationship between our personal freedom and the *Willkür* of the species is not entirely clear under this reading. Kant may think, like Schelling, that we were somehow implicit within the species, transcendentally considered—although in a less individualistic sense than Schelling would offer. Or Kant may simply refrain from judgment on this point. Whatever Kant's views on this particular nuance, his overall scheme is reflective of the Augustinian notion that we, as humans, are not exempt from the freely appropriated guilt of our species.[52] We are human, and the chosen disposition is chosen by *humanity*: what is individuated in us and common among all other individuals is this secondary substance. Drawing on the Adamic metaphor, then, there is a very real sense in which, for Kant, " 'in Adam we have all sinned' and still sin—except that a prior innate propensity to transgression is presupposed in us but not in the first human being" (6:42).

The above understanding of the formal ground of human freedom helps clarify a number of issues. First, we find here an explanation of how Kant can blame freedom alone for the moral character of the supreme maxim, while also claiming that radical evil is universal. Although there is no necessity in the human species for the choosing of evil, if the species does not incorporate the moral law into the supreme maxim as supreme incentive, then all particular members of the species who bear this maxim as innate will display a corrupt character. Evil, then, is not an a priori feature of our species in this scheme; *humanity*, rationally considered, does not require the predicate *evil*. That humanity has a moral nature is a priori and necessary—we are a *moral* species —but the actual moral bent of our nature is contingent on the choice of *Willkür*. Once evil is chosen, however, it becomes a characteristic of the species and a universal characteristic of each individual human—we as humans display the freely chosen character of our species.

Second, we begin to see why humans manifest a propensity to evil. If the supreme maxim endures throughout and underlies our moral decision-making as humans, and this supreme maxim subordinates the moral law to other incentives, we as humans engage in particular maxim-making with other competing incentives already alongside the moral law—this is part of our innate moral nature. Yet, for Kant, this process itself is evil. The grounding order of incentives is so fundamental in Kant's world that even an act that on the surface appears good is corrupt if motivated by an incentive other than the moral law. As Kant puts it, "In this reversal of incentives . . . actions can still turn out to be as much in conformity to the law as if they had originated from true principles. . . . The empirical character is then good but the intelligible character still evil" (6:36–37). Thus, the radicality of evil lies not in the particular exercise of freedom in time, but in the very way we generate our moral maxims: non-moral incentives already have a foothold in the process.

The distinction between the particular members of humanity and the species also offers a third insight regarding why Kant speaks of gradations of corruption. Since the corruption of the supreme maxim tells us only that in time humans operate under a rule that does not treat the moral law as supreme incentive, there is still a sense in which the outworking of this evil (that is, our free response to the supreme maxim) is spontaneous. Some of us may, in response to the predisposition to personality, attempt to operate under the moral law as supreme incentive, but find ourselves incapable of doing so since, given the nature of the supreme maxim, the moral law seems subjectively weaker than other non-moral incentives (per Kant's notion of *frailty*). Others of us may simply choose to operate in an overtly evil manner, affirming the subordination of the moral law as supreme incentive, and thereby display outright wickedness (per Kant's definition of *depravity*). While the underlying, supreme maxim may be corrupt, the specific ways in which and degrees to which this evil manifests itself are subject to the spontaneous exercise of freedom in the individual members of the species.

Fourth and finally, we are able to better grasp why Kant thinks the supreme maxim, if corrupt, cannot be extirpated through human force. With Kant's investigation of the species being outside the individual sphere, the supreme maxim is not an individual affair. If the corrupt maxim were an individual affair, the change of maxim, it would seem, would be within the individual's power to undo. But since the adoption of the supreme maxim is by the species, it stands beyond the power of the individual to affect. Kant avers, "This evil is *radical*, since it corrupts the ground of all maxims; as natural propensity, it is also not to be *extirpated* through human forces, for this could only happen through good maxims—something that cannot take place if the subjective supreme ground of all maxims is presupposed to be corrupted."[53] This, it seems, is why, in 6:31, Kant so boldly calls the radical evil of the supreme maxim *peccatum originarium* (original sin).

If the foregoing is right, then the image we get of Book One is roughly as follows: Kant engages in an examination of what humanity's moral nature must look like, transcendentally considered. Per the predicate *moral*, this nature must be a maxim that is freely chosen, and this maxim must regard our posture toward the moral law generally—that is, as supreme incentive. As such, per moral rigorism, this maxim must either embrace the moral law as supreme incentive or subordinate it to other non-moral incentives. Yet, per the concept of *nature*, this maxim must be an essential property of our species—even if the specific bent of our species is non-essential. *Moral nature* therefore indicates that the human species, or *humanity* as secondary substance, must possess *Willkür*, at least with regard to the single act of generating the supreme maxim that defines our moral nature—a nature for which we are culpable as members of *humanity*. Apparent from the empirical exercise of freedom, the supreme maxim must reject the moral law as supreme incentive. As a result, we empirical members of the species bear an innate, corrupt disposition and display the corrupt character of the supreme maxim. And since we bear this disposition *qua* human, this corruption is universal. This underlying maxim creates in us a propensity to evil because we, by nature, consider other non-moral incentives in our decision-making. Yet, the specific outworking of this corruption appears in varying degrees, since we, as individuals, continue to exercise our personal *Willkür* in particular acts of maxim-making and continue to display a level of spontaneity, despite our corrupting tendency to consider other incentives alongside the moral law.

With these lenses in hand, Kant's comments in 6:20–21, which set the tone for Book One, are worth returning to and quoting at length. Kant writes:

But lest anyone be immediately scandalized by the expression *nature*, which would stand in direct contradiction to the predicates *morally* good or *morally* evil if taken to mean (as it usually does) the opposite of the ground of actions [arising] from *freedom*, let it be noted that by "the nature of a human being" we only understand here the subjective ground—wherever it may lie—of the exercise of the human being's freedom in general (under objective moral laws) antecedent to every deed that falls within the scope of the senses. But this subjective ground must, in turn, itself always be a deed of freedom (for otherwise the use or abuse of the human being's power of choice with respect to the moral law could not be imputed to him, nor could the good or evil in him be called "moral"). Hence the ground of evil cannot lie in any object *determining* the power of choice through inclination, not in any natural impulses, but only in a rule that the power of choice itself produces for the exercise of its freedom, i.e., in a maxim. One cannot, however, go on asking what, in a human being, might be the subjective ground of the adoption of this maxim rather than its opposite. For if this ground were ultimately no longer itself a maxim, but merely a natural impulse, the entire exercise of freedom could be traced back to a determination through natural causes—and this would contradict freedom. Whenever we therefore say, "The human being is by nature good," or, "He is by nature evil," this only means that he holds within himself a first ground (to us inscrutable) for the adoption of good or evil (unlawful) maxims, and that he holds this ground *qua* human, universally—in such a way, therefore, that by his maxims he expresses at the same time the character of his species.

In this excerpt, we see Kant offering an overview of his intentions in Book One that echoes with striking clarity the conclusions of our foregoing exposition. And therefore, as peculiar as it may seem to read Kant as adopting a more Aristotelian understanding of the human species and assigning to this secondary substance the power of choice in a single act of maxim-making, the ability of this hermeneutic shift to explain Kant's claims and alleviate the apparent conundrums in Book One gives reason to follow this trajectory on into Book Two.

With all this said, the major question that emerges under such an understanding of radical evil as ours is the question of, not only moral hope, but moral freedom. If Kant's presumption that humanity bears a moral nature leads to the conclusion that our individual moral freedom is bent toward evil, does not radical evil rob us of moral hope and conflict with the *ought*-implies-*can* principle? The answers to this question make themselves known as we press ahead with this interpretation into Book Two. As we will see, this way of reading Book One pays even greater dividends as we move into Kant's discussion of moral renewal. If our investigation of Book One is right, then Book Two becomes not a moralist's poetic reinterpretation of the Christian gospel, but a robust transcendental theology. This theology we will refer to as "Kant's Prototypical Theology," and as we move into Book Two we will see how this theology answers the problem of radical evil, restores human freedom, and secures moral hope.

6
Book Two of *Religion*

Without question, one of the most striking features of Book Two of *Religion* is Kant's use of Christic imagery. Kant's talk of the "prototype," who is the "Word" or "[God's] only-begotten Son," is rather shocking to those familiar with the Kantian paradigm. In many ways, Kant's philosophy epitomizes the rationalist emphasis on reason over history. And while Kant consistently asserts, "no human being can hold it impossible that . . . God might have given to it, in a higher revelation, certain truths" (28:1119), Kant is equally consistent with reference to the epistemological limitations humans face regarding revelatory possibilities. To use Kant's words in *Conflict*, "if God should really speak to a human being, the latter could still never *know* that it was God speaking" (7:63). Or, in Allen Wood's words, "though divine revelation itself is not impossible, it is impossible for any man to know through experience that God has in any instance actually revealed himself."[1] For Kant to draw explicitly on "revelatory" resources raises serious questions over exactly what he is up to in Book Two of *Religion*.

The interpretative approaches to this content are roughly three in number. First, we find the translation approach of John Hare and Bernard Reardon. By construing Kant's entire argument in *Religion* as a translation of Christian concepts, per the second experiment in the Second Preface, Hare and Reardon are able to offer an explanation of why Kant draws on historical Christology. Simply put, his experiment necessitates it. Under the guide of *Religion*-as-Translation, Reardon suggests that Kant finds the rational usefulness of Christ to lie in his embodiment (at least symbolically) of the ideal of virtue, which we must emulate. Reardon writes:

Kant turns to the doctrine of the incarnation as alone expressing the humanly realized moral ideal in all its perfectness. . . . The historical example thus sets before us, as of one who goes about disseminating good by both word and deed, is completed by afflictions, even to the extreme of an ignominious death, which he endured wholly undeservedly for the sake of the world and even his enemies. . . . [Kant] insists that the only way for man to please God and gain salvation is through a practical faith in the incarnate Son of God; a faith, that is, whereby he makes his own the dispositions of which the incarnate is the ideal exemplar.[2]

In other words, the Christ of Christian theology is the union of divine perfection and human nature, and therefore provides a picture of the moral ideal Kant's practical philosophy suggests we ought to emulate.

Hare also sees this motif in *Religion*, but goes even further, drawing out an entire Trinitarian theology from Book Two. Says Hare: "We have in these translations a reading of the three persons of the Trinity. Christ is understood as humanity in its full moral perfection. . . . God the Spirit is translated as the good disposition, which exists within us, is seen as our 'Comforter,' and provides us with assurance (through our actions, which are its fruits) of its own presence within us. God the Father is translated as the idea of holiness."[3] In short, the Christic imagery under the guide of *Religion*-as-Translation is merely the outworking of Kant's experiment, which is fixed on testing a specific purported revelation. The appearance of Christic imagery (if not full-blown Trinitarian theology) should, therefore, not be surprising.

A second way of dealing with Kant's apparent Christology in Book Two is the *Religion*-as-Symbol approach, found in readers such as Keith Ward and Stephen Palmquist. Both Ward and Palmquist see Kant's Christology as a symbol meant to spur on moral progress in the face of our personal moral failings. As Ward sees it, religious symbols "express what is indefinable in a particular mental state in such a way that it can be communicated to others."[4] Under such a reading, Jesus is the chosen historical-religious symbol Kant draws upon to invigorate moral exertion. But this does not indicate that Kant has exclusive commitments to Christianity or that Kant thinks Jesus actually is the moral prototype of humanity made manifest. The symbol could be drawn from any historical faith. Only insofar as Kant has chosen Christianity to be the vehicle for his symbolic theology does the moral ideal take on a Christological character. As Ward puts it:

In Book Two of the *Religion*, Kant develops a view of Christian doctrines as symbolic of the conflict of the good and evil principles, which are expressed in man's freely chosen ultimate maxims. Thus the Devil symbolizes the power of one's own evil choice: Heaven and Hell symbolize the radical gulf between the pure and impure will; the Holy Spirit becomes our confidence in our own moral disposition; and Christ symbolizes that moral perfection which is the final end of creation. But such ideas "reside in our morally-legislative reason"; their empirical instantiation, if any, is morally worthless. Whether Jesus ever existed or not is beside the point; he is the "archetype of the pure moral disposition," which all men must imitate in themselves.[5]

And likewise, Palmquist asserts, "Kant's purpose in devoting a whole section to [the gospel narrative] is not to ridicule those who believe it is true. . . . Rather, it is to confirm its *suitability* to serve as a symbolic vehicle for true religion."[6] In the end, however, this imagery is just that—imagery. The symbol may serve a practical function, but it does not require Christian commitments or tell us Kant's personal beliefs about Jesus.

One final way of addressing Kant's use of Christic imagery is to read Book Two as Kant's uncritical dependence upon revelatory resources, given a lack in his critical resources. Gordon Michalson and Vincent McCarthy both read Kant as drawing explicitly on Christian theology without strong justification for doing so. Michalson presumes that Kant, in the face of radical evil, runs out of critical resources and ultimately defaults back to ideas from his Pietistic upbringing:

> There is an important, intrinsic connection for Kant between the figure of Christ and what he at one point calls the "breaking" of the "power" of radical evil to hold rational beings under its spell. Apparently, apart from the existence of Jesus, the power of evil to hold us remains unbroken. The issue is not one of certain beliefs we are to hold about this historical figure, but concerns the occurrence of a past event that is evidently the necessary condition for the possibility of overcoming radical evil. It is Jesus of Nazareth, rather than anybody else, who is the personified version of the rational principle, residing in all rational beings, that turns out to be the basis of our own hope for moral regeneration.[7]

McCarthy also takes this approach, understanding Kant's discussion of radical evil to itself be an awkward mixing of Enlightenment moralism and Christian theology, and this awkward mixture spills over, according to McCarthy, into the Christic images of Book Two. As McCarthy characterizes it, "Kant's repeated singling out of Christianity and Christ (even when he does not refer to them by name) are, in fact, unjustified by his method of inquiry."[8] To quote Michalson along similar lines, "In the specific instance of the discussion of moral regeneration, Kant's response to this [severe intellectual limitation imposed by radical evil] is to quote from the Bible."[9] In short, such interpreters think there simply is no critical justification for Kant's importation of Christology in *Religion*, and the results ultimately reveal only Kant's personal religious commitments.[10]

Following the trajectory of our interpretation of Book One in the previous chapter, we will offer an understanding of Kant's Christic language in Book Two that is quite distinct from the above triad of interpretations. Kant's prototypical theology takes on the same transcendental character as our reading of humanity's corrupt moral disposition in Book One. The prototype, on our reading, represents a cognized ideal, or (more boldly) a transcendental entity of sorts. The prototype is not a translation of Christian theology or a symbolic rendition of Jesus of Nazareth, nor is Kant, in our view, defaulting to his

Pietistic Christian roots. Rather, Book Two, as part of the first experiment, falls within the purview of Kant's development of rational religion. And while Kant may draw upon biblical language (a point discussed above in chapter 4), we take his turn to the prototype to constitute a transcendentally chastened form of Platonic idealism, which is rooted in practical reason. As Kant puts it in Book Three of *Religion*, "The living faith in the prototype . . . refers . . . to a moral idea of reason" (6:119).

As we move into the details of Book Two, we submit that Kant is arguing the case that, in order to maintain moral freedom and hope in the face of radical evil, we must go beyond the cognition of an evil disposition and cognize a perfect human disposition to which we can have access through moral faith. In this light, Hare is quite right to associate Kant's discussion of moral redemption with "Spener's problem." As Hare notes, "The problem [Philipp Jakob Spener raises] is, how can we become *other* men and not merely better men (as if we were already good but only negligent about the degree of our goodness)?"[11] Book Two, as we understand it, certainly addresses this question, but it does so not via a translation of Christianity but by Kant's ongoing development of transcendental theology.

Our interpretation of Book Two is presented in three parts. The first centers on the particulars of how Kant cognizes the perfect human disposition, which draws us directly into Kant's introduction of the prototype. Section two focuses on those areas where Kant explains what moral faith looks like and the degree of assurance we may have regarding our moral redemption. The third and final section of this chapter centers on the anatomy of moral conversion, its relationship to the prototype, and the ways this relationship serves to ground moral hope.

The Prototype of Perfect Humanity

In the opening of Book Two, Kant links the world as an object of divine decree and the prototypical ideal. In 6:60, Kant draws a direct connection between the pleasure of the deity and this moral ideal: "from [this ideal of moral perfection] happiness follows in the will of the Highest Being directly as from its supreme condition." The exact rationale behind this particular statement is inexplicit, but the basic idea seems to be that only morally perfect humanity is pleasing to God, and such is the divinely ordained *telos* of our species. But unclear from this particular statement is whether Kant has in mind an existing ideal that precedes the creation of our world and stands as our moral exemplar, or whether perfect humanity is a mere possibility. Our reading opts for the former, but either way, such humanity is necessary to the meaningfulness of our world and subsequently necessary for moral hope and redemption. That is to say, the rational idea of God, in Kant's world, is such that God is principally concerned with morality, or, to use Nicholas Wolterstorff's words, "all we know of God is that God honors and ensures the requirements of morality—i.e., of rights and obligations."[12] If, therefore, the world is meaningful, being the product of divine decree, the ideal of perfect humanity or full moral perfection must be possible (that is, attainable by our species), if not somehow or somewhere already actual. As Michalson points out, "God enters Kant's scheme by riding on the coattails of the principle of proportionality. . . . On Kantian grounds, I cannot conceive of a universe in which, in the long run, the wicked prosper and the virtuous or innocent—such as the little girl in Ivan's story [from *The Brothers Karamazov*]— find only suffering and wretchedness."[13] Based on this "principle of proportionality," as Michalson calls it, Kant feels justified, on practical grounds, in following practical reason to a solution to radical evil; and in so doing, Kant cognizes the prototype of perfect humanity.

To be sure, we do not take Kant to move forward merely on practical grounds by defaulting to the *ought*-implies-*can* principle. Kant cannot merely presume that moral perfection is possible for our species, despite his conclusions in Book One, the way Davidovich, for example, suggests Kant does when she writes, "All that reflective faith allows us is to believe that our nature makes our rebirth possible. Kant calls it 'grace' because this reflection depends on thinking of God as the moral designer of the universe."[14] The reason Kant cannot employ such raw practical optimism was pointed out in our discussion of Philip Quinn in chapter 2: if Kant were to presume the possibility of moral goodness, despite his findings in Book One, his examination of redemption would undercut the *ought*-implies-*can* principle. It will be recalled that Quinn, while recognizing Kant's intent to affirm the possibility of moral renewal, argues that Kant's premises in Book One undercut the possibility of such renewal. Quinn argued that "there is no possible world in which (i) the thesis of rigorism is true, (ii) every human adopts a morally evil supreme maxim, and (iii) some human adopts a morally good supreme maxim."[15] Insofar as radical evil establishes that a corrupt nature resides within humanity, and Kant's concept of corruption is such that this evil cannot be extirpated through human force, Kant cannot merely assert that individuals must, nevertheless, be capable of reversing the disposition of the species. Such would result in blatant contradiction. Rather, Kant must cognize a moral ideal *outside of* and *distinct from* our corrupt species, which comes to our aid in the predicament of radical evil if practical reason is to remain stable. This aid is the prototype.[16]

Kant's cognizing of the prototype takes place in the opening of Book Two under the heading "The Personified Idea of the Good Principle" (6:60). Kant uses *the good disposition* and *the good principle* interchangeably throughout *Religion*. Therefore, the personification of the good principle we understand as a cognizing of the personified ideal disposition, which stands in juxtaposition to our corrupt disposition or the evil principle. Here, in the personification of the good principle, we find Kant's most explicit Christological language. As mentioned above, Kant refers to "*Humanity . . . in its full moral perfection*" (*die Menschheit . . . in ihrer moralischen ganzen Vollkommenheit*), which is the personified ideal. Kant names this personified ideal the "prototype" (*Urbild*), calling him the "Word (the *fiat!*)"; Kant even goes so far as to dub this prototype of moral perfection "[God's] only-begotten Son" (*sein [Gottes] eingeborner Sohn*). "This human being, alone pleasing to God," Kant boldly asserts, "'is in him from all eternity'; the idea of him proceeds from God's being [*Wesen*]; he is not, therefore, a created thing but God's only-begotten Son" (6:60). Such language is what has led interpreters such as McCarthy and Michalson to see Kant as merely defaulting to Christian theology in the face of radical evil, and this type of language has also funded the translation readings of Hare and Reardon. Given the reading of Book One offered in the previous chapter, however, we find an alternative way of understanding Kant's Christic language.

In his "Lectures on Religion," Kant uses language nearly identical to what we find at the opening of Book Two; yet, this language appears in the context of a "remark concerning the Platonic idea." Kant summarizes Plato's metaphysic as follows:

> The term *idea* properly signifies *simulacrum*, and therefore in human philosophy it signifies a concept of reason insofar as no possible experience can ever be adequate to it. Plato thought of the divine ideas as archetypes of things, according to which these things are established, although, to be sure, they are never posited as adequate to the divine idea. For example, God's idea of the human being, as archetype, would be the most perfect idea of the most perfect human being. Particular individuals, as particular human beings, would be formed in accord with this idea, but never in such a way that they completely corresponded to it.—In consequence, Plato was blamed for treating these ideas in God as pure substances. (28:1058–59)

While Kant does not offer this summary as a representation of his own view, this language may serve to explain what exactly he has in mind when he makes the aforementioned Christological claims in *Religion*. It may, in fact, be the case that Kant's answer to radical evil moves from an Aristotelian understanding of the unity of our human species in Book One to a type of Platonism (albeit transcendental) for his solution to radical evil in Book Two.[17] That is, it may be that the "personified *idea*" of the good principle is not an empty idea of the imagination but a Platonic Idea in God that is in fact a pure substance.

If Kant's prototypical theology does represent a transition in Kant's thinking to a transcendental Platonism of sorts, this movement, in combination with the above passage, makes plain the meaning of the titles Kant gives the Christic figure of Book Two, as well as the juxtaposition of the prototype and our corrupt species. In the above passage, Kant avers that, in the mind of God, the idea of a human being "would be the most perfect idea of the most perfect human being"; or, said differently, this idea is the exemplar of humanity in its full moral perfection. Kant makes plain that this "most perfect human being" would serve as the "archetype" or "prototype" of humanity. That is, the moral nature of the prototype would be the ideal after which we must strive to model ourselves, and is representative of our divinely ordained moral *telos*. This prototype of perfect humanity, moreover, would signify "a concept of reason insofar as no possible experience can ever be adequate to it"—a claim in keeping with Kant's notion that the disposition, which is the prototype's perfection, is not a possible object of experience. We also find that this idea *exists* within God, not merely as a concept but as a being, or substance, that proceeds from God's own being. Finally, since Kant takes as given that God cannot exist within time and is "unalterable" (see 28:1043–44), it follows that this prototype of perfect humanity has existed within God from all eternity; it proceeds from God's very being and is not a created thing.

If we approach the opening of Book Two in this manner, we are able to make better sense of why Kant turns to the prototype as an answer to moral hope. Reading Kant's prototypical theology under the guide of transcendental Platonism (as opposed to a discussion of the Christ of Christian theology), what we find is that Kant draws a distinction between created humanity and the idea of the most perfect human being in God from all eternity. The former constitutes our created species that ought to model itself after the most perfect human being within God; yet, insofar as we are a moral species, our created humanity (in the Aristotelian sense) must choose our moral disposition, and we therefore have the ability to instantiate a disposition that will place us at some remove from our prototype. By contrast, the prototype is an ideal within God that possesses a good and perfect disposition from eternity.

Despite providing some explanation of the difference between our created humanity and its prototype, this Platonic turn in Book Two may seem odd to some, given that we have argued for an Aristotelian reading of *species* in Book One. Yet, several considerations speak in favor of this Aristotelian-Platonic coupling. Leroy E. Loemker points out that mixing Aristotelianism and Platonism was not uncommon in the seventeenth century. As noted in the previous chapter, Loemker argues that the dominant concept of species in the early sixteenth century was Aristotelian in nature, similar to what we find in Julius Caesar Scaliger. The ideas are forms, first *in potentia* as "seeds" in matter, which are brought forth *in actu*; and these "seeds" are passed on and further individuated in the process of generation. Human concepts were therefore held to be signs of things known through contact with the species or form individuated in matter.[18] Yet, Loemker also notes that during the sixteenth-century, debate existed over whether Platonism or Aristotelianism constituted the more sure foundation for things like mathematics. The result in the seventeenth century was a merger between Platonism and Aristotelianism, which retained the Aristotelian notion of immanent form, while also affirming the existence of "archetypal" ideas in God, which may not always find an empirical manifestation.[19] Loemker summarizes:

> The unifying bonds between Platonism and Aristotelianism in the seven-
> teenth century were found in a complex of principles—the immanence of
> forms in the particulars, the completion of analysis in intuition, a concep-
> tualistic theory of mathematical forms existing as "exemplary" or "arche-
> typal" in the mind of God, and a dynamic theory of the potency of these
> forms; ideas are active or, as Leibniz put it, have an exigency to actualize
> themselves, and are therefore discoverable in things by scientific analysis.[20]

What is particularly interesting for our purposes about this seventeenth-
century development is that it provides historical precedence for Aristotelian-
Platonic admixture, which distinguishes active, immanent form from ideas as
"archetypes" (or prototypes) in God.

In addition to the general shift toward such a merger in the seventeenth
century, Loemker notes that Gottfried Leibniz was of the "old ways," which
sided with the realist notion of ideas or form over against nominalism.[21] Leibniz is quite explicit in his *Discours de métaphysique* that a return to something
akin to Aristotelian form is needed for philosophical coherence.[22] Moreover,
we find that Christian Wolff, the often-dubbed systematizer of Leibniz, offers a
definition of existence that moves strikingly close to an Aristotelian-Platonic
merger. Wolff distinguishes the possibility of a thing in the mind of God (akin
to Platonic form) from immanent form, and suggests that the correspondence
of something outside of God to the idea within God is the very notion of
existence (*de notione entis*).[23] Given that both Leibniz and Wolff were influential on Kant in his early years, it would not be surprising to find echoes of this
Aristotelian-Platonic admixture in *Religion*.

One final consideration is the medieval background of the Platonic-Aris-
totelian merger. Looking again to Loemker, we find, "In the seventeenth
century there was an accommodation of the two viewpoints [Aristotle and
Plato], which derived indirectly from the Scotist doctrine of the univocity."[24]
The prospect of a Scotistic underpinning to the Aristotelian-Platonic merger is
intriguing, given that Ludger Honnefelder has argued that John Duns Scotus's
univocity doctrine is, in fact, the background of Kant's transcendental philosophy generally. Honnefelder links his argument with N. Hinske, who identifies
three main influences on Kant's notion of the "transcendental": (1) the notion
of transcendental philosophy in the seventeenth century, (2) Christian Wolff's
understanding of the transcendental, on which he bases his *cosmologia tran-
scendentalis*, and (3) the conception of transcendental in Baumgarten's com-
pendium of metaphysics.[25] Honnefelder not only argues that Hinske is correct
in identifying these influences but has suggested that the background to all
three influences Hinske identifies is Scotus's univocity doctrine.[26]

Scotus links his univocity doctrine with his understanding of metaphysics
as the "science of transcendentals."[27] Contrary to Thomas Aquinas, who denied the possibility of univocal language about God,[28] Scotus suggests that one
word does exist that is applied univocally to God and creatures, namely, the
word "being" (*ens*).[29] According to Scotus, being is the quidditative concept

that emerges when abstracting from particulars, be they genera, species, or individuals; and in this sense, being stands above all such divisions. Moreover, being constitutes the quidditative concept underlying the even more basic division between infinite and finite.[30] This quality not only makes being the one univocal concept applied to God and creatures alike, but also makes being transcendental, as that reality arrived at, indifferent to all divisions. As Scotus puts it, "Whatever pertains to 'being,' then, in so far as it remains indifferent to finite and infinite, or as proper to the Infinite Being, does not belong to it as determined to a genus, but prior to any such determination, and therefore as transcendental and outside any genus."[31]

By identifying being as indifferent to divisions, Scotus is not suggesting that being is without attributes, as if it were merely an amorphous substratum, like the Stoics' *proton hypokeimenon*. To the contrary, Scotus maintains that being must possess the essential attributes of that for which it supplies the quidditative concept, both those attributes that are "coextensive with [being], such as 'one,' 'true' and 'good,'" as well as those that are "opposed to one another such as 'possible-or-necessary,' 'act-or-potency,' and suchlike."[32] This is not to say that Scotus thinks all particular beings possess all the attributes of being. As he puts it, " '[W]isdom,' or anything else, for that matter, which is common to God and creatures, can be transcendental. A transcendental, however, may also be predicated of God alone, or again it may be predicated about God and some creature. It is not necessary, then, that a transcendental as transcendental be predicated of every being, unless it be coextensive with the first of the transcendental, namely, 'being.' "[33] Scotus's univocity doctrine is meant to establish that the essential attributes of creatures lies not in their actualized specific genera but in being itself, prior to all division.

Important to note is that Scotus is part of the Augustinian tradition. Thus, when he speaks about being proper, he is ultimately speaking about God. Standard metaphysics for Augustinians take God and being to be synonymous and interchangeable.[34] We saw this interchangeability in Scotus's talk of "Whatever pertains to 'being' . . . in so far as it remains indifferent to finite and infinite, or as proper to the Infinite Being [etc.]."[35] Therefore, the univocity doctrine affirms that all essential creaturely attributes are implicit, not simply in being *in abstracto*, but in God himself. To be sure, Scotus is neither a pantheist nor a panentheist on this point. Scotus is a voluntarist with regard to the will, and God's will is no exception.[36] Therefore, while the content of the Great Chain of Being may be known necessarily by God, and be rooted in God's own perfections, the actualization of this chain in creation is only a possibility. God retains voluntaristic freedom regarding whether to create the world and to actualize and individuate the Great Chain of Being within matter. Creaturely being is thus identified with immanent form, mingled with matter, even though the perfections and attributes that inform matter are first found implicitly in God's own being. In this light, we may say Wolff's "notion of existence" as the correspondence of something immanent in matter to an idea first in God is quite Scotistic.

The likelihood of Scotus's univocity doctrine lying in the background of Kant's thought is not only bolstered by the historical case of Loemker, Hinske, and Honnefelder, but is echoed in Kant's dispersed definitions of God as the "highest being" (A578/B606), the "being of all beings" (A578/B606), "the highest reality" (A579/B607), the "necessary all-sufficient original being" (A621/B649), and "a being having all reality" (A631/B659). This last definition in particular hints toward Kant's tendency to associate infinite predication or all reality with God (the *ens realissimum*), a tendency that is intimately tied up with the Kantian understanding of deity: "It already lies in my concept of an *ens realissimum* that he must be a thing, and therefore I have to ascribe to him every reality which can be predicated of him as a thing" (28:1020); and again, "Thus if the thoroughgoing determination in our reason is grounded on a transcendental substratum, which contains as it were the entire storehouse of material from which all possible predicates of things can be taken, then this substratum is nothing other than the idea of All of reality (*omnitudo realitatis*)" (A575–76/B603–604).

If Kant does, in fact, have a Scotistic understanding of divine being, then the Platonic turn of Book Two is not a turn from immanent form to a supersensible entity in the "world of the forms," but is a turn to the very concept of humanity implicit in the divine being itself. Hence, unlike our creaturely humanity that is made immanent in matter and is thus empirically accessible, the *Idea* of the prototype "proceeds from God's being" (*die Idee desselben* [*des Urbilden*] *geht von seinem* [*Gottes*] *Wesen aus*) and "is not, therefore, a created thing but God's only-begotten Son" (6:60). While Kant clearly develops the notion of the transcendental in ways divergent from Scotus—specifically as it relates to the turn to the subject—underlying Kant's understanding of God and predication, there remains an apparent indebtedness to Scotus and those in the seventeenth century (and beyond) who built on the univocity doctrine.

Assuming Kant is, in fact, suggesting that hope requires that we look outside of created, immanent humanity to a type of transcendental human, who proceeds from God's own being, this scheme does raise a potential problem: if immanent humanity and ideal humanity are both universals, but these universals have distinct moral natures, then it would seem these so-called universals are not universals at all, but particulars, predicated by some higher, morally neutral or bifurcated universal, *human*. Given the aims of this chapter, we will not go into a lengthy discussion of the fine nuances in Scotus's thought on nature and individuation and the distinction between essential properties and universals,[37] but suffice it to say that for Scotus, there is a distinction between the essential attributes of creatures, which belong to being, and created substance. The former, as rooted in uncreated being, "has a primacy of commonness in regard to the primary intelligibles, that is, to the quidditative concepts of the genera, species, individuals, and all their essential parts, and to the Uncreated Being."[38] Scotus maintains that being is what moves the intellect, even in the case of creaturely accidents; and therefore, being is what allows for knowledge of the essential parts of substance (*de partibus essentialibus substantiae*).[39] Scotus thus takes the transcendental, essential attributes of a given nature to be prior to and to stand above the categories of experience and the accidental properties of creation and individuation. Therefore, if Kant's Platonic turn in Book Two is a turn to humanity as implicit in or, in Kant's terms, proceeding from God's own being, which is not created, then Kant may rightly distinguish the prototype of humanity from our created species.

As for whether both the prototype and our created species are rightly dubbed *human*, given their disparate moral natures, we must consider the difference between essential and non-essential properties. A non-essential property, *p*, is a property that is in a subject, *A*, but is not part (that is, part of the concept or definition) of *A*. Conversely, if a property, *q*, is part of the concept or definition of *A*, then *q* is an essential property. If moral agency is part of (that is, part of the concept or definition) of *human*, as Kant suggests, then moral agency is an essential property. In Kant's defense of moral rigorism, over against moral indifferentism and syncretism, Kant is clear that he does not think humanity can be non-moral in nature; humanity must be good or evil. Therefore, by Kant's lights, the presence of a moral nature or disposition is an essential property of *human*. Yet, we must remember that Kant rejects out of hand the possibility that evil is the product of natural predispositions since the predicate *moral* requires that this disposition be freely chosen. In other words, Kant does not understand *evil* (or *good*) to be part of the nature, *human*; good and evil are contingent or non-essential properties. That humanity bears a moral disposition and bears one of these two moral leanings has been shown to be essential, but which of these postures toward the moral law is actually taken by humanity is contingent, resulting from freedom.

Since Kant does not understand our dispositional bent to be an essential property of humanity, the fact that the prototype bears a dispositional bent distinct from our own should in no way require that the prototype be something other than human. Radical evil is not one of the species' essential properties; evil is a contingent property. We do, however, face the question of why the prototype, if constituting the essential properties of our species, has a moral disposition at all, given that the dispositional bent is non-essential. According to the foregoing, the prototype must possess a disposition (the presence of *a* disposition is essential), but what of the dispositional bent? Is the prototype's dispositional bent freely chosen and contingent? Here we move outside the bounds of Kant's explicit comments, and so we must step cautiously. But we may note two possible responses.

First, Kant's talk of the prototype links the prototype with God's own being, making him a *divine*, not a creaturely, human. Therefore, if part of the very concept of God is eternal goodness, then the divine-human prototype can be cognized no other way than morally good. Such goodness, however, would not be contingent, creaturely goodness, but a participation in the eternal goodness of God (cf. 6:66).

Second, if Kant is genuinely influenced by Scotus, Kant may be aware of Scotus's exultation of Christ above Adam. In Scotus's thought, Christ, the God-man, is identified as the exemplar of the teleological end of humanity, and therefore does not come into our world and to our species purely in response to Adam's sin; Christ is instead logically prior to Adam.[40] Kant's language in Book Two continually upholds the prototype as humanity's teleological end by talking of our need to emulate the prototype, presenting the prototype as our only hope to be well-pleasing to God, and even designating the prototype our *prototype*. Of course, for Scotus, the logical priority of Christ over Adam, while stepping outside the realm of pure historical theology, was nevertheless attached to historical Christianity and explicitly Christian concerns. Kant, by contrast, seems to move toward a similar concept driven purely by the question of hope in the face of radical evil. But in the end, whether from natural theology or from Christian concerns, the outcome is quite similar: we must cognize human nature as it proceeds from God's own being, not as morally neutral, but as morally good, and in this sense, we find in God the uncreated exemplar of perfect humanity, who is logically prior to our created species and who constitutes the teleological end of our moral striving. Only by union with him and his nature can we hope to be found well-pleasing to God.

Taking up this understanding of the prototype, we find Kant's prototypical theology in Book Two to make a good deal of sense. The univocity doctrine explains Kant's talk of the dual nature of the prototype without presuming that Kant is defaulting to the dual nature of Jesus Christ in the Nicene-Chalcedonian sense. For Kant, the prototype is *divine* in the sense that he exists within God from all eternity; he proceeds (eternally) from the being of God and is not a created thing, and as such, he is rightly called the Son of God. Yet, Kant in no way develops this transcendental Platonism into a Trinitarian metaphysic regarding the relationship between *ousia* and *hypostasis* within the Godhead. The prototype is an ideal *human* within God from all eternity. Thus, there is a sense in which the prototype bears a divine nature; he is unique, representing the most perfect human being that is implicit in or eternally proceeds from God's own being; yet, he is the prototype of *humanity*. Or, as Kant puts it in 6:64, the prototype is a "divine human being [who] had actual possession of his eminence and blessedness from eternity."

This understanding of the prototype's nature sets up the basic concept that grounds the entirety of Book Two. The prototype, Kant tells us, is our only hope for overcoming dispositional corruption: "only in him and through the

adoption of his disposition can we hope 'to become children of God', etc."
(6:60–61). Here, in Kant's emphasis on our adoption of the prototype's disposition (*Annenhmung seiner [des Urbildes] Gesinnungen*), we see the heart of how
Kant understands the prototype to offer moral hope. For Kant, the prototype
provides hope for our species, not because he is a moral exemplar, but because
he possesses and actualizes the ideal disposition that we lack. By adopting this
pristine disposition—that is, by participating in or laying hold of this disposition, or nature, in the most literal sense—we too can hope to become pleasing
to God: the disposition from which happiness follows in the Highest Being is
now found in us.

Kant understands the prototype's disposition, or moral nature, to be available to us for adoption as a result of a gracious condescension on the prototype's part. As mentioned, Kant speaks of the prototype's descent to and
union with our corrupt, created species—we should cognize the prototype as
having "*come down* to us from heaven, . . . it has taken up humanity" (6:61).
This descent does not refer principally to an empirical appearance in a particular individual (e.g., Jesus of Nazareth), since, as Kant makes clear in 6:63,
emulation of the prototype is part of our universal human duty and is therefore
not contingent on an empirical appearance—a point we will return to later.
The descent of the prototype is, instead, what elsewhere has been called a
"transcendental incarnation."[41] In the context of answering the problem of
radical evil, Kant's concern is not the *appearance* of the God-man but the
availability of his disposition or moral nature to corrupt humanity. Therefore,
the prototype offers moral hope by descending to our species in the secondary-
substance sense. By his union with corrupt humanity, he makes availability to
us his pristine disposition. Hope emerges because there is present within our
species a new disposition, an ideal disposition, contrary to our innate disposition; and this ideal we may adopt as our own. The prototype is, therefore, not
merely an ideal "presented by reason for emulation" (although Kant affirms
that the prototype is that), but the prototype is "the prototype of moral disposition in its entire purity"; and only "the adoption of his disposition" can make us
pleasing to God (6:61): "In the *practical faith in this Son of God* . . . the human
being can thus hope to become pleasing to God (and thereby blessed); that is,
only a human being conscious of such a moral disposition in himself . . . is
entitled to consider himself not an unworthy object of divine pleasure" (6:62).

This top-down access to the good disposition emerges, as said before,
because Kant cannot see how "the *human being, evil* by nature, would renounce evil on his own and *raise* himself up to the ideal of holiness" (6:61),
especially if we presume our supreme maxim is corrupt. As we saw in Book
One, under such a presumption, "[the corrupt disposition] is also not to be
extirpated through human forces" (6:37). What moral hope requires is a new
nature be made available to us from without. The descent of the divine Son of
God is thus a provision of divine grace, which makes available to us a disposi-

tion that is not naturally our own. As Kant states in 6:61, "This union with [humanity] may therefore be regarded as a state of *abasement* of the Son of God. . . . The human being . . . who is never free of guilt . . . [is] hence unworthy of the union of his disposition with such an idea, even though this idea serves him as prototype." Despite Kant's concession that the prototype's union with our corrupt species is an abasement of this prototypical ideal, he does not take this to be a hindrance to this union, for though our species displays a corrupt disposition, this disposition is a *chosen* disposition; we are not evil by necessity. Kant therefore has no difficulty cognizing the prototype as "tak[ing] up humanity—which is not evil in itself—by *descending* to it" (6:61). But this self-abasement does highlight the gracious nature of the prototype's descent; the prototype's disposition is available to us only as a result of its transcendental (as opposed to historical) incarnation. Kant is clear that "we are not [the prototype's] author"; the prototype should instead be cognized as having "*come down* to us from heaven, . . . it has taken up humanity" (6:61), and, as such, is a proper object of rational religious faith.

The picture we then get of Kant's movement from Book One to Book Two is as follows. In Book One, Kant's examination of moral nature presses him toward a type of Aristotelian unity to the human species, and the corporate disposition of our species is found to be corrupt. In Book Two, Kant addresses the corruption of our species by introducing the prototype of humanity, who is ideal humanity implicit in God's own being. This ideal of virtue exists within God from all eternity and is not created. Rather, the prototype is a type of divine humanity, which constitutes the *telos* of our created species. Yet, our created species, as temporal, contingent, and created, must choose our moral disposition, and therefore has within its power the ability to opt for a disposition at a distance from its divine prototype. Our exercise of freedom in time indicates that such dispositional distance is, in fact, what our created species has chosen. Hence, Kant cognizes the prototype as coming down to our species via a transcendental incarnation in order to make his own disposition available to our species for adoption. Only by adopting this disposition in place of our corrupt disposition can we hope to be found pleasing to God. In short, Kant's dispositional philosophy in Books One and Two presents humanity as bound under one of two moral principles: we are innately bound under the corrupt disposition of our species, but the gracious descent of the prototype makes available to our species a new dominion of moral freedom and hope. Or, as Kant himself characterizes *Religion* in the First Preface, "I represent the relationship of the good and the evil principles as two equally self-subsisting transient causes affecting men" (6:11).

This vision of competing principles and the role of the prototype's willful descent within this conflict are important to keep in mind when scrutinizing Kant's notion of grace. As discussed at length in chapter 2, Kant's introduction of grace raises a number of difficulties in the minds of his interpreters. Grace, in Kant's scheme, is often presumed to refer to God's willingness to forgive moral debts and offer a mysterious assistance in stirring our wills toward the good. As Wood puts it, "Kant maintains, the good man may trust that for the sake of this which is in his power to do, God will complete by His verdict of forgiving grace these imperfect efforts to attain complete moral perfection."[42] We will address the former (i.e., divine forgiveness) in the subsequent sections of this chapter. Regarding the latter, we begin to see in the above reading of Book Two how Kant can hold together both divine assistance and the spontaneous, self-moving quality of the moral will. Under the reading of Book One offered in the previous chapter, humanity has no natural moral resources for overcoming radical evil. The spontaneity of *Willkür* may be employed in individuals in various ways despite the corruption of our supreme maxim. But insofar as the supreme maxim constitutes the chosen nature of the species, all of the human individual's moral acts—even those that happen to coincide with the dictates of the moral law—display the corrupt character of our species. Moral freedom is therefore placed in jeopardy. Kant's arguments in Book Two indicate that only the descent of the prototype can restore the possibility of genuine moral freedom. That is to say, only if another disposition is made available to us for adoption is it possible that we display a new nature, engage in untainted maxim-making, and perhaps attain a level of virtue that would make us pleasing to God.

Kant confirms quite clearly in 6:82–83 that only the descent of the prototype restores moral freedom in the face of radical evil. In these General Remarks, Kant uses the Christian picture of humanity bound under Satan and redeemed by Christ as an illustration of the two opposing dispositions:

> So the moral outcome of this conflict [between the good and the evil principle], on the part of the hero of the story (up to his death), is not really the *conquering* of the evil principle—for its kingdom still endures . . .—but only the breaking up of its controlling power in holding against their will those who have so long been subject to it, now that another moral dominion (since the human being must be subject to some dominion or other) has been revealed to them as freedom, and in it they can find protection for their morality if they want to forsake the old one.

We find here a development in Kant's thinking on moral freedom rooted in the development of his anthropology in *Religion*. Through a critical examination of the moral disposition, Kant comes to the realization that "the human being must be subject to some dominion or other" (6:83)—that is, humanity must possess a moral nature or disposition, and that disposition must be either good or evil, per moral rigorism. Because the disposition provides the innate character of our species, there is no such thing as the autonomous individual, if by this we mean an individual functioning apart from a moral disposition or with an "undetermined will," to use Schelling's phrase. Hence, if the human being, who is bound under the evil disposition, is to be morally free, this can happen only if an alternative good disposition is made available to her. Kant tells us this good disposition is available only because of the condescension of the prototype.

The importance of this relationship between Kant's prototypical theology and moral freedom is that it helps make sense of Kant's admixture of grace and moral freedom. Grace, for Kant, is not a divine overriding of human choice or even a mystical stirring of the will to do good. We cannot agree with Palmquist when he writes, "I am able to confess with a clear conscience and an uncompromised intellect that the change of heart is an effect of God's grace; yet I believe God somehow does this while preserving both my free choice and my responsibility to act in a way consistent with a good disposition."[43] Or, to use Reardon's words, "although we are not in a position to deny that works of grace do occur, they must remain incomprehensible to us, and so can have no place in a religion circumscribed by reason."[44] Kantian grace is first and foremost the willful descent of the prototype, which restores to our species moral freedom and the possibility of genuine moral goodness. Grace, in this sense, is not in conflict with human freedom, for the prototypical disposition must still be adopted by moral agents, and in this sense, Kant's soteriology is plainly synergistic. Stated briefly, Kantian grace speaks principally of the *availability* of the prototypical disposition, not a mystical stirring of the will to become like the prototype. Moral agents still bear the responsibility to lay hold of this grace.

While Kantian grace and *human* free will may be compatible, what of divine freedom? If grace speaks principally of the availability of the prototype's disposition, which is available only as a result of the gracious condescension of this moral ideal, we run headlong into Wolterstorff's concern: grace, by definition, is offered without obligation; therefore, "Kant cannot have it both ways: he cannot hold that we can expect God's forgiveness, since God's failure to forgive would violate the moral order of rights and obligations, and also hold that God's granting of forgiveness is an act of grace on God's part"[45]—or, in the case of the above reading, is an act of grace on the prototype's part. When considering such an objection, we must remember two things. First, assuming a Scotistic background to Kant's prototypical theology, the existence of the prototype is rationally grounded and is not a contingent matter. Even if God chooses to not create humanity, the moral archetype of our species would still proceed from God's own being from eternity, per the univocity doctrine. The question of divine freedom, therefore, concerns only the descent of the prototype to our species, not the prototype's existence. As for this descent, we must remember a second point, namely, that practical reason proceeds on the assumption that the world is meaningful. Kant's program moves ahead under the *presumption* of moral hope, granting something like the principle of proportionality. Kant does not know that moral hope is justified; the world may be meaningless; moral reason may be unstable; God may not exist. But *if* moral hope is real, and *if* the world is meaningful (for us) then we must believe in moral redemption. And when we follow the guide of practical reason in reference to the problem of radical evil, only our union with the prototype of perfect humanity offers legitimate moral hope.[46]

As we come to the close of this treatment of Kant's vision of the prototype, we reach Kant's cognizing of the prototypical narrative. In keeping with the predicate *moral*, Kant's cognizing of the prototype does not leave this moral ideal as a stagnant ideal. Instead, Kant submits that we must have an accompanying cognition of the prototype's moral narrative:

> We cannot think the ideal of a humanity pleasing to God . . . except in the idea of a human being willing not only to execute in person all human duties, and at the same time to spread goodness about him as far wide as possible through teaching and example, but also though tempted by the greatest temptation, to take upon himself all sufferings, up to the most ignominious death, for the good of the world and even for his enemies. (6:61)

The prototype's purpose, namely, "to deliver [his enemies] from eternal damnation" (6:64), shows that Kant's thinking on the prototype is more dynamic than mere condescension. The particulars of this account are rooted, for Kant, in the utter perfection of the prototypical disposition. Kant writes, "[H]uman beings cannot form for themselves any concept of the degree and the strength of a force like that of a moral disposition except by representing it surrounded by obstacles and yet—in the midst of the greatest possible temptations—victorious" (6:61). It will be remembered that, according to Kant, the disposition is not a possible object of experience. Since empirical cognition cannot yield the disposition itself, which is the prototype's true perfection, our epistemic limitations require such a narrative in order for the human mind to grasp the prototype's moral perfection. Hence, this narrative is a type of symbolic theology meant to help us grasp the nature of the prototypical disposition we ought to appropriate. "The abasement" of the Son of God points, therefore, not only to the prototype's union with our humanity, but also to the suffering he endures in the cognized narrative. "[Although] not bound to submit to sufferings," Kant tells us, "[the prototype] nonetheless takes these upon himself in the fullest measure for the sake of promoting the world's greatest good" (6:61).

As with the prototype's incarnation, it should be remembered that this prototypical narrative is not, for Kant, an actual history, but a transcendental narrative. The prototype is "presented to us by reason" (6:61), and is part of pure cognition driven by practical concerns, not empirical cognition. This is important for Kant because conformity to the prototype is part of "our universal human duty" (6:61). Therefore, the prototypical ideal cannot be contingent on historical happenings. As tied to our universal duty, prototypical theology can be thought of as necessary and universally accessible only via reason. Kant draws out the distinction between necessary and contingent religious beliefs most clearly in Book Three. There, Kant distinguishes between a religion grounded in a historical event, which "carries . . . the consciousness of its contingency," and a religion grounded in reason, which "can be recognized as necessary" (6:115). The prototypical narrative falls into the latter category, for empirical cognition "yields no example adequate to the idea; as outer it does not disclose the inwardness of the disposition but only allows inference to it" (6:63). Hence, "the required prototype," Kant tells us, "always resides only in reason" (6:63)—that is, in pure cognition—and is "perfectly valid for all human beings, at all times, and in all worlds" (6:66).

In discussing the relationship between the prototypical narrative and empirical history, Kant argues explicitly against the *need* for an empirical cognition of the prototype by drawing on the *ought*-implies-*can* principle. Says Kant: "[The prototype] has complete reality within itself. For it resides in our morally-legislative reason. We *ought* to conform to it, and therefore we must also *be able to*" (6:62). To rephrase, the prototype provides us with the picture of our moral duty, the same duty testified to by the moral law; and conformity to the prototype's image thus falls within the purview of humanity's universal duty. If we must first establish an example from experience of someone who conforms to the prototypical ideal in order to validate this idea, we would likewise need to demand such an example for the moral law to validate its authority and the ideals it commends. To Kant's mind, "even if there never had been one human being capable of unconditional obedience to the law, the objective necessity that there be such a human being would yet be undiminished and self-evident" (6:62). The prototypical ideal, in like manner, retains the same type of validity as the moral law: "There is no need, therefore, of any example from experience to make the idea of a human being morally pleasing to God a model to us; the idea is present as model already in our reason" (6:62). If one demands such an outward experience, such a one only confesses what Kant calls "moral *unbelief*" (6:63). This practical commendation of belief in the prototype and the link between this moral ideal and our universal duty is what we take to lie behind Kant's ascription of "objective reality" to the prototype (6:62). Despite the fact that from the theoretical vantage point, practical ideals cannot be granted objective reality (i.e., empirical verification), from the practical vantage point they must be presumed.

Noteworthy is that Kant's concern to guard against making the prototype contingent on a historical appearance is clearly not meant to defeat the *possibility* of such an appearance. On the contrary, after arguing against the need for an empirical manifestation of the prototype, Kant submits that such a manifestation must, nevertheless, be possible. Kant again uses the *ought*-implies-*can* principle, arguing, "an experience must be possible in which the example of such a human being [pleasing to God] is given" (6:63). Kant qualifies this admission by noting that this possibility exists only "to the extent that one can . . . ask for evidence of [the] inner moral disposition from external experience" (6:63) since, as already noted, the "outer . . . does not disclose the inwardness of the disposition but only allows inference to it, though not with strict certainty" (6:63). Nevertheless, the possibility of an empirical manifestation of the prototype is in no way diminished by this epistemic gap. Even if not practically necessary, the appearance is a necessary possibility, given the ought-implies-can principle. We find, then, a careful balance in Kant's thinking on this point. The *required* prototype is a universally valid pure cognition, but an empirical cognition of this ideal must be possible to whatever extent outward deeds provide evidence of an inward disposition.

This balance does not mean that if we find a historical individual (e.g., Jesus) who seems to emulate perfectly the prototype we should presume him to be the prototype. Quite the contrary, Kant tells us that in such a scenario, "we would have no cause to assume in him anything else except a naturally begotten human being (because he too feels to be under the obligation to exhibit such an example in himself)" (6:63). Said differently, since human duty is to conform to the prototypical ideal, we should not think that one who emulates the prototype is unique. Kant is equally cautious, however, that we not "absolutely deny that he might indeed also be a supernaturally begotten human being" (6:63). Kant suggests instead that, since our duty is to conform to such an image regardless of the empirical appearance of the prototype (or lack thereof), the quandary itself "from a practical point of view . . . is of no benefit to us" (6:63).

Practical Faith in the Son of God

In 6:62, we find the first mention of moral faith in Book Two—or what Kant calls "the *practical faith in this Son of God.*" In the context of Kant's argument, this refers to our need to adopt the prototypical disposition in place of our innate, corrupt disposition. The logical force compelling moral faith emerges in the context of duty: "it is our universal human duty to *elevate* ourselves to this ideal of moral perfection [*Ideal der moralischen Vollkommenheit*], i.e. to the prototype of moral disposition in its entire purity" (6:61). As with readers such as Reardon or Hare, who see the prototype as the embodiment of the moral ideal, we find Kant's language to be more explicit in its transcendental implications: we must adopt the disposition of this ideal, which is available to the species only as a result of divine grace. This said, we still face the epistemological difficulty that the disposition is beyond empirical cognition, for we do not have empirical access to even our own disposition (see 6:63). One's quest to adopt the prototype's disposition can therefore be worked out practically in the moral life only by cultivating a character that reflects the prototype's perfect disposition. This practical application of Kant's prototypical theology provides the context for how we understand moral faith within *Religion*.

Kant's movement from the quest for moral hope to the object of moral faith becomes the practical import of the prototypical narrative. Moral hope requires that we believe our disposition is of such a kind that, if subjected to the same temptations, trials, and sufferings we cognize the prototype as undergoing, we too would emulate the prototype. This litmus test, which uses outward evidence to infer the inward disposition, alone gives assurance of a renewed nature:

> [O]nly a human being conscious of such a moral disposition in himself as enables him to *believe* and self-assuredly trust that he, under similar temptations and afflictions (so far as these are made the touchstone of that idea), would steadfastly cling to the prototype of humanity and follow this prototype's example in loyal emulation, only such a human being, and he alone, is entitled to consider himself not an unworthy object of divine pleasure. (6:62)

On first blush, such a standard would seem to be a barrier to moral hope. As Kant himself acknowledges, the "human being . . . is never free of guilt even when he has taken on [the prototype's] disposition" (6:61). How, then, can a human being ever say with confidence that he or she has laid hold of the prototypical disposition?

This difficulty for moral hope centers on what Kant calls "*moral happiness*," which is "the assurance of the reality and *constancy* of a disposition that always advances in goodness (and never falters from it)" (6:67). Kant acknowledges the common desire for internal assurance of having already procured redemption and final perseverance. He likens this desire to a search for the inward testimony of the Holy Spirit in Christian theology, which tells Christian believers they are children of God (see Rom 8:16). The search for such an inward witness is, to Kant's mind, a search by the convert to "feel of himself that he can never fall so low as to regain a liking for evil" (6:68). The difficulty Kant sees with such a self-assuring solution is the danger of self-deception, for "one is never more easily deceived," Kant quips, "than in what promotes a good opinion of oneself" (6:68). More problematic than this kind of self-deception, however, is the suffocation of all moral motivation resulting from such assurance, since "the constant 'seeking after the Kingdom of God' would be equivalent to knowing oneself already in possession of this kingdom" (6:67–68). From Kant's perspective, it is better for human beings to, in the words of the apostle Paul, "work out their salvation with fear and trembling" (6:68; Phil 2:12).

This said, Kant acknowledges that "without *any* confidence in the disposition once acquired, perseverance in it would hardly be possible" (6:68). Some moral assurance must, therefore, be possible. But whatever modicum of confidence Kant allows, he does not intend this confidence to be unshakeable. Given his contention, "a human being's inner experience of himself does not allow him so to fathom the depths of his heart," (6:63) whatever confidence we have must, in Kant's words, come "by comparing our life conduct so far pursued with the resolution we once embraced" (6:68). Assurance must be based on one's personal moral momentum and trajectory, which yield only one of two possible results. On the one hand, one may find that "from the time of his adoption of the principles of the good . . . [he] has perceived the efficacy of these principles on what he does, i.e. on the conduct of his life as it steadily improves, and from that has cause to infer . . . a fundamental improvement in his disposition" (6:68). On the other hand, one may observe that despite "often repeated resolutions to be good . . . [he] has always relapsed into evil" (6:68); and this observation can only rouse the "conscience to judgment" (6:69). Thus, while we cannot observe the disposition itself, Kant holds that moral progress and regress provide legitimate testimony of the inward disposition.

Significantly, the type of moral progress required for confidence in our dispositional improvement is not, for Kant, indicative of moral perfection. Certainly if one possessed personal perfection, one would be "entitled to consider himself not an unworthy object of divine pleasure" (6:62). Yet, Kant is clear that even the one who has legitimate grounds to think that he will "come ever closer to his goal of perfection" (6:68) cannot expect to attain perfection in this life: "[He] can . . . reasonably hope that in this life he will no longer forsake his present course . . . and come ever closer to his goal of perfection, *though it is unattainable*" (6:68, emphasis added). Hence, while hope of genuine dispositional change is possible, the moral convert still has moral failings.

As realistic as Kant's expectations are, the reality of continued failings does raise a question for Kant's scheme: how can someone with a new disposition continue to fail morally if any moral failing gives reason to think of the disposition as corrupt? Reardon aptly draws out this problem when he writes, "The theological doctrine is not inconsistent with attributing conversion to the grace of God, and sin to the corrupted will of man. But Kant's effort to attribute both the good and the evil to one and the same human volition, which yet must adopt the maxim *either* of duty *or* of self-love, surely indicates a discrepancy in Kant's reasoning that does not admit of easy solution."[47] And again, "do not bad actions, on Kant's reckoning, proceed from *radical* evil in human nature, so that the heart is not after all regenerate?"[48]

Certainly this is a noteworthy challenge to Kant's argument. We will, however, delay our response to this particular difficulty until the next chapter since it helps to contextualize our understanding of Kant's arguments in Book Three. For now, suffice it to say Kant thinks that, in the face of such transgressions, moral progress may provide comfort, but it cannot make one "*absolutely assured of the unchangeableness of . . . [his or her] disposition*" (6:67). And again, Kant is quite clear that "we cannot base this confidence upon an immediate consciousness of the immutability of our disposition" (6:71). The convert may therefore take comfort in an improved life, but this comfort is not certainty. Instead, it is a reasonable hope based on the outward evidence of a change of inward disposition.

The Anatomy of Moral Hope

Heretofore, we have made clear that Kant's argument roots moral faith in the adoption of the prototype's disposition through moral faith in, or emulation of, the cognized prototype. Yet, this in itself does not explain exactly how Kant expects this adoption to make us pleasing to God. In a basic sense, the prototypical disposition provides for us a new moral nature that is, in itself, pleasing to God. Therefore, if this nature becomes our own, being found within us, we too should be found pleasing to God. Yet, Kant recognizes a number of difficulties that must be addressed in order to show this dispositional renewal to be sufficient for moral redemption and hope. Under the section titled "Difficulties That Stand in the Way of the Reality of This Idea and Their Solution," Kant sets forth three potential problems for a moral hope rooted in the prototype and provides his answers to the exact way dispositional renewal addresses these issues. These problems and Kant's solutions will occupy the remainder of this chapter and lay bare the anatomy of moral hope in Book Two.

The first of the difficulties Kant raises is straightforward and easily resolved. It concerns the question of how we can hope to be judged pleasing to God if our outward deeds, which allow inference to the disposition, are not perfected. This problem is not identical with the quandary raised by Reardon in the previous section. Rather, Kant's response indicates that this is an epistemological question, surrounding the issue of how *God* can judge our disposition to be upright if the evidence points away from this conclusion. Does God judge our disposition inductively by considering our outward deeds? Kant's answer is simply this: we will be "judged by him who scrutinizes the heart" (6:67). Even though the particular "deed is *every time* . . . defective," Kant assures us that the "*disposition* from which it derives and which transcends the senses" is what God judges (6:67). If someone has genuinely adopted the prototype's disposition, he or she "can still expect to be *generally* well-pleasing to God, at whatever point in time his existence be cut short" (6:67)—that is, despite the failings present throughout the empirical process of moral transformation.[49] Succinctly put, Kant thinks we can take comfort in the fact that God, unlike us, knows the disposition as it is, and if we have adopted the prototypical disposition, we can trust that God will judge our disposition righteous, even if our deeds have not yet achieved perfection.

Kant's second difficulty focuses on the challenges facing moral happiness, given our epistemological limitations. Since we have already isolated and addressed this difficulty above in our treatment of moral faith, we will simply move to the third difficulty in Kant's triad. Kant's analysis of the third difficulty, more than any other, draws out the specific dynamics of how a revolution of disposition satisfies divine justice and grounds moral hope—dynamics that are of particular interest to us here.

Kant summarizes the third difficulty for moral hope as follows: "[E]very human being, even after he has entered upon the path of goodness, [is] still a reprobate in the sentencing of his entire life conduct before a divine *righteousness* . . . however steadfastly a human being may have persevered in such a disposition . . . *he nevertheless started from evil*" (6:72). This evil starting point speaks of the innate, corrupt disposition that belongs to our species. The challenge this dispositional starting point presents for moral hope lies in the unfortunate reality that this original debt "is impossible for [the convert] to wipe out" (6:72). Kant gives three reasons for this impossibility. First, even if the convert perseveres in the good disposition to such a degree as to avoid incurring new debts, this is not "equivalent to his having paid off the old ones" (6:72). Second, the convert cannot produce through the "future conduct of a good life, a surplus over and above what he is under obligation to perform each time," for the convert's "duty at each instant is to do all the good in his power" (6:72). Third, dispositional evil "is not a *transmissible* liability which can be made over to somebody else. . . . [It is] the *most personal* of all liabilities, namely a debt of sins which only the culprit, not the innocent, can bear" (6:72). This dispositional debt of sin is non-transmissible, Kant explains, "because the evil is in the *disposition* and the maxims in general (in the manner of *universal principles* as contrasted with individual transgression)" (6:72).

Kant's solution to this tripartite set of difficulties has three corresponding answers that lay bare the anatomy of moral hope. Kant's answers center on (1) the resolution of infinite dispositional guilt through moral conversion itself, (2) the vicarious suffering of the prototype for finite non-dispositional guilt (or particular transgressions), and (3) the imputation of the prototype's surplus of righteousness to the convert for the securing of divine favor.

Beginning with the problem of dispositional evil, Kant notes that the moral debt resulting from such corruption is not like a financial debt or even a particular legal transgression in a human court. Financial debts are finite and transferable. Dispositional debt, by contrast, is infinite and non-transferable. Kant's talk of infinite moral debt is reminiscent of a discussion between Gottfried Leibniz and Ernst Sonner, relayed in Leibniz's *Theodicy*, which was later picked up by Lessing in his essay "Leibniz on Eternal Punishment." The discussion centered on the issue of hell and the question of its judicial proportionality relative to human guilt. Leibniz writes:

> Ernst Sonner . . . had composed a little discourse entitled: *Demonstration against the Eternity of Punishment*. It was founded on this somewhat trite principle, that there is no proportion between an infinite punishment and a finite guilt. . . . I replied that there was one thing to be considered which had escaped the late Herr Sonner: namely that it was enough to say that the duration of the guilt caused the duration of the penalty. Since the damned remained wicked they could not be withdrawn from their misery; and thus one need not, in order to justify the continuation of their sufferings, assume that sin has become of infinite weight through the infinite nature of the object offended, who is God.[50]

Notice that here Leibniz understands the enduring moral nature, or the wellspring of wickedness within the heart of the damned, to be what necessitates the eternality of hell. Leibniz sees the ongoing presence of evil and guilt in the moral nature itself to be what makes the guilt of the damned infinite—their corrupt moral nature, which is the object of divine wrath, persists throughout eternity. The evil nature can therefore pay its debt only by its final obliteration. But since this cannot happen to those in hell (assuming the immortality of the soul), their guilt is infinite.

Kant's talk of infinite guilt echoes this notion, with specific emphasis on the disposition as an unredeemable, enduring quality in moral agents. Kant suggests that the transgression that brings infinite guilt is "in the manner of *universal principles*" (6:72), that is, in the disposition itself. The disposition "brings with it an *infinity* of violations of the law," for the disposition is the supreme maxim from which all corrupt maxims and moral transgressions flow. To use Kant's words, it is "the subject of all inclinations that lead to sin" (6:74). Hence, dispositional corruption "brings with it . . . an *infinity* of guilt . . . because the evil is in the *disposition*" (6:72). As a result, "every human being," Kant concludes, "has to expect *infinite* punishment and exclusion from the Kingdom of God" (6:72). Kant, with Leibniz, maintains that a corrupt disposition or moral nature cannot pay off its moral debt with anything less than its obliteration, for this corrupt nature is the very *source* of guilt and all other transgressions. Its guilt is infinite.

Kant's solution to this infinite dispositional guilt emerges as he considers the divine judge who "knows the heart of the accused" (6:72). While it may seem that God is without judicial resources and must simply condemn the moral perpetrator, Kant suggests that God cannot mete out justice so simplistically. Such a heavy-handed solution, aside from ending humanity's moral hope and prospects for meaningful teleology, is not actually justice if the moral agent has, in fact, undergone a revolution in disposition. Kant argues that the punishment of the corrupt disposition cannot be rightly extended to the moral convert post-conversion, for the convert, in his new disposition is "a human being well-pleasing to God," even though in his former disposition he was "the subject of God's displeasure" (6:73). For Kant, an individual's moral identity is wrapped up in the disposition he possesses. If a moral convert undergoes a dispositional revolution, the convert's moral identity changes. To then execute judgment upon the convert based on his old identity would constitute injustice, not justice. Clearly, God must carry out justice in some way, thinks Kant, but the deity can no longer carry out the punishment of the "old person" after conversion, for the penalty would fall on only the "new person." Therefore, justice, in Kant's view, must move beyond a blind condemnation of the moral convert to something much more dynamic.

In Kant's careful attention to the judicial puzzle of moral conversion, we find his first step toward fleshing out the inner workings of moral hope as it relates to dispositional renewal. Kant submits that, since justice was executed "neither *before* nor *after* conversion," "the punishment must be thought as adequately executed in the situation of conversion itself" (6:73). In other words, if justice is to be rendered, but it has not been rendered pre-conversion and cannot be rendered post-conversion, then the "*punishment* whereby satisfaction is rendered to divine justice" must be found in "the very concept of moral conversion" (6:74). Kant thus turns to an examination of the dynamics of conversion in the dispositional philosophy for his solution.

In keeping with the link between one's moral identity and one's moral disposition, Kant defines moral conversion in Pauline terms as "the putting off of the old man and the putting on of the new" (6:74; Col 3:9–10). In the context of Book Two, this *putting off* refers specifically to the revolution in disposition, where the convert adopts the disposition of the prototype in place of his or her innate, corrupt disposition. Dispositional revolution is not indicative of two acts "separated by a temporal interval," says Kant, as if the convert were momentarily morally neutral; rather, this revolution is two sides of the same coin. As Kant puts it, "conversion is . . . a single act, since the abandonment of evil is possible only through the good disposition that effects the entrance into goodness, and *vice versa*" (6:74). Therefore, while the empirical character of the individual remains unchanged in moral conversion, Kant emphasizes the *moral* shift in identity that takes place at conversion: while "[p]hysically . . . still the same human being," the convert "in the sight of a divine judge . . . is *morally* another being" (6:74). The old man's identity, Kant tells us, is wrapped up in the individual's union with the corrupt disposition of the species. In the moral convert's adoption of a new disposition, the old man is put to death. The convert's new moral identity is defined by a wholly distinct disposition, and thus, "The emergence from the corrupted disposition into the good is in itself already sacrifice (as 'the death of the old man,' 'the crucifying of the flesh')" (6:74; Gal. 2:19).

To bring us back to the issue of the infinite debt of our moral nature, Kant's argument is this. The old moral nature that bears infinite guilt is not the nature of the moral convert. If the moral nature itself is what requires our exclusion from the kingdom of God, then, in abandoning the corrupt disposition of our species for the disposition of the prototype, the moral convert also abandons that which brings infinite guilt. In the process, the "old man," who bore the corrupt disposition as his moral nature, is put to death—he is no more. If, therefore, punishment requires that the man who bears a corrupt disposition be executed for his debt—since this debt cannot be paid off so long as the old man lives on—Kant sees moral conversion as satisfying this demand. The old man is not forgiven in conversion; he is put to death. The nature that bore an infinity of guilt is not the nature of the convert; the convert (morally speaking) is a new man. Punishment for the infinite dispositional debt is thereby rendered, according to Kant, at the moment of conversion with the simultaneous execution of the old person and birth of the new.

Conversion, while satisfying our infinite dispositional guilt, still leaves unaddressed the particular transgressions that arise after conversion. Yet, in Kant's emphasis on the *infinity* of guilt associated with dispositional debt, we find a way forward. Notice that Kant suggests that part of the reason dispositional guilt could not be atoned for is its *infinite* status—it stands as the source of moral failings and retains its guilt so long as it persists. Yet, in linking the infinity of guilt with the disposition itself, Kant implies that non-dispositional guilt does not carry the same infinite character. Particular moral failings, while the by-product of a corrupt disposition, do not persist throughout time. If, then, failings can occur after the dispositional revolution (which Kant's dispositional philosophy presumes is possible), these debts do not carry the *infinite* guilt of the disposition, which persists throughout time. They are *finite* debts.

If Kant indeed distinguishes between infinite dispositional guilt and the finite guilt of particular failings, we find here the possibility of a Kantian openness to the idea of atonement for finite guilt. While readers of Kant are quite familiar with his claim that moral debt "is not a *transmissible* liability," what is missed is that this claim comes in the context of Kant's discussion of dispositional guilt: "this **original debt** . . . cannot be erased by somebody else. For it is not a *transmissible* liability" (6:72, bold emphasis added). If Kant's notion of infinite guilt is reminiscent of Leibniz in the way we have suggested, then infinite guilt is not to be applied to any moral failing; it applies only to the enduring moral nature (i.e., the disposition). And since Kant links non-transferability explicitly with the original debt and its infinity, we have reason to think this non-transferability does not apply to non-original, finite debts. Therefore, it is entirely possible that Kant thinks post-conversion failings, which bring non-dispositional (and thus finite) guilt, are debts for which atonement can take place.[51]

This possibility may help explain the talk of atonement in the moments following Kant's solution to dispositional debt. As is well-known, in 6:74 Kant speaks of our disposition serving an atoning role for moral failings: "And this disposition which [the convert] has incorporated in all its purity of the Son of God—or (if we personify this idea) this very **Son of God**—bears as *vicarious substitute* the debt of sin for him, and also for all who believe (practically) in him." Interpreters of Kant often recognize that the disposition "bears as *vicarious substitute*" the debt of sin for the convert in this passage, but this language is typically taken poetically. Because God considers our inward disposition and counts this disposition as a completed righteousness, despite our distance from perfection, the disposition, it is argued, can symbolically be said to atone for our personal moral failings, bearing the pains of moral progress and conversion required by the failings of the "old man." As Palmquist writes:

> As a philosophical theologian, Kant cannot appeal to the vicarious atonement of Jesus, since it can be known only through revelation. Moreover, taken literally, Kant thinks it could be detrimental to our moral improvement. In hopes of guarding against this danger while preserving the essential meaning of the Christian doctrine, he transfers the same imagery to each individual believer. Each person must, in a moment of conversion, symbolically go to the cross and (though now morally good, due to the change in disposition) suffer a punishment on behalf of "the old man."[52]

The imagery of atonement is, on such a reading, a symbol that assures us that God will wipe out our moral debts on account of our own renewed moral resolve and suffering for righteousness' sake.

The problem with this reading is that it runs headlong into the very questions Kant is attempting to answer. The section in which Kant's talk of atonement appears begins by noting that (1) not accruing new moral debts is not equivalent to paying off old ones, and (2) we cannot produce a surplus of righteousness over and above what duty requires of us (6:72). Either in answering these two problems Kant is rejecting both of his earlier premises—our pursuit of the good does pay off old debts and produce a surplus of righteousness (see 6:75)—or he is suggesting something quite different.

If we are right in understanding the prototype as an eternal (transcendental) entity who proceeds from God's own being and is a cognized object of rational faith—not a mere symbol—and if Kant's prohibition on vicarious atonement applies only to infinite dispositional guilt, then Kant's language of vicarious atonement in this passage may refer to an actual atonement performed by the prototype. While Kant certainly identifies the disposition as that which bears debt as vicarious substitute, we should not be too quick to take Kant to be speaking poetically, as if somehow a mere change of heart in the convert atones for past sins. Notice that Kant quite clearly identifies the disposition with the entity from whom this new disposition comes, namely, the prototype: "And this disposition which [the convert] has incorporated in all its purity of the Son of God—or (if we personify this idea) this very **Son of God**" (6:74). This link becomes clear in both Kant's reference to the disposition's personification in the Son of God and Kant's emphasis on practical faith, which parallels his earlier talk of the *practical faith in the Son of God*. The disposition, Kant tells us, bears the sins of the convert, as well as the sins of those who "believe (practically) in him." The *him* in whom converts believe practically cannot refer to the hypothetical moral convert, since this would yield the absurdity that the hypothetical convert would atone for his own debts by his change in disposition, while also proceeding to atone, via his change of heart, for the debts of those who believe in "him," that is, in the convert. Instead, the one in whom converts believe practically must refer to the personified disposition to whom the convert is united. Thus, Kant is equating the disposition with its personification in the Son of God, and practical faith with the practical faith in the Son of God. The prototype is the one who atones for the moral convert and for all moral converts who display practical faith.

If the prototype is the sort of cognized entity described throughout this chapter, then it seems Kant is suggesting here a genuine vicarious atonement performed by the prototype for the finite moral guilt of moral converts. In this light, the disposition, which the convert "has made his own," provides the link between the convert and the prototype that makes possible the prototype's vicarious suffering for non-dispositional guilt, and not only the guilt of the convert, but also the non-dispositional guilt of all who believe practically in him (i.e., adopt the prototype's disposition). Moral converts are united with the prototype as a result of moral conversion—his disposition is within them. Incidentally, this link may also serve to address the issue of *how* debts are transmitted, given that Kant has already indicated in Book One some level of moral reciprocity between humanity (in a secondary-substance sense) and members of the species (in a primary-substance sense). In this union between the moral convert and the prototype, the debt of sin can be borne by the prototype, not only because this debt does not carry the same infinite character as dispositional debt, but also because the prototype is united with moral converts; his disposition now constitutes their moral nature. The prototypical atonement can, therefore, offer legitimate satisfaction: "as *savior*, he satisfies the highest justice through suffering and death, and, as *advocate*, he makes it possible for them to hope that they will appear justified before their judge" (6:75).

Atonement offers only half of Kant's equation for moral hope, however. With both infinite and finite moral debts paid, the convert, Kant suggests, still stands in need of positive righteousness before the divine judge. The convert's moral debts may be paid, but duty demands more of us than the avoidance of evil; we are under obligation to do the most good in our power at every instant (see 6:72). We might say that the moral convert is guilty of both sins of commission and sins of omission. Significant here is that Kant retains, from Book One, the notion of moral imputability between the individual and her disposition. Just as the demerits of the corrupt disposition are imputable to human individuals (see 6:21 and 31), so Kant assumes that this same imputability applies to the convert's appropriation of the prototypical disposition—only by a consciousness of such a perfect disposition within us can we hope to be well-pleasing to God. Kant suggests that the convert's adoption of the prototype's disposition enables the imputation of the prototype's positive righteousness to the convert, for the prototype's disposition, which is the wellspring of his goodness, now resides in the moral convert. Thus, the convert's adoption of this ideal disposition not only makes possible the removal of the convert's moral debt (both infinite and finite) but also allows the prototype's surplus of righteousness or "surplus over the merit from works" (6:75) to be "imputed to" the convert. This imputation provides for the convert a positive righteousness with which the deity is well-pleased and which fills in the gap, as it were, in the convert's efforts to perform perfectly her duty over the course of the moral life.

Kant's vision of moral conversion, the atoning work of the prototype, and the imputation of the prototype's righteousness to us provide the anatomy of moral hope. And in this anatomy, we are better able to grasp how Kant understands divine grace to come to humanity. Grace comes to humanity principally in the form of the availability of the prototypical disposition, without which we would be bereft of moral options. If adopted, however, this disposition provides a basis for the wiping away of guilt, which secures hope of being well-pleasing to God. Rather than Kant's suggesting that God simply chooses to forgive sin, or perhaps ignore sin, Kant's account of moral renewal offers a clear basis in the act of conversion for the payment of infinite dispositional guilt. And in distinguishing between the non-transferable infinite guilt of the disposition and the finite guilt of non-dispositional failings, Kant is able to consider the legitimate possibility of atonement for remaining finite moral debts. Our union with the prototype and Kant's notion of moral reciprocity between humans and their dispositions provides a basis for considering how the prototype may bear these finite failings on our behalf, as well as a basis for how the prototype may impute his surplus of righteousness, springing from his disposition, to moral converts with whom he is united. Grace in this scheme is not judicial fudging, but a thoroughgoing examination of the implications of a transcendental theology faced with the problem of radical evil.

7

Book Three of *Religion*

As we move into Book Three, we approach the *vision* portion of the problem-solution-vision shape of Kant's first experiment in *Religion*. Prior to analyzing this vision from the vantage point of our reading of Books One and Two, however, we should say a word regarding how interpreters typically approach Book Three. As mentioned above in chapter 3, Gordon Michalson's research on Kant began with an emphasis on Kant's notion of historical faith as a vehicle for rational religion. This emphasis represents an influential trend in the field of Kant-studies, which reads *Religion* through a Book-Three lens. The later career of Allen Wood is in many ways typical of the field in this regard. Wood avers, "The historical function of ecclesiastical faith is to serve as the *vehicle* for pure rational religion. But it is also to serve as the *shell* in which rational religion is encased and from which humanity's historical task is to free the religion of reason. . . . The plain intent here is to abolish the church's hierarchical constitution."[1] With this abolishment of the church's hierarchical constitution on the horizon of Wood's understanding of *Religion*, Kant's prototypical theology becomes less important to Kant's rational religion than the corporate struggle to realize the good principle here on earth.

The recent work of Peter Byrne and Sharon Anderson-Gold echo the sentiments of the later Wood. Their respective interpretations provide what we might term a moral-humanist approach to interpreting *Religion*. In his book *The Moral Interpretation of Religion*, Byrne emphasizes the Book-Three presentation of an ethical commonwealth as the argumentative apex of *Religion*. To juxtapose Byrne's interpretive strategy with our own, Byrne sees Book

Three not as the *vision* portion of *Religion*, but as the *solution* portion. Where we see the solution to radical evil taking place in Kant's articulation in Book Two of rational faith in the prototype, Byrne sees Kant's so-called solution to radical evil in Book Two to be controversial and wholly inadequate. The real solution in *Religion*, for him, is found in the collective moral agency of humanity in Book Three.

Citing the difficulties noted by Michalson and others, Byrne writes, "It is a key part of Kant's argument in *Religion* that the creation of the 'Kingdom of God,' which is the society of all people on earth ruled by moral laws alone, is possible only through 'a public form of obligation.'"[2] The genius of *Religion*, as Byrne sees it, is not the anatomy of moral redemption laid out in Book Two, but the meta-ethical implications of seeing the moral law (which was shown to be personally taxing to the point of despair in Books One and Two) as a *corporate* set of ethical demands that humans can strive to achieve in unison. This movement to the corporate allows Kant's moral philosophy to use the strength of civil institutions to make the quest for moral renewal more plausible. Byrne writes, "Kant's underlying thought here—surely a plausible one—is that only in and through cooperative human effort can the full human power to combat evil and pursue good be realized and enhanced."[3] In brief, Byrne finds Kant's solution to radical evil in the collective moral agency of human beings and the socio-political implications of this ethical community.

Like Byrne, Anderson-Gold argues in *Unnecessary Evil: History and Moral Progress in the Philosophy of Immanuel Kant* that collective moral agency is the key to understanding *Religion*. As she puts it:

> Kant's analysis of the conditions of enlightenment points beyond the individual and identifies the need for the development of an enlightened public. If evil is rooted in the sociocultural aspects of the human condition, it goes deeper than external institutions. External institutions are the result of sociocultural processes that must become the subject of moral improvement. By reconceptualizing the overcoming of evil as a social process, it is possible to build a bridge between Kant's ethics and his philosophy of history.[4]

Anderson-Gold theorizes that in order to overcome the conundrums created by the introduction of radical evil, Kant's philosophy of religion needs more than merely individual resolutions to pursue the good; it needs a corporate resolution in conjunction with sociocultural processes aimed at producing justice. Anderson-Gold writes, "In introducing the idea of the highest good as an object of moral volition Kant did more than simply 'make room' for happiness as a legitimate pursuit subordinated to the moral law. This notion is also ultimately social in significance."[5] Both Byrne and Anderson-Gold argue that Kant's solution to humanity's moral failings is a moral-humanism, which has as its *telos* the eroding away of historical religions in order to make room for the type of ethical society the moralists envisioned and believed unbound reason *must* ultimately produce.

The difficulty with this moral-humanistic reading of *Religion* is that it must move straight from the problem of radical evil to its solution in the pursuit of the ethical commonwealth. Kant still dribbles on his philosopher's cloak in this reading, but the stain is less pervasive, being limited to Book Two. Yet, the bypassing of Book Two is quite problematic, for as Philip Quinn points out, Kant's premises in Book One make the successful pursuit of moral goodness, on the face of it, a natural impossibility: "there is no possible world in which (i) the thesis of rigorism is true, (ii) every human adopts a morally evil supreme maxim, and (iii) some human adopts a morally good supreme maxim."[6] Quinn recognizes that insofar as radical evil establishes the corruption of humanity's moral nature and Kant's concept of our moral nature is such that this evil cannot be extirpated through human force, Kant cannot assert that individuals must, nevertheless, be capable of reversing the disposition of the species. Such an assertion, as Quinn demonstrates, would result in a formal contradiction.[7] While Kant may be justified in appealing to practical reason in the absence of theoretical resources, practical reason cannot overcome a formal contradiction. Prior to suggesting that humans must band together in pursuit of moral redemption, therefore, Kant must first establish that moral redemption is somehow possible despite the premises of Book One—a possibility that, we have argued, is explicable only as a result of Kant's prototypical theology.

If this difficulty is not enough, Kant is clear in Book Three that human communities are as corrupting on moral agents as they are redeeming. Speaking of those who have not been converted to the good, Kant writes, "[I]t suffices that they are there, that they surround [the moral convert], and that they are human beings, and they will mutually corrupt each other's moral [predisposition] and make one another evil."[8] Unless such communities consist of moral converts whose natures have *already* undergone a dispositional revolution, the banding together of humans, discussed in Book Three, will yield only further corruption, not moral progress. There exists, therefore, a logical priority in Kant's work, which requires moral conversion to occur prior to building an ethical community. While we may affirm Byrne's and Anderson-Gold's notion that the pursuit of the ethical commonwealth is an essential feature of Kant's understanding of moral hope—Kant does not think the dominion of the good principle over humanity can be established without moral communities fixed on this end—Kant's teleological vision of the ethical commonwealth cannot get off the ground, as it were, without first establishing the possibility of moral renewal and requiring this renewal of those who would join together in the pursuit of this vision.

Frederick Beiser recognizes quite clearly this logical priority in Kant's thought and how Kant's rational religion is thereby necessarily distinct from a humanist sociopolitical vision. In reference to Kant's understanding of the highest good, Beiser writes, "Kant had . . . powerful arguments against a purely secular and humanistic conception of the highest good. He was perfectly aware of such a conception and rejected it utterly."[9] Citing some of Kant's writings in the 1790s, Beiser highlights three Kantian premises (each of which we will echo in our treatment of Book Three to follow) that are particularly relevant:

> First, the individual efforts of finite human beings are not by themselves sufficient to bring about a collective result. . . . Second, Kant does not think that human beings themselves are able to completely subdue radical evil, which constantly tempts them to exempt themselves from the moral law, even when it is contrary to their conscience. . . . Third, unlike his more idealistic successors, Kant does not think that the highest good can be a political ideal, one achieved through the state. The highest good demands that happiness be given according to virtue, which involves knowledge of a person's inner disposition and motives. But such an internal realm can never fall under the jurisdiction of the state, whose laws direct and control only external actions.[10]

The bottom line, for Beiser, is that the prospects for successful human striving and the rational necessity of moral faith are reciprocally related.[11] Humanity, considered on its own merits, cannot hope to pull itself up by its moral bootstraps and attain the ideals of the moral law (collectively or individually), nor do we have the ability to scrutinize the heart, yet less to transform the innermost being of a person. "Kant's conception of both the world and humanity," argues Beiser, "was far too pessimistic for him to believe that a Promethean humanity could approach, let alone attain, the highest good."[12]

In the light of these points, we must take an approach contrary to Byrne and Anderson-Gold. In what follows, we will look at the content of Book Three as the continuation of Kant's program in Books One and Two. After establishing the corrupt nature of the human species in Book One and sketching the contours of moral redemption in Book Two, Kant moves, in Book Three, to the communal application of this moral redemption and its relationship to corporate redemption in the teleological vision of the highest good. Kant has already established in Book Two that the practical faith in the Son of God involves moral striving, but this linchpin for resolving the problem of radical evil, by itself, is incomplete. Moral converts, as mentioned in the previous chapter, still retain the capacity to fail morally, despite possessing a new disposition. Thus, while Kant's prototypical theology shows that moral renewal is possible, this possibility requires a corporate promotion of moral renewal in the form of an aiding moral community. The pursuit of moral renewal through practical faith in the Son of God within these communities ultimately becomes the concretized pursuit of the corporate redemption of humanity in the highest good. This being said, Kant is all too aware that such societies must emerge out of the well-tilled soil of the existing religious landscape, which is already littered with a variety of historical-ecclesiastical faiths. This reality leads to Kant's discussion of the ongoing relationship between historical faiths and rational religion in the pursuit of the ethical commonwealth, as well as his discussion of the role of the biblical scholar relative to the philosopher in promoting the highest good.

In our treatment of Book Three to follow, we center our examination on four main topics: the pursuit of the ethical commonwealth, or "a Kingdom of God on earth," by moral converts, the relationship between historical faith and rational religion, the role of the biblical scholar as understood by the philosopher who advocates rational religion, and the way Kant's vision affects his perspective on Christianity. We will divide our treatment of these topics into three sections. The first section focuses on 6:93–101. There, Kant emphasizes the need for moral converts to unite with one another in order to defeat the evil principle and safeguard moral hope. In banding together, converts form moral communities that, Kant maintains, must be corporately fixed on more than simply personal redemption if they are to serve their proper purpose. Such communities must work toward the common end (albeit an unattainable end in this life) of actualizing the ethical commonwealth. In making this argument, Kant names several essential characteristics of the ethical commonwealth, which make plain its teleological nature and relatedness to the highest good. One such feature is its universality. This particular feature gives way to Kant's discussion in 6:102–24 of the need for moral communities to be rooted in pure rational religion. In this discussion, Kant submits that only rational religion is a sufficient foundation for a universal church, for only a religion rooted in the universal faculty of reason can be accessible to all. But Kant also makes plain that there exists a necessary relationship between rational religion and ecclesiastical or historical faith, given the realities of human nature and the world in which we find ourselves. Kant's discussion of the relationship between pure rational religion and historical faith, including the role of the biblical scholar, is the focus of our second section. The material discussed in our opening two sections leads to Kant's case for Christianity as rational religion in 6:124–36, which is the topic of our third section. Original Christianity is, in Kant's assessment, the seminal example of rational religion. While Kant does not affirm Christendom's later ecclesial developments, he does provide his own rendition of Christianity's origin that he uses as the example par excellence of how rational religion must advance if it is to achieve its teleological ends.

The Need for and Nature of the Ethical Commonwealth

As covered in the previous chapter, Kant's dispositional philosophy faces one rather serious and heretofore unanswered question: how is it possible for those who have undergone a dispositional revolution to continue to fail morally? This problem was drawn out by Reardon, who formulates the difficulty as follows:

> Kant certainly would not have argued that conversion results in immediate virtue, in clearly recognizable "newness of life"; he is all too well aware that the reform process is gradual; and he also concedes that a man can also never be wholly sure of the genuineness or the durability of his change of heart. Thus there is bound to be moral failure, despite the recovered will to good. All the same, do not bad actions, on Kant's reckoning, proceed from *radical* evil in human nature, so that the heart is not after all regenerate?[13]

This conundrum presents itself as a serious difficulty for any account of moral hope in Kant's philosophy of religion. As Reardon notes, "The theological doctrine is not inconsistent with attributing conversion to the grace of God, and sin to the corrupt will of man. But Kant's effort to attribute both the good and the evil to one and the same human volition, which yet must adopt the maxim *either* of duty *or* of self-love, surely indicates a discrepancy in Kant's reasoning that does not admit of easy resolution."[14] Kant's moral rigorism and doctrine of conversion create a peculiar difficulty for Kant's philosophy of religion. The fact that humans who have supposedly converted to the good principle still invert the moral order of incentives presents a serious challenge to Kant's idea that a change in disposition is genuinely possible.

Quinn and others attempt to soften this difficulty by identifying the inevitable rift between the moral ideal and empirical entities. As Quinn puts it, "Since we begin from evil, the good disposition manifests itself in time as unending progress from bad to better. . . . So even if an evil person can acquire a morally good disposition . . . , it looks as if the ideal of complete moral perfection remains elusive."[15] Of course, when opting for such a solution, we run headlong into two problems. First, Kant gives indication that we can infer something about the disposition from the empirical character. Yet, if inferring the disposition's character from the empirical cannot take place with regard to conversion, why is such an inference valid in regard to depravity? Can Kant make a legitimate distinction between the two inferences? If Quinn's brand of solution is adopted, it is not clear why Kant makes this distinction or whether the distinction is valid. We may, in the end, simply be left with an inconsistency in Kant's idea of dispositional inference. Second, either Quinn's solution presumes that humans, empirically considered, can never display a character adequate to the ideal of virtue, in which case moral failings are *necessary* (as is radical evil) in the empirical realm, or his position is that a human, empirically considered, can reflect the ideal of virtue, but only *if* she *begins* with a good disposition. The former option Kant clearly rejects—both in his rejection of the necessity of evil and in his defense of the possibility of an empirical appearance of the prototype—and, in the case of the latter, Reardon's question is not answered: why does beginning from evil prevent us from reflecting an ideal disposition if the disposition that brings corruption has been abandoned?

Our interpretation offers an alternative way of addressing this difficulty. It will be remembered that we argued for reading Book One as a transcendental examination of the human species in a unified, Aristotelian sense; and, in our movement to Book Two, we contended that the prototype constitutes an uncreated divine-human implicit in the being of God, who serves as our moral prototype and teleological aim. The ideal of virtue exists within God from all eternity and parallels (transcendentally) Plato's forms. The unified humanity of Book One, by contrast, constitutes creaturely immanent form, individuated and actualized in matter. Our created species must choose its dispositional bent and has within its power the ability to actualize a disposition at some distance from its prototype. Our exercise of freedom in time indicates that such distance is, in fact, what our species has chosen. For our redemption, therefore, the prototype has come down to humanity in a type of transcendental incarnation, both presenting to us his own perfection for emulation and making his very disposition available to our species for adoption. Only by adopting this pristine disposition in faith can we hope to be found pleasing to God.

Notice that in this scheme there exist two dispositions within our species. The first is the disposition our species has chosen for itself. This disposition is corrupt and innate in every individual human—it is the moral nature of our species. The second disposition is that of the prototype. Humans ought to adopt this ideal disposition and live a life worthy of its nature. Yet, this disposition is only made *available* to us by the descent of the prototype; it lies dormant in humanity unless grabbed hold of in moral faith. When adopted, this disposition serves as the defining mark of the new person. The opening of Book Three, however, makes the startling claim that a revolution in disposition does not entail the obliteration of the old disposition's influence. Rather, the new disposition or good principle is merely dominant over the old disposition or evil principle. Kant lays the groundwork for this duality at the close of Book Two: "So the moral outcome of this conflict [between the good and the evil principle] . . . is not really the *conquering* of the evil principle—for its kingdom still endures . . . —but only the breaking up of its controlling power in holding against their will those who have so long been subject to it, now that another moral dominion . . . has been revealed to them as freedom" (6:82–83). In conversion, the new disposition gains "the upper hand over the evil principle" (6:73), says Kant, but both the good and evil dispositions continue to reside in humanity, per the transcendental narrative of corruption and redemption in Books One and Two. We might say that insofar as moral converts remain *human*, they cannot completely separate themselves from the evil principle; they can only supplant its rule by adopting the prototype's divine disposition. But in the end, Kant holds that, even after conversion, "the good and evil principles . . . [are] two equally self-subsisting transient causes affecting men" (6:11). Thus, the moral convert must continually engage in the subduing of evil, actively exercising the practical faith in the Son of God.

Book Three opens by highlighting this conflict between good and evil within the moral convert. Kant describes this inner conflict in battle-like terms: "every morally well-disposed human being must withstand in this life, under the leadership of the good principle, against the attacks of the evil principle . . . and assert his freedom, which is constantly under attack" (6:93). Kant tells us that the moral convert bears the responsibility of undoing the threat of evil. But how can he fulfill this duty? This question sets the tone for Book Three: "[The convert] is *bound* at least to apply as much force as he can muster in order to extricate himself from [the evil principle]. But how? That is the question."[16] The importance of this question is tied directly to Kant's vision for the sustaining of moral hope. If faith in the prototype grounds hope and is practically worked out in the throwing off of evil, Kant's argument must answer the question of how the moral convert is to "remain forever armed for battle" (6:93). This is, of course, a different question than the one raised by the moral-humanist reading of *Religion*. In our reading of the opening of Book Three, individual converts gain the upper hand over the evil principle in their adoption of the prototypical disposition, not by a collective good will. The question of Book Three is, therefore, one that oscillates between personal assurance of moral conversion (which remains hidden in the convert's disposition) and readiness to stay the course in the face of the convert's necessary fellowship with depraved humanity.

As Kant engages this question of how we must "arm ourselves," he submits that an examination of "the causes and the circumstances that draw [the convert] into this danger" indicates that the tendency to moral regress does not come "from [the convert's] own raw nature" (6:93). Rather, Kant suggests that "malignant inclinations . . . assail [the convert's] nature, which on its own is undemanding, *as soon as he is among other human beings*" (6:94). Kant essentially argues that since the good principle has already bettered the evil principle within the moral convert, the threat of evil must be an external threat, one that arises not from the subdued evil within, but from the influence of those without in whom the evil principle is still dominant. Kant has already established in Book One that all individuals bear a corrupt disposition as innate; hence, he thinks it inevitable that humans (prior to conversion) will display the character of their species and have a corrupting influence on one another. Moral stifling, and even regress, is simply the inevitable result of the convert's being a part of humanity in association with humanity: "[I]t suffices that they are there, that they surround [the convert], and that they are human beings, and they will mutually corrupt each other's moral [predisposition] and make one another evil" (6:94).

Kant's solution to this contextual moral challenge involves the establishment of "a union which has for its end the prevention of this evil and the promotion of the good" (6:94). This union is envisioned by Kant as "an enduring and ever expanding society, solely designed for the preservation of morality by counteracting evil with united forces" (6:94). In other words, in order to combat moral degeneration and persevere in the good, the moral convert must unite with other moral converts. Without such a communal effort, the convert will be ill-equipped to persevere in the good; and, more importantly, the final establishment of the good principle's dominion over humanity generally will be impossible. As Kant notes, "If no means could be found to establish a union which has for its end the prevention of this evil and the promotion of the good in the human being . . . however much the individual human being might do to escape from the dominion of this evil, he would still be held in incessant danger of relapsing into it" (6:94). Only with such a union of moral converts, Kant tells us, "can we hope for a victory of the good principle over the evil one," and without it, "the dominion of the good principle is not otherwise attainable" (6:94). What we see here is that, while Kant offers his prototypical theology as that which makes available a new disposition and makes possible moral renewal, Kant is clear that such individual moral renewal has little chance of stability without the communal aid of other moral converts.

The need for communal aid brings Kant to his vision of moral communities that press toward what he calls the "ethical commonwealth," and this, in turn, makes plain the relationship between personal redemption in the prototypical theology and corporate renewal in the instantiation of the highest good. As Kant explains the moral convert's need for moral community, it becomes clear that Kant thinks the type of community the moral convert is in need of is one that reflects, on a small scale, the ideal society envisioned in the highest good. Hence, Kant sets out to explicate the nature of the ethical commonwealth in order to make plain the teleological ideal that particular moral communities must pursue in their promotion of moral renewal. Kant presents some basic definitions, which set the stage for how he thinks the ethical commonwealth must be envisioned. First, Kant distinguishes between what he calls the *state of nature* and the *civil state*. The state of nature is a type of private self-governing, wherein "each individual prescribes the law to himself" (6:95). This private governance contrasts with the civil state, where "laws are public" (6:94). Next, Kant distinguishes between the *ethical* and the *juridical*. The ethical is a heading for humans ruled by the laws of virtue. Such laws are non-coercive—those ruled by them choose to be ruled by them—while the juridical involves laws "which are all coercive laws" (6:95). Under these definitions, Kant's definition of the *ethico-civil* (or ethical community) naturally follows: the ethical community is an association of non-coerced human beings united under the laws of virtue, which are made public. Kant's entire vision for the ethical commonwealth expands from this basic definition.

Kant sets out three main features that define the ethical commonwealth. First, we find that individuals, all of whom begin in an ethical state of nature, cannot be forced to enter into an ethical civil state by any ruling power. By definition, one cannot be *coerced* into an ethical civil state since it is built on *non-coercive* laws. Or, as Kant puts it, "it would be a contradiction (*in adjecto*) for the political community to compel its citizens to enter into an ethical community, since the latter entails freedom from coercion in its very concept" (6:95). The ethical commonwealth, therefore, must be a community composed of individuals who are united under the good principle without coercion.

Second, Kant argues that, "since the duties of virtue concern the entire human race, the concept of an ethical community always refers to the ideal of a totality of human beings" (6:96). Kant draws a link between the universal duties of humanity and the universal call for all to adopt the prototypical disposition over and against the evil principle. In light of the universality of this call, individual ethical societies can never constitute the ethical commonwealth proper. Each particular society is only part of a greater whole, striving toward a common end, to wit, the realization of the ethical commonwealth and the highest good. This common end, along with the societies' sharing of a unifying principle (viz., the good principle), makes them only part of a greater whole. The ethical commonwealth is this greater whole and must therefore comprise the totality of all particular ethical societies: "each partial society is only a representation [of an absolute ethical whole]" (6:96).

Third, we find that the ethical commonwealth, as a union of individuals under a common principle, is rightly called a kingdom. Here, there is a movement in Kant's thinking from individual efforts to organize particular societies that promote the practical faith in the Son of God to a presiding authority over the ethical commonwealth proper. This movement ultimately leads to Kant's identification of the ethical commonwealth with the people of God. Such a designation is based on the need for organized unity and moral governance in this ideal community. The ethical commonwealth, Kant submits, "will need the presupposition of . . . a higher moral being through whose universal organization the forces of single individuals . . . are united for a common effect" (6:98). Kant suggests in 6:99 that such universal organization demands a public lawgiver with three essential characteristics: this lawgiver must be able to (1) institute laws as part of a "prior sanction," as opposed to an arbitrary extension of his will, (2) know "the most intimate parts of the dispositions of each and everyone"—that is, know the inward disposition—and (3) be able to "give to each according to the worth of his actions," or exercise true justice. Such characteristics, in Kant's estimation, are found in only one being: "this is the concept of God." Therefore, Kant contends that the ethical commonwealth "is conceivable only . . . as a *people of God . . . in accordance with the laws of virtue*" (6:99).

This threefold picture of the ethical commonwealth is an ideal Kant admits is "never fully attainable" in this life. It stands as the central component of the philosophical representation of the highest good; and, as such, the teleological pursuit of the ethical commonwealth represents a unique duty in two senses. First, unlike most human duties, instantiating the ethical commonwealth is a duty of the species, not the individual. As Kant states in 6:97, "For every species of rational beings is objectively . . . destined to a common end, namely the promotion of the highest good as a good common to all." The fulfillment of this duty cannot come about by individual effort; it requires "a union . . . into a whole toward that very end" (6:97–98). Second, Kant thinks it evident that, even with the fervent efforts of particular moral societies, we cannot presume human power is sufficient to bring about this ideal end—a nuance that shows this duty to differ "from all others in kind and in principle" (6:98). The highest good is something that moral converts, as a redeemed people of God united under the good principle, must work toward; but the establishment of such an ideal community is ultimately teleological and outside human power.

Given this gap between (redeemed) humanity's corporate abilities and the ideals of the highest good, Kant submits (in keeping with his talk in other writings about the highest good) that the convert must move forward in faith, believing that God is the one who will ultimately establish the ethical commonwealth on earth. This is not to say that the convert has license to be idle regarding the ethical commonwealth's formation, letting each "go after his private moral affairs and entrust to a higher wisdom the whole concern of the human race" (6:100–101). To the contrary, each person must, in Kant's view, "conduct himself as if everything depended on him" (6:101)—that is, as if establishing the ethical commonwealth were both her personal responsibility and within her power to actualize. Only when pursuing this end with such tenacity does Kant think the moral convert is justified in hoping God "will provide the fulfillment of his well-intentioned effort" (6:101), namely, the eventual formation of the ethical commonwealth.

Beiser recognizes the rather strong emphasis on providence in Kant's talk of the highest good, arguing that Kant is far too sober-minded to think the coming of such an ideal kingdom is within the power of corrupt humanity—or, for that matter, even redeemed humanity. The highest good for the human race requires more than individual effort; it requires divine grace and providence on a corporate and historical scale, working in and through the collective efforts of redeemed individuals to bring about this end. Beiser puts it thus:

> So, in the end, the highest good is indeed a goal of human striving, but the problem is that it cannot be approached, still less achieved, through human effort alone. What we also need, Kant believes, is that fundamental Christian virtue: hope, or faith in divine grace and providence. We can believe that all our efforts to create a better world will come to something. Kant argues, only if we also assume that there is a divine providence that has so organized nature and history that finite human efforts constantly progress toward their ultimate ideal. Without this faith all the labors of Prometheus will be no better than those of Sisyphus.[17]

Therefore, while the duty to form the ethical community belongs to the species, Kant maintains that humans, individually and corporately, must cling to the hope that God himself will bring into being the ethical commonwealth.

With this teleological ideal before us, we are better able to grasp the interplay between Kant's prototypical theology and the teleological vision of the ethical commonwealth in the highest good. As we have seen, Kant's prototypical theology makes possible moral renewal; and this renewal, in turn, allows for the formation of moral communities with a supporting—rather than corrupting—influence on the moral convert's pursuit of practical faith in the Son of God. In making such communities possible, there is a sense in which the birth pains of the ethical commonwealth are already felt. While particular moral communities cannot themselves form the ethical commonwealth, they do, nevertheless, begin to concretize some of the essential characteristics of the ethical commonwealth: their members are willful, non-coerced subjects under the laws of virtue, who are universally united with one another by the good principle and, as such, form a people of God. But these particular moral communities are at some remove from the ideal kingdom envisioned in the highest good. In order to fulfill their purpose for humanity in general and moral converts in particular, these communities (and the converts within these communities) must fix their sights on the corporate duty of instantiating the teleological ideal of the ethical commonwealth, trusting that providence will honor these efforts by one day actualizing the highest good.

Notice that, unlike in the moral-humanist reading of Book Three, Kant's vision, as presented here, does not allow us to see Kant's commendation of faith in providence as identical with personal renewal through practical faith in the Son of God. The moral community in view throughout Book Three is the union of already redeemed humans under God and the prototype, striving to realize the ideals of the moral law. But this moral community is not possible (nor is its pursuit of the ethical commonwealth) without the prototypical redemption, which offers to the individual genuine moral renewal. Having said this, Kant's vision does not allow for a sharp division between personal renewal and the highest good. Individual redemption and the pursuit of corporate redemption are mutually dependent upon one another. Without redeemed humanity, the moral societies that pursue the ethical commonwealth are not possible, and without the communities that corporately pursue the ethical commonwealth, the moral convert cannot secure a stable moral hope. Kant, therefore, creates a dynamic interplay between personal and corporate redemption. There exists a bilateral relationship between the individual's moral hope through practical faith in the Son of God and the *telos* of the species in the vision of the highest good. In the end, however, Kant's vision will not permit the conflating of personal renewal in this life with the teleological renewal of humanity in the philosophical vision of the highest good. This relationship is dynamic. Practical faith in the Son of God solves the problem of radical evil and makes moral community possible, while pursuit of the ethical commonwealth through the banding together of converts reciprocally stabilizes the process of moral renewal.

Ecclesiastical Faith as the Vehicle of Pure Religious Faith

Kant's vision of the ethical commonwealth is clearly intended to be a religious vision. This intent is evident both in Kant's emphasis on the future members of the ethical commonwealth being moral converts united under the good principle and in his emphasis on the headship of God over the ethical commonwealth. Yet, Kant is not so optimistic as to think that the insights of rational religion can simply level the religious playing field, replacing all world religions with purely moralistic societies in pursuit of the highest good. Even if the doctrines of radical evil and prototypical theology are practically defensible and Kant's vision of the ethical commonwealth follows accordingly, this vision of religion within the boundaries of mere reason must deal with the realities of the religious landscape in which we find ourselves.

In Section Four of Book Three, Kant therefore moves into his discussion of the distinction between and the interplay of ecclesiastical faith and rational religion. His treatment of this topic is an extension of his discussion of the moral community needed to aid the moral convert. Kant suggests that the idea of a moral community united as a people of God can be realized only in the form of a church. But in order for a church to play the role discussed in our previous section, it must be grounded in what Kant calls "pure religious faith" (6:102). By *pure religious faith*, he means a faith rooted in reason and the moral law. Only the content of such a faith can, according to Kant, be "convincingly communicated to everyone" (6:103)—its content is rational and accessible to all with the faculties of reason. Historical faith, by contrast, requires that humans have access to records of contingent, historical events (viz., the purported revelatory happenings on which they are built), and this historical faith can only be tested through an examination of its historical credibility. This universal-versus-contingent distinction is what Kant sees as the primary difference between pure religious faith and pure historical faith. Given Kant's Enlightenment concern for that which is rational and universally valid, Kant takes pure religious faith to have a natural priority over historical faith. Says Kant: "So if the question How does God wish to be honored? is to be answered in a way that is universally valid for every human being, *each considered simply as a human being,* there is no second thought that the legislation of his will might not be simply *moral.* For a statutory legislation (which presupposes a revelation) can be regarded only as contingent" (6:104). The universality of pure religious faith is significant because the ethical commonwealth and its relationship to the highest good concerns the entire human species. Establishing the ethical commonwealth is a universal duty, Kant insists. Therefore, only a *universal* church (i.e., one built on pure religious faith accessible to all) can validly serve humanity in the quest for the ethical commonwealth.

Despite his confidence in the universal validity and communicability of pure religious faith, Kant does not feel that such a faith can establish a community and be successfully propagated without the help of a historical faith—a point recognized by readers such as Michalson. "To a great extent, the bulk of Book Three of *Religion* is," according to Michalson, "Kant's account of how his ideal ethical commonwealth is achieved by means of—and only by means of—the historical church."[18] The problem, as Kant identifies it, is that "due to a peculiar weakness of human nature, pure faith can never be relied on as much as it deserves, that is, to found a Church on it alone" (6:103). Kant recognizes that the religious landscape of this world has established itself for good reason. It speaks to a certain felt need in humanity. Therefore, while pure religious faith may be sufficiently universal in content, it is insufficient, given the realities of our world, for propagation unless coupled with a historical faith.

Kant discusses this "peculiar weakness" that bids an ecclesial precursor to rational religion in the context of what he calls "religion of *divine service*" (6:103). In Kant's assessment, "a morally good life is all that God requires . . . to be his well-pleasing subjects in his Kingdom" (6:103). Humanity's moral obligations are revealed in reason, and these obligations are what concern the divine judge in Kant's world. Nevertheless, Kant thinks it clear that humans, for whatever reason, tend to feel that simply being moral is somehow insufficient to please God—perhaps because we universally fail to fulfill our moral duty or because we model God on human rulers, who need to be flattered. As a result, humans often feel a need to pay homage to God in ways analogous to homage paid to earthly rulers. Such acts of service, Kant tells us, go beyond the requirements of duty—not in terms of difficulty, of course, but in the sense that they unnecessarily expand the list of what is required of humanity by God. These non-moral rituals, which humans imagine "they must perform for God," are the basis for what Kant calls "religion of *divine service*" (6:103).

This inclination to perform deeds undefined by moral reason is what Kant sees as the driving force behind the search for divine revelation and is what gives to purported revelatory texts their weight of authority. Reason testifies only to our moral duty, presumes Kant. If, therefore, we deem the fulfillment of duty inadequate to please God, we must turn to something other than reason for instruction. Revelation is required. Hence, there emerges a sea of historical faiths, built on accounts of supposed revelatory happenings meant to address the question: what does God require of us? Given humanity's inclination toward such "revelatory accounts," Kant contends that in order to establish itself, rational religion must come to terms with humanity's felt need for revelation of what God requires. In this context we find Kant's idea that the natural relationship between historical faith and rational religion is one wherein historical faith serves as a vehicle for rational religion.

The relationship between ecclesiastical faith and rational religion that Kant sets up is such that "ecclesiastical faith naturally precedes pure religious faith" (6:106). This idea of a natural ecclesial precursor brings us to a difficulty noted by Michalson, which we dubbed "the Unnecessary Necessity Paradox." Michalson finds a paradox in Kant's Book Three vision insofar as Kant maintains that rational religion is self-sufficient, universal, and alone necessary to humanity's religious life, while historical faiths are contingent and unnecessary to humanity's religious life. Yet, in the end, Kant seems to indicate that rational religion could not thrive without the empirical counterpart. That is, Kant seems to make rational religion, which is necessary and self-sufficient, contingent upon historical faith for its survival and propagation.

It should be noted that Michalson's objection, when looked at in context, is actually a fallacy of false identification, centering around two different kinds of *necessity*. The necessity of rational religion—that is, its universality and self-sufficiency—is a rational necessity. The *truths* of rational religion are not contingent on historical happenings; thus, rational religion is universally accessible insofar as its doctrines are necessary truths of reason. By contrast, when talking about the necessity of a historical-faith vehicle, Kant is discussing a pragmatic need regarding the dissemination of rational religion, given the realities of this world and the human condition. There exists a weakness in corrupt humanity that creates the need for a historical-faith vehicle, but this weakness is a *contingent* weakness, arising out of humanity's contingent corruption. The *need* for a historical faith is a subjectively felt need, resulting from a common human inclination to feel direct service to God is needed in order to be pleasing to God. From a purely rational perspective, then, only rational religion is necessary for moral hope—it supplies all that is necessary to be well-pleasing to God—while from a pragmatic perspective of dissemination, rational religion must come to grips with humanity's search for revelation, and in this pragmatic sense, historical faith is a necessary vehicle, first step, or catalyst for the spread of rational religion; it does not add anything to our moral duty before God.

In this light, we may say the need for a historical-faith vehicle is the result of radical evil. Corrupt humans under the evil principle are naturally unable to perform their duty before God. While practical reason offers hope of moral renewal and restores moral freedom, humans in their weakness tend to look outside the stringent demands of the moral realm (which are no less stringent when it comes to moral conversion) and seek means of securing divine favor that are less difficult to perform. Thus, rather than striving after moral conversion, humans tend to search for a revelation that makes plain what non-moral services one might do for God directly in order to make up for our moral inadequacies. This tendency, argues Kant, is the weakness in corrupt humanity that rational religion must overcome if it is to establish a universal church in the present religious landscape. Insofar as radical evil is not the necessary condition of our species, there are possible worlds in which neither this weakness nor the need for a historical-faith vehicle exists. But, given the realities in which we find ourselves, rational religion must begin with the ecclesial precursor as its vehicle to reach corrupt humanity—a vehicle that would be unnecessary had our species chosen at its inception to mirror its moral prototype.

All this takes us some distance toward answering the Unnecessary Necessity Paradox, but one dimension of the question still remains: does Kant think that without historical faith, rational religion could not emerge or be established among humanity in this world? Or, put another way, if no historical faith vehicle were available, would rational religion be incapable of disseminating its doctrines? This particular question, we believe, is best addressed in the context of Book Four. Thus, we will delay our response to this issue until the next chapter. For now, suffice it to say, Kant's schematic of the relationship between rational religion and historical faith is simply intended to be more a sober judgment of human weakness than an abrupt admixture of historical doctrine and rational religion.

Now, given our understanding of the link between humanity's affinity for religion of divine service and the quest for divine revelation, we can better understand why Kant sees holy books principally as "a revelation to present and future generations" (6:107) of what God requires. Despite Kant's pessimistic outlook on the origin of holy books, he does not deem all purported revelations to be without value. Instead, Kant suggests that purported revelation has a significant value for rational religion, and in the context of Book Three this value regards the usefulness of sacred texts in disseminating rational religion. (In Book Four the possibility of rational religion gaining insight from a purported revelation is explored, but this prospect is far afield from Kant's concerns here in Book Three.) Kant in Book Three finds that such "revelation" has intrinsic value for the propagation of pure religious faith, given its implicit authority in addressing the peculiar weakness of humanity: "A holy book commands the greatest respect even among those . . . who do not read it" (6:107), quips Kant; and again, "no subtle argument can stand up to the knockdown pronouncement, *Thus it is written*" (6:107). Kant finds this authoritative voice within ecclesiastical faith quite useful to the goals of pure religious faith, given the weakness that hinders its propagation. Here, Kant uses his well-known metaphor of a "vehicle" to explain this usefulness: "a statutory *ecclesiastical faith* is added," says Kant, "to the pure faith of religion as its vehicle and means for the public union of human beings promoting it" (6:106). Since a religious faith, based on an authoritative text, has an inalienable authority all its own (at least in human eyes), the faith and its sacred text is able to command authority among those who are otherwise uncompelled by the authority of practical reason. If, therefore, such texts can be made to carry the moral doctrines, they would constitute an effective vehicle for transporting pure religious faith to corrupt humanity. Hence, for Kant, the best holy book is one that contains the "purest moral doctrine of religion" (6:107), for such a book would satisfy the (corrupt) human affinities for a revelation, while also affirming the moral doctrines of practical reason.

We begin to see here an important interplay between ecclesiastical faith or "revealed faith," which is diverse in its manifestations, and rational religion, which, Kant maintains, yields an exclusive set of moral doctrines. According to Kant, there are many different revealed faiths, but only one religion. Two passages are much-discussed and noteworthy on this point. Firstly, we have 6:107–108:

> There is only *one* (true) *religion*; but there can be several kinds of *faith.*—We can say, further, that in the various churches divided from one another because of the difference in their kinds of faith, one and the same true religion can nevertheless be met with. It is therefore more appropriate (as it is in fact more customary) to say: This human being is of this (Jewish, Mohammedan, Christian, Catholic, Lutheran) *faith,* than: He is of this or that religion.

Kant claims that various revealed faiths can meet with the "one and the same true religion." When this claim is coupled with Kant's metaphor of a vehicle in 6:106 and again in 6:115, confusion can—and often does—ensue over what exactly he means. Kant's clearest use of the vehicle metaphor comes in 6:115: "Thus, even though (in accordance with the unavoidable limitation of human reason) a historical faith attaches itself to pure religion as its vehicle, yet, if there is consciousness that this faith is merely such and if, as the faith of a church, it carries a principle for continually coming closer to pure religious faith until finally we can dispense with the vehicle, the church in question can always be taken as the *true* one." Judaism, Islam, and Christianity do not, in Kant's view, represent disparate religions, but disparate faiths. To Kant's mind, only one true religion exists, namely, the religion of reason, but the world is filled with a diversity of faiths, each of which may be a vehicle for the one true religion.

There are two ways one can read Kant on this point, given the language in these and related passages. First, Kant's use of the vehicular metaphor in reference to historical religions could serve as evidence for his affirmation of religious pluralism. In reading Kant this way, one would follow Michalson's conclusion: "Thus, the correct way to appreciate the historical dimensions of Kant's rational faith is to inquire into the moral core which he seems to think is present in all faiths, given the universality of practical reason."[19] Ronald Green and others develop this notion into a fully worked out philosophy of religion. Since all faiths contain the seed of rational religion, one should be able to find within their inner workings the pure religion of reason. This approach not only serves as a basis for religious tolerance but also makes Kant's philosophy useful to practitioners of comparative religion who want to uncover the common moral core of the diverse spectrum of world religions. Green develops this so-called Kantian strategy in his second book on Kant's *Religion*, entitled *Religion and Moral Reason*: "My aim is to show that religion has its basis in a process of moral and religious reasoning common to all human beings. I term this process 'religious reasoning,' and I believe it constitutes a 'deep structure' of thought underlying historical religious traditions."[20] Conclusions and applications such as these are somewhat oversimplistic, however, given Kant's careful nuances in such matters.

The second way one could understand Kant on this point, which we maintain is truer to Kant's intent, is that any historical faith is a candidate for the historical-faith vehicle, but not all historical faiths necessarily serve this function. In other words, if a historical faith is to become a historical-faith vehicle, then it must be so utilized by rational religion. Kant is careful not to assert that all faiths *are* vehicles for religion, but only that all faiths *can* meet with the one true religion and serve as its vehicle. Although we will reserve our lengthy examination of Kant's comments on Judaism for the next section, worth noting here is that Kant rejects outright the idea that pre-Christian Judaism contains the truths of rational religion (see 6:125). It would seem a mischaracterization of Kant's thought, therefore, to read him as espousing a naïve form of religious pluralism. Kant does not take it to be true prima facie that any given historical faith *is* a vehicle for rational religion. On the contrary, each faith must be tested regarding the extent to which it "harmonizes with the universal practical rules of a pure religion of reason" (6:110). If it fails this test, Kant holds that the given faith must be transformed into something that rises to the level of rational religion. But if it passes this test, it will either be an example of rational religion in its current form or be in need of some level of purification so as to better manifest its rational essence.

In the case of faiths in need of transformation and faiths in need of purification, universal principles of morality are, for Kant, the supreme interpreters. A revealed faith must be morally reinterpreted, bringing its texts and doctrines in line with the universal principles of reason if it is to be made a vehicle for rational religion. Kant acknowledges that such a reinterpretation may lead to a forced reading of the specific faith's sacred text, but this is neither new—this is, according to Kant, "how all types of faith . . . have always been treated, . . . teachers . . . kept on interpreting them until, gradually, they brought them . . . in agreement with the universal principles of moral faith" (6:110–11)—nor should it be troubling. To Kant's mind, the particular historical meaning is distinct from that which "is to make better human beings"; and since the historical meaning "contributes nothing to this end," Kant thinks "one can do with [the historical] what one wills" (6:111).

Kant offers a number of historic examples of religious reinterpretations in defense of his point. He writes:

> [The moral philosophers among the Greeks and, later, among the Romans] knew . . . how to interpret even the coarsest polytheism as just a symbolic representation of the properties of the one divine being; and how to invest all sorts of depraved actions, and even the wild yet beautiful fancies of their

poets, with a mystical meaning that brought popular faith (which it would never have been advisable to destroy, for the result might perhaps have been an atheism even more dangerous to the state) close to a moral doctrine intelligible to all human beings and alone beneficial. Late Judaism, and Christianity too, consist of such in part highly forced interpretations, yet, [in] both [instances], directed to ends undoubtedly good and necessary to every human being. The Mohammedans know very well (as Reland shows) how to inject a spiritual meaning in the description of their paradise, other-wise dedicated to every sensuality, and the Indians do the same with the interpretation of their *Vedas*, at least for the more enlightened part of their people.—That this, however, can be done without ever and again greatly offending against the literal meaning of the popular faith is due to the fact that, long before this faith, the predisposition to moral religion lay hidden in human reason.[21]

Three points are noteworthy about this passage. First, we see that Kant views the inclination to reinterpret historical faiths morally as a natural tendency in faiths that develop and mature, given the innateness of the moral doctrines in human reason (not necessarily in the faith itself). We might say this is the complement to our natural human weakness: while we naturally seek non-moral ways to please God, as we develop morally and religiously, the pure moral doctrines more readily rise to the surface. Second, Kant gives indication that the renovation, as opposed to demolition, of existing faiths is important in that a complete deconstruction of a popular faith could lead to skepticism and ultimately atheism, thereby making such deconstruction a hindrance rather than a help to rational religion. Third, when coupling what we see in this passage with Kant's later comments on Christianity (comments we will explore in detail in the next section), it becomes apparent that Kant thinks numerous faiths have been and continue to reinterpret themselves so as to move closer to a moral faith, but ultimately Kant will argue that Christianity at its founding is the example par excellence of rational religion; it is the faith that, at its incep-tion, most fully balanced the pure moral doctrines with the historical faith vehicle.[22]

From these three points, we can gather a clearer picture of Kant's view of providence in humanity's religious development. Kant's understanding of God's providential hand in actualizing the ethical commonwealth is not en-tirely unlike what we find in G. W. F. Hegel. Seeds of truth can be found littered throughout the current religious landscape, and even glimpses of re-ligious progress and growth can be found as humans seek to nurture these seeds into something more via "spiritual interpretations" of holy books or monotheistic interpretations of polytheism. Humanity's religious history shows signs of upward mobility. But, as we will see in the next section, Christianity at its founding is, for Kant, the "consummate religion," to use Hegel's phrase.[23] The great difference between Kant and Hegel on this point, however, is Kant's sober coupling of human responsibility with the providential thrust of this vision. Unlike Hegel's objective idealism, which understands humanity's religious development to move upward necessarily, given the dialectical relationship between God and world, Kant's vision of humanity's religious momentum emphasizes personal responsibility, and thus cannot presume that our religious development will be necessarily upward—hence Kant's emphasis on *original* Christianity as opposed to Christianity after its robust ecclesial developments, which Kant sees as degenerative. Kant's vision of humanity's religious momentum is not necessarily upward—hence Kant's emphasis on *original* Christianity as opposed to Christianity after its robust ecclesial developments, which Kant sees as degenerative.[24] Kant's sober emphasis on converts' personal responsibility in the forming of the ethical commonwealth is precisely why we see Kant flesh out the anatomy of religious progress in the interplay of historical faith and rational religion. This interplay essentially becomes an explication of the providential method of religious progress, as it were, which is laid bare so that moral converts may be properly equipped to join this process of religious progress and corporate renewal. Moral converts must proceed as if the ushering in of the ethical commonwealth depended entirely on them.

As Kant develops his understanding of how moral converts and communities may aid in the birthing of rational religion (and eventually the ethical commonwealth), his emphasis on the historical-faith vehicle, or, more specifically, the sacred-text vehicle, moves into a discussion of the role biblical scholars must play in this transformative process. The human demand for sacred scripture naturally gives rise to the additional demand for scriptural scholars—that is, those who examine the origin, language, and historicity of the sacred "to preserve the authority of a church based on holy Scripture" (6:112). Such scholarship, Kant points out, draws on resources inaccessible to laypersons (e.g., ancient languages) and pulls from the text "the understanding of the church community" (6:113). These official doctrinal interpretations are what contain the true authority of the purported revelation, for they constitute the authoritative reading of the sacred text and the official understanding of the church. When this doctrine-forming aspect of the scriptural scholar's role in the faith community is coupled with Kant's distinction between faiths and religion, we find the meeting place of the rational and the historical.

According to Kant, only "the *religion of reason* and *scholarship*" (6:114) constitute legitimate expositors of scripture. That is to say, the former, what Kant calls "*authentic*," represents the sure moral content commended by reason and expounded by the philosopher, while the latter, what Kant calls "*doctrinal*," represents the authoritative doctrine pulled from the text by the scriptural scholar. When combined toward a common end, the goal is "the transformation of the ecclesiastical faith for a given people at a given time into a definite and self-maintaining system" (6:114). Put otherwise, Kant's vision for the scriptural scholar is one in which she draws from the sacred text the pure moral doctrines and presents them to the community as the understanding of the church. Essentially, Kant hopes for an awakening in the biblical scholar, in which she realizes the natural human inclination to reinterpret historical faith morally—an inclination already present in her interpretive work. And, in this realization, Kant hopes the biblical scholar will embrace her role as official (re)interpreter of her particular sacred text, thereby progressing with the self-aware intention of drawing out the pure moral doctrines for the sake of moving the faith's members from weakness to pure religious faith. The community will then be able to embrace rational religion, even if still subject to the common human weakness for revealed religion, since rational religion now comes to them via the sacred text. For this reason, "the authority of Scripture," in Kant's assessment, is "the worthiest and . . . only instrument of union of all human beings into one church" (6:112).

This notion of utilizing biblical revelation in the propagation of rational religion brings us back to a difficulty noted by Michalson, which we called "the Hermeneutic Circularity Crisis." Michalson essentially argues that Kant's hermeneutic in Book Three creates a vicious circularity. Presuming something akin to the *Religion*-as-Translation approach, Michalson assumes that Kant is here speaking about the type of hermeneutic he employs in his translation experiment throughout *Religion*. Such a hermeneutic, according to Michalson, casts suspicion on *Religion* as a whole because Kant is not really *testing* Christianity; he is presuming Christianity to contain rational religion and forcing its sacred text to assert rational religion, even when it does not. Here, the distinction between the *Religion*-as-Translation reading of Kant's two experiments and the understanding we have been arguing for is quite helpful. On our reading, Kant establishes within Book Three the relationship desired by the philosopher between the biblical scholar and rational religion. His concern is how moral communities are best formed, given the current religious landscape, and how they are best able to assist in the coming of the kingdom of God or ethical commonwealth. Contrary to the entailments of the *Religion*-as-Translation thesis, Kant has yet to engage Christianity directly in our reading—the second experiment does not come until Book Four. Kant's own experiments, discussed in the Second Preface, are something quite different than what is in view in Book Three. Moreover, unlike Michalson, we have argued that Kant does not presume all religions are rational; and therefore, Kant's philosophy of religion quite readily allows for the second experiment to conclude that Christianity is not naturally conformable to rational religion—even though this is not Kant's final conclusion. If Kant's second experiment were to fail and Christianity were shown to be at odds with the sphere of pure moral doctrine, the transformation of Christianity via the aforementioned hermeneutic would be the job of Christian biblical scholars, not the Kantian philosopher.

While this nuance in Book Three may help address a potential logical difficulty internal to Book Three, a word should be said regarding the general palatability of Kant's vision here. Likely, many readers will think Kant's suggestion that biblical scholars should use their position to manipulate sacred texts is offensive insofar as it condones and even encourages an ethically questionable practice. Some may think it outright immoral to use a trusted office to move individuals from one belief-set (viz., the belief-set of whatever historical faith to which they hold) to another belief-set (viz., the belief-set of rational religion) without these individuals being made aware of this transaction. Kant's apparent methodology here may be construed either as a moral failure on his part or as simply the result of an elitist tendency—part of the dark side of Kant's Enlightenment heritage. In either case, if such questionable tactics are required for the establishment of rational religion, it would seem we are morally obligated to resist striving after the establishment of rational religion.

This difficulty, to our minds, is far more serious than Michalson's concern over hermeneutic circularity, especially for those quite happy with revealed religion over and against Kant's "rational religion." While, in the end, there may be no vindicating Kant's vision of transforming members of various historical faiths into thoroughgoing Kantians, two points are worth noting that may help alleviate the potential offense of Kant's proposed strategy here. First, Kant presumes that revelation, if genuine, must reveal something rational. Kant is willing to concede that revelation could tell us mysteries that are "above" reason, so to speak, but the only things we are obliged before God to heed (even within a genuine revelation) are its rational truths, which are testable and accessible to all via reason.[25] In this light, while the religiously minded may object to Kant's suggested hermeneutic to the extent that it runs the danger of emasculating or significantly altering a genuine revelation, Kant's conviction is that, while he cannot know whether a given text is divine revelation, the faculties of reason are a sure test of purported revelation. The surety of the test is rooted not in the ability of reason to assess whether some purported revelation actually is revelation but in its ability to test whether the purported revelation conflicts with reason and is thereby clearly *not* revelation (see, e.g., 28:1118). Put another way, we may say that Kant intends to let the sure revelation of reason test and correct, if needed, those purported revelations of whose genuineness we cannot be sure. Kant's conviction, however, is that if a given text actually is genuine revelation, no correction will be needed (except, perhaps, where it has been corrupted); it will already accord with reason. And, in this light, Kant sees his suggested hermeneutic for the biblical scholar not as the gagging of God but as the human side of the providential movement toward the ethical commonwealth and the highest good.

Second, Kant does not offer a unilateral relationship between "revelation" and reason. Kant notes in Book Four the possibility that revelation may awaken in reason something that it had not yet come to on its own (see 6:155). We will not here develop this point (we will wait for our direct treatment of Book Four in the next chapter), but for now suffice it to say that Kant has more than merely a reason-over-revelation hermeneutic. In Kant's estimate, reason certainly has the more sure footing, but he does intend a reason-in-dialogue-with-revelation relationship (both in practice and in the academy), which has built into it the possibility of a purported revelation awakening or correcting something in the philosopher. Such awakening would, of course, be an awakening of things "human beings *could and ought to have* arrived at . . . on their own through the mere use of reason" (6:155)—that is, it would awaken something rational—but such would be an awakening nevertheless. These points are likely inadequate to make Kant's hermeneutic desirable to faithful adherents of revealed religion, but given Kant's assumptions, his hermeneutic is neither surprising nor as anti-theistic, or even anti-revelation, as it may seem on first blush.

Now, our treatment of Kant's vision for the propagation of rational religion would not be complete if we did not discuss the content of pure moral doctrine as presented in Book Three. For Kant, pure moral doctrine clearly includes the moral philosophy of the second *Critique* and *Groundwork*, but we submit that pure moral doctrine, as Kant presents it, also includes the doctrines of dispositional corruption and redemption in Books One and Two of *Religion*. As argued in chapter 4, Kant's first experiment, announced in the Second Preface, is not a reference to the religion of the second *Critique*. Kant's explication of rational religious faith in the first experiment refers specifically to Books One, Two, and Three of *Religion*. Throughout Book Three, therefore, we find indications that Kant's prototypical theology is an integral part of the rational religion to be propagated. Kant's emphasis on saving faith in 6:116 is a good example. "Saving faith holds two conditions for its hope of blessedness," Kant tells us. The first condition is the hope of "reparation of guilt, redemption, reconciliation before God," or the "the lawful undoing (before a judge) of actions done"; the second is the hope of conversion to "a new life conformable to its duty" or "faith in the ability to become well-pleasing to God in a future good conduct of life." Saving faith, as a solution to radical evil, finds its footing nowhere else than in the prototypical theology of Book Two. Thus, as Kant puts it in 6:119, "The living faith in the prototype of a humanity well-pleasing to God (the Son of God) refers, *in itself*, to a moral idea of reason," making the prototypical theology both the condition of true saving faith and part of the pure moral doctrines to be propagated in the vision of Book Three.

This clarification is useful for understanding Kant's vision for reinterpreting historical faith. Kant's focus in the reinterpreting process is not on a simple replacement of history with morality; instead, his focus is on the role sacred history can play in *awakening* and *establishing* rational faith.[26] When using faith in the prototype as an example, Kant makes clear that one can legitimately be awakened to the prototype of reason by a purported historical manifestation of the prototype (e.g., Jesus of Nazareth). According to Kant, whether one is awakened to the prototype by reason or by history, both means of awakening can set one on the path of pure moral faith. The question is not one of the means of awakening but of the object of faith. Certainly, if one makes the historical manifestation *the condition* for faith (e.g., you must believe in the historical Jesus to be saved), this would no longer be a universal faith in the prototype of reason, but faith in a contingent history to which not all humans have access. Such a contingent faith would, for Kant, be distinct from rational faith. If, however, the empirical manifestation is believed to be a revelatory means of awakening something rational—namely, the prototype already embedded in reason—then, for Kant, there is no rift between this faith and the faith of reason; both look to the same prototype for hope. Kant summarizes this point in 6:119:

> The living faith in the prototype . . . refers . . . to a moral idea of reason . . . By contrast, faith in this very same prototype according to its appearance . . . is not, as empirical . . . one and the same as the principle of a good life conduct (which must be totally rational); and it would therefore be something quite different to wish to start with such a faith and derive a good life conduct from it. . . . However, in the appearance of the God-man the true object of the saving faith is not what in the God-man falls to the senses, or can be cognized through experience, but the prototype lying in our reason which we put in him (since from what can be gathered from his example, the God-man is found to conform to the prototype), and such a faith is all the same as the principle of a good life conduct. Hence we do not have two principles here that differ in themselves, so that to start from the one or the other would be to enter on opposite paths, but only one and the same practical idea from which we proceed.

This nuance in Kant's thinking serves to illuminate two often-missed features of *Religion*. First, the rational religion Kant seeks to propagate must possess the full spectrum of moral doctrines, including Kant's dispositional philosophy in *Religion*. Rational religion is not mere moralism. Second, Kant will admit that we can believe that a certain person (e.g., Jesus) is the prototype made manifest. However, Kant submits that in order for our religious faith to remain rational in such a case, we must maintain a certain priority of belief: the rational narrative of redemption must be the place where we find hope, and only then may we believe rationally that the corresponding history is the manifestation of this redemption. For Kant, we cannot make redemption contingent on a particular history that itself is contingent and inaccessible to all persons. If the hope of redemption is truly rational, it must be accessible to all who possess the faculties of reason.[27]

Here we see that Kant's vision for rational religion in Book Three, when preceded by the reading of Books One and Two offered in the previous two chapters, looks significantly different than what we see in interpreters such as Michalson. Rather than a strictly moralistic society in which ecclesiastical faiths are done away with, the vision of rational religion glimpsed above retains much of the appearance of revealed religion. Kant retains the notion of a church, both particular and universal, as well as the headship of God and providential guidance of this community. Kant also retains the presence of scripture and of scriptural scholars who expound the pure moral features of the venerated text for communities that sit under this revelatory authority. Kant, in addition to seeing glimmers of progress in humanity's religious development—specifically in those instances of moral reinterpretations of religious doctrine—opposes the complete disbandment of historical faiths, realizing that this could lead to skepticism and even atheism. He therefore does not oppose belief in historical-religious figures or events that may support rational belief, so long as the rational ground takes priority. And as we transition to our next section, we will see that, for Kant, original Christianity represents a rational religion that has already latched hold of a historical-faith vehicle and then done away with that vehicle, leaving in its place a rational religion. If such is an accurate reading of Kant's perspective on Christianity, Kant sees original Christianity—with its sacred text and its emphasis on dispositional corruption, prototypical redemption, and moral renewal—as the seminal example of rational religion.

The Rational Merits of Christianity

On one level, Kant's understanding of the history of religion is quite pessimistic. He holds that the various "revelatory" histories in the array of historical faiths are not unified; and insofar as they are based on contingent events, they never can be unified. On another level, however, there is hope for religious unity, a sense that humanity is progressing morally, and faith that the hand of providence is positively involved in this groping after moral religion. The pendulum does not swing toward naïve optimism, however. Two or more histories can find unity, according to Kant, only if restricted "to that portion of the human race in which the predisposition to the unity of the universal church has already been brought close to its development" (6:124)—that is, if restricted to true moral converts. Religious unity is reserved, in Kant's view, for those who share a commitment to the good principle and pure religious faith. Without the universal guiding light of pure religious faith and a unifying principle, the church would be in a constant state of war and forever prone to schism. Kant is therefore not concerned with disparate, contingent histories, but only with tracing the lineage of the "true church"—that is, the church in which pure religious faith and the good principle were present at its founding. For this reason, Kant's work in Division Two of Book Three focuses on that church "which from the beginning bore within it the germ and the principles of the objective unity of the true and *universal* religious faith" (6:125). To Kant's mind, Christianity in its original form is that church.

Before looking at Kant's comments regarding original Christianity, we should first note that his discussion of Christianity in the context of Book Three does not yet mark Kant's official turn to the second experiment. As noted in chapter 4, Kant makes plain this transition in 6:156–57 of Book Four. His remarks about original Christianity in Book Three come in the context of his suggested method for propagating rational religion. While Kant tips his hand in Book Three regarding his final posture toward the Christian religion, indicating that the focus of Christian doctrine fits well the concerns of rational religion, his case in Book Three centers more directly on how he understands the origin of Christianity. More specifically, Kant's interest in Book Three is on the relationship between pre-Christian Judaism and the birth of Christianity since, in Kant's assessment, this relationship epitomizes the vehicle motif he commends in the propagation of rational religion.

Kant's case for marking the origin of the true church with the birth of Christianity begins with his claiming that pre-Christian Judaism does not naturally contain the seed of rational religion. In Kant's view, Judaism only "provided the physical occasion for the founding of this church (the Christian)" (6:125). Kant asserts rather forcefully that "[s]trictly speaking Judaism is not a religion at all" (6:125)—a declaration built on Kant's distinction between faiths and religion. In support of this rather bold assessment, Kant highlights the emphasis in Judaism on ceremonial laws, political solidarity, and blood descent, and suggests that its moral laws were merely "*appended* to it . . . [and] do not in anyway belong to Judaism as such" (6:125). In Kant's version of Judaism, the Hebraic laws are ritualistic, are concerned with external conduct rather than the disposition, and, far from being universal, are exclusivist and ruled by a God hostile to all other peoples. Kant's rather uncharitable portrait of the Jewish faith should not be taken as anti-Semitic rhetoric. Rather, this characterization is part of a broader claim on Kant's part regarding pre-Christian faiths in general. In Kant's account, these non-rational, ritualistic features are not unique to pre-Christian Judaism. Quite the contrary, Kant avers, the "doctrine of faith [of other ancient religions] equally tended in this direction" (6:127). Kant's indictment of Judaism is therefore part of a broader judgment that all pre-Christian religions naturally lack the seed of universal religion in their doctrinal and ceremonial emphases.

In showing (or attempting to show) pre-Christian religions to be void of rational religion, Kant brings additional clarity to his earlier claim that any faith can be a vehicle for rational religion. To Kant's mind, although there are many candidates for a historical faith that might precede pure religious faith, only those candidates to which rational religion actually latches on serve as its vehicle—a point we discussed in the previous section. In the latter portions of Book Three, original Christianity is identified by Kant as unique, insofar as its rational elements emerge, not through later reinterpretations—the way Kant characterized the burgeoning rational elements of non-Christian faiths in 6:111—but as part of its very constitution. Christianity, at its inception, was a rational religion, in Kant's view, not a historical-faith vehicle. It contained the pure moral doctrines—presumably including the doctrines of dispositional corruption and prototypical redemption—and it proceeded from the mouth of its teacher explicitly with a view to pointing humanity to these doctrines over against religion of divine service. Kant sees the rationality of Christianity as something that was clouded as the religion advanced, but he thinks rational religion is undeniably present in Christianity's original form as found in the teachings of Jesus—teachings Kant will look at more closely in Book Four in his turn to the second experiment. Moreover, this original form, as Kant understands it, was propagated via the use of an existing historical-faith vehicle (viz., pre-Christian Judaism). And this feature is what Kant finds most interesting in Book Three.

As Kant tells the story, Christianity laid hold of Judaism as its vehicle and then dispensed with it. Christianity sought, for the sake of human weakness, to draw a link between itself and the Jewish faith, but it replaced Jewish law with a concern for the disposition (both its corruption and its redemption), earthly concerns with the afterlife (or immortality), and ritualistic concerns with freedom from the ceremonial law. Thus, "the new faith . . . was to contain a religion valid for the world" (6:127). The New Testament emphasis on Christ as the fulfillment of the Law—a fulfillment that thereby makes ceremonial practices obsolete—is, according to Kant, a transformative reinterpretation of Judaism on the part of Christ and his followers, not a natural trajectory of the Jewish faith. For these reasons, Kant thinks, "[w]e cannot, therefore, begin the universal history of the Church . . . anywhere but from the origin of Christianity" (6:127). Christianity in its original form is seen by Kant as the example par excellence of rational religion, which not only introduced the pure moral doctrines in their most explicit form but did so by latching hold of a historical faith and using it as its vehicle. Kant's account of the origin of Christianity is thus intended to provide a tangible illustration of the reinterpretation of ecclesiastical faith into a pure religion that Kant commends.[28]

All this is not to say that, for Kant, Christianity in all its forms constitutes rational religion or that this pristine origin went untainted as Christianity developed. Kant does not endorse Christianity's later ecclesial advances, its exclusivity, or its form as he knew it. Instead, Kant admits that Christianity often demands the exaltation of its historical elements, making them a condition for faith, and in so doing, Christianity distinguishes itself from rational religion. Kant writes, "[T]o this teaching there are nonetheless added in a holy book miracles and mysteries, and the propagation of these is itself a miracle requiring historical faith" (6:129). Moreover, Kant acknowledges that the often pervasive Christian emphasis on that which is only historically verifiable (e.g., miracles), in combination with the various blemishes in Christian history (e.g., strife, division, persecution, hierarchies, etc.), would seem to indicate that Christianity is not a pure religion at all but a historical, dogmatic faith.

    In the face of this potential objection, Kant emphasizes that it was "a learned public from whom the history of the political events of the time has been transmitted to us" (6:130). Here, Kant has in mind the Romans, and his point is that their records do not recognize or focus on the religious revolution that was original Christianity, but on only the political results of this revolution. According to Kant, it is only "later, after more than one generation" that the Romans investigated Christianity's nature (but not its origin). We do not, therefore, have a record of the moral nature of Christianity's adherents until after "Christianity developed a learned public of its own" (6:130). Based solely on its political history, Kant admits there is nothing to commend Christianity as true religion—and there may only be evidence to the contrary. Nevertheless, Kant contends that when considering the religious origin of Christianity, "the fact still clearly enough shine[s] forth from its founding. . . . Christianity's true first purpose was none other than the introduction of a pure religious faith, over which there can be no dissension of opinions" (6:131).

8
Book Four of *Religion*

To this point, Kant's arguments throughout *Religion* have been focused on matters of natural or rational religion. In understanding Kant's Book One examination of the human species as a transcendental examination of how we must cognize humanity's moral nature or disposition, we offered an interpretation of Kant's arguments very different from the ones presented under the *Religion*-as-Translation and *Religion*-as-Symbol theses. Additionally, we found that by reading Kant's discussion of the prototype as a continuation of his dispositional philosophy, which moves into the resources available in transcendental theology for sustaining moral hope, Kant's prototypical theology becomes a remarkably significant extension of his philosophy of religion rather than a reinterpretation of the Christ story of Christianity. Kant's discussion of the ethical commonwealth likewise takes on a slightly different form when the pursuit of this community is understood as a communal aid in promoting the moral convert's exercise of practical faith in the Son of God. We saw how Kant's engagement of historical faith takes on a pragmatic significance toward this end, given his sober estimate of the human condition under the dominion of radical evil. Rational religion must address the weakness of humanity that gives way to religions of divine service if it is to establish itself amid the current religious landscape, and Christianity, as Kant relays its origin, exemplifies ideally his suggested strategy.

While Kant certainly engages matters of historical faith in *Religion* prior to Book Four, the material of Books One, Two, and Three makes the most sense if we understand it as a matter of pure philosophy of religion. Without the lenses of translation or symbol, Kant's dispositional philosophy and discussion of *faiths* versus *religion* represents a complex interplay between Kant's transcendental theology and his understanding of how rational religion establishes itself among corrupt humanity. In moving into Book Four, we reach the threshold of Kant's much-awaited second experiment. Book Four is where Kant applies his understanding of rational religion, based on his philosophy of religion in Books One, Two, and Three, to one particular historical faith, namely, New Testament Christianity. Book Four therefore offers perhaps the greatest insight into how Kant understands his philosophy of religion to affect the religious landscape of our world.

Despite its obvious importance within our interpretation, Book Four remains the least studied Book of *Religion*. The reasons behind this state of affairs revolve primarily around four points. Firstly, Kant's numerous distinctions within the opening of Book Four are generally thought to be coherent relative to the content of Books One, Two, and Three. Quite a few interpreters mention one or more examples of these philosophical distinctions, but few criticize them as a source of conundrums.[1] Secondly, traditional interpreters such as Allen Wood, Nicholas Wolterstorff, and Gordon Michalson, among others, almost never mention this part of Kant's work (except for the distinctions made in its early pages), and the book has therefore generated little scholarly discussion. Thirdly, Book Four, as a stand-alone contribution to Kant's philosophy of religion, appears to chasten Christianity robustly via its attacks on "priestcraft" (*Pfaffentum*) and counterfeit service to God. For this reason, it seems to fit well with the standard account of Kant as the metaphysical "all-destroyer," which has caused theologically minded interpreters to shy away from this portion of *Religion*. The fourth and most telling reason why Book Four is often overshadowed by the preceding books, however, is that *Religion* is often approached in the field of Kant-studies as a single experiment. When *Religion* is read in this way, Book Four is simply metaphysical overkill. Kant goes after Christianity in an effort, not to conduct his second experiment and find ways of purifying what was once the pure religion of reason, but to decimate its historical components.

When we approach *Religion* as a work containing both Kant's first and second experiments, however, Book Four takes on a greater level of significance for Kant's philosophical program, as well as for discerning its intended impact on philosophical and theological discussions of the day. Since this portion of *Religion* is often ignored, so much so that we find a surprising dearth of conundrums raised so as to challenge its coherence, we have some freedom to explore its historical context in this chapter. We will, therefore, take the opportunity in this chapter to look at Book Four as an extension of our interpretation of the previous three books, focusing less on reorienting the reader's understanding of the book and more on a few of Kant's more significant distinctions and their relationship to debates of the day that may help further illuminate Kant's purposes and vision in *Religion*.

This chapter is divided into three sections. In the first section, we will explore Kant's much-debated distinction between the naturalist, supernaturalist, rationalist, and pure rationalist. We will offer a rereading of this insertion in Part One of Book Four with a view to recasting how these distinctions are typically understood and where Kant's own position lies. After addressing this perennial problem in Kant's philosophy of religion, we turn in our second section to Kant's second experiment. Here, we find Kant examining Christianity from two angles: the angle of natural religion and the angle of a learned religion. This dual perspective on Christianity makes way for the reaffirmation of Kant's claim in Book Three that original Christianity is in fact a rational religion. But, to the extent that Kant's examination is of original Christianity and he distinguishes between *religion* and *faiths*, his claim here does not allow the Christian religion to sit comfortably in the seat of rational religion without continual self-examination. Rather, Kant thinks that even with the birth of rational religion corruption can arise. Thus, we will look in our third and final section at Kant's discussion of priestcraft and counterfeit service of God, highlighting those things that Kant thinks hinder the rational core of Christianity and threaten to hurl it back to the state of a historical faith. In addressing these remaining issues we will bring to a close our understanding of Kant's two experiments and present the final evidence in our defense of Kant's *Religion*.

Kant on Revelation and Rationalism

In the opening of Book Four, Kant reiterates a number of points discussed in the previous three books of *Religion*, and then, in Part One of Book Four, he gives indication that he is turning to his second experiment. Therein, he holds up the transcendental theology of Books One, Two, and Three as the test of a particular historical faith, namely, New Testament Christianity. Between Kant's reiteration of what has been established and his turn to the second experiment, however, he discusses four stances on the relationship between revelation and religion: (1) naturalism, (2) rationalism, (3) pure rationalism, and (4) supernaturalism. Kant is typically thought to define each of these positions roughly as follows: The naturalist is one who rejects all revelation out of hand and adheres only to the religion of reason. The rationalist also holds to the religion of reason, but, unlike the naturalist, cannot dismiss revelation as impossible. A supernaturalist moves most decidedly toward "revelation," embracing it as necessary in matters of faith and the only reliable source of religion. The pure rationalist allows for and even embraces revelation but does not view any purported revelation as universally necessary in matters of faith for all people of all times.

This fourfold set of distinctions raises two questions: (1) Why does Kant introduce these distinctions? (2) Which position represents Kant's own stance on the matter? Within the field of Kant-studies, discussion has centered on the second question and done so with little success. Disagreement exists over which of these positions is Kant's own, for as Wood notes, "Kant is a trifle coy about exactly where he stands."[2] Kant's rejection of naturalism and supernaturalism is evident enough to most interpreters. Thus, the dispute in Kant-studies is typically over whether Kant holds to rationalism or pure rationalism. More theologically affirmative interpreters tend to read Kant as a pure rationalist, seeing this position as more nuanced and conducive to Kant's lingering Christian commitments. More traditional readers, however, see pure rationalism as no less suspect from a Kantian vantage point than naturalism or supernaturalism and, therefore, read Kant as a rationalist. The interpretations of Allen Wood and John Hare are good examples of these divergent interpretative trends.

As discussed in chapter 2, the later Wood finds that Kant's philosophy leaves no legitimate room for the embrace of revelation. Wood sees Kant's transcendental theology as deistic in thrust and points out, "Essential to any deism is the view that there is such a thing as rational or natural religion, religion based on natural reason and not on supernatural revelation."[3] On Wood's reading of Kant, rational religion is not only possible but sufficient; there is no need for supernatural insight into our duties toward God. "Kant is emphatic," argues Wood, "that there need not be any special duties to God in order for there to be religion . . . What does seem requisite to religion is that (1) we have duties, (2) we have a concept of God, and (3) we are capable of regarding our duties as something God wills us to do."[4] All rational beings who "use their reason honestly" can engage in legitimate religious expression, doing the will of God and pleasing him by adhering to the moral law.[5]

Under such a reading of Kant, Wood suggests that we must understand the "pure rationalist" as follows: "[Pure rationalism] apparently takes the position that God has given us certain commands supernaturally while denying that we are morally bound to carry them out."[6] Said differently, Kant presumes that only the tenets of rational religion constitute humanity's universal religious duty. If, therefore, the pure rationalist affirms this premise but admits the possibility of additional revealed commands, his position must be that such revelatory commands are possible but do not obligate anyone—they cannot be known a priori or even be known to be revelation. The idea that we may have commands revealed to us that add to our natural, moral obligations is, Wood argues, (1) suspect as lending itself to the type of anthropomorphic view of God that Kant unabashedly criticizes in his critique of religions of divine service, and (2) reducible to absurdity, given that the pure rationalist must see these non-moral, revealed commands as non-obligatory obligations. Wood thinks it self-evident that this is not Kant's position. In the end, Kant's inclusion of pure rationalism as a soft middle ground between naturalism and supernaturalism must, according to Wood, represent Kant's way of rhetorically "cushioning his evident denial of pure supernaturalism" from the Prussian censors.[7] Hence, "Kant is plainly a rationalist because he is simply an agnostic about supernatural revelation."[8]

John Hare's rendition of 6:153–55 differs dramatically from Wood's. Like Wood, Hare recognizes Kant's siding with natural religion over revealed religion and, again like Wood, Hare sees supernaturalism as synonymous with a purely revealed, historical religion. Therefore, "Kant is, in the terms of this passage, a rationalist (and is therefore committed to denying pure supernaturalism)."[9] Moreover, Hare recognizes, as does Wood, Kant's rejection of naturalism, since its rejection of the very possibility of revelation "transcends the limits of human insight just as supernaturalism does."[10] Yet, unlike Wood, Hare thinks it quite evident that Kant's endorsement falls to pure rationalism.

Hare gives three main reasons for taking Kant to be an affirmer of pure rationalism. Hare writes, "The first question to ask is why Kant should have introduced the category of pure rationalist at all. . . . The second reason is that the term 'pure rationalist' is the sort of phrase we should expect Kant to use as honorific. . . . Third, Kant sees special revelation as a 'vehicle' in God's dealings with human beings."[11] For Hare, Kant's program in *Religion* and positive casting of the pure rationalist indicate that pure rationalism is more than a proxy. Kant himself is best described as a pure rationalist, argues Hare, because such a one "accepts special revelation but nevertheless does not think that its acceptance is without qualification necessary to religion."[12] Even though the definition of the rationalist seems broadly in keeping with Kant's rejection of naturalism and supernaturalism, Hare argues that the designation of *pure rationalist* is simply a better fit for Kant and makes the most sense of the text as it stands.

Michel Despland offers an assessment of this passage similar to that of Hare. Says Despland: "In keeping with his general solution to the problem of the parerga Kant eliminated the positions of rationalism and naturalism which both deny that reason could have a moral interest in such 'supernatural' conceptions. There remain only the claims of the pure rationalist and those of the pure supernaturalist. The solution for Kant is to be found with the pure rationalist."[13] Despland sees Kant's refusal to deny the possibility of revelation as moving counter, not only to naturalism, but also to any form of rationalism that makes the possibility of revelation a superfluous possibility, one that, while possible, may as well be impossible. Thus, the only two possible positions that remain regarding revelation are the pure rationalist and the supernaturalist. Kant clearly thinks natural religion is possible; and therefore, if the supernaturalist is the prototypical Barthian, who says *Nein!* to all natural religion, the scales must tip, for Kant, toward pure rationalism.

Of course, as noted in chapter 2, even if Hare (and Despland) are right in Kant's affirmation of pure rationalism, Wood raises a very good question surrounding the relevance of such a position. Since Kant thinks that reason sufficiently reveals the will of God, the pure rationalist must maintain, argues

Wood, "that God has given us certain commands supernaturally while denying that we are morally bound to carry them out."[14] Such a position seems
pedantic and superfluous, if not outright absurd, to Wood. Even if Hare is right
in attributing a more charitable reading of pure rationalism to Kant's project
and applying this rendering of pure rationalism to *Religion,* Wood's assessment—to wit, that the pure rationalist position draws its additions from the
tenets of revealed religion (tenets no one is obligated to heed)—still stands as a
noteworthy criticism. Kant may be justified in holding this position since there
is nothing internally inconsistent about the view, but the position would be
curious to say the least.

When looking at Part One of Book Four in a way akin to what is assumed
in the aforementioned dialogue in Kant-studies, it is certainly difficult to adjudicate the discussion. Much of Kant's corpus, thinks the later Wood, displays deistic leanings that would make the concession of pure rationalism odd.
Yet, Hare is right to note that features of Kant's *Religion,* under a certain
reading, point in this direction. In the dialogue as it stands, all agree that
Kant rejects the naturalist position. As he states in his "Lectures on Religion,"
"no human being can hold it impossible that . . . God might have given to
it, in a higher revelation, certain truths" (28:1119). Thus, any position that
would dismiss out of hand the very possibility of revelation is necessarily a non-
option for Kant. Moreover, if the supernaturalist is rightly understood as
one who rejects the religion of reason in favor of a purely revealed, historical
faith, Kant cannot embrace this position either. Thus, the dispute would
rightly be said to regard whether Kant affirms the pure rationalist or the
rationalist.

There may, however, be another way forward in this debate that, to our
knowledge, has yet to be explored and that, we believe, serves not only to bring
clarity to Kant's stance on the issue, but also to shed light on why he raises the
issue in his transition to the second experiment. This alternative approach is to
take three of Kant's titles (viz., naturalism, pure rationalism, and supernaturalism) as three subheadings or available options underneath the main heading,
rationalism. According to this understanding, Kant begins by introducing the
broad distinction between revealed religion and natural religion; he then
identifies the *rationalist,* broadly conceived, as one who holds that natural
religion is alone morally necessary and then provides three positions on the
role (or lack thereof) of revelation relative to the instantiation of natural
religion that are available to the rationalist: (1) he may deny the very possibility
of revelation and be called a *naturalist;* (2) he may allow for the possibility of
revelation in the instantiation of true religion, but suggest that it is not required
for religion, and be called a *pure rationalist;* or (3) he may hold that natural
religion is in need of revelation for its awakening and establishment and be
called a *supernaturalist.* To clarify this third option, it may be that the supernaturalist is one who holds that religious truths are rational and a priori in

principle, but they require the catalyst of a historical revelation in order to awaken, lest they continually lie dormant within human reason. Hence, the supernaturalist would differ from adherents of a purely revealed religion that opposes natural religion insofar as the supernaturalist affirms natural religion, but believes natural religion requires revelation for its awakening, fleshing out, and establishment among humanity.

On such a read, naturalism, pure rationalism, and supernaturalism each represents a rationalist position. Each holds that duty, not revealed acts of divine service, is sufficiently pleasing to God. And each maintains that natural religion is possible, given that the truths of reason are a priori. They differ only with regard to their stance on the role revelation plays (or does not play) in the instantiation and establishment of true religion.

In support of such a reading, we may note the contrast between the matter-of-fact way Kant introduces the rationalist and the conditional way he introduces the three stances on revelation. In regard to the rationalist, Kant simply asserts, "Anyone who declares natural religion as alone morally necessary . . . can also be called *rationalist*" (6:154). Yet, Kant switches to the conditional when discussing the following three subheadings.[15] Kant writes: "**If he** denies the reality of any supernatural divine revelation, he is called *naturalist*; **should he,** however, allow this revelation, yet claim that to take cognizance of it and accept it as actual is not necessarily required for religion, then he can be named *pure rationalist*; but, **if he** holds that faith in divine revelation is necessary to universal religion, then he can be called pure *supernaturalist* in matters of faith" (6:154–55; bold emphasis added). Certainly, this can be read as providing three additional categories, but the shift to the conditional may indicate that the personal pronoun "he" (*er*) is not meant to play the same role as the indefinite pronoun "anyone" (*welcher*), in the previous sentence. Instead, "he" may be intended to refer back to the rationalist broadly conceived by providing three subsets of rationalism available to "him" (i.e., the rationalist).

There are two textual points that speak in favor of understanding the shift to the conditional in this way. First, the naturalist, the pure rationalist, and the supernaturalist are identified and distinguished from one another by their disparate stances on the possibility and subsequent role of revelation in the instantiation of true religion. The rationalist, however, is not defined relative to this issue. The rationalist is identified only as one who holds to natural religion as opposed to revealed religion—that is, as opposed to the religion of service. But the rationalist's stance on the role revelation may or may not play in the instantiation of true religion is not specified. This seems to indicate that the rationalist should not be lumped in with the positions to follow, becoming one of *four* stances on the role of revelation in the instantiation of true religion, but should be set apart as a main heading under which the following *three* positions fall.

The second bit of textual evidence in favor of this reading can be found in the paragraph that follows. There, Kant submits that the rationalist "must of his own accord hold himself within the limits of human insight" (6:155). Given this requirement, Kant dismisses outright the naturalist position, suggesting that to deny the very possibility of revelation cannot be done within the limits of human insight: "Hence [the rationalist] will never deny in the manner of a naturalist . . . the intrinsic possibility of revelation" (6:155). While this denial of naturalism is not surprising, Kant goes on to make plain that the rationalist will also not deny the supernaturalist's claim that revelation is needed to introduce true religion. As Kant puts it, "[N]or will [the rationalist] ever contest the intrinsic possibility of revelation in general or the necessity of a revelation as a divine means for the introduction of true religion; for no human being can determine anything through reason regarding these matters" (6:155). Since the rationalist will not deny the possibility or necessity of revelation for the introduction of true religion, the rationalist has available to her the road either of pure rationalism or of supernaturalism. As Kant notes, "The point of dispute can therefore concern only the reciprocal claims of the pure rationalist and the supernaturalist in matters of faith, or what either accepts as necessary and sufficient, or only as accidental, to the one and only true religion" (6:155).

When reading the passage in this way, the point of dispute Kant seems to have in mind is one raised by G. E. Lessing.[16] Written in response to Johann Heinrich Ress's *The Historical Resurrection of Jesus Christ,* which attacks the historical "proofs" for Christianity, Lessing's *A Rejoinder* argues that Christianity does not rest on its historically contingent proofs (e.g., miracles or even the accuracy of its historical record). Rather, Christianity is a faith with a rational core, and its historical dimensions are mere scaffolding for the erecting of its grand rational system. Assuming this perspective on Christianity, Lessing attacks historically rooted critiques of the Christian faith, submitting:

> How strange that people are so rarely satisfied with what they have before them!—The religion which triumphed over the pagan and Jewish religions through the message of the risen Christ is *there*. And are we to suppose that this message was not credible enough at the time when it triumphed? Am I to believe that it was not considered credible enough then, because I can no longer prove its complete credibility now?[17]

Lessing argues that miracles and historical testimony were the mere means of establishing Christianity's rational core. Historical "facts" are an unsure foundation for metaphysics, concedes Lessing, but this should not be a concern to the Christian faith, for Christianity does not hang on historical "facts"; it hangs on reason.[18]

In keeping with this conviction, Lessing would claim that Christianity's existence is not dependent upon its historical occurrences at all. As Lessing puts it, "The Christian religion could exist even if the Bible were to become entirely lost, if it had long ago been entirely lost, if it had never existed." This claim would ignite his dispute with Goeze in Lessing's *Necessary Answer to a Very Unncessary Question of Herr Haupt-Pastor Goeze in Hamburg* and the *Anti-Goeze* writings to follow. This statement seems to indicate Lessing's own inclination to think that the core of the Christian religion (a core Lessing thought to be summed up in the *regula fidei* of the patristic writers) is fully rational, embedded in reason, and bound to emerge regardless of whether any revelatory events had intervened in humanity's religious progress and search for rational insight.

In 1777, Lessing published the first fifty-three sections of *The Education of the Human Race*. Lessing compares revelation to the process of education, where what the individual is taught is not something irrational, but something rational and embedded in reason (much like mathematics). The teaching process merely aids in drawing out truths already in reason, but it does so in a quicker manner. Lessing writes: "Education gives man nothing which he could not also get from within himself; it gives him that which he could get from within himself, only quicker and more easily. In the same way too, revelation gives nothing to the human race which human reason could not arrive at on its own; only it has given, and still gives to it, the most important of these things sooner."[19]

Lessing would later publish the remaining forty-seven sections, which offer a slightly revised stance on the relationship between revelation and reason. Lessing writes in the later-added §77 the following: "And why should not we too, by means of a religion whose historical truth, if you will, looks dubious, be led in a similar way to closer and better conceptions of the divine Being, of our own nature, of our relation to God, which human reason would never have reached on its own?"[20] Notice that in §4, Lessing presents revelation as drawing out truths of reason in a fashion that is far more efficient than natural reasoning would yield on its own. Yet, in §77, Lessing gives indication that the human race would not have come to these insights at all without the revelatory catalyst.

Clearly it is difficult to discern Lessing's own position. He rarely writes in a systematic fashion, and his debates are often prone to rhetoric that changes depending on whom he is attacking—defenders of historically rooted Christian apologetics clash swords with the rationalist Lessing, while skeptics who attack Christianity on the unreliability of its historical accounts meet with the rebuke of Lessing as defender of Christianity, the supremely rational religion. Yet, we see here two opposing positions on revelation that presume, nevertheless, the same grounding premise. In Lessing's earlier claim, we find the contention that Christianity would emerge whether the revelatory catalyst had emerged or not, while in his latter work, especially §77, we find the claim that the revelation was needed for the emerging insight. Both positions assume natural religion and even presume that the Christian religion is rooted in natural religion. The difference between the positions is the question of whether the truths of Christianity would ever have been discovered by reason, despite their innate presence there, without the catalyst of revelation. According to the latter position, the answer is No, while the former answers Yes.

Henry Chadwick points out that, regardless of Lessing's own stance on the matter, *The Education of the Human Race* contains Lessing's recommended view for orthodox defenders of Christianity.[21] In this light, it may in fact be the case that Lessing himself holds a position closer to that of the deists—revelation does not offer anything that human reason would not have come to on its own—but intends the stronger claim regarding the need for revelation to be a suggested option for a more rationally defensible form of Christian orthodoxy. If this take on Lessing is right, Lessing intends to change the debate between the orthodox and the deists. As Chadwick puts it, "[F]or Lessing and the Enlightenment as much as for Goeze and the orthodox, the natural and the supernatural appear in radical antithesis to one another. *The Education of the Human Race* shows Lessing using language which in some degree cuts across the traditional antithesis. He wants to change the terms of reference of the debate."[22] It may, in fact, be the case that Lessing intends the debate to shift to a dispute over whether the revelatory catalyst is needed or merely useful. And, as Chadwick points out, Lessing's attempts were not entirely without success: "The theologians of the Enlightenment did not reject the Bible; they found in it only natural religion."[23]

Drawing this back to Kant's comments in Part One of Book Four, the dispute between the supernaturalist and the pure rationalist may refer to the very dispute Lessing sparked, in which case the pure rationalist (rationalist) is contrasted with the supernaturalist rationalist. The former holds that revelation is useful in hastening rational religion, while the latter holds that revelation is necessary for the awakening of rational religion; the matter does not concern natural versus revealed religion. Scholars in the realm of English-speaking Kant-studies often overlook the fact that German historians of ideas, such as August Dorner and Emanuel Hirsch, identify the supernaturalist rationalist as a form of German rationalism, devoting entire chapters to this school of thought.[24] Moreover, John Nevin, an astute nineteenth-century student of German thought, speaks explicitly of "rationalistic supernaturalism," suggesting, "The term, it is hardly necessary to say, is not one of my own invention. It has its well known application in Germany to a certain order of Christian life and theology there, the constitution and historical meaning of which are just as well settled and understood, as the nature of orthodoxy and rationalism under any other view."[25] He goes on to cite Dorner's *History of Protestant Theology*, "where the mode of thought in question is clearly accounted for and confirmed"; and he argues that "[t]he rationalistic supernaturalism of Germany, in the latter part of the last century [viz., at the time when Kant wrote *Religion*], was in its time highly respectable."[26] Nevin goes on to remark that proponents of rationalistic supernaturalism stood firmly and convincingly against the anti-theological rationalists who sought to undo the Christian faith.[27]

Taking this understanding of the supernaturalist, Kant's final word on the dispute between pure rationalism and supernaturalist rationalism is agnosticism, which Kant voices in 6:155: "Hence [the rationalist] will never . . . contest either the intrinsic possibility of revelation in general or the necessity of a revelation as divine means for the introduction of true religion; for no human being can determine anything through reason regarding these matters." If 6:153–55 can be rightly read as Kant's examination of three options available to rationalism—naturalism, pure rationalism, and supernaturalism— it would not be surprising to find Kant dismissive of the naturalist, but agnostic regarding the debate spawned by Lessing and carried on after him. The naturalist oversteps the limits of human knowledge from a Kantian perspective and can, therefore, be readily dismissed. Yet, the issue of whether a revelatory catalyst may serve to only hasten certain insights or prove a necessary catalyst for the awakening of certain insights is a matter that moves beyond the Kantian boundary lines of human understanding. Kant's philosophy cannot give justification for empty speculation over whether key philosophical insights would have emerged without whatever catalyst has given rise to them. We would, therefore, expect from Kant the response, "The point of dispute can therefore concern only the reciprocal claims of the pure rationalist and the supernaturalist in matters of faith, or what either accepts as necessary and sufficient, or only as accidental, to the one and only true religion" (6:155).

When we read Kant's discussion of the forms of rationalism under the above approach, the haziness Wood identifies disappears. As traditional readers argue, Kant affirms rationalism. But this affirmation does not answer which of the three forms of rationalism Kant affirms. Kant quite readily denies the naturalist position as untenable but runs headlong into the limits of reason in the dispute between the pure rationalist and the supernaturalist rationalist. In identifying his agnosticism on this point, Kant makes plain in this prelude to the second experiment that his concern in *Religion* is not to address this specific quandary; the debate between the deists and the orthodox must dissolve as outside the bounds of reason. Kant's concern is more modest. He admits, per the dispute between the pure rationalist and the supernaturalist, that "a religion can be *natural*, yet also *revealed*, if it is so constituted that human beings *could and ought to have* arrived at it on their own through the mere use of reason, even though they *would* not have come to it as early or as extensively as is required" (6:155). But rather than resolving the dispute between the pure rationalist and the supernaturalist rationalist, Kant merely hopes to establish whether by beginning from within the sphere of a particular revealed religion, one can arrive at the tenets of rational religion. Hence, he intends to test a historical faith, looking at it from two perspectives—the perspective of natural religion and the perspective of learned religion. This shift marks Kant's turn to the second experiment.

Christianity as a Natural and Learned Religion

In 6:151–52, Kant prepares the reader for the task of Book Four by summarizing what he feels has been established in Books One, Two, and Three. In particular, he recounts his vision for rational religion in Book Three with a view to the comparison he is about to perform with Christianity. He asserts that the kingdom of God is at hand because the principles that ground it have already taken root, "even though the complete development of its appearance in the world of the senses is postponed to an unseen distance" (6:151). Moral converts must unite, Kant reminds us, with a view to establishing this visible kingdom, and this union, he reiterates, is a duty of a special kind. While such corporate unity may take place due to "*accidental agreement* of all in a common good" (6:151), true hope requires proactive measures or "special organization" to resist the evil principle, lest "human beings . . . otherwise tempt each other to serve as tools [of the evil principle]" (6:151). This special organization represents a community under God, "**as a Kingdom of God**" (6:151), and must be brought about in a public setting—which, according to Kant, requires a church. Moral converts with a good disposition must seek to organize moral communities fixed on this end, but the kingdom of God itself must ultimately be divinely established. "God himself is in the last instance the author of the *constitution* as founder," says Kant, "whereas human beings, as members and free citizens of this kingdom, are in all instances the authors of the *organization*" (6:152).

With this reiteration of his vision for rational religion in hand, and with his clarification in 6:153–55 of his intentions relative to the pure rationalist-supernaturalist debate, Kant is able to move into his second experiment, beginning in 6:156. It will be recalled that, as Kant explains it, the first experiment considers only natural or rational religion. The second experiment looks at a specific "alleged revelation" and compares its doctrines to the doctrines of natural religion in order to "see whether it does not lead back to the same pure *rational system* of religion" (6:12). We find Kant's transition to this second experiment in the introductory paragraphs of Part One of Book Four. As mentioned, Kant holds that "a religion can be *natural*, yet also *revealed*, if it is so constituted that human beings *could and ought to have* arrived at it on their own through the mere use of their own reason" (6:155). What this means is that if a religion commends to its adherents the pure moral doctrines expounded in Books One, Two, and Three of *Religion*, then that religion is natural, despite its historical constitution and dependence on the erudition of biblical scholars. With the pure moral doctrines clearly displayed in Books One, Two, and Three, Kant is ready to turn and "consider a revealed religion as yet *natural,* on the one hand, but on the other hand, a *learned* religion; we shall test it and be able to sort out what, and how much, it is entitled to from the one source or the other" (6:156).

Unlike the dispute between the pure rationalist and the supernaturalist, Kant's concerns are more epistemologically humble. Since reason cannot adjudicate whether the "revelatory" history of a faith is no more than an expendable means of establishing certain insights or a necessary catalyst for awakening key rational insights, Kant's approach is to look at the faith in question from a dual vantage point, first scrutinizing its doctrines from the perspective of natural religion and after this considering it as a learned religion, dependent upon texts and histories. Kant's intent, as he explains it, is to examine the given faith in order to discover how much of its content is dependent upon its historical apparatus and how much is attributable to a rational core. Kant identifies New Testament Christianity as the revealed religion he will utilize in this test.

Beginning with New Testament Christianity as natural religion, Kant thinks this examination will make clear (1) that Christianity most certainly bears the rational core of the pure moral doctrines expounded in the first experiment, and (2) as such, the most central Christian doctrines, propagated by Jesus, do not depend on the Jewish scriptures. Original Christianity (i.e., Christianity as expounded by Jesus) stands instead on rational insights of which all can be convinced simply by reason. As Kant states in 6:158:

> If we now assume a teacher of whom the story . . . has it that he was the first to advocate a pure and compelling religion, one within the grasp of the whole world (i.e., a natural religion) and of which the doctrines, as preserved for us, we can therefore test on our own; . . . if we find that he made this universal religion of reason the supreme and indispensable condition of each and every religious faith, and then added certain statutes to it . . . as means for the establishment of a church founded upon those principles: then, despite the accidentality and arbitrariness of what he ordained to this end, we cannot deny to the said church the name of the true universal church. . . . After this description one will not fail to recognize the person [viz., Jesus] who can be revered, not indeed as the *founder* of the *religion* which, free of every dogma, is inscribed in the heart of all human beings . . . , but as the founder of the first true *church*.[28]

Kant looks, in 6:159–63, at various points of Jesus's teachings, specifically in the Sermon on the Mount, in order to show their congruence with the pure moral doctrines. Kant suggests that Jesus denies the moral efficacy of civil, statutory ordinances—a denial central to Kant's idea of the *ethico civil.* Jesus emphasizes instead the non-coerced inner moral character of the human being or "the pure moral disposition of the heart [that] can make a human being well-pleasing to God" (6:159; cf. Mt 5:20–48; emphasis added). Highlighting Jesus's teaching that "sins in thought are regarded in the eyes of God as equivalent to deed" (see Mt 5:28), that "holiness is above all the goal for which the human being should strive" (see Mt 5:48), that "hate in one's heart is tantamount to killing" (see Mt 5:22), and the like, Kant seeks to make plain the dispositional emphasis of Jesus's instruction (6:159).

Kant also notes the way Jesus cites Jewish law: *You have heard it said, but I say to you*, and so on. Jesus, to Kant's mind, expounds the pure moral doctrines by reinterpreting Judaism's "merely external" ordinances with a dispositional focus. For example, Kant sees Jewish laws as condoning revenge—*an eye for an eye*. Recognizing corrupt humanity's tendency toward revenge, Jesus taught that this natural tendency "ought to be completely reversed, that the sweet feeling of revenge must be transformed into tolerance" (6:160; cf. Mt 5:39–40). Kant sees such critical uses of Jewish law as exemplifying a vehicular use of Judaism. Jesus, to Kant's mind, consistently grabs hold of this historical-faith vehicle but reinterprets it under the guide of rational religion: "Thus [Jesus] says he does intend to satisfy the Jewish law in full, whence it is obvious that not scholarship but pure religion of reason must be its interpreter, for, taken according to the letter, the law allows the very opposite of all this" (6:160; Mt 5:17). The juxtaposition of Jesus's teachings (which echo the clear insight of natural religion) with the Jewish law (which Jesus regularly reinterprets) demonstrates, to Kant's satisfaction, (1) Jesus's intent to establish the Christian religion on the doctrines of rational religion, and (2) Jesus's recognition of the fact that without a vehicular use of the historically rooted Jewish faith, rational religion could in no way be established among Jesus's hearers.

In addition to seeing in Jesus's teaching an emphasis on the disposition and an exemplary vehicular use of Judaism, Kant sees Jesus combating the human tendency toward religion of divine service. Kant reads Jesus's talk of the narrow gate that leads to life and the wide gate that leads to destruction as a warning against religion of divine service. In these two roads, Kant sees the common folly of corrupt humanity to seek acts of divine service (the wide gate) rather than true moral conversion (the narrow gate): "[Jesus] does not leave unnoticed the misinterpretation of the law which human beings allow themselves in order to evade their true moral duty and make up for it by fulfilling the ecclesiastical duty" (6:160; cf. Mt 7:13). Kant understands Jesus's continual emphasis on dispositional transformation to contrast starkly with the false pietism of those engaged in religion of divine service. Kant writes, "[Jesus] . . . requires of these pure dispositions that they should also be demonstrated in *deeds*, and, by contrast, he rebuffs the crafty hope of those who, through innovation and praise of the supreme lawgiver in the person of his envoy, would make up for their lack of deeds and ingratiate themselves into his favor" (6:160; cf. Mt 5:16 and 7:21).

Finally, Kant highlights Jesus's teachings regarding the teleological vision of the highest good. In Jesus's teaching, Kant finds the appropriate balance (from a practical perspective) that "as regards happiness [a human's] lot will be proportionate to his moral conduct" (6:161; cf. Mt 5:11–12), but this principle should not prompt humans to seek virtue *for the sake of* this future compensation. Jesus balances the call of duty and the relatedness of virtue and happiness, suggests Kant, by noting that the future reward is "of a different kind for those who did their duty *for the sake of the reward* (or also for release from a deserved punishment) that [*sic*] for those better human beings who performed it for its own sake" (6:161). Kant argues that Jesus presents the true elect of the kingdom of God as those who exemplify the moral motivation that comes "simply by duty" (see 6:161–62; cf. Mt 25:35–40). Ultimately, the teleological "recompense" of which Jesus speaks is held out not as an incentive alongside duty, but as a vision of the providential push toward the highest good, which concerns human destiny as a whole. Says Kant: "[W]hen the teacher of the Gospel speaks of a recompense in the world to come, he did not mean thereby to make this recompense an incentive of actions but only (as an uplifting representation of the consummation of divine goodness and wisdom in guidance of the human race) an object of the purest admiration and greatest moral approval for a reason which passes judgment upon human destiny as a whole" (6:162).

Finally, and perhaps most notable is that, for Kant, not only do the teachings of Jesus bring into sharp relief the pure moral doctrines, but in Jesus's very person and work, the prototype "has been made visible in an example" (6:162). When this is coupled with the foregoing exposition of Jesus's teaching, Kant thinks one cannot fail to see Jesus as the founder of the one true church, which is established on the foundation of natural religion:

> Here we then have a complete religion, which can be proposed to all human beings comprehensibly and convincingly through their own reason; one moreover, whose possibility and even necessity as a prototype for us to follow . . . has been made visible in an example, without either the truth of those teachings or the authority and the worth of the teacher requiring any other authentication (for which scholarship or miracles, which are not matters for everyone, would be required). (6:162)

In short, Kant sees the rational foundation of original Christianity shining through so clearly that he is confident we can rightly conclude that the true foundation on which Christianity stands is one of natural religion.

In Kant's examination of Christianity as natural religion, we hear echoes of Book Three, where Kant presents the Christian religion as latching hold of Judaism as its historical-faith vehicle. Presuming this rendition of Christianity's origin, Kant argues that without the rational core found in Jesus's teachings, Judaism faced a significant difficulty in its propagation. Kant writes, "The security of the ecclesiastical faith based on [Judaism's sacred texts] . . . requires that there should be learned individuals knowledgeable in the Hebrew language . . . at all times and among all peoples" (6:166–67). Without such universal linguistic knowledge, the Jewish faith could never hope to be a valid faith for all people of all times and all places, for its original teachings were not, to Kant's mind, built on reason and natural religion. By contrast, Kant argues that Christianity "has the great advantage over Judaism of being represented as coming *from the mouth of the first teacher* not as a statutory but as a moral religion. And since it thereby treads in the closest proximity to reason, it was capable through reason to propagate with the greatest assuredness by itself, even without historical scholarship, at all times and among all peoples" (6:167). What Christianity rests on, argues Kant, is not the surety of its historical foundation or the accessibility of its historical record, but its rational foundation that can be embraced by rational humans everywhere and at all times by the mere use of reason.

In offering such an assessment, Kant echoes the approach to rational religion commended by Lessing. While Lessing was a defender of the reasonableness of Christianity, he was no advocate of historically rooted Christian apologetics. In his highly influential *On the Proof of the Spirit and of Power* (1777), written in response to Johann David Schumman's historical apologetic, *On the Evidence for the Truth of the Christian Religion*, Lessing, like Kant, distinguishes between contingent truths of history and necessary truths of reason.[29] In so doing, Lessing seeks to undercut Schumman's use of so-called historical proofs for Christianity, proofs commonly employed in orthodox Lutheran apologetics of the day. Necessary truths of reason, Lessing argues, are immutable by definition, while a rational truth remains rational regardless of historical occurrences—if an idea is endorsed by reason (or is contrary to reason), no historical event can change this fact. Thus, *"contingent truths of history can never become the proof of necessary truths of reason."*[30] Lessing sees the religious application of this historical-rational gap as this: "[T]o make the leap from this historical truth into a quite different class of truths, and to require me to revise all my metaphysical and moral concepts accordingly; to expect me to change all my basic ideas on the nature of the deity because I cannot offer any credible evidence against the resurrection of Christ—if this is not a 'transition to another category,' I do not know what Aristotle meant by that phrase."[31] This gap between history and reason and its application constitutes Lessing's well-known ditch: "This, this is the broad and ugly ditch [*einer grausamen, breiter Graben*] which I cannot get across, no matter how often and earnestly I have tried to make the leap. If anyone can help me over it, I beg and implore him to do so. He will earn a divine reward for this service."[32]

Noteworthy is that Lessing, while seeking to undercut historically rooted Christian apologetics, did not intend to nullify Christianity. As Henry Allison points out:

> This . . . is Lessing's polemic against the historical proofs of the Christian religion, and . . . he is here in perfect accord with Spinoza and the deists. However, Lessing differs from both in that he endeavors to combine the

rejection of the historical foundation of Christianity with the acceptance of the actual content of Christian doctrine. This positive aspect of Lessing's attitude toward Christianity is suggested by the final, and generally neglected paragraphs of the work.[33]

The paragraph to which Allison refers is where Lessing makes plain that he sees the Christian faith standing not on historical proofs for its miraculous inauguration but upon the rational import that Christian doctrine carries and that lies behind Christianity's longevity. As Lessing puts it, what binds him to the teachings of Jesus are "these teachings themselves."[34] While these teachings may have required miracles and fulfilled prophecy "before the mass of people would pay any attention to them," Lessing thinks their longevity testifies to their "inner truth," which has outlived any transient proof of the spirit and power.[35]

Kant's two experiments allow for a duality similar to that of Lessing. Lessing's distinction between the historical occurrences surrounding the birth of Christianity and the rational foundation on which Christianity stands echoes in the corridors of Kant's two experiments in general and Kant's consideration of Christianity as natural and learned religion in particular. Like Lessing, Kant maintains that Christianity stands on the rational ground of natural religion, not on any supposed historical proofs. Kant's first experiment in *Religion*, in this light, is a thoroughgoing attempt to explicate the doctrines of natural religion on practical grounds, and Kant's turn to the Christian religion in the second experiment utilizes these grounds as the test that more firmly establishes Lessing's claim that, to the extent Christianity stands, it stands on rational, not historical, merits:

> Of the evil that lies in the human heart and of which nobody is free; of the impossibility of ever retaining ourselves justified before God on the basis of our life-conduct and yet of the necessity of such a valid justification before him; of the futility of substituting ecclesiastical observances and pious servile works for the lack of righteousness and yet of the inescapable obligation to become a new man: [of all this] everyone can be convinced through his reason, and to be convinced of it is part of religion. (6:163)

To be sure, the foregoing does not indicate that *Religion* is a Christian apologetic. Kant does not, and indeed cannot, conclude with certainty, given his epistemic strictures, that Jesus *is* the prototype manifest in history. Nor does Kant suggest that Christianity, as a religion that proceeded from the mouth of its first teacher as a rational religion, has any exclusive rights to the pure moral doctrines. Any historical faith could serve as a vehicle for their propagation. Moreover, original Christianity, in Kant's view, is certainly not impervious to corruption. Despite its rational foundation, its historical vehicle and development always threaten to cloud, rather than enhance, the pure moral doctrines if given precedence over these doctrines—which is most certainly, in Kant's estimate, a very real danger.

For this reason, Kant's two experiments do not end with the mere explication and affirmation of Christianity's rational foundation. Rather, Kant must consider the apparatus surrounding this foundation and the potential excesses that threaten to cloud or even undermine it. Switching to his examination of Christianity as a learned religion, therefore, Kant reiterates the Book Three theme that communicability is the true measure of whether a religion is natural or learned—that is, is historical and linguistic erudition required to grasp and communicate the faith (as was the case in—Kant's reading of—Judaism), or are its merits rational and communicable to all with the faculty of reason? The Christian doctrines highlighted in Kant's assessment of Christianity as natural religion are, in Kant's estimate, universally communicable. Yet, when assessing Christianity as learned religion, Kant's focus shifts to the need for scriptural scholars, who utilize their erudition to decipher and communicate doctrines found in sacred texts—texts that are "a sacred possession entrusted to the care of the *learned*" (6:163).

While Kant is confident that the rational foundation of Christianity in the teachings of Jesus can be communicated to all through mere reason, to the extent that Christianity has a sacred text in the possession of the learned, "We shall have to consider the Christian faith, therefore, on the one hand as pure *rational faith,* and on the other as *revealed faith* (*fides statutaria*)" (6:163). To whatever extent Christianity has come to emphasize and elevate its historical contingencies, it "is no longer called simply the Christian *religion,* but the Christian *faith*" (6:164). Kant's two perspectives on Christianity are therefore intended to identify its rational core, while also discerning what outside of this core has, by Kant's practical lights, been unduly elevated to a requisite of saving faith.

In keeping with Kant's comments in Book Three on humanity's felt need for revelation and historical faith, Kant admits that the dual aspects of Christianity cannot finally be separated—"the second not from the first, because the Christian faith is a religious faith; and the first not from the second because it is a learned faith" (6:164). In searching out Christianity's rational core, Kant does not intend to purge Christianity of contingent elements, lest it no longer meet our peculiar human weakness and, per the warning of Book Three, pave the way for skepticism and even atheism. Kant's emphasis in Book Four, as in Book Three, is instead on the priority of belief in Christianity. Only if belief in the historically contingent elements is made into a duty and condition for salvation does this learned dimension rob Christianity of its status as rational or "free." Thus, Christianity's rational elements must retain priority over its contingent components. As Kant puts it:

> Were it a pure faith of reason, it would still have to be regarded as a free faith even though the moral laws upon which it is based as faith in a divine legislator command unconditionally. . . . Indeed, if only this believing were not made into a duty, even as historical it could be a theoretically free faith,

if all human beings were learned. If, however, it is to be valid for all human beings, even the unlearned, it is a faith not merely commanded but one which obeys the command blindly (*fides servilis*), i.e., it does not investigate whether the command is actually divine. (6:164)

Here, Kant's concern is that humans universally have access to their religious duty before God. If a religious faith exalts its contingent elements that only the learned have access to, and if these elements are made the condition for salvation, then humanity lacks universal access to its religious duty before God and can have access to its duty only by blindly following the learned. Only by sustaining the centrality of its rational elements, argues Kant, can it remain a universally valid religion.

Kant realizes that a blind trail of laity behind the learned is, in some sense, unavoidable—hence Kant's discussion of the need for a historical-faith vehicle and biblical scholars in Book Three. But Kant again reiterates that wherever the learned have this authority, they bear the responsibility of declaring not historical doctrines (which only lead back to religion of divine service) but the true foundation of Christianity, namely, natural religion. As Kant puts it, "If this [blind embrace of revelation] is not . . . to happen, universal human reason must be recognized and honored as supreme commanding principle in a natural religion within the Christian doctrine of faith; whereas the doctrine of revelation . . . must be cherished and cultivated as a mere means, though a most precious one, for giving meaning" (6:165).

Kant's understanding of the biblical scholar's role in propagating rational religion establishes his distinction between true and counterfeit service (*After-dienst*) to the one true Church, which is essential to his arguments throughout the remainder of Book Four. Kant calls the biblical scholar's role in propagating rational religion "the true *service* of the church under the dominion of the good principle" (6:165). This true service is a ministry to the unlearned, discussed in Book Three, which overcomes humanity's natural weakness for religion of divine service by teaching rational religion by means of a purported revelation. Kant contrasts true service with counterfeit service, which declares the conditional, "revelatory" elements of a faith as its true foundation. Counterfeit service is "that service in which revealed faith is to come ahead of religion" (6:165). This juxtaposition serves as Kant's indictment of ecclesial "officials" who would bury the rational core of a faith for the sake of their own authority. "A church founded upon this last principle does not have true *servants* (*ministri*), like those of the first constitution," proclaims Kant, "but commanding high *officials* (*officiales*), and these . . . in fact wish to be regarded as the exclusive chosen interpreters of a holy Scripture, having robbed the pure religion of reason of its due dignity as at all times its highest interpreter, and having commanded scriptural scholarship for use solely in the interests of ecclesiastical faith" (6:165).

Such an indictment captures Kant's assessment of post-first-century Christianity as learned religion. According to Kant, while Christianity proceeded from the mouth of its teacher as a rational religion, the Christian religion did not long remain on this path. Kant argues that the historical elements of Christianity quickly gave way to the very type of counterfeit service he describes. As Kant tells the story, "the first founders of *congregations* found it yet necessary to intertwine the history of Judaism with it, and this, granted the founders' situation at the time was the sound thing to do" (6:167). Kant finds this decision to be sound, however, only "with respect to that situation." Following Christianity's birth, counterfeit service fast crept in alongside Jesus's rational doctrines: "These founders of the *church*, however, took up those fortuitous means of advocacy into the essential article of faith themselves" (6:167). In the light of this narrative, Kant sees Christianity as a faith that contains a rational core in need of liberation. Thus, his consideration of Christianity from the angle of learned religion gives way to his discussion of the effects of counterfeit service in Christianity that must be pruned.

Concerning Counterfeit Service to God

Given what the dual perspective of the two experiments concludes regarding Christianity, Kant sees no terminal threat in embracing the Christian faith. One may readily begin from Christianity and arrive at rational religion. Having said this, Kant's assessment of the Christian religion is an assessment of original Christianity. With this rational foundation now clouded and even subordinated to contingent historical happenings and non-moral ceremonial rituals, Christianity begins to recede back to a historical faith. Thus, Kant spends a good deal of time in Book Four identifying those issues that he see as fruit of counterfeit service and that must be addressed if Christianity is to be of use to moral converts and conducive to the providential hastening of the highest good.

The latter portions of Book Four become, in many ways, a catalogue of and commentary on excesses that are of little concern to the current project. Cataloguing this material (which, as mentioned at the opening of this chapter, is not considered a source of conundrums) has already been done efficiently and can be found elsewhere.[36] Our concern here is not, therefore, to discuss at length the various excesses that concern Kant, but to offer only a general overview of what Kant presents in the latter portions of Book Four as the specific danger to the rationality of the Christian religion.

Kant's criticisms of post-first-century learned Christianity center principally on matters that he sees as leading back to a religion of divine service. Anthropomorphism is of great significance in this regard. With those of his day, Kant saw the biblical language of God as wrathful, sorrowful, regretful, and the like as contrary to the rational understanding of God.[37] Such anthropomorphisms, in Kant's estimate, are dangerous, not merely because they are counter to the "rational" understanding of God, but because they promote religion of divine service. Anthropomorphic imagery promotes in the human mind the idea that God is likened to earthly rulers. And to the extent religion of divine service is based on this very type of analogical reasoning, the promotion of these images of God carries the implicit danger of leading away from rational religion. Kant admits, in a manner akin to the *Religion*-as-Symbol motif of Ward and Palmquist, that in practice non-moral rituals or symbols may have value as visual aids in "harmonizing [the sensible faculty of representation] with the ideas of the end" (6:169). Yet, in practice, these deeds of service, more often than not, are treated as means of pleasing the deity that take the place of genuine moral improvement. So, while the morally weak show in these practices their eagerness to obey, ultimately this inversion of the means over the end becomes a "hidden inclination to deceit" (6:170).

Kant is confident that only "good life conduct"—that is, the practical faith in the Son of God—is pleasing to the divine judge. As Kant boldly states in 6:170–71: "I accept the following proposition as a principle requiring no proof: *Apart from a good life-conduct, anything which the human being supposes that he can do to become well-pleasing to God is mere religious delusion and counterfeit service of God.*" Recognizing that the appeal of divine service is its ability to appease humanity's sense of moral failure, Kant is quick to point out the rational resources of the prototypical theology for addressing moral failings and radical evil. Reason, therefore, does not leave us without hope, Kant assures, but tells us to pursue the good by dispositional revolution, and here alone do we find true divine pleasure and forgiveness. If we heed our moral duty, God will grant aid, provide a good disposition, and supply the ground for true moral hope.

Here, Kant seeks to again emphasize the practical nature of faith in the Son of God. Kant recognizes the danger of making mere knowledge and understanding of transcendental theology an act of divine service. He warns that, if we seek too great a knowledge of the conditions and dynamics of grace, we run the risk of making such knowledge the condition of finding favor with the divine judge. This warning echoes a distinction Kant makes in 6:116–17 of Book Three between the practical faith in the Son of God and the more Lutheran brand of faith, which places belief in the gospel narrative prior to the pursuit of moral renewal—a priority Kant thinks absurd; how could any rational person, aware that he deserves punishment, think himself absolved of guilt merely by believing the "news of a satisfaction . . . rendered for him" (6:116)? In like manner, we find in Book Four Kant warning against this more Lutheran approach to faith. While reason offers hope of moral renewal through prototypical redemption, Kant maintains that too great an emphasis on understanding the anatomy of grace or when and where this grace occurs runs the risk of making an act of service (viz., the non-moral act of knowing transcendental theology) the counterfeit source of divine pleasure. To seek transcendental understanding in this way moves dangerously close to religion of divine service. In the end, Kant assures us, what matters before God is the disposition itself, not a cognitive affirmation of the dispositional philosophy void of practical faith and genuine moral renewal.

A second of Kant's concerns in Book Four with Lutheran-like approaches to grace is that they seek to explicate not merely the possibility of grace but its actuality. As Kant's prototypical theology indicates, grace is transcendental. All such matters are non-empirical and at an infinite remove from knowledge proper under Kant's definitions. The anatomy of grace is hidden from us, and our faith must therefore be practical, driven by a hope that we have undergone (or will undergo) a dispositional revolution. We can admit the possibility of grace and even the need for grace; we can even reasonably (though tentatively) infer a change of disposition based on steady moral improvement, but, according to Kant, to move beyond this and suggest, based on some feeling, that we have, in fact, received grace is mere enthusiasm.

"Enthusiasm" (*Schwärmerei*) is, of course, Kant's well-known term for the belief that cultic practices, which do not affect one's character, somehow make one pleasing to God.[38] Kant sees enthusiasm as rooted in two facets of corrupt human nature. First, enthusiasm arises out of mere feeling. It seeks to *feel* the divine presence and, by this feeling, to assert a knowledge or apprehension of the divine presence that cannot be apprehended by the five senses. This is the form of enthusiasm Kant criticizes in the search for the *where* and the *when* of divine grace. This feeling is strongly tied to the second source of negative enthusiasm, namely, fear. Kant suggests that primordial cultic service originated from fear and a sense of powerlessness, which, in recognition of the stain of radical evil on humanity's moral nature, sought non-moral means of appeasing the deity.

Kant does not, of course, oppose service to the deity, but he does oppose service built upon anthropomorphic conceptions of the deity, which fuel these primordial forms of enthusiasm. True service to God, Kant argues, is found only in the moral life. "Only those whose intention is to find this service solely in the disposition to good life-conduct," submits Kant, "distinguish themselves from those others by crossing over into an entirely different principle" (6:176). Recognizing that religion of divine service is built on the search for divine favor, Kant argues that if God is rightly cognized as a moral being, the good life is necessarily what pleases him. Conversely, the idea that non-moral rituals would please (or appease) such a supremely moral entity is evidently false.

Toward the end of Book Four, Kant raises the question of whether rituals of divine service are of any consequence if they turn out to be of no value before God. Kant notes what he understands to be the opposing perspectives of Protestants and Catholics on this matter. Protestants throw off the religious practices and beliefs they see as unnecessary, while Catholics find it better to hold more than less—some of the practices may prove pleasing to God, but if not, they do no harm. The difficulty Kant finds in adjudicating this issue is that, when it comes to judging the genuineness of non-moral "revelation," Kant submits, "I cannot indeed believe and assert as certain, but just as little can I reject it as certainly false" (6:189). In other words, if reason can assess revelation only by what it finds reasonable, in matters of religion it can be certain only of that which practical reason commends (viz., the moral law, radical evil, prototypical theology, etc.). The only safety Kant feels is therefore on the ground of the dispositional philosophy itself: "I count on the fact that whatever saving content [this 'revelation'] may have, it will come to good for me only so far as I do not render myself unworthy of it through a defect of the moral disposition in a good life-conduct" (6:189).

Kant closes Book Four by attempting to persuade his readers of the relative surety of this dispositional ground via a thought experiment. He asks his readers to consider themselves before the divine judge in order to test the surety of their convictions. Kant writes:

> Let the author of a creed or teacher of a church, indeed; let every human being, so far as he inwardly stands by the conviction that certain propositions are divinely revealed ask himself: Do you really dare to avow the truth of these propositions in the sight of him who scrutinizes the heart, and at the risk of relinquishing all that is valuable and holy to you? I would have to have a very unfavorable conception of human nature (which is, after all, at least not altogether incapable of good) not to suppose that even the boldest teacher of the faith must quake at the question. (6:189–90)

To Kant's mind, no one can honestly claim a faith conviction in non-moral matters with great enough assurance to profess such beliefs unreservedly before God. If, in the face of such a test, one's beliefs cannot stand as certain, then the elevation of these beliefs to the level of duty violates the duty to act with understanding. Only a good life conduct, argues Kant, can, without reservation, be presented before the divine judge as universally required of humanity. Thus, Kant is confident that the only faith that can be held unshakably as universally valid is the dispositional philosophy, which makes the prototype's disposition the only sure source of divine pleasure. Hence, Kant extends this thought experiment, with the testimony of conscience, as a call to the biblical scholar to abandon all counterfeit service to God and to begin, instead, the work needed to liberate Christianity's rational core from the excesses that hinder this pure religion of reason first propagated in the teachings of Jesus.

Closing Statement

Kant's *Religion* has been both a seminal text for determining the contours of Kant's philosophy of religion and an increasingly maligned text because of its supposed incoherence. Our goal in part 1 was to provide an overview of the metaphysical motivations and philosophical character of *Religion* by examining various approaches to the text in the literature. In the process, we brought into sharp relief the difficulties thought to inhabit the text and established the nature of the indictment against it. By drawing out the debilitating conundrums in *Religion* expressed in the work of Philip Quinn, Nicholas Wolterstorff, and Gordon Michalson, we found that, to date, no reading of *Religion* seems capable of answering these objections without simultaneously stripping Kant's argumentative specifics of their philosophical precision and intended significance. Either one has to accept that the text is guilty of incoherence and adopt from it only those portions that can be made to cohere with the rest of the critical philosophy, or one must offer another way of understanding the text that has yet to be expressed in the literature. The interpretations of Ronald Green, Adina Davidovich, John Hare, Bernard Reardon, Peter Byrne, and Sharon Anderson-Gold, in their own respective ways, follow the first pathway. The goal throughout our treatment of *Religion*, by contrast, has been to follow the road less traveled, offering a reading of *Religion* that remains close to the textual and argumentative specifics and addresses head-on the plethora of alleged conundrums noted in part 1.

The results of this endeavor, at a number of points, display novelty. This should not be surprising, however, since one would expect that in the attempt to vindicate a text thought to be filled with conundrums, novelty inevitably arises. We have sought to follow the simple rule of justice—"Innocent until proven guilty"—and to show how Kant's arguments, though often difficult and sometimes obscure, can be understood coherently. Throughout our exposition of *Religion* in part 2, we have also sought to make clear the way in which our interpretation of the text answers the conundrums identified in part 1 of this work. Since our goal has been a defense of Kant's *Religion*, the final verdict hinges on the success (or failure) of the rejoinders our reading of the text offers. However, before one renders a final verdict for or against Kant's *Religion*, a few points should be kept in mind.

Undoubtedly, *Religion* is a text that is clever enough, complex enough, and controversial enough to allow for a diversity of opinions about its philosophical and religious significance. Book One, for instance, presents plenty of passages that lend themselves to the view that Kant is primarily concerned with individual autonomy and moral philosophy and that the main implications of *Religion* for the religious life are traceable to these concerns. Book Two can give the impression that Kant's language and doctrines are simply borrowed from Christianity, schematized into rational terms, and placed into or alongside his philosophy of religion. If we downplay the significance of Book Two and play up the significance of Book Three, one can viably interpret Kant's philosophy of religion as placing the solution to radical evil in the collective moral striving of human beings toward an ethical commonwealth. When, in Book Four, Kant challenges the rational merit of many Christian positions and practices, we could get the impression, should we simply focus there, that Kant wants to eliminate historical religion from the sociopolitical scene and replace it with a merely ethical or "enlightened" community. Not surprisingly, all such foci can be found in the current literature on Kant.

By contrast, we have argued that Kant's *Religion* is equally amenable, and perhaps more so, to a holistic and linear interpretation—one where its arguments are understood to build on one another by unpacking underdeveloped concepts from his critical philosophy in ways that are intricate and insightful, and in ways that are not only coherent, but also religiously and theologically affirmative. Kant's turn to a transcendental analysis of the moral disposition via pure cognition is perhaps the most important new element of his philosophy of religion. Expanding on this concept, we noted the significance of Kant's unified conception of the human species in *Religion*, and this recognition paid dividends when we turned to the very difficult and much maligned Book Two of *Religion*. While Kant's Christic imagery in Book Two appears quite amenable to biblical imagery, we found that the prototype of perfect humanity may easily and fruitfully be read not (or, at least, not necessarily) as the historical God-man of Christianity, but as the perfect divine-human ideal, conceived to be in God from all eternity. Only by holding fast to the disposition of the prototype in rational religious faith can we hope to please God, attain moral freedom, and progress in virtue. Additionally, we found, in Book Three, that Kant's understanding of the ethical commonwealth can quite meaningfully be understood as the vision portion of a problem-solution-vision structure of Kant's rational religion in Books One, Two, and Three. Kant's philosophical representation of the kingdom of God on Earth shows what the world would look like if moral converts band together in pursuit of the practical faith in the Son of God and the highest good. Moreover, we saw how neither Kant's religious vision nor his second experiment is adverse to the existence and persistence of historical faiths, but together under our reading make for a very capable rejoinder to the problem posed by Lessing's ditch and other issues of the time surrounding the relationship between contingent historical facts and rational truths.

While the various Kant experts we have cross-examined throughout this work have much textual merit in support of their respective interpretations, what we have seen is that debilitating conundrums, paradoxes, and even outright contradictions have continually reemerged in their midst. If these interpretations display all the resources and arguments available when interpreting Kant, *Religion* would have to be judged guilty as charged. What we have shown, however, is that there exists at least one alternative way into the text that is still available, quite promising and, until this volume, untried. Our interpretation throughout has capitalized on the convergence of a unified conception of humanity's moral disposition, a fresh understanding of Kant's two experiments, and nuances in Kant's use of cognition. When moving into the text from this vantage point, we saw that the alleged philosophical failings began to quickly disappear. Gone was the temptation to truncate the text in order for it to make sense; gone was the alleged anti-religious emphasis in Kant's philosophy of religion; and gone was the supposed incoherence in the text. Herein we find an interpretation of *Religion* that preserves the text's consistency and profundity and addresses successfully the plethora of objections to the text from Kant's critics. Since this interpretation overcomes the many objections facing *Religion* and provides a consistent and stable understanding of *Religion*, the only decision any reasonable jurist can make regarding the indictment is to acquit the text of the charges leveled against it.

Having said this, the interpretation of *Religion* we have defended, if right, or even if only on the right track, represents a mere beginning. Much work still needs to be done to understand precisely how this later development in Kant's thought may affect our understanding of Kant's trajectory leading up to *Religion*. Our goal has not been to offer a rereading of Kant's corpus in light of our rereading of *Religion* but only to understand *Religion*, and to come to this understanding informed by the various ways it has been interpreted, with a view to resolving the most common conundrums forwarded by Kant's critics. In the process, these interpretations and conundrums have identified promising interpretive avenues as well as dead ends that have been met with when navigating this classic work. Without these charts and navigational tools to mark out the rocks that have shipwrecked many interpretations, navigating the treacherous seas of Kant's philosophy of religion would be nearly impossible. Much is owed to Kant's interpreters and critics in this regard. Nevertheless, in light of the foregoing analysis and interpretation, the charges of incoherence against *Religion* are not sufficiently strong as to render a guilty verdict, and should therefore be dropped. Our hope is that the methods and standards of interpretation presented here will facilitate further inquiries into Kant's work, so that, should the above interpretation one day be overcome, its replacement will be of such a kind as does not again cast suspicion on the metaphysical motivations or philosophical character of Kant's *Religion*.

NOTES

People vs. *Religion*

1. While most English quotations of Kant will be based on *The Cambridge Edition of the Works of Immanuel Kant,* for the sake of clarity, we will refer to the four major divisions of *Religion* as "Books" (per Greene and Hudson) rather than "Parts" (per Cambridge). See *Religion within the Limits of Reason Alone,* Theodore M. Greene and H. H. Hudson, trans. (New York: Harper and Brothers, 1960).

2. See "Editors' Introduction," in *Kant and the New Philosophy of Religion,* ed. Chris L. Firestone and Stephen R. Palmquist (Bloomington: Indiana University Press, 2006).

3. See Allen W. Wood, "Kant's Deism"; and Denis Savage, "Kant's Rejection of Divine Revelation and His Theory of Radical Evil," both in *Kant's Philosophy of Religion Reconsidered,* ed. Philip J. Rossi and Michael W. Wreen (Bloomington: Indiana University Press, 1991). In the next chapter, we make a distinction between the early Wood, whose work is optimistic about the prospects of grounding religion and theology in Kant's philosophy, and the later Wood, whose work has a decidedly pessimistic tone.

4. See Keith Ward, *The Development of Kant's View of Ethics* (Oxford: Basil Blackwell, 1972); and Don Cupitt, "Kant and the Negative Theology," in *The Philosophical Frontiers of Christian Theology: Essays Presented to D. M. MacKinnon,* ed. Brian Hebblethwaite and Stewart Sutherland (Cambridge: Cambridge University Press, 1982).

5. Matthew Alun Ray, *Subjectivity and Irreligion: Atheism and Agnosticism in Kant, Schopenhauer and Nietzsche* (Aldershot, UK: Ashgate Publishing, 2003). See also Yirmiahu Yovel, *Kant and the Philosophy of History* (Princeton, N.J.: Princeton University Press, 1980).

6. Ronald M. Green, *Religious Reason: The Rational and Moral Basis of Religious Belief* (New York: Oxford University Press, 1978); Ronald M. Green, *Religion and Moral Reason: A New Method for Comparative Study* (New York: Oxford University Press, 1988); Ann L. Loades, *Kant and Job's Comforters* (Newcastle upon Tyne, UK: Avero Publications, 1985); Stephen R. Palmquist, *Kant's System of Perspectives* (Lanham, Md.: University Press of America, 1993); Stephen R. Palmquist, *Kant's Critical Religion* (Aldershot, UK: Ashgate Publishing, 2000); Adina Davidovich, *Religion as a Province of Meaning: The Kantian Foundations of Modern Theology* (Minneapolis: Fortress Press, 1993); John E. Hare, *The Moral Gap: Kantian Ethics, Human Limits, and Divine Assistance* (New York: Oxford University Press, 1996); and Elizabeth Cameron Galbraith, *Kant and Theology: Was Kant a Closet Theologian?* (San Francisco: International Scholars Publications, 1996).

7. Philip Quinn, "Saving Faith from Kant's Remarkable Antinomy," *Faith and*

Philosophy 7, no. 4 (1990); Nicholas P. Wolterstorff, "Conundrums in Kant's Rational Religion," in *Kant's Philosophy of Religion Reconsidered*, 44.

8. See, e.g., Wolterstorff, "Conundrums in Kant's Rational Religion," 44–45; and Vincent A. McCarthy, *Quest for a Philosophical Jesus: Christianity and Philosophy in Rousseau, Kant, Hegel, and Schelling* (Macon, Ga.: Mercer University Press, 1986), 69 and 74–80.

9. Gordon E. Michalson, Jr., *Fallen Freedom: Kant on Radical Evil and Moral Regeneration* (Cambridge: Cambridge University Press, 1990), 1–10.

10. Yovel, *Kant and the Philosophy of History*, 202.

11. See Kant's 1793 letter to Carl Friedrich Staüdlin (11:429). For a useful discussion of Kant's religious sincerity, see Palmquist, *Kant's Critical Religion*, 192ff.

12. See Philip J. Rossi, "Reading Kant through Theological Spectacles," in *Kant and the New Philosophy of Religion*, 114.

13. For an assessment of the implications and desirability of our reading of *Religion* for Christian thought, see Nathan Jacobs, "Kant's *Apologia*: A Look at the Usefulness of Kantian Insights for Christian Thought," *Philosophia Christi* 9, no. 1 (2007).

14. Because this book is the product of several years of research, portions of parts 1 and 2 inevitably overlap with both existing and forthcoming publications, which include the following: Chris L. Firestone, "Kant and Religion: Conflict or Compromise?" *Religious Studies* 35 (1999); Chris L. Firestone, "Kant's Two Perspectives on the Theological Task," *International Journal of Systematic Theology* 2, no. 1 (2000); Nathan Jacobs, "Kant's Prototypical Theology: Transcendental Incarnation as a Rational Foundation for God-Talk," and Chris L. Firestone, "Making Sense Out of Tradition," both in *Kant and the New Philosophy of Religion*, ed. Chris L. Firestone and Stephen R. Palmquist (Bloomington: Indiana University Press, 2006); Jacobs, "Kant's *Apologia*," and Chris L. Firestone and Nathan Jacobs, "Kant on the Christian Religion," both in *Philosophia Christi* 9, no. 1 (2007); and Chris L. Firestone, *Theology at the Transcendental Boundaries of Reason: Toward a New Kantian Theology* (Aldershot, UK: Ashgate Publishers, forthcoming). Any overlapping material is used with permission of the aforementioned publishers.

1. The Metaphysical Motives behind *Religion*

1. Allen W. Wood, *Kant's Rational Theology*, (Ithaca, N.Y.: Cornell University Press, 1978), 18–19.

2. Ibid., 84.

3. McCarthy, *Quest for a Philosophical Jesus*.

4. Ibid., 56.

5. Ibid., 72.

6. McCarthy uses the symbolic interpretation of Kant's Christic imagery to explain why Kant gives only an "unnamed Jesus." See ibid., 72.

7. Ibid., 58.

8. Ibid., 59.

9. Ibid., 60.

10. Ibid., 60.

11. Ibid., 61.

12. This development McCarthy links with Kant's 1791 essay, "On the Failure of All Philosophical Theodicies," and Kant's lectures on religion. See McCarthy, *Quest for a Philosophical Jesus*, 61.

13. McCarthy, *Quest for a Philosophical Jesus*, 71.

14. Ibid., 69.

15. McCarthy points to the original title of the piece, which contained the term *Lehre* (theory, teaching, or doctrine), as an indicator that the essays that make up *Religion* were not intended to be a fourth *Critique*. See McCarthy, *Quest for a Philosophical Jesus*, 66.

16. McCarthy, *Quest for a Philosophical Jesus*, 64.

17. Ibid., 74.

18. Ibid., 76.

19. Ibid., 73.

20. Ibid., 74.

21. Ibid., 70.

22. Ibid., 77.

23. Ibid., 80–81.

24. Ibid., 78.

25. Ibid., 80.

26. Ibid., 71.

27. Ibid., 84.

28. Ibid., 87.

29. Ibid., 92–95.

30. Ibid., 83.

31. Ibid., 83.

32. Ibid., 101.

33. Gregory Johnson, in the introduction to the latest translation of "Dreams of a Spirit-Seer," joins Palmquist in disagreeing with this conventional wisdom. Johnson points to the possibility that Kant was "two-faced" in his dealings with Swedenborg, being as interested in career advancement as he was in being transparent about his real affinities for such a controversial figure. See Gregory R. Johnson, "Introduction," in Immanuel Kant, *Kant on Swedenborg: "Dreams of a Spirit-Seer" and Other Writings*, ed. Gregory R. Johnson, and trans. Gregory R. Johnson and Glenn Alexander Magee (West Chester, Pa.: Swedenborg Foundation, 2002), xiii–xv.

34. Palmquist, *Kant's System of Perspectives*, 321.

35. Palmquist, *Kant's Critical Religion*, 25 (F12).

36. Ibid., 303.

37. Palmquist, *Kant's System of Perspectives*, 61. The capitalization of "Transcendental Perspective" signifies the overarching nature of this perspective. In *Kant's Critical Religion*, the Transcendental Perspective becomes crucial to Palmquist's understanding of Kant's residual affinity for metaphysics after his critical turn in the first *Critique* as well as Kant's bold return to metaphysics in the *Opus Postumum*.

38. Palmquist, *Kant's System of Perspectives*, 61.

39. Ibid., 58.

40. For a brief summary of Palmquist's interpretation of the critical philosophy, see Stephen R. Palmquist, "Philosophers in the Public Square: A Religious Resolution of Kant's *Conflict*," in *Kant and the New Philosophy of Religion*; for a more-lengthy defense, see Palmquist, *Kant's System of Perspectives*.

41. Palmquist, "Philosophers in the Public Square," 238.

42. Ibid.

43. Ibid., 239. For a detailed summary of Kant's third *Critique* and its relation to his architectonic, see Palmquist, *Kant's System of Perspective*, ch. 9. Palmquist further

examines the focus on symbolism in Kant's thought in Palmquist, *Kant's Critical Religion*, ch. 5.

44. Palmquist, *Kant's Critical Religion*, 114.

45. Ibid., 129.

46. Ibid.

47. Ibid.

48. Ibid., 187.

49. Ibid., 130.

50. Ibid.

51. Ibid., 131.

52. Ibid., 187–88.

53. Ibid., 161.

54. Ibid.

55. Ibid., 166.

56. Ibid., 171–72.

57. Ibid., 172.

58. Ibid., 173.

59. Ibid., 175.

60. Ibid., 181.

61. Ibid., 150.

62. Ibid.

63. Ibid., 155.

64. Ibid.

65. Ibid., 157.

66. Ibid., 158.

67. See ibid., 158.

68. Ibid., 159.

69. For more on Palmquist's understanding of grace and works, see Stephen R. Palmquist, "Kantian Redemption: A Critical Challenge to Christian View of Faith and Works," *Philosophia Christi* 9, no. 1 (2007).

70. Ward, *Kant's View of Ethics*, 28.

71. Ibid., 3.

72. Ibid.

73. Ibid., 4.

74. Ibid.

75. Ibid.

76. Ibid., 41.

77. Ibid.

78. Ibid., 59.

79. Ibid., 159.

80. Ibid., 79.

81. Ibid., 62.

82. This point is brought into sharpest relief with Ward's understanding of Kant on fanaticism. See ibid., 63.

83. Ibid., 155.

84. Ibid., 168.

85. Ibid., 146.

86. Ibid., 147.

87. Ibid.

88. Ibid.
89. Ibid., 148.
90. Ibid.
91. Ibid.
92. Ibid., 150.
93. Ibid., 154.
94. Ibid., 151.
95. Ibid., 149.
96. Ibid., 147.
97. Ibid., 148.
98. Ibid., 153–54.
99. See ibid., 147–48.
100. Ibid., 149.

101. Common in Kant-studies are references to "Pelagianism" and "semi-Pelagianism" without explanation. The basic Pelagian doctrines that are thought to echo in Kant include the natural fecundity of humanity's moral nature and the *ought*-implies-*can* principle. For these doctrines in Pelagius's words, see Pelagius, "To Demetrias," in *The Letters of Pelagius and His Followers*, ed. and trans. B. R. Rees (New York: Boydell Press, 1991).

102. Ward, *Kant's View of Ethics*, 153.

103. Ibid.

104. Ibid., 154.

105. Ibid., 155.

106. Ibid., 166.

107. Ibid., 151.

108. Allen W. Wood, *Kant's Moral Religion* (Ithaca, N.Y.: Cornell University Press, 1970).

109. Wood, *Kant's Rational Theology*, 147.

110. Wood, *Kant's Moral Religion*, 161.

111. Ibid., 164.

112. Wood, "Kant's Deism," 5; and Allen W. Wood, "Rational Theology, Moral Faith, and Religion," in *The Cambridge Companion to Kant*, ed. Paul Guyer (Cambridge: Cambridge University Press, 1992).

113. Wood, "Kant's Deism," 2.

114. For the stark contrast between the early and later Wood, compare the section on "Moral Faith in God" in *Kant's Moral Religion* (160–76) with "Kant's Deism."

115. Wood, *Kant's Rational Theology*, 17.

116. Ibid., 79–80.

117. See ibid., 150–51.

118. Ibid., 18–19.

119. Ibid., 80–81.

120. Ibid., 19.

121. Ibid., 24.

122. Ibid., 92.

123. Ibid., 82–83.

124. Ibid., 26.

125. Wood, *Kant's Moral Religion*, 21.

126. Ibid., 25.

127. Ibid.

128. Ibid., 26.
129. Ibid., 34.
130. Ibid., 147.
131. Ibid.
132. Ibid.
133. Ibid., 162.
134. Ibid., 121.
135. Ibid., 151.
136. Ibid., 160.
137. Ibid.
138. Ibid., 193.
139. Ibid., 193–94.
140. Ibid., 194.
141. Ibid., 195.
142. Ibid., 197–98.
143. Ibid., 199.
144. Ibid.
145. Ibid., 209.
146. Ibid., 211.
147. Ibid.
148. Ibid., 212.
149. Ibid., 214.
150. Ibid., 220–21.
151. Ibid., 217.
152. Ibid., 225.
153. Ibid.
154. Ibid.
155. Ibid., 218.
156. Ibid., 228.
157. Ibid., 228–29.
158. Ibid., 228.
159. Ibid., 239.
160. Ibid., 240.
161. Ibid., 241.
162. Ibid., 242.
163. Ibid., 236.
164. Ibid., 248.

2. The Philosophical Character of *Religion*

1. This title for the traditional understanding of Kant's God comes from Theodore M. Greene, "The Historical Context and Religious Significance of Kant's *Religion*," in *Religion within the Limits of Reason Alone*, trans. Theodore M. Greene and Hoyt H. Hudson (New York: Harper and Bros., 1960), lxiv.

2. See Chris L. Firestone, "Kant and Religion: Conflict or Compromise?" *Religious Studies* 35 (1999); and Chris L. Firestone, "Kant's Two Perspectives on the Theological Task," *International Journal of Systematic Theology* 2, no. 1 (2000).

3. Wolterstorff, "Conundrums in Kant's Rational Religion"; Nicholas P. Wolterstorff, "Is It Possible and Desirable for Theologians To Recover from Kant?," *Modern Theology* 14, no. 1 (1998).

4. Quinn often speaks quite favorably of Kant's insights. See, e.g., Philip L. Quinn, "Original Sin, Radical Evil and Moral Identity," *Faith and Philosophy* 1, no. 2 (1984), 197. Yet, Quinn's use of Kant always ends with criticism and reformulation.

5. Philip L. Quinn, "Christian Atonement and Kantian Justification," *Faith and Philosophy* 3, no. 4 (1986); Quinn, "Saving Faith from Kant's Remarkable Antinomy."

6. See, e.g., Wolterstorff, "Conundrums in Kant's Rational Religion," 46.

7. Ibid., 48–49.

8. Ibid., 49.

9. Ibid.

10. Quinn, "Saving Faith from Kant's Remarkable Antinomy," 422.

11. Ibid., 423.

12. Ibid.

13. Wood, *Kant's Moral Religion*, 248.

14. Ibid., 242.

15. Wolterstorff, "Conundrums in Kant's Rational Religion," 45.

16. Quinn, "Original Sin, Radical Evil and Moral Identity," 198–99.

17. Ibid., 199.

18. Ibid., 199–200.

19. Quinn, "Christian Atonement and Kantian Justification," 449.

20. Ibid.

21. Quinn, "Original Sin, Radical Evil and Moral Identity," 196.

22. Quinn, "Christian Atonement and Kantian Justification," 449.

23. Ibid.

24. One anomaly of Quinn's reading of *Religion* is that he sees Kant as desiring to import the notion of Christ's vicarious atonement and imputable righteousness (see Quinn, "Christian Atonement and Kantian Justification," 451ff.; and Quinn, "Saving Faith from Kant's Remarkable Antinomy," 425ff.). On this score, Quinn seems alone among Kant's interpreters. Almost all Kant scholars recognize Kant's rejection of vicarious atonement. Quinn, in his defense, points to Allen Wood's response to John Silber (see Wood, *Kant's Moral Religion*, 236ff.). Silber argues that Kant rejects atonement as violating the moral law (see John R. Silber, "The Ethical Significance of Kant's *Religion*," in *Religion within the Limits of Reason Alone*, trans. Theodore M. Greene and Hoyt H. Hudson [New York: Harper and Brothers, 1960], cxxxi–iii). Wood certainly denies Silber's claim that forgiveness is necessarily unavailable to Kant's God, but contrary to Quinn's assessment, Wood does not suggest that Kant affirms the Christian view of atonement. Wood only allows for the mystery of God's resources in this regard and suggests that *forgiving* is a predicate of one who is morally good and is thus rightly applied to God. Given that Quinn seems alone on this point of interpretation, we will not consider this aspect of Quinn's reading in this section.

25. Quinn, "Christian Atonement and Kantian Justification," 452.

26. See ibid., 449–52.

27. See ibid., 447ff.

28. Wolterstorff, "Conundrums in Kant's Rational Religion," 46.

29. Ibid.

30. See Quinn, "Christian Atonement and Kantian Justification," 458.

31. See ibid., 458.

32. Silber, "The Ethical Significance of Kant's *Religion*," cxxxii.

33. Wood attempts to address Silber's formulation of the problems facing Kant's talk of divine grace (see Wood, *Kant's Moral Religion*, 236ff.). We will not here explore Wood's attempted solution, but suffice it to say, even within Wood's response, the moral

convert remains morally defective and divine grace comes nevertheless, leaving the basic problem of God's justness untouched. Perhaps the only possible remaining route, which Wood does utilize, is to draw out the nuance that, while admitting that vicarious atonement is difficult to reconcile with reason, Kant does not use this difficulty as a basis for concluding that God has no resources by which he can wipe out guilt. Hence, an appeal to mystery could be in order. Even on this score, however, Quinn, who agrees broadly with Wood's rejection of the Silber critique, still finds numerous problems with Kant allowing room for the removal of guilt (mysteriously or otherwise). See Quinn, "Christian Atonement and Kantian Justification," 447ff.

34. One of the chief advocates of the severity of these strictures and the limitations they place on transcendent metaphysics is P. F. Strawson. See P. F. Strawson, *The Bounds of Sense: An Essay on Kant's Critique of Pure Reason* (London: Metheun, 1966), 16.

35. Wolterstorff, "Is It Possible and Desirable for Theologians to Recover from Kant?" 9.

36. Ibid., 13.

37. Ibid., 18.

38. Green, *Religious Reason*, 34.

39. Green, *Religion and Moral Reason*, 6.

40. Ronald M. Green, *Kierkegaard and Kant: The Hidden Debt* (Albany: State University of New York Press, 1992), 45.

41. Green, *Kierkegaard and Kant*, 50.

42. Green, *Religious Reason*, 35.

43. Ibid., 54.

44. Green, *Religion and Moral Reason*, 20.

45. Green, *Religious Reason*, 68–69.

46. Green admits that Kant wants to establish something more than merely a logical flaw in human persons, but also thinks that this is wrongheaded. In personal correspondence (2000), Green states that he interprets Kant on religion in this way, not because it necessarily provides the most accurate reading of Kant, but because it is the only way to make Kant cogent in light of the realities facing us today.

47. Davidovich, *Religion as a Province of Meaning*, 40, emphasis added.

48. Michel Despland, in his book *Kant on History and Religion* (Montreal: McGill-Queen's University Press, 1973), also focuses on the faculty of judgment as a too-often neglected aspect of Kant's work that provides crucial resources for understanding Kant's philosophy of religion. We have chosen to focus on Davidovich's interpretation rather than Despland's, however, because of her clear focus on the third *Critique* and more systematic examination of the particulars of *Religion*.

49. Davidovich, *Province of Meaning*, 33.

50. Ibid., 70.

51. Ibid., 71.

52. Ibid.

53. Adina Davidovich, "How to Read *Religion within the Limits of Reason Alone*," *Kant-Studien* 85 (1994): 1.

54. Davidovich, "How to Read *Religion*," 1.

55. Ibid., 4.

56. Ibid.

57. Ibid., 3.

58. Ibid., 4.

59. Ibid., 4–5.

60. Ibid., 5.

61. Wood, *Kant's Moral Religion*, 28.

62. Davidovich, "How to Read *Religion*," 5.

63. Ibid.

64. Ibid., 6.

65. Ibid., 5.

66. Ibid., 11.

67. Ibid., 13.

68. Ibid.

69. Ibid., 14.

70. Paul Guyer, *Kant and the Claims of Taste* (Cambridge, Mass.: Harvard University Press, 1979), 65.

71. Ibid., 50.

72. This explains the hermeneutic importance of what we might call "the theory of the supremacy of aesthetic judgment" for judicial reasoning relative to its rival, "the theory of the supremacy of reflective judgment." See ibid., 50–51.

73. Davidovich, *Province of Meaning*, 89.

74. See Bernard M. G. Reardon, *Kant as Philosophical Theologian* (Totowa, N.J.: Barnes and Noble Books, 1988). For a compact presentation of Reardon's interpretation, see Bernard M.G. Reardon, "Kant as Theologian," *Downside Review* 93 (1995).

75. See, e.g., Hare, *The Moral Gap*; John E. Hare, "The Rational Instability of Atheism," in *Kant and the New Philosophy of Religion*, ed. Chris L. Firestone and Stephen R. Palmquist (Bloomington: Indiana University Press, 2006); John E. Hare, "Augustine, Kant, and the Moral Gap," in *The Augustinian Tradition*, ed. Gareth B. Matthew (Berkeley: University of California Press, 1999).

76. Reardon, *Kant as Philosophical Theologian*, 87.

77. Ibid., 88.

78. Ibid.

79. See ibid., 88.

80. Ibid., 89–90.

81. See ibid., 89f. Reardon titles his treatment of *Religion* "Interpreting Christianity," which seems a clear indication that he takes *Religion* in its entirety to be the second experiment.

82. Hare, "Augustine, Kant, and the Moral Gap," 253. Cf. Hare, "The Rational Instability of Atheism," 64–65.

83. Hare, "Augustine, Kant, and the Moral Gap," 253.

84. Hare, *The Moral Gap*, 40–41.

85. Reardon, *Kant as Philosophical Theologian*, 90.

86. Hare, "Augustine, Kant, and the Moral Gap," 253.

87. Ibid.

88. Reardon, *Kant as Philosophical Theologian*, 91.

89. Hare postulates a third experiment in Kant's philosophy of religion that Kant nowhere makes explicit. In this third experiment, "We investigate the inner circle to see whether the beliefs and practices we find there require support from beliefs and practices in the territory of the outer circle." Hare, *The Moral Gap*, 41.

90. Reardon, *Kant as Philosophical Theologian*, 92.

91. Ibid., 94.

92. Ibid.

93. Ibid.

94. Ibid.

95. Hare, "Augustine, Kant, and the Moral Gap," 254.

96. Ibid. This objection presumes, of course, that *ought* implies *can*, and thus, if we *cannot* live thus, we *ought* not live thus.

97. Ibid., 254.

98. Reardon only offers the observation that Kant seems to think radical evil (i.e., the corruption of humanity's disposition) is evident from experience. See Reardon, *Kant as Philosophical Theologian*, 88 and 96.

99. Hare, "Augustine, Kant, and the Moral Gap," 254.

100. Ibid.

101. Ibid.

102. Ibid.

103. Reardon, *Kant as Philosophical Theologian*, 96–97.

104. Ibid., 96.

105. Hare, "Augustine, Kant, and the Moral Gap," 254.

106. Reardon, *Kant as Philosophical Theologian*, 97. Cf. John E. Hare, "Kant on Depravity: The Opening of *Religion within the Boundaries of Mere Reason*" (Eastern Regional Meeting of the Society of Christian Philosophers, 2006).

107. Reardon, *Kant as Philosophical Theologian*, 101.

108. Ibid., 101–102.

109. Ibid., 102.

110. Ibid., 112.

111. Ibid.

112. Hare, "Augustine, Kant, and the Moral Gap," 257.

113. By "justification," we mean, of course, the doctrine in Protestant theology, wherein Christ's atoning death wipes out the sinner's debt of sin, and Christ's own righteousness is imputed to the sinner, making her righteous (despite herself) in the sight of God.

114. Hare, "Augustine, Kant, and the Moral Gap," 257.

115. Reardon, *Kant as Philosophical Theologian*, 103.

116. Ibid., 102.

117. Ibid., 106.

118. Hare, "Augustine, Kant, and the Moral Gap," 254–55.

119. Ibid., 256.

120. Ibid., 255.

121. Reardon, *Kant as Philosophical Theologian*, 108.

122. Wood, "Kant's Deism," 5.

123. Ibid., 7.

124. Ibid.

125. See ibid., 8.

126. Ibid., 11.

127. Ibid.

128. Hare, "Augustine, Kant, and the Moral Gap," 252–53 and n6.

129. Ibid., 252–53.

130. Hare, "Augustine, Kant, and the Moral Gap," 253.

131. Ibid.

132. Ibid.

133. Johann Wolfgang von Goethe, *Goethes Briefe*, 4 vols. (Hamburg: Christian

Wegner Verlag, 1964), 536:5. Ernst Cassirer describes Goethe's bitter reaction to Kant's doctrine of radical evil in *Kant's Life and Thought* (New Haven, Conn.: Yale University Press, 1981), 391–2.

134. Hare, "Augustine, Kant, and the Moral Gap," 257.

135. Ibid., 258.

136. Ibid.

137. Ibid., 257.

138. See, e.g., Augustine, *The Spirit and the Letter*, para. 5ff.

139. See Hare, "Augustine, Kant, and the Moral Gap," 259.

140. Wood, *Kant's Moral Religion*, 209.

3. The Indictment of *Religion*

1. Gordon E. Michalson Jr., *The Historical Dimensions of a Rational Faith: The Role of History in Kant's Religious Thought* (Washington, D.C.: University Press of America, 1979); and Michalson, *Fallen Freedom*. In a third book, *Kant and the Problem of God* (Oxford: Blackwell, 1999), Michalson assesses the impact of Kant's philosophy of religion on contemporary theology. Michalson's growing pessimism regarding Kant's philosophy of religion comes to a head in this third work. Michalson asserts that Kant's primary influence on Western thought has been negative; and this negative influence is traceable to (1) "The consistent subordination of divine transcendence to the demands of autonomous rationality," (2) the limitations his philosophical system places on theology, and (3) Kant's own inadequate efforts to ameliorate these limitations. Michalson, *Kant and the Problem of God*, 137. *Kant and the Problem of God* will be addressed only indirectly in the indictment to follow.

2. Gordon E. Michalson Jr., "The Role of History in Kant's Religious Thought," *Anglican Theological Review* 59, no. 5 (1977).

3. Ibid., 421.

4. Michalson, *Fallen Freedom*, 37.

5. Ibid.

6. Ibid., 42.

7. Ibid., 41.

8. Ibid., 40.

9. Ibid., 38.

10. Ibid., 41–42.

11. Ibid., 45.

12. Ibid., 43.

13. Ibid., 45.

14. Ibid., 46.

15. Ibid., 56.

16. Wood, *Kant's Moral Religion*, 209–10.

17. Quinn, "Original Sin, Radical Evil and Moral Identity," 197.

18. Ward, *The Development of Kant's View of Ethics*, 146.

19. Michalson, *Fallen Freedom*, 46.

20. Ibid., 56.

21. Ibid., 31.

22. Ibid., 56.

23. Ibid., 65.

24. Ibid., 69.

25. Ibid.

26. Ibid.

27. Quinn, "Original Sin, Radical Evil and Moral Identity," 194.

28. Ibid.

29. Ibid.

30. Ibid., 196–97.

31. Michalson, *Fallen Freedom*, 69.

32. Ibid.

33. Ibid.

34. Ibid.

35. Michalson's reading of *Religion* is not, of course, identical to that of Wolterstorff and Quinn. Michalson tends to read Kant's talk of divine grace as a type of moral psychology that is very similar to Ward's view, where grace becomes an image that spurs on moral progress. Yet, even under this reading, Michalson does not think the consistency of Kant's mixture of autonomy and grace improves. In fact, it only creates additional instability, given that Kant's use of *Christian* images "hints at the possibility that Kant's commitment to radical evil forces his position back to some sort of reliance on a specific historical occurrence—in the form of Christ's breaking the 'power' of the evil principle to hold us against our will." Michalson, *Fallen Freedom*, 92.

36. Michalson, *Fallen Freedom*, 97.

37. Ibid., 89.

38. Ibid., 90.

39. Ibid., 91.

40. Ibid., 94–95.

41. Ward, *Kant's View of Ethics*, 149.

42. Michalson, *Fallen Freedom*, 85.

43. Ibid.

44. Reardon, *Kant as Philosophical Theologian*, 105.

45. See Quinn, "Original Sin, Radical Evil and Moral Identity," 196.

46. Michalson, *Fallen Freedom*, 87.

47. Michalson, *The Historical Dimensions of a Rational Faith*, 77.

48. Ibid., 90.

49. Ibid., 90–91.

50. Ibid., 91.

51. Ibid.

52. Hare, "Augustine, Kant, and the Moral Gap," 253.

53. Michalson, *The Historical Dimensions of a Rational Faith*, 115.

54. Ibid., 116.

55. Ibid.

56. Ibid., 117.

57. Ibid., 116.

58. Ibid., 118.

59. Michalson, *Fallen Freedom*, 8–9.

4. Kant's Philosophy of Religion Reconsidered—Again

1. Byrne, "Kant's Moral Proof of the Existence of God."

2. Ibid., 333.

3. Ibid., 335.

4. Cf. ibid., 335f.

5. Ibid., 335.

6. Don Wiebe, "The Ambiguous Revolution: Kant on the Nature of Faith," *Scottish Journal of Theology* 33 (1980): 516.

7. Ibid., 518–19.

8. Ibid., 519.

9. Ibid., 520.

10. Ibid.

11. Ibid., 522.

12. Ibid., 525. Wiebe submits that this extension of theoretical knowledge through practical reason appears as early as the first *Critique* (ibid., 527).

13. J. C. Luik, "The Ambiguity of Kantian Faith," *Scottish Journal of Theology* 36 (1983): 341.

14. Ibid., 342.

15. Ibid.

16. Ibid., 339.

17. Ibid., 345.

18. Some Kant translators, such as Norman Kemp Smith, translate both *Erkenntnis* and *Wissen* as "knowledge."

19. See, esp., Rolf George, "*Vorstellung* and *Erkenntnis* in Kant," in *Interpreting Kant*, ed. Moltke S. Gram (Iowa City: University of Iowa Press, 1982).

20. See Johann Christoph Adelung, *Grammatisch-Kritisches Wörterbuch der Hochdeutschen Mundart mit beständiger Vergleichung der übrigen Mundarten, besonders aber der Oberdeutschen* (Leipzig: Breitkopf und Hartel, 1793–1801; New York: Georg Olms Verlag, 1990), 1906–1907.

21. George, "*Vorstellung* and *Erkenntnis* in Kant," 34.

22. Ibid., 35.

23. Friedrich Paulsen, *Immanuel Kant: His life and Doctrine* (New York: Charles Scribner's Sons, 1902), 110.

24. A829/B857. This particular quote we have taken from J. M. D. Meiklejohn's translation of the first *Critique* (New York: Prometheus Books, 1990). The Cambridge edition renders "moral sentiments" (the chosen translation of both Meiklejohn and Norman Kemp Smith) as "moral disposition," which may only muddle matters in the context of discussing *Religion*. (Cf. *Immanuel Kant's Critique of Pure Reason*, trans. Norman Kemp Smith [London: Macmillan Press, 1929].) We think it clear that Kant is not here giving a prelude to the dispositional philosophy of *Religion*, but making a broader point regarding the role of practical reason in rational belief. To avoid confusion, therefore, we have chosen an alternate translation.

25. Leslie Stevenson, "Opinion, Belief or Faith, and Knowledge," *Kantian Review* 7 (2003): 88.

26. Ibid., 95.

27. See Reardon, *Kant as Philosophical Theologian*, 89–90. See also Hare, *The Moral Gap*; and Hare, "Augustine, Kant, and the Moral Gap."

28. Hare, "Augustine, Kant, and the Moral Gap," 253.

29. This quotation, for reasons of clarity, is taken from the Greene/Hudson translation. Immanuel Kant, *Religion within the Limits of Reason Alone*, trans. Theodore M. Greene and Hoyt H. Hudson (New York: Harper and Brothers, 1960).

30. Wood, *Kant's Moral Religion*, 199.

31. Silber, "The Ethical Significance of Kant's *Religion*," cxiv–cxv.

32. Ibid., cxvi.

33. Ibid.

34. Ibid., cxvii.

35. Wood, *Kant's Moral Religion*, 177.

36. Frederick Beiser criticizes the usual formulations of Kant's *absurdum practicum* argument, but believes the argument to have a cogent form. See Frederick C. Beiser, "Moral Faith and the Highest Good," in *The Cambridge Companion to Kant and Modern Philosophy*, ed. Paul Guyer (Cambridge: Cambridge University Press, 2006), 604–607.

37. Wood, *Kant's Moral Religion*, 178.

38. Ibid., 179–80.

39. This emphasis, it seems, is compatible with Hare's emphasis on "Spener's problem," which asks how we can become different men, not merely better men. See Hare, "Augustine, Kant, and the Moral Gap," 254.

40. The title for Kant's philosophy of religion in Book Two, "Kant's prototypical theology," first appears in Nathan Jacobs, "Kant's Prototypical Theology: Transcendental Incarnation as a Rational Foundation for God-Talk," in *Kant and the New Philosophy of Religion*, ed. Chris L. Firestone and Stephen R. Palmquist (Bloomington: Indiana University Press, 2006).

5. Book One of *Religion*

1. Wood, *Kant's Moral Religion*, 209.

2. Silber, "The Ethical Significance of Kant's *Religion*," cxvii.

3. See Silber, "The Ethical Significance of Kant's *Religion*," xcivff.

4. Henry E. Allison, *Kant's Theory of Freedom* (Cambridge: Cambridge University Press, 1990), 129–35.

5. See ibid., 132.

6. See ibid., 130.

7. Ibid., 131.

8. See Donald Greene, "Latitudinarianism and Sensibility: The Genealogy of the 'Man of Feeling' Reconsidered," *Modern Philology* 75, no. 2 (Nov. 1977).

9. We owe this objection to David Sussman, who raised this very point at a special eastern regional meeting of the Society of Christian Philosophers in response to Nathan Jacobs's paper, "On the Only Possible Reading of Kant's *Religion*: Books One and Two" (2006).

10. Reardon, *Kant as Philosophical Theologian*, 97. See Hare, "Augustine, Kant, and the Moral Gap," 254. Hare also makes his leanings toward this reading of moral rigorism plain in "Kant on Depravity."

11. Silber, "The Ethical Significance of Kant's *Religion*," cxix.

12. Sharon Anderson-Gold, *Unnecessary Evil: History and Moral Progress in the Philosophy of Immanuel Kant* (New York: State University of New York Press, 2001), 42.

13. Michalson, *Fallen Freedom*, 67.

14. Quinn, "Original Sin, Radical Evil and Moral Identity," 194. For a defense of a purely empirical reading of Kant's anthropology, see Patrick R. Frierson, *Freedom and Anthropology in Kant's Moral Philosophy* (Cambridge: Cambridge University Press, 2003), 31–47.

15. Gary Banham, *Kant's Practical Philosophy: From Critique to Doctrine* (New York: Palgrave MacMillan, 2003), 124.

16. See *Anlage* in Adelung, *Grammatisch-Kritisches Wörterbuch*.

17. Michalson, *Fallen Freedom*, 40.

18. Wood, *Kant's Moral Religion*, 211.

19. Michalson, *Fallen Freedom*, 42.

20. Wood, *Kant's Moral Religion*, 212.

21. Thomas admits this notion is not his creation, but is drawn from Aristotle. See Aristotle, *Nicomachean Ethics*, bk.I. See Aquinas, *Summa Theologiae*, II.1, q.90, art.2. This same notion can be found in Plato as well. See, e.g., Plato, *Meno*, 77c–78a.

22. See Aquinas, *Summa Theologiae*, II.1, q.90, art.2.

23. While Augustine is typically credited for privation theory, it can certainly be found in Christian thought prior to Augustine. See, e.g., Origen, *De Principiis*, bk.II, ch.9, §2; Athanasius, *Contra Gentes*, §7 and *De Incarnatione*, §§4–5; and Basil of Caesarea, *Hexameron*, Hom.II, §§4–5.

24. Augustine, *De civitate Dei*, bk.XI, ch.22. See also *De civitate Dei*, bk.XI, ch.10 and chs.22–23; *Confessiones*, bk.III, chs.11–2; *Enchiridion*, chs.11–4. In pointing to Plotinus as Augustine's key influence, we are echoing the common sentiment among Plotinian (and Augustinian) scholars. See, e.g., Emile Brehier, *The Philosophy of Plotinus* (Chicago: University of Chicago Press, 1958), 103; and Grace H. Turnbull, *The Essence of Plotinus: Extracts from the Six Enneads and Porphyry's* Life of Plotinus (New York: Oxford University Press, 1934), 249. In L. Grandgeorge, *Saint Augustin et le néo-platonisme* (Frankfurt, a.M., Minerva GmbH.: Unveränderter Nachdruck, 1967) the plethora of parallels between Augustine and Plotinus's texts are thoroughly laid out.

25. See Aquinas, *Summa Theologiae*, I, qq.48–49.

26. Plotinus, *Enneads*, Enn.I, Trac.8, §3. Plotinus, while being one of the fathers of privation theory, did not see evil as identical with nothingness. Rather, Plotinus equated evil with *matter*, in the Platonic sense, and thus, attributed to it more positive properties than is often seen in the Christian tradition. See, e.g., Plotinus, *Enneads*, Enn.I, Trac.8, §5. W. R. Inge rejects the title "non-being," often used by Plotinus, for this very reason. See W. R. Inge, *The Philosophy of Plotinus* (London: Longmans, Green, 1929), 1:134.

27. Here Kant echoes the Augustinian tradition regarding the *ordo amoris*. See Augustine, *De civitate Dei*, XV, 22; and Augustine, *De libero arbitrio voluntatis*, bk.I. See also Aquinas, *Summa Theologiae*, I.2, q.26, art.3; and John Duns Scotus, *Ordinatio*, IV, d.49, q.5.

28. Wood, *Kant's Moral Religion*, 211.

29. Ibid., 221.

30. Quinn, "Original Sin, Radical Evil and Moral Identity," 196.

31. Michalson, *Fallen Freedom*, 69.

32. Wood, *Kant's Moral Religion*, 225.

33. Michalson, *Fallen Freedom*, 60. See also Quinn, "Original Sin, Radical Evil and Moral Identity," 192–93.

34. In the very brief sketch of Leibniz on freedom and preestablished harmony above, we are, of course, siding with incompatibilist readers such as R. Cranston Paull, "Leibniz and the Miracle of Freedom," *Noûs* 26, no. 2 (1992), over against compatibilist readers such as Jack Davidson, "Imitators of God: Leibniz on Human Freedom," *Journal of the History of Philosophy* 36, no. 3 (1998), or deterministic readers such as Robert Sleigh Jr., Vere Chappell, and Michael Della Rocca, "Determinism and Human Freedom," in *The Cambridge History of Seventeenth-Century Philosophy*, 2 vols., ed. Daniel Garber and Michael Ayers (Cambridge: Cambridge University Press, 1998), 2:1195–1278.

35. Quinn, "Original Sin, Radical Evil and Moral Identity," 194.

36. Ibid.

37. See F. W. J. Schelling, *Of Human Freedom*, 384–85. All citations of *Of Human Freedom* reference the standard German pagination found in *Friedrich Wilhelm Joseph von Schelling Sämmtliche Werke, VII Band, I Abteilung*, 1805, 1810, ed. K. F. A. Schelling (Stuttgart and Augsburg: J. G. Cotta, 1860), vol. 7. English quotations are based on F. W. J. Schelling, *Of Human Freedom*, trans. James Gutmann (Chicago: Open Court, 1936). See also F. W. J. von Schelling, *On the History of Modern Philosophy*, trans. Andrew Bowie (Cambridge: Cambridge University Press, 1994), 94–106.

38. See David Hume, *A Treatise of Human Nature* (Oxford: Clarendon, 1967), 411.

39. Schelling, *Of Human Freedom*, 384.

40. See ibid., 385.

41. Ibid., 386.

42. Ibid.

43. Ibid., 336.

44. Wood, *Kant's Moral Religion*, 214.

45. Ibid., 224.

46. Ibid.

47. To justify his rejection of the species emphasis, Wood offers only a single quote, where Kant suggests that we must regard each individual "as though" he had fallen into evil from a state of innocence. See Wood, *Kant's Moral Religion*, 224.

48. The interpretive controversy centers on Aristotle, *Metaphysica*, Z.13. For a sampling of Aristotle interpreters who affirm the individuation of universals, see G. E. R. Lloyd, *Aristotle: The Growth and Structure of His Thought* (Cambridge: Cambridge University Press, 1968); Frank A. Lewis, *Substance and Predication in Aristotle* (Cambridge: Cambridge University Press, 1991); and Joseph Owens, *Cognition: An Epistemological Inquiry* (Houston, Tex.: Center for Thomistic Studies, 1992).

49. Leroy E. Loemker, *Struggle for Synthesis: The Seventeenth Century Background of Leibniz's Synthesis of Order and Freedom* (Cambridge, Mass.: Harvard University Press, 1972), 118–19. See also Tom Sorell, ed., *The Rise of Modern Philosophy: The Tension between the New and Traditional Philosophies from Machiavelli to Leibniz* (Oxford: Clarendon Press, 1993). The authors argue that, contrary to the common narrative, Aristotelianism did not disappear in the Enlightenment, but continued on, taking various forms in figures like Leibniz.

50. Loemker, *Struggle for Synthesis*, 118.

51. Ibid., 106.

52. See, e.g., Augustine, *Enchiridion*, XLV–XLVII.

53. While Kant holds that moral regeneration is beyond the individual's power to affect, he suggests that the necessity of moral hope, a hope we will explain in our treatment of Book Two, must be presumed: "Yet it must equally be possible to *overcome* this evil, for it is found in the human being as acting freely" (6:37).

6. Book Two of *Religion*

1. Wood, *Kant's Moral Religion*, 204.

2. Reardon, *Kant as Philosophical Theologian*, 112.

3. Hare, "Augustine, Kant, and the Moral Gap," 257.

4. Ward, *Kant's View of Ethics*, 154.

5. Ibid., 151.

6. Palmquist, *Kant's Critical Religion*, 211.

7. Michalson, *Fallen Freedom*, 109.

8. McCarthy, *Quest for a Philosophical Jesus*, 83.

9. Michalson, *Fallen Freedom*, 81.

10. A fourth approach we could mention is to simply ignore Kant's Christology. Wood, for example, never mentions or addresses the prototype figure in *Kant's Moral Religion*. Wood simply moves straight to Kant's discussion of the "postulate of grace" as an answer to the *absurdum practicum* argument. The one appearance of the prototype appears in a lengthy quote from Book Two. See Wood, *Kant's Moral Religion*, 233.

11. Hare, "Augustine, Kant, and the Moral Gap," 254. Kant's explicit acknowledgment of this problem can be found in *The Conflict of the Faculties*. See 7:54.

12. Wolterstorff, "Conundrums in Kant's Rational Religion," 46.

13. Michalson, *Fallen Freedom*, 24–25.

14. Davidovich, "How to Read *Religion within the Limits of Reason Alone*," 5.

15. Quinn, "Original sin, Radical Evil and Moral Identity," 199.

16. The question of realism versus non-realism seems to hinge on this concept of meaning. If the world is meaningful, then it will be because of the existence of perfect humanity. If the world is not meaningful, then the need for perfect humanity evaporates. Ultimately, Kant's argument does not address the realist–non-realist issue, but presumes the meaningfulness of our world and presses ahead, most likely on the basis of something like the principle of proportionality.

17. While hearing echoes of Platonism in Kant's account of rational religious faith may seem unusual, Michalson notes that a number of Kant interpreters, including J. Bohatec, Michel Despland, and Friedrich Paulsen, have suggested similar echoes. See Michalson, *The Historical Dimensions of a Rational Faith*, 117.

18. Loemker, *Struggle for Synthesis*, 118–9.

19. Ibid., 105–106.

20. Ibid., 106.

21. Ibid., 125–26. See Gottfried Wilhelm Freiherr von Leibniz, *Discours de métaphysique*, §11ff. in *Samtliche schriften und briefe/herausgegeben von der Deutschen akademie der wissenschaften zu Berlin*, 49 vols. (Berlin: Akademie, 1950). For an English translation see *Philosophical Writings*, ed. and trans. Mary Morris and G. H. R. Parkinson (London: Dent, 1973).

22. See Leibniz, *Discours de métaphysique*, §11ff.

23. Christian Wolff, *Philosophia Prima Sive Ontologia*, ed. Joannes Ecole (Georg Olms Verlagsbuchhandlung Hildesheim, 1962), Pt.I, §2 ch.3, §132.

24. Loemker, *Struggle for Synthesis*, 105.

25. N. Hinske, "Die historischen Vorlagen der Kantischen Transzendentalphilosophie," *Archiv für Begriffsgeschichte* 12 (1968).

26. Ludger Honnefelder, "Metaphysics as a Discipline: From the 'Transcendental Philosophy of the Ancients' To Kant's Notion of Transcendental Philosophy," in *The Medieval Heritage of Early Modern Metaphysics and Modal Theory, 1400–1700*, ed. Russell L. Friedman and Lauge O. Nielsen (Boston: Kluwer Academic Publishers, 2003).

27. John Duns Scotus, *Philosophical Writings*, ed. and trans. Allan B. Wolter (London: Nelson, 1962), 2. This collection of writings contains both the original Latin and an English translation.

28. See, e.g., Aquinas, *Summa Theologiae*, I, q.13, a.5.

29. Scotus, *Philosophical Writings*, 6–7.

30. Ibid., 2–3.

31. Ibid., 2.

32. Ibid., 3.

33. Ibid.

34. See, e.g., Augustine, *De civitate Dei*, bk.XI, ch.22. Though the interchangeability of being and goodness is typically attributed to Augustine, the metaphysical assumption has a long history in Christian theology as a defense against Manicheistic dualism: evil is not a thing, but a privation of goodness. See, e.g., Origen, *De Principiis*, bk.II, ch.9, §2; Athanasius, *Contra Gentes*, §7 and *De Incarnatione*, §§4–5; and Basil of Caesarea, *Hexameron*, hom.II, §§4–5. Within the Augustinian tradition, the link between being and goodness is often taken to be traceable to Neoplatonism. See, e.g., Grandgeorge, *Saint Augustin et le néo-platonisme*. See also Augustine, *conf.* blks. VII–VIII, esp. bk. VII, ch. 9.

35. Scotus, *Philosophical Writings*, 2.

36. For a treatment of Scotus's voluntarism, see Berard Vogt, "The Metaphysics of Human Liberty in Duns Scotus," in *Proceedings of the American Catholic Philosophical Association*, 16 vols., ed. Charles A. Hart (Washington, D.C.: Catholic University of America, 1940); Eef Dekker, "The Theory of Divine Permission according to Scotus' *Ordinatio* I 47," *Vivarium* 38, no. 2 (2000); Bernardine M. Bonansea, "Dun Scotus' Voluntarism," in *John Duns Scotus, 1265–1965*, ed. John K. Ryan and Bernardine M. Bonansea (Washington, D.C.: Catholic University of America Press, 1965); John Cresswell, "Duns Scotus on the Will," *Franciscan Studies* 13 (1953); Joseph M. Incandela, "Duns Scotus and the Experience of Human Freedom," *Thomist* 56, no. 2 (1992); John Duns Scotus, *Contingency and Freedom: Lectura I.39*, trans. A. Vos Jaczn, et al. (Dordrecht: Kluwer Academic Publishers, 1994); and John Boler, "The Moral Psychology of Duns Scotus: Some Preliminary Questions," *Franciscan Studies* 50 (1990).

37. For an manifold grappling with the problem of Scotus on nature and individuation, which includes a translation of *Ordinatio* I d.8 p.1 q.3 nn.138–40, see Peter King, "Duns Scotus on the Common Nature," *Philosophical Topics* 20 (1992): 50–76.

38. Scotus, *Philosophical Writings*, 4.

39. Ibid., 5–6.

40. For a survey of Scotus on the primacy of Christ, see Francis Xavier Pancheri, *The Universal Primacy of Christ*, trans. Juniper B. Carol (Front Royal, Va.: Christendom Publications, 1984), ch.2.

41. See Jacobs, "Kant's Prototypical Theology," esp. §3. The notion that Kant's philosophy requires empirical (as opposed to transcendental) incarnation is the view of Jeffrey S. Privette in "Must Theology Re-Kant?" *Heythrop Journal* 40 (1999). Jacobs shows Privette's views problematic, demonstrating that Kant requires transcendental incarnation commended by practical reason in order for this cognition to have universal validity. See Jacobs, "Kant's Prototypical Theology," §§1–2.

42. Wood, *Kant's Moral Religion*, 245.

43. Palmquist, *Kant's Critical Religion*, 282.

44. Reardon, *Kant as Philosophical Theologian*, 108. See also Ward, *Kant's View of Ethics*, 150; and Wood, *Kant's Moral Religion*, 240ff.

45. Wolterstorff, "Conundrums in Kant's Rational Religion," 45.

46. This same point is made and expanded on (albeit in a slightly broader context) in Jacobs, "Kant's *Apologia*," 58–62.

47. Reardon, *Kant as Philosophical Theologian*, 105.

48. Ibid.

49. The emphasis here on the *empirical* process is pivotal, since, for Kant, the revolution in disposition is not something that takes place gradually. Only our *pursuit* of this revolution is a process, for we do not know when or if a dispositional revolution has taken place, and therefore must simply press on in the hope that our moral progress is indicative of a change of inward disposition.

50. G. W. Leibniz, *Theodicy: Essays on the Goodness of God the Freedom of Man and the Origin of Evil*, trans. E. M. Huggard (Chicago: Open Court, 1990), §266. Sonner was not unique in offering this line of argument for the eternal damnation of sinners. Jonathan Edwards in the early eighteenth century develops and defends the same line of argumentation attributed to Sonner in "The Justice of God in the Damnation of Sinners," found in *The Works of Jonathan Edwards*, ed. Harry S. Stout (New Haven, Conn.: Yale University Press, 2001), vol. 19.

51. Reading Book Two in a way that affirms atonement is quite unique in Kant-studies. Nearly all of Kant's readers recognize Kant's intent to deny atonement, but most also fail to recognize that this denial comes in the context of infinite dispositional guilt. The distinction between infinite and finite guilt is crucial to making sense of Kant's claims here. Quinn is one of the few who reads Kant as affirming atonement. But, regrettably, Quinn's own reading of atonement does not build on the infinite/finite-guilt distinction; rather, it is the result of a dubious reading of *Religion*. He sees Kant as desiring to import the notion of Christ's vicarious atonement and imputable righteousness. See Quinn, "Christian Atonement and Kantian Justification," 451ff.; and "Saving Faith from Kant's Remarkable Antinomy," 425ff. For comments on this oddity in Quinn, see note 24 of chapter 2 of this volume.

52. Palmquist, *Kant's Critical Religion*, 460–61.

7. Book Three of *Religion*

1. Wood, "Kant's Deism," 5.

2. Byrne, *The Moral Interpretation of Religion*, 152.

3. Ibid., 152.

4. Anderson-Gold, *Unnecessary Evil*, 26.

5. Ibid., 30.

6. Quinn, "Original Sin, Radical Evil and Moral Identity," 199.

7. See chapter 2 above for a full explication of Quinn's argument on this point.

8. The bracketed change in the above quote replaces "disposition" with "predisposition" based on the German, which shows *Anlage*, not *Gesinnung*. Cf. the Greene/Hudson translation, which translates "predisposition." This change is important in that, assuming our interpretation of Book One is correct, the human disposition is corrupt outside of time, prior to any exercise of freedom; thus, Kant cannot root dispositional corruption in communal interaction that takes place within time. Instead, he must have in mind here the communal corruption of the predisposition to personality.

9. Beiser, "Moral Faith and the Highest Good," 602.

10. Ibid., 602–603.

11. We do not mean to suggest here that Beiser assumes a reading of *Religion* in general or moral faith in particular that parallels what we have argued for in the two previous chapters. Beiser's essay focuses less on the specifics of *Religion* and more on the general case that Kant has a robust emphasis on providence in his vision of the highest good—an emphasis we will echo in this chapter. See, e.g., Beiser, "Moral Faith and the Highest Good," 603–604.

12. Ibid., 603.

13. Reardon, *Kant as Philosophical Theologian*, 105.

14. Ibid., 105.

15. Quinn, "Christian Atonement and Kantian Justification," 236ff.

16. Worth noting is that Kant suggests that this internal moral battle is the human's "own fault" (6:93). Such language we read as an extension of Kant's notion of dispositional imputability, discussed in our treatment of Book One above, not as confirmation that dispositional corruption is a personal affair.

17. Beiser, "Moral Faith and the Highest Good," 603–604.

18. Michalson, *The Historical Dimensions of a Rational Faith*, 122.

19. Ibid., 115.

20. Green, *Religion and Moral Reason*, xi.

21. Careful readers may notice that in this passage Kant indicates that Judaism and Christianity have undergone forced interpretations that draw out pure moral doctrines. Such a claim may seem to move contrary to our comments above regarding Kant's rejection of Judaism as a rational religion and our claim in the next section that Kant sees Christianity as the example par excellence of rational religion. Yet, it should be noted that the emphasis here is on "Late" Judaism and Christianity. Kant's rejection of Judaism as rational religion is based on his understanding of pre-Christian Judaism, and his case for Christianity as rational religion is a case regarding original Christianity, not the later developments of Christianity, which may again be in need of purification.

22. When Kant speaks of late Christianity undergoing renovation back to its moral roots via moral readings of texts, he may have in mind figures such as Augustine, who suggests that if something in the Old Testament appears immoral, then one should give it an allegorical meaning. See Augustine, *De Doctrina Christiana*, bk.III, ch.10, §14.

23. In Hegel's *Lectures on the Philosophy of Religion*, Hegel dedicates Part II to "Determinate Religion," engaging Daoism, Buddhism, Judaism, and so on, while in Part III, Hegel turns to "The Consummate Religion," offering his understanding of Christianity. See Georg Wilhelm Friedrich Hegel, *Vorlesungen über die Philosophie der Religion*, Walter Jaeschke, ed. (Hamburg, 1983–1985), vols. 3–5. English quotations are based on Georg Wilhelm Friedrich Hegel, *Lectures on the Philosophy of Religion: The Lectures of 1827*, one-vol. ed., ed. Peter C. Hodgson, and trans. R. F. Brown, Peter C. Hodgson, and J. M. Stewart (Berkeley: University of California Press, 1988). Citations of Hegel refer to the standard German pagination in *Vorlesungen über die Philosophie der Religion*.

24. Kant's emphasis on original Christianity captures well the contrast between Kant and Hegel on the providential trajectory of religious progress. Hegel clearly thinks the ongoing development of Christian doctrine in doctrinal decisions surrounding the Trinity, which were the first steps into the philosophy of religion, represented great advances; and ultimately, the greatest advance was yet to come in Hegel's own philosophy of religion. See, e.g., Hegel, *Lectures on the Philosophy of Religion*, pt. III, 184–89.

25. Of course, Kant recognizes that God could command any number of things not testified to by reason (e.g., do not wear a garment made out of two different types of fabric; see Lv 19:19), but because knowing that God is the one speaking presents an epistemic difficulty for Kant (see, e.g., 28:1118), Kant thinks humans are bound only by what reason affirms. Thus, revelation may serve the function of awakening something rational (see 6:155), but the revelation itself does not carry authority unless reason testifies that such revelatory dictates are in keeping with what God has revealed already in our morally legislative faculties. See Wood, "Kant's Deism"; and Jacobs, "Kant's *Apologia*," §5.

26. See Firestone, "Making Sense Out of Tradition," §3.

27. See, e.g., 6:104. Here in Kant we hear echoes of G. E. Lessing's "ugly ditch" (*grausamen Graben*), with its accompanying distinction between rational truths that are embedded in reason and remain unaffected by historical happenings, and the historical happenings that may awaken us to such truths. See Gotthold Ephraim Lessing, *On the Proof of the Spirit and of Power*, in *Philosophical and Theological Writings*, ed. and trans. H. B. Nisbet (Cambridge: Cambridge University Press, 2005). We will return to this parallel in our treatment of Book Four of *Religion*.

28. Kant's retelling of Christianity's birth, which embraces discontinuity between Judaism and the Christian religion, is not entirely novel for his time. Lessing, for example, seeks to offer a theory of revelation that shows revelation to be merely part of an upward movement in humanity's religious maturity or education. Thus, discontinuity between early, "immature" ideas in Judaism and "mature" Christian ideas is to be expected. See Gotthold Ephraim Lessing, *The Education of the Human Race*, in *Lessing's Theological Writings*, trans. Henry Chadwick (Stanford, Calif.: Stanford University Press, 1957), esp. §§4 and 77.

8. Book Four of *Religion*

1. See, e.g., Palmquist, *Kant's Critical Religion*; and Sidney Axinn, *The Logic of Hope: Extensions of Kant's View of Religion* (Atlanta, Ga.: Rodopi B.V., 1994), 120–38.

2. Wood, "Kant's Deism," 10.

3. Ibid., 7.

4. Ibid.

5. Ibid., 8.

6. Ibid., 11.

7. Ibid.

8. Ibid.

9. Hare, *The Moral Gap*, 42.

10. Ibid., 42.

11. Ibid., 42–43.

12. Ibid., 44–45.

13. See Despland, *Kant on History and Religion*, 220.

14. Wood, "Kant's Deism," 11.

15. In the German, Kant inverts the subject and the verb, and follows the clause containing this inversion with the (German) word *so* (English equivalent "then"), indicating an if-then construction.

16. References to Lessing's works in their original German are taken from *Lessings sämtliche Werke*, 6 vols., ed. Robert Petsch (Berlin, 1907). Given the brevity of many of Lessing's writings (often no longer than a few pages), we will cite the pagination in the English translations from which quotations are drawn, unless standardized section divisions are available. Quotations of *On the Proof of the Spirit and of Power* and of *A Rejoinder* are based on Nisbet's translation in *Philosophical and Theological Writings*; quotations of *The Education of the Human Race* are based on Chadwick's translation in *Lessing's Theological Writings*.

17. Lessing, *A Rejoinder*, 104–105.

18. See Ibid., 109.

19. Lessing, *The Education of the Human Race*, §4.

20. Ibid., §77.

21. See Lessing, *Lessing's Theological Writings*, 38–42.

22. Ibid., 37.

23. Ibid., 45.

24. See I. A. Dorner, *History of Protestant Theology, Particularly in Germany, Viewed According to Its Fundamental Movement and Connection with the Religious, Moral, and Intellectual Life* (Edinburgh: T and T Clark, 1871), vol.2, bk.2, div.2, pt.3, ch.1ff.; and Emanuel Hirsch, *Geschichte der Neuern Evangelischen Theologie. Im Zusammenhang mit den allgemeinen Bewegungen des europäischen Denkens* (C. Bertelsmann Verlag Gutersloh, 1949), vol.1, pt.1, chs.47 and 48.

25. John W. Nevin, *My Own Life: The Early Years*, Papers of the Eastern Chapter, Historical Society of the Evangelical and Reformed Church, No.1 (Lancaster, Pa., 1964), 117.

26. Ibid., 117.

27. See ibid., 118.

28. Kant's nuance at the close of this quote is rather important. Note that Kant does not think the birth of Christianity marks the birth of rational religion in the sense that these insights came into being with original Christianity. The insights of rational religion are a priori, for Kant. Rather, the origin of Christianity marks the origin of the first church built upon these rational insights. As stated in the previous chapter, any faith can be made to contain the insights of reason; and thus, the unique status of Christianity does not, for Kant, speak in favor of a religious exclusivism. Christianity may be the "consummate" religion, but it has no exclusive rights to the insights or doctrines of natural religion.

29. Lessing's distinction between necessary and contingent truths is drawn from §33 of Leibniz's *Monadology*. Terry H. Foreman notes that Lessing clearly recognizes there are more than two kinds of truth-claims, since in *The Freethinker*, Lessing "lampooned those who used such excluded middles." Terry H. Foreman, "Difference and Reconciliation: G. E. Lessing as Partner in Ecumenical Conversation," in *Christian Faith Seeking Historical Understanding: Essays in Honor of H. Jack Forstmann*, ed. James O. Duke and Anthony L. Dunnavant (Macon, Ga.: Mercer University Press, 1997), 98. And in this light, Foreman suggests "the ditch between the accidental truths of history and the necessary truths of reason would appear to be a rhetorical device" (Foreman, "Difference and Reconciliation," 97–98).

30. Lessing, *On the Proof*, 85. See also J.C. Thomas, "Faith and History: A Critique of Recent Dogmatics," *Religious Studies* 18 (1982): 327–28.

31. Lessing, *On the Proof*, 87.

32. Ibid.

33. Henry E. Allison, *Lessing and the Enlightenment: His Philosophy of Religion and Its Relation to Eighteenth-Century Thought* (Ann Arbor: University of Michigan Press, 1966), 103.

34. Lessing, *On the Proof*, 87.

35. Ibid. This reference to "of the Spirit and power" is meant to be a reference to 1 Corinthians 2:4, which Lessing understands as testimony to the continuation of miraculous proofs in the apostles after the Ascension of Christ. Likewise Lessing opens *On the Proof* by quoting Origen's *Contra Celsum*, bk. 1, ch. 2, which also testifies to such ongoing miraculous proofs. Lessing quotes this passage and uses it to frame his argument throughout principally because it was employed by Schumman in his reaffirmation of the historical proofs. See Allison, *Lessing and the Enlightenment*, 101.

36. See, e.g., Palmquist's quite idiosyncratic cataloguing of the religious excesses identified in *Religion* (or parerga) in Palmquist, *Kant's Critical Religion*, appendix 7.

37. Cf. Lessing, *The Education of the Human Race,* §5ff.

38. See Gregory Johnson, "The Tree of Melancholy: Kant on Philosophy and Enthusiasm," in *Kant and the New Philosophy of Religion,* ed. Chris L. Firestone and Stephen R. Palmquist (Bloomington: Indiana University Press, 2006), which focuses on Kant's more positive use of "enthusiasm," a use that should not be confused with the more derogatory use of "enthusiasm" above.

Selected Bibliography

Adelung, Johann Christoph. *Grammatisch-Kritisches Wörterbuch der Hochdeutschen Mundart mit beständiger Vergleichung der übrigen Mundarten, besonders aber der Oberdeutschen*. Leipzig: Breitkopf und Hartel, 1793–1801. New York: Georg Olms Verlag, 1990.

Allison, Henry E. *Idealism and Freedom*. Cambridge: Cambridge University Press, 1996.

———. *Kant's Theory of Freedom*. Cambridge: Cambridge University Press, 1990.

———. *Kant's Theory of Taste: A Reading of the Critique of Aesthetic Judgment*. Cambridge: Cambridge University Press, 2001.

———. *Kant's Transcendental Idealism: An Interpretation and Defense*. New Haven, Conn.: Yale University Press, 1983.

———. *Lessing and the Enlightenment: His Philosophy of Religion and Its Relation to Eighteenth-Century Thought*. Ann Arbor: University of Michigan Press, 1966.

Anderson-Gold, Sharon. "God and Community: An Inquiry into the Religious Implications of the Highest Good." In *Kant's Philosophy of Religion Reconsidered*, ed. Philip J. Rossi and Michael Wreen. Bloomington: Indiana University Press, 1991.

———. *Unnecessary Evil: History and Moral Progress in the Philosophy of Immanuel Kant*. New York: State University of New York Press, 2001.

Aquinas, St. Thomas. *Summa Theologiae*. Vols. 1–60. New York: McGraw-Hill, and London: Eyre and Spottiswoode, 1966.

Aristotle. *Categories, Metaphysics, Nicomachean Ethics*, and *On Generation and Corruption*. In *The Basic Works of Aristotle*, ed. Richard McKeon. New York: Random House, 2001.

———. *Categoriae, De Generatione et Corruptione, Ethica Nicomachea*, and *Metaphysica*. In *Aristotelis Opera*, ed. Immanuelis Bekkeri. Oxonii e Typographeo Academico, 1837.

Athanasius of Alexandria. *Against the Heathen* and *On the Incarnation of the Word of God*. In *The Ante-Nicene Fathers: Translations of the Writings of the Fathers down to A.D. 325*, ed. Alexander Roberts and James Donaldson. Grand Rapids, Mich.: William B. Eerdmans, 1950–51.

———. *Athanase d'Alexandrie, évêque et écrivain: une lecture des traités Condre les Ariens*. Théologie historique, 70. Ed. Charles Kannengiesser. Paris: Beauchesne, 1983.

Augustine. *De Civitate Dei, Confessiones, De Doctrina Christiana*, and *Enchiridion*. In *Patrologia Latina Cursus Completus*, ed. J. P. Migne. 221 vols. Paris: Vives, 1844–55.

———. *The City of God*. London: Penguin, 1984.

———. *Confessions*. New York: Oxford University Press, 1998.

———. *The Enchiridion: On Faith, Hope and Love*. Washington, D.C.: Regnery Publishing, 1996.

——. *On Free Will*. In *Augustine: Earlier Writings*, ed. J. H. S. Burleigh. Philadelphia: Westminster Press, 1953.

——. *The Spirit and the Letter*. In *The Works of Saint Augustine: A Translation for the 21st Century*, trans. Edmund Hill, and ed. John E. Rotelle. New York: New City Press, 1996.

——. *Teaching Christianity*. In *The Works of Saint Augustine: A Translation for the 21st Century*, trans. Edmund Hill, and ed. John E. Rotelle. New York: New City Press, 1996.

Axinn, Sidney. *The Logic of Hope: Extensions of Kant's View of Religion*. Atlanta, Ga.: Rodopi B.V., 1994.

Banham, Gary. *Kant's Practical Philosophy: From Critique to Doctrine*. New York: Palgrave MacMillan, 2003.

Barth, Karl. *Christus und Adam, nach Röm. 5. [Ein Beitrag zur Frage nach dem Menschen und der Menschheit]*. Zollikon-Zürich: Evangelischer Verlag, 1952.

——. *Protestant Theology in the Nineteenth Century: Its Background and History*. London: S.C.M. Press, 1972.

Basil of Caesarea. *Hexameron*. In *The Ante-Nicene Fathers: Translations of the Writings of the Fathers down to A.D. 325*, ed. Alexander Roberts and James Donaldson. Grand Rapids, Mich.: William B. Eerdmans, 1950–51.

——. *Homélies sur l'Hexaéméron*. Ed. Stanislas Giet. Paris: Editions du Cerf, 1968.

Beck, Lewis White. *Early German Philosophy: Kant and His Predecessors*. Bristol, England: Thoemmes Press, 1969.

Beiser, Frederick C. *The Fate of Reason: German Philosophy from Kant to Fichte*. Cambridge, Mass.: Harvard University Press, 1987.

——. "Moral Faith and the Highest Good." In *The Cambridge Companion to Kant and Modern Philosophy*, ed. Paul Guyer. Cambridge: Cambridge University Press, 2006.

Bird, Graham. *Kant's Theory of Knowledge*. London: Routledge and Kegan Paul, 1962.

Boler, John. "The Moral Psychology of Duns Scotus: Some Preliminary Questions." *Franciscan Studies* 50 (1990).

Bonansea, Bernardine M. "Dun Scotus' Voluntarism." In *John Duns Scotus, 1265–1965*, ed. John K. Ryan and Bernardine M. Bonanasea. Washington, D.C.: Catholic University of America Press, 1965.

Brehier, Emile. *The Philosophy of Plotinus*. Chicago: University of Chicago Press, 1958.

Byrne, Peter. "Kant's Moral Proof for the Existence of God." *Scottish Journal of Theology* 32 (1979).

——. *The Moral Interpretation of Religion*. Grand Rapids, Mich.: William B. Eerdman, 1998.

Caird, Edward. *The Critical Philosophy of Immanuel Kant*. Vols. 1 and 2. Glasgow: James Madehose and Sons, 1889.

Cassirer, Ernst. *Kant's Life and Thought*. New Haven, Conn.: Yale University Press, 1981.

Cassirer, H. W. *Grace and Law*. Grand Rapids, Mich.: William B. Eerdmans, 1988.

Collins, James. *The Emergence of Philosophy of Religion*. New Haven, Conn.: Yale University Press, 1967.

——. *Interpreting Modern Philosophy*. Princeton, N.J.: Princeton University Press, 1972.

Copleston, Frederick. *A History of Philosophy*. Vol. 6. New York: Doubleday, 1963 and 1964.

Cresswell, John. "Duns Scotus on the Will." *Franciscan Studies* 13 (1953).

Cupitt, Don. "Kant and the Negative Theology." In *The Philosophical Frontiers of Christian Theology: Essays Presented to D. M. MacKinnon*, ed. Brian Hebblethwaite and Stewart Sutherland. Cambridge: Cambridge University Press, 1982.

Davidovich, Adina. "How to Read *Religion within the Limits of Reason Alone.*" *Kant-Studien* 85 (1994).

——. *Religion as a Province of Meaning: The Kantian Foundations of Modern Theology.* Minneapolis: Fortress Press, 1993.

Davidson, Jack. "Imitators of God: Leibniz on Human Freedom." *Journal of the History of Philosophy* 36, no. 3 (1998).

Davidson, Robert F. *Rudolf Otto's Interpretation of Religion.* Princeton, N.J.: Princeton University Press, 1947.

Dekker, Eef. "The Theory of Divine Permission according to Scotus' *Ordinatio* I 47." *Vivarium* 38, no. 2 (2000).

Despland, Michel. *Kant on History and Religion.* Montreal: McGill-Queen's University Press, 1973.

Dorner, I. A. *History of Protestant Theology, Particularly in Germany, Viewed according to Its Fundamental Movement and Connection with the Religious, Moral, and Intellectual Life.* Vol. 2. Edinburgh: T and T Clark, 1871.

Duke, James O., and Anthony L. Dunnavant, eds. *Christian Faith Seeking Historical Understanding: Essays in Honor of H. Jack Forstmann.* Macon, Ga.: Mercer University Press, 1997.

Edwards, Jonathan. *The Works of Jonathan Edwards.* Ed. Harry S. Stout. New Haven, Conn.: Yale University Press, 2001.

England, F. E. *Kant's Conception of God.* George Allen and Unwin, 1929.

Fichte, Johann Gottlieb. *Attempt at a Critique of All Revelation.* Trans. Garrett Green. Cambridge: Cambridge University Press, 1978.

Firestone, Chris L. "Kant and Religion: Conflict or Compromise?" *Religious Studies* 35, no. 2 (1999).

——. "Kant's Two Perspectives on the Theological Task." *International Journal of Systematic Theology* 2, no. 1 (2000).

——. "Making Sense Out of Tradition." In *Kant and the New Philosophy of Religion*, ed. Chris L. Firestone and Stephen R. Palmquist. Bloomington: Indiana University Press, 2006.

Firestone, Chris L., and Nathan Jacobs. "Kant and the Christian Religion." *Philosophia Christi* 9, no. 1 (2007).

Firestone, Chris L., and Stephen R. Palmquist. "Editors' Introduction." In *Kant and the New Philosophy of Religion*, ed. Chris L. Firestone and Stephen R. Palmquist. Bloomington: Indiana University Press, 2006.

——, eds. *Kant and the New Philosophy of Religion.* Bloomington: Indiana University Press, 2006.

Fischer, Kuno. *A Critique of Kant.* London: Swan Sonnonshein, Lowrey, 1888.

Florschütz, Gottlieb. *Swedenborg and Kant: Emanuel Swedenborg's Mystical Vision of Humankind, and the Dual Nature of Humankind in Immanuel Kant.* West Chester, Pa.: Swedenborg Foundation, 1993.

Foreman, Terry H. "Difference and Reconciliation: G. E. Lessing as Partner in Ecumenical Conversation." In *Christian Faith Seeking Historical Understanding: Essays in Honor of H. Jack Forstmann*, ed. James O. Duke and Anthony L. Dunnavant. Macon, Ga.: Mercer University Press, 1997.

Frei, Hans. *The Eclipse of Biblical Narrative.* New Haven, Conn.: Yale University Press, 1974.

Frierson, Patrick R. *Freedom and Anthropology in Kant's Moral Philosophy.* Cambridge: Cambridge University Press, 2003.

Galbraith, Elizabeth Cameron. *Kant and Theology: Was Kant a Closet Theologian?* San Francisco: International Scholars Publications, 1996.

George, Rolf. *"Vorstellung* and *Erkenntnis* in Kant." In *Interpreting Kant,* ed. Moltke S. Gram. Iowa City: University of Iowa Press, 1982.

Goethe, Johann Wolfgang von. *Goethes Briefe.* 4 vols. Hamburg: Christian Wegner Verlag, 1964.

Gram, Moltke S., ed. *Interpreting Kant.* Iowa City: University of Iowa Press, 1982.

Grandgeorge, L. *Saint Augustin et le néo-platonisme.* Frankfurt, a.M., Minerva GmbH.: Unveränderter Nachdruck, 1967.

Green, Ronald M. *Kierkegaard and Kant: The Hidden Debt.* Albany: State University of New York Press, 1992.

——. *Religion and Moral Reason: A New Method for Comparative Study.* New York: Oxford University Press, 1988.

——. *Religious Reason: The Rational and Moral Basis of Religious Belief.* New York: Oxford University Press, 1978.

Greene, Donald. "Latitudinarianism and Sensibility: The Genealogy of the 'Man of Feeling' Reconsidered." *Modern Philology* 75, no. 2 (Nov. 1977).

Greene, Theodore M. "The Historical Context and Religious Significance of Kant's *Religion.*" In *Religion within the Limits of Reason Alone,* trans. Theodore M. Greene and Hoyt H. Hudson. New York: Harper and Brothers, 1960.

Guyer, Paul, ed. *The Cambridge Companion to Kant and Modern Philosophy.* Cambridge: Cambridge University Press, 2006.

——. *Kant and the Claims of Knowledge.* Cambridge: Cambridge University Press, 1987.

——. *Kant and the Claims of Taste.* Cambridge, Mass.: Harvard University Press, 1979.

Guyer, Paul, and Allen W. Wood, gen. eds. *The Cambridge Edition of the Works of Immanuel Kant.* Cambridge: Cambridge University Press, 1993–2004.

Hare, John E. "Augustine, Kant, and the Moral Gap." In *The Augustinian Tradition,* ed. Gareth B. Matthew. Berkeley: University of California Press, 1999.

——. *God's Call.* Grand Rapids, Mich.: William B. Eerdmans, 2001.

——. "Kant on Depravity: The Opening of *Religion within the Boundaries of Mere Reason.*" Eastern Regional Meeting of the Society of Christian Philosophers, 2006.

——. *The Moral Gap: Kantian Ethics, Human Limits, and God's Assistance.* New York: Oxford University Press, 1996.

——. "The Rational Instability of Atheism." In *Kant and the New Philosophy of Religion,* ed. Chris L. Firestone and Stephen R. Palmquist. Bloomington: Indiana University Press, 2006.

Hebblethwaite, Brian, and Stewart Sutherland, eds. *The Philosophical Frontiers of Christian Theology: Essays Presented to D. M. MacKinnon.* Cambridge: Cambridge University Press, 1982.

Hegel, Georg Wilhelm Friedrich. *Lectures on the Philosophy of Religion: The Lectures of 1827.* One-vol. ed. Ed. Peter C. Hodgson, and trans. R. F. Brown, P. C. Hodgson, and J. M. Stewart. Berkeley: University of California Press, 1988.

——. *Vorlesungen über die Philosophie der Religion.* Ed. Walter Jaeschke. Hamburg, 1983–1985.

Hinske, N. "Die historischen Vorlagen der Kantischen Transzendentalphilosophie." *Archiv für Begriffsgeschichte* 12 (1968).

Hirsch, Emanuel. *Geschichte der Neuern Evangelischen Theologie. Im Zusammenhang mit den allgemeinen Bewegungen des europäischen Denkens.* Vol. 1. Gütersloh: C. Bertelsmann Verlag, 1949.

Honnefelder, Ludger. "Metaphysics as a Discipline: From the 'Transcendental Philosophy of the Ancients' To Kant's Notion of Transcendental Philosophy." In *The Medieval Heritage of Early Modern Metaphysics and Modal Theory, 1400–1700,* ed. Russell L. Friedman and Lauge O. Nielsen. Boston: Kluwer Academic Publishers, 2003.

Hume, David. *A Treatise of Human Nature.* Oxford: Clarendon Press, 1967.

Incandela, Joseph M. "Duns Scotus and the Experience of Human Freedom." *Thomist* 56, no. 2 (1992).

Inge, W. R. *The Philosophy of Plotinus.* London: Longmans, Green, 1929.

Jacobs, Nathan. "Kant's *Apologia:* A Look at the Usefulness of Kantian Insights for Christian Thought." *Philosophia Christi* 9, no. 1 (2007).

———. "Kant's Prototypical Theology: Transcendental Incarnation as a Rational Foundation for God-Talk." In *Kant and the New Philosophy of Religion,* ed. Chris L. Firestone and Stephen R. Palmquist. Bloomington: Indiana University Press, 2006.

———. "On the Only Possible Reading of Kant's *Religion:* Books One and Two." Eastern Regional Meeting of the Society of Christian Philosophers, 2006.

Johnson, Gregory R. "The Tree of Melancholy: Kant on Philosophy and Enthusiasm." In *Kant and the New Philosophy of Religion,* ed. Chris L. Firestone and Stephen R. Palmquist. Bloomington: Indiana University Press, 2006.

Kant, Immanuel. *Anthropology from a Pragmatic Point of View.* Trans. Mary J. Gregor. The Hague: Martinus Nijhoff, 1974.

———. *Correspondence.* Ed. and trans. Arnulf Zweig. Cambridge: Cambridge University Press, 1999.

———. *Critique of the Power of Judgment.* Ed. Paul Guyer, and trans. Paul Guyer and Eric Matthews. Cambridge: Cambridge University Press, 2000.

———. *Critique of Pure Reason.* Ed. and trans. Paul Guyer and Allen W. Wood. Cambridge: Cambridge University Press, 1997.

———. *Critique of Pure Reason.* Trans. J. M. D. Meiklejohn. New York: Prometheus Books, 1990.

———. *Immanuel Kant's Critique of Pure Reason.* Trans. Norman Kemp Smith. London: Macmillan Press, 1929.

———. *Kant on Swedenborg: "Dreams of a Spirit-Seer" and Other Writings,* ed. Gregory R. Johnson, trans. Gregory R. Johnson and Glenn Alexander Magee. West Chester, Pa: Swedenborg Foundation, 2002.

———. *Kants gesammelte Schriften.* Berlin: G. Reimer, 1902.

———. *Lectures on Ethics.* Ed. Peter Heath and J. B. Schneewind, and trans. Peter Heath. Cambridge: Cambridge University Press, 1997.

———. *Lectures on Logic.* Ed. and trans. J. Michel Young. Cambridge: Cambridge University Press, 1997.

———. *Lectures on Metaphysics.* Ed. and trans. Karl Americks and Steve Naragon. Cambridge: Cambridge University Press, 1997.

———. *Opus Postumum.* Ed. Eckart Förster, and trans. Eckart Förster and Michael Rosen. Cambridge: Cambridge University Press, 1993.

——. *Practical Philosophy.* Ed. and trans. Mary J. Gregor. Cambridge: Cambridge University Press, 1996.

——. *Religion and Rational Theology.* Ed. and trans. Allen W. Wood and George di Giovanni. Cambridge: Cambridge University Press, 1996.

——. *Religion within the Limits of Reason Alone.* Trans. Theodore M. Greene and Hoyt H. Hudson. New York: Harper and Brothers, 1960.

——. *Theoretical Philosophy, 1755–1770.* Ed. and trans. David Walford. Cambridge: Cambridge University Press, 1992.

King, Peter. "Duns Scotus on the Common Nature." *Philosophical Topics* 20 (1992).

Körner, Stephan. *Kant.* London: Penguin Books, 1955.

Kroner, Richard. *Kant's Weltanschauung.* Chicago: University of Chicago Press, 1956.

Leibniz, G. W. Confessio philosophi: *Papers Concerning the Problem of Evil, 1671–1678.* Ed. and trans. Robert C. Sleigh Jr. New Haven, Conn.: Yale University Press, 2005.

——. De Summa Rerum: *Metaphysical Papers, 1675–1676.* Trans. G. H. R. Parkinson. New Haven, Conn.: Yale University Press, 1992.

——. *Die Philosophischen Schriften von G.W. Leibniz.* Ed. C. J. Gerhardt. 7 vols. Berlin, 1875–1890.

——. *Discourse on Metaphysics and Related Writings.* Trans. and ed. R. N. D. Martin and Stuart Brown. New York: Manchester University Press, 1988.

——. *G.W. Leibniz's* Monadology: *An Edition for Students.* Ed. and trans. Nicholas Rescher. Pittsburgh, Pa.: University of Pittsburgh Press, 1991.

——. *New Essays on Human Understanding.* Trans. and ed. Peter Remnant and Jonathan Bennet. New York: Cambridge University Press, 1996.

——. *Philosophical Papers and Letters.* Ed. and trans. Leroy E. Loemker. Chicago: University of Chicago Press, 1956.

——. *Philosophical Writings.* Ed. and trans. Mary Morris and G. H. R. Parkinson. London: Dent, 1973.

——. *Samtliche schriften und briefe/herausgegeben von der Deutschen akademie der wissenschaften zu Berlin.* 49 vols. Berlin: Akademie, 1950.

——. *Theodicy: Essays on the Goodness of God the Freedom of Man and the Origin of Evil.* Trans. E. M. Huggard. Chicago: Open Court, 1990.

Lessing, Gotthold Ephraim. *The Education of the Human Race.* In *Lessing's Theological Writings,* trans. Henry Chadwick. Stanford, Calif.: Stanford University Press, 1957.

——. *The Freethinker.* In *The Dramatic Works of G. E. Lessing.* Ed. Ernest Bell, Gotthold Ephraim Lessing, and Helen Zimmern. London: G. Bell, 1878.

——. *Lessings sämtliche Werke.* Ed. Robert Petsch. 6 vols. Berlin, 1907.

——. *On the Proof of the Spirit and of Power.* In *Philosophical and Theological Writings.* Ed. and trans. H. B. Nisbet. Cambridge: Cambridge University Press, 2005.

——. *Philosophical and Theological Writings.* Ed. and trans. H. B. Nisbet. Cambridge: Cambridge University Press, 2005.

——. *A Rejoinder.* In *Philosophical and Theological Writings,* ed. and trans. H. B. Nisbet. Cambridge: Cambridge University Press, 2005.

Lessing, Gotthold Ephraim, Hermann Samuel Reimarus, and Johann Heinrich Ress. *Die Auferstehungs-Geschichte Jesu Christi gegen einige im vierten Beytrage zur Geschichte und Litteratur aus den Schätzen der Herzoglichen Bibliothek zu Wolfenbüttel gemachte neure Einwendungen vertheidiget.* Braunschweig: Verlag der Fürstl. Waisenhaus-Buchhandlung, 1777.

Lewis, Frank A. *Substance and Predication in Aristotle.* Cambridge: Cambridge University Press, 1991.

Lindsay, A. D. *Kant.* London: Oxford University Press, 1934.

Lloyd, G. E. R. *Aristotle: The Growth and Structure of His Thought.* Cambridge: Cambridge University Press, 1968.

Loades, A. L. *Kant and Job's Comforters.* Newcastle upon Tyne, UK: Avero Publications, 1985.

Loemker, Leroy E. *Struggle for Synthesis: The Seventeenth Century Background of Leibniz's Synthesis of Order and Freedom.* Cambridge, Mass.: Harvard University Press, 1972.

Luik, J. C. "The Ambiguity of Kantian Faith." *Scottish Journal of Theology* 36 (1983).

Matthew, Gareth B., ed. *The Augustinian Tradition.* Berkeley: University of California Press, 1999.

McCarthy, Vincent A. *Quest for a Philosophical Jesus: Christianity and Philosophy in Rousseau, Kant, Hegel, and Schelling.* Macon, Ga.: Mercer University Press, 1986.

Michalson, Gordon E., Jr. *Fallen Freedom: Kant on Radical Evil and Moral Regeneration.* Cambridge: Cambridge University Press, 1990.

——. *The Historical Dimensions of a Rational Faith: The Role of History in Kant's Religious Thought.* Washington, D.C.: University Press of America, 1979.

——. *Kant and the Problem of God.* Oxford: Blackwell, 1999.

——. "The Role of History in Kant's Religious Thought." *Anglican Theological Review* 59, no. 5 (1977).

Nevin, John W. *My Own Life: The Early Years.* Papers of the Eastern Chapter, Historical Society of the Evangelical and Reformed Church, No.1. Lancaster, Pa., 1964.

Origen. *De Principiis.* In *The Ante-Nicene Fathers: Translations of the Writings of the Fathers down to A.D. 325,* ed. Alexander Roberts and James Donaldson. Grand Rapids, Mich.: William B. Eerdmans, 1950–51.

——. *Oreginis Contra Celsum: libri VIII.* Ed. M. Marcovich. Boston: Brill, 2001.

Otto, Rudolf. *The Idea of the Holy.* Oxford: Oxford University Press, 1931.

Owens, Joseph. *Cognition: An Epistemological Inquiry.* Houston, Tex.: Center for Thomistic Studies, 1992.

Palmquist, Stephen R. "Kantian Redemption: A Critical Challenge to Christian View of Faith and Works." *Philosophia Christi* 9, no. 1 (2007).

——. *Kant's Critical Religion: Volume Two of Kant's System of Perspectives.* Aldershot, UK: Ashgate Publishing, 2000.

——. *Kant's System of Perspectives: An Architectonic Interpretation of the Critical Philosophy.* Lanham, Md.: University Press of America, 1993.

——. "Philosophers in the Public Square: A Religious Resolution of Kant's *Conflict.*" In *Kant and the New Philosophy of Religion,* ed. Chris L. Firestone and Stephen R. Palmquist. Bloomington: Indiana University Press, 2006.

Pancheri, Francis Xavier. *The Universal Primacy of Christ.* Trans. Juniper B. Carol. Front Royal, Va.: Christendom Publications, 1984.

Paton, H. J. *The Categorical Imperative: A Study in Kant's Moral Philosophy.* Philadelphia: University of Pennsylvania Press, 1947.

Paull, R. Cranston. "Leibniz and the Miracle of Freedom." *Noûs* 26, no. 2 (1992).

Paulsen, Friedrich. *Immanuel Kant: His Life and Doctrine.* New York: Charles Scribner's Sons, 1902.

Pelagius. "To Demetrias." In *The Letters of Pelagius and His Followers,* ed. and trans. B. R. Rees. New York: Boydell Press, 1991.

Plantinga, Alvin. *Warranted Christian Belief.* Oxford: Oxford University Press, 2000.

Plato. *Meno.* In *Plato: Five Dialogues,* trans. G. M. A. Grube. Indianapolis: Hacket Publishing, 1981.

Plotinus. *Enneads.* London: Penguin Books LTD, 1991.

Prichard, H. F. *Kant's Theory of Knowledge.* Oxford: Clarendon Press, 1909.

Privette, Jeffrey S. "Must Theology Re-Kant?" *Heythrop Journal* 40 (1999).

Quinn, Philip L. "Christian Atonement and Kantian Justification." *Faith and Philosophy* 3, no. 4 (1986).

——. "Original Sin, Radical Evil and Moral Identity." *Faith and Philosophy* 1, no. 2 (1984).

——. "Saving Faith from Kant's Remarkable Antinomy." *Faith and Philosophy* 7, no. 4 (1990).

Rabel, Gabriele. *Kant.* Oxford: Clarendon Press, 1963.

Raschke, Carl A. *Moral Action, God, and History in the Thought of Immanuel Kant.* Dissertation Series, No. 5. Missoula, Mont.: American Academy of Religion and Scholars Press, 1975.

Ray, Matthew Alun. *Subjectivity and Irreligion: Atheism and Agnosticism in Kant, Schopenhauer and Nietzsche.* Aldershot, UK: Ashgate Publishing, 2003.

Reardon, Bernard M. G. *Kant as Philosophical Theologian.* Totowa, N.J.: Barnes and Noble Books, 1988.

——. "Kant as Theologian." *Downside Review* 93 (1995).

Rossi, Philip J. "Reading Kant through Theological Spectacles." In *Kant and the New Philosophy of Religion.* Chris L. Firestone and Stephen R. Palmquist, eds. Bloomington: Indiana University Press, 2006.

Rossi, Philip J., and Michael Wreen. *Kant's Philosophy of Religion Reconsidered.* Bloomington: Indiana University Press, 1991.

Savage, Denis. "Kant's Rejection of Divine Revelation and His Theory of Radical Evil." In *Kant's Philosophy of Religion Reconsidered,* ed. Philip J. Rossi and Michael W. Wreen. Bloomington: Indiana University Press, 1991.

Schelling, Friedrich Wilhelm Joseph von. *Friedrich Wilhelm Joseph von Schelling Sämmtliche Werke, VII Band, I Abteilung,* 1805, 1810. Ed. K. F. A. Schelling. Stuttgart and Augsburg: J. G. Cotta, 1860.

——. *Of Human Freedom.* Trans. James Gutmann. Chicago: Open Court, 1936.

——. *On the History of Modern Philosophy.* Trans. Andrew Bowie. Cambridge: Cambridge University Press, 1994.

Schelling, Friedrich Wilhelm Joseph von, and Manfred Schröter. *Schellings Werke.* München: C.H. Beck, 1979.

Scotus, John Duns. *Contingency and Freedom: Lectura I.39.* Trans. A. Vos Jaczn et al. Dordrecht: Kluwer Academic Publishers, 1994.

——. *Opera Omnia, jussu et auctoritate . . . totius Ordinis Fratrum Minorum ministry generalis studio et cura Commissionis Scotisticae ad fidem codicum edita.* Civitas Vaticana: Typis Polyglottis Vaticanis, 1950–.

——. *Philosophical Writings.* Ed. and trans. Allan B. Wolter. London: Nelson, 1962.

Sidgwick, Henry. *The Philosophy of Kant and Other Lectures.* London: Macmillan Press, 1905.

Silber, John R. "The Ethical Significance of Kant's *Religion.*" In *Religion within the Limits of Reason Alone,* trans. Theodore M. Greene and Hoyt H. Hudson. New York: Harper and Brothers, 1960.

Sleigh, Robert, Jr., Vere Chappell, and Michael Della Rocca. "Determinism and Human Freedom." In *The Cambridge History of Seventeenth-Century Philosophy*, 2:1195–1278, ed. Daniel Garber and Michael Ayers. Cambridge: Cambridge University Press, 1998.

Sorell, Tom, ed. *The Rise of Modern Philosophy: The Tension between the New and Traditional Philosophies from Machiavelli to Leibniz.* Oxford: Clarendon Press, 1993.

Stevenson, Leslie. "Opinion, Belief or Faith, and Knowledge." *Kantian Review* 7 (2003).

Strawson, P. F. *The Bounds of Sense: An Essay on Kant's Critique of Pure Reason.* London: Metheun, 1966.

Swedenborg, Emmanuel. *Kant on Swedenborg: "Dreams of a Spirit-Seer" and Other Writings.* Ed. Gregory R. Johnson, and trans. Gregory R. Johnson and Glenn Alexander Magee. West Chester, Pa.: Swedenborg Foundation, 2002.

Thomas, J. C. "Faith and History: A Critique of Recent Dogmatics." *Religious Studies* 18 (1982).

Turnbull, Grace H. *The Essence of Plotinus: Extracts From the Six Enneads and Porphyry's* Life of Plotinus. New York: Oxford University Press, 1934.

Vogt, Berard. "The Metaphysics of Human Liberty in Duns Scotus." In *Proceedings of the American Catholic Philosophical Association*, ed. Charles A. Hart. 16 Vols. Washington, D.C.: Catholic University of America, 1940.

Wallace, William. *Kant.* Edinburgh: William Blackwood and Sons, 1905.

Ward, James. *A Study of Kant.* Cambridge: Cambridge University Press, 1922.

Ward, Keith. *The Development of Kant's View of Ethics.* Oxford: Basil Blackwell, 1972.

Watson, John. *The Philosophy of Kant Explained.* Glasgow: J. Maclehose and Sons, 1908.

Webb, Clement C. J. *Kant's Philosophy of Religion.* Oxford: Clarendon Press, 1926.

Wiebe, Don. "The Ambiguous Revolution: Kant on the Nature of Faith." *Scottish Journal of Theology* 33 (1980).

Wolff, Christian. *Philosophia Prima Sive Ontologia.* Ed. Joannes Ecole. Georg Olms Verlagsbuchhandlung Hildesheim, 1962.

Wolterstorff, Nicholas P. "Conundrums in Kant's Rational Religion." In *Kant's Philosophy of Religion Reconsidered*, ed. Philip J. Rossi and Micheal Wreen. Bloomington: Indiana University Press, 1991.

———. "Is It Possible and Desirable for Theologians to Recover from Kant?" *Modern Theology* 14, no. 1 (1998).

Wood, Allen W. "Kant's Deism." In *Kant's Philosophy of Religion Reconsidered*, ed. Philip J. Rossi and Michael Wreen. Bloomington: Indiana University Press, 1991.

———. *Kant's Moral Religion.* Ithaca and London: Cornell University Press, 1970.

———. *Kant's Rational Theology.* Ithaca and London: Cornell University Press, 1978.

———. "Rational Theology, Moral Faith, and Religion." In *The Cambridge Companion to Kant*, ed. Paul Guyer. Cambridge: Cambridge University Press, 1992.

Yovel, Yirmiahu. *Kant and the Philosophy of History.* Princeton, N.J.: Princeton University Press, 1980.

Index

Chris L. Firestone is Associate Professor of Philosophy at Trinity College in Deerfield, Ill. He has authored many articles on Kant and is editor, with Stephen R. Palmquist, of *Kant and the New Philosophy of Religion* (Indiana University Press, 2006).

Nathan Jacobs is Assistant Professor of Theology in the School of Biblical and Religious Studies at Trinity College in Deerfield, Ill. He has authored many articles on Kant and other topics and is a contributor to *Kant and the New Philosophy of Religion.*

Printed and bound by CPI Group (UK) Ltd, Croydon, CR0 4YY

13/04/2025

14656547-0007